Cops,
Crooks
and other
Crazies

©Copyright 2008 by George C. Nuttall
ISBN 978-1-890035-74-2

All rights reserved.
No part of this publication may be reproduced, stored in a retrieval system, or transmitted in any form, electronic, recording or otherwise, without the prior permission of the copyright owner.

Published in the United States by:
New Century Press
1055 Bay Blvd., Suite C
Chula Vista, CA 91911
1 800 519 2465
www.newcenturypress.com

Imagination Is
More Important Than Knowledge.

— Dr. Albert Einstein

INTRODUCTION

You have to be half crazy to be a cop. And if you become a motor cop, that takes care of the other half.

I spent the first two years, two months, two weeks and two days of my diverse 31-year California peace officer career on the San Diego Police Department. There, we had to type all of our reports, except the Daily Activity Report, which we completed by hand as events occurred during the shift. Our reports had to be typed in carbon-copy triplicate for civilian cases and quadruplicate for cases involving military personnel. The fourth copy was sent to the cited or arrested military member's district commander. For Naval and Marine Corps personnel, it was Admiral Dyer of the 11th Naval District.

At the end of each shift a bunch of hunt-and-peck typists were rapidly plucking away trying to avoid overtime. That's because there was no such thing as overtime on the San Diego Police Department at that time. Our time was the department's time, period. If and when an officer had accumulated 16 court subpoenas that were stamped by a court clerk as proof that the officer had actually appeared in court, the officer's captain just might generously give him one day off with pay as full compensation. In over two years, I never reached that magic number of 16. It didn't take long for me to learn that complete, well-written reports would minimize court time.

Occasionally, an officer would cry out, "Oh, shit," or some other expression of pain or misery. All would laugh because they knew he had made a mistake on the small pile of carbon copies. Then some genius would volunteer to bulldoze through the mistake or concoct an end run. Not always easy reading, but good enough for government work. Run-of-the-mill arrest reports weren't very important anyway, because it was the days before free defense attorneys and almost everyone was automatically guilty in Judge John J. Brennan's Police Court.

But overtime or not, the end-of-shift typing sessions were also our entertainment hour. Nearly every day at least one officer would relate a hilarious event during the shift. After the laughter subsided, someone would say, "Somebody should take notes on this stuff and write a best seller when they retire." We all agreed, but to my knowledge nobody ever did. I agreed, but I hated typing so much I always figured it was some other fool's job to do it.

With the public's interest in cop shows at an all-time high, I decided to disclose what police work is really like as I observed and experienced it during the greatest evolution of law enforcement in American history. Many of the changes have been positive, but far too many have been needlessly negative.

The incidents range from tragic fatal shootings of unarmed persons to hilarious capers by cops, crooks and other crazies. For example, I was at the scene of a wild San Diego police shootout in April 1954. It was like some of the veteran police officers had been possessed by mob mentality. One returned fire on the shotgun shooter in an apartment, and it was as if it were the first day of hunting season.

In between the violent and humorous events and situations were the emotionally wrenching ones, such as delivering death notifications. There is no way to soften the news, because it is so absolutely final. And no officer I ever knew could bear to investigate or be close to the serious injury or death of a child, because the child was never at fault. It was nearly always the irresponsible negligence of parents that had caused the problem.

What is presented in this over 30 years of experience is straight from the street and other scenes without any Hollywood screening, glamour, romance or other fantasies.

Of the hundreds of police-related movies and TV productions I have seen, the TV sitcom "Barney Miller" was the most realistic. I have known many cops like Nick with his racing form, Wojo and his ragged lifestyle, Harris writing his book, Fish's woes with his wife, and the intellectual and ancient Inspector Luger. It was the crazy antics of many cops I knew that made the job tolerable, enjoyable and entertaining.

From the humorous to the sad, tragic, violent and incredible, here it is — and straight from the street, the only place where true police work can be learned.

> Many of the names have been changed to protect the guilty and the innocent alike — including cops, crooks and other crazies.

ABOUT THE AUTHOR

When George Clifton Nuttall was born on August 6, 1930, nearly everyone in his large, extended family of more than 60 members expected him to grow up to be a San Diego firefighter. After all, his grandfather was Fire Department Battalion Chief John Andrew Wood, and his father was Captain George Patrick Nuttall.

Author's grandfather, John Andrew Wood on right, in about 1908.

But fate took a hand. When George was only five months old, his father and grandfather died three days apart of pneumonia they contracted in the aftermath of a devastating house fire a week earlier. Yet George's mother and San Diego Fire Chief George Courser still hoped he would carry on the family tradition and become a fireman.

With no father or grandfather as role models, George was drawn to his next-door neighbor, John Golden, a scrupulously honest and frugal Irish Catholic who had been a San Diego police officer since 1908. From the age of three, George spent most of his time with his childless neighbors "Nanno" and his wife, learning about guns and what policemen did, mooching dinners and listening to "Calling All Cars" and "Gangbusters" on the radio.

Another big influence was the Junior Traffic Patrol, which the San Diego Police Department started in 1935 to train sixth grade boys to serve as crossing guards at their schools. George was appointed a sergeant in the patrol when he was 11 and began his lifelong love affair with motorcycles when his police officer supervisor gave him rides on his motor and let him listen to the police radio.

By the time he was 19, George had decided he wanted to be a California Highway Patrol officer. Achieving that goal in 1954 after two years on the San Diego Police Department, he served in many California communities, working his way up to sergeant, lieutenant and captain and initiating many innovations and reforms promoting greater safety for both CHP officers and the general public.

As a CHP captain in Santa Barbara, George partnered with the Secret Service to orchestrate the most complex state visit in Secret Service history — the meeting of President Ronald Reagan and Queen Elizabeth of England.

Even after retirement, George couldn't give up police work. He and his former San Diego partner joined forces for an exhaustive investigation of the unsolved D.B. Cooper skyjacking case. Together they concluded with certainty that

Author's father, San Diego Fire Department Captain George Patrick Nuttall

Author's surrogate father, San Diego Police Department Officer John Edward Golden and his horse, Dan, in about 1908.

Cooper's scattered remains are on a Columbia River island and discovered why the Cooper case is the only one of the 2,111 reported skyjacking cases in the 1960s and 1970s that has not yet been solved.

Table of Contents

PART TWO - Princes Of The Highways

CHAPTER I

The Good and Bad Police Years

The substation closures and the loss of ambulance service, the emergency hospital and the Police Athletic League were the first gigantic steps the San Diego Police Department took to distance itself from the public it was sworn to protect and serve.

During the 1930s and after World War II, the San Diego Police Department, San Diego Sheriff's Office and the California Highway Patrol had excellent reputations with law-abiding citizens. Their officers were all friendly, courteous, fair and reasonable. However, the San Diego Police Department earned a less than favorable reputation during World War II, especially with Naval and Marine personnel. Even when I joined the police department in 1952, many sailors still called San Diego police officers "chicken shit." And the police department did hire some undesirable officers during the war.

My friend Gary Gray explained. First of all, he said after Pearl Harbor was attacked, San Diego police officers went on 12-hour shifts seven days a week. After a few weeks of that marathon, tempers shortened and cops got pretty rough with the unruly sailors and marines.

Then, he said, even though San Diego was well known to be a "Navy town" and needed ample policing, the government drafted a large number of San Diego police officers into the military. Because of the zero unemployment rates during the war, the police department actually hired many people who had been kicked out of the military with bad conduct discharges. Among the wartime hires

1

were two motorcycle officers who terrorized my end of town — East San Diego.

When I joined the police department, one of those "terrorist" cops was no longer on the force. After about a year the second officer asked me where I was from. When I told him East San Diego, he quickly became defensive and apologetic. He said he and his partner were ordered by the traffic division captain commander to clean up East San Diego at any cost and in any way they saw fit. It was obvious he regretted their conduct.

He was actually a good officer and very likeable, so I played dumb and didn't let on that I had ever heard of him. But, his and his partner's abusive and unprofessional conduct was well known and did much damage to the reputation of the San Diego Police Department. Since it was during the busy war years they got away with it because with so many new residents and the focus on the war effort, San Diego was in major turmoil.

The Junior Traffic Patrol

In 1935, the San Diego Police Department initiated the Junior Traffic Patrol for elementary schools. It was composed mostly of sixth grade boys wearing red sweaters, chrome badges and yellow caps with red trim, who served as crossing guards. My two older brothers, Don and Ed, were on the patrol before me, and I was appointed as a sergeant in September 1941.

We were supervised by a car or motorcycle traffic officer, and at Edison Elementary, our supervisor was Motor Officer Bill Ward, who came to Edison every Tuesday about noon for a meeting with the Junior Patrol members. I was always waiting for him at the corner of 35th and Polk. When he got off his motorcycle, I got on before he crossed the sidewalk.

Officer Ward gave each of the patrol boys a ride on his motorcycle for two blocks from 35th and Polk to Wilson and University. I lucked out, and he gave me two rides. Each time after he turned southbound on Wilson, he poured the gas on wide open. What a thrill! The forward surge was like an amusement park ride. I was hooked on motors from that time on.

2

The police department put on a large Christmas pit barbecue for all of the Junior Patrol boys every year at the Police Pistol Range at Home Avenue and Federal Boulevard. They also put on a firearms demonstration with different guns, including a Thompson submachine gun. Our barbecue was held on December 6, 1941. Little did we know what was in store for San Diego and the rest of the world the next morning at Pearl Harbor.

In 1940, Clifford E. Peterson became police chief, and the San Diego Police Department started the Police Athletic League, better known as "PAL." It was mostly or exclusively baseball for boys from about 12 to 16 years of age, and it was managed by juvenile officers from the police department.

In addition to the main San Diego police station at 801 West Market Street, there had been three substations since 1923. They were in East San Diego, La Jolla and Ocean Beach. The East San Diego station was incorporated with a fire station. It also housed the police ambulance and included what was called an emergency hospital, which was manned by a physician who was always on duty or on call.

It wasn't until after I joined the police department that I learned that San Diego was almost completely unprotected after the attack on Pearl Harbor. Upon receiving the report of the attack, the San Diego fleet immediately left for the high seas to avoid being caught at the docks.

In addition, there was absolutely no military protection from San Diego north to San Clemente in Orange County. The only emergency protection was the immediate deployment of San Diego motorcycle officers equipped with Spanish American War surplus 30.40 Krag rifles and no radio transmitters to patrol U.S. Highway 101 with instructions to spread the alarm if they spotted any Japanese activity. They were to report sightings by telephone, which were few and far between.

We didn't know it, but we were in trouble. Being a major "Navy town" with the Naval Training Center and Marine Corps Recruit Depot and the home of the Consolidated Vultee (Convair) aircraft plant that produced B-24s and PBYs, San Diego was a prime military target.

In 1947, the California Highway Patrol was established as an independent department. Since August 14, 1929 when it was established as a state-operated and controlled agency, it was the enforcement division of the Department of Motor Vehicles. Upon being established as a department, Governor Earl Warren appointed Clifford E. Peterson as the first CHP commissioner.

Upon Peterson's departure, Adam Elmer Jansen was promoted to chief of the San Diego Police Department. Under his command, the East San Diego and Ocean Beach Substations were almost immediately closed, the police department ambulance service was terminated, and the Police Athletic League was transferred to the Parks and Recreation Department. But the outstanding Junior Patrol program was retained.

The La Jolla Substation was retained. Although it may have been justified due to its distance from the main station at Market and Pacific Coast Highway, there were suspicions of covert politics. The assignment of a captain who lived in La Jolla to command the substation and the well-known "better-than-thou" attitude of many La Jolla residents was a sore subject with most of the police department officers. It was like the La Jolla Police Department.

About that time and for years after — into the 1950s — the powers to be in La Jolla badgered the Postal Service to assign La Jolla its own exclusive postmark. They objected to being clumped in with the "commoners and riffraff" of the city of San Diego. But, they didn't win the campaign at that time.

Very simply, with strategic overlapping deployment of patrol division units from the main station, the La Jolla Substation also could have been closed.

The substation closures and loss of ambulance service, emergency hospital and PAL were the first gigantic steps the San Diego Police Department took to distance itself from the public it was sworn to protect and serve. The next less obvious movement started in 1953 with rapidly increasing pressure to issue more and more traffic tickets to generate "money in the pot" — since cities get half of traffic ticket fines.

The termination of the police ambulance service was probably the most damaging to equal and fair public service. It was replaced by contracting with private ambulance companies. Contracts were let based on the lowest bidder for payment by the city when the ambulance company could not collect their fee from the transported patient or responsible party.

The successful bid figures I heard about while on the police department were $3.50 and $4.00 per indigent patient passenger. Not really attractive payment, if there is an alternative.

As I experienced one time in 1954, indigents could and did receive second-class citizen service. If an ambulance company had only one ambulance available to take a call and received a call from the police department and one from a private party in Point Loma at the same time, which one would they take first? Right! And, would they admit to the police department dispatcher that they couldn't respond to the call for 30 to 45 minutes? Not likely! With that scenario, it was quite easy to predict that the police department call could be delayed — for 45 minutes in one of my cases.

Tragically, during my two years, two months, two weeks and two days on the police department, the environment on the job went from enjoyable and fun to management-imposed stress, over-control and confusion. And things got much worse after I left.

CHAPTER 2

Welcome Aboard

"This work gets in your blood real fast and spoils you for any other kind of work. If you don't have a good sense of humor, this job can be hell, and you probably won't last very long."

In 1949 when I was 19, I decided without reservation that I wanted most of all to be a California Highway Patrolman. CHP officers had an enviable reputation, and they were actually called "the princes of the highways" by many California and out-of-state citizens alike. And they were few and far between. For example, in 1945, there were only 954 CHP officers, and 335 were on military leave of absence at the end of the war, with only 619 on active duty.

The entrance exam for "State Traffic Officer," as CHP officers were officially called, was given only about every two to three years, and 10,000 to 12,000 people took each written test. The eligibility lists had a legal lifetime of one to four years. A test was given in October 1950, but I was only 20, and the minimum age to apply to take the written test was 21.

Dying to get into police work and to get away from my boring job of installing and repairing telephones, I took the San Diego Police Department test in December 1951, four months after I turned 21. Not being a war veteran, and without the five veterans' preference points, I ranked 11 on the eligibility list out of about one hundred people who took the written test. It wasn't the CHP, but the San Diego Police Department had an excellent reputation at that time, and there was no guarantee I could get into the California Highway Patrol.

So, on July 14, 1952 the San Diego Police Department hired me and 25 others, which was the greatest number of officers hired in one day in the history of the department. We were administered a sworn oath of office to uphold the law. It only took a minute, and when it was over we were officially California peace officers.

6

Our initial orientation was conducted by an impressive, super sharp lieutenant. He told us to be effective police officers we had to be curious by nature and think police work 24 hours a day, seven days a week. He said we should mentally plan emergency actions in our leisure time so they would come automatically when confronted by dangerous situations when there was no time to make instant, effective decisions. He even emphasized that we should imagine life-threatening tight spots and mentally plan survival actions before going to sleep. Later when I tried to come up with ideas on how to save my life, I got so keyed up I couldn't go to sleep, so, I did my planning during the daytime.

The lieutenant also stressed that our wives would have to make sacrifices to tolerate our being police officers — not only the hours and days we had to work, but also the scrutiny and rejection by some others for being a cop's wife. With that, he strongly stressed making it up to our wives in every way possible for letting us play cops and robbers. I was later told by one of my training officer partners that the lieutenant's first wife had divorced him.

The lieutenant stressed that the two common things that ended many police officers' careers were women and booze, but he didn't mention burglary, grand theft and compulsive gambling at poker parlors. Before, during and after my time on the San Diego Police Department, five cops were fired for burglary, one went to prison for grand theft, and one went to prison for writing bad checks to cover gambling losses — and those were only the ones I knew of.

We were then issued badges, cap pieces, new Smith and Wesson six-inch-barrel service revolvers still in the boxes and 20 rounds of .38-caliber ball ammunition. We were then led by a young sergeant to the first aid clinic next to the jail for physical examinations.

Dr. "Thumbs"

Our physical exams were conducted by the police surgeon, Dr. Williams. I was later told by one of my training officers that Williams was also known to some older officers as "Thumbs." That nickname stuck after one very bad diagnosis. He had counted Motorcycle Officer Johnnie Wilson out in error.

After seeing critically injured Motorcycle Officer Johnny Wilson in the hospital, Dr. Williams went to the main police station. As he walked through the large drive-through archway between the business office and the captain's office, the captain asked him how Johnnie was doing. Without slowing, Dr. Williams made a thumbs-down gesture, meaning Johnnie was a goner — when in fact Johnnie was still patrolling downtown San Diego, terrorizing motorists and pedestrians alike as Dr. Williams gave the 26 of us the speediest physical exams in medical history. Johnnie continued to "clean up" downtown, for which he was a legend.

Within about 90 minutes, Dr. Williams had administered physical exams to all 26 of us — so quickly that my usually excellent memory fails me on what happened. All I can guess is if we had normal body temperature, were breathing and had a somewhat regular heartbeat, we passed with flying colors. Accordingly, we all passed. That later explained to me how he had counted Johnnie out so quickly. His most sterling quality was making lightning-fast decisions. Dr. Williams was a good reason not to get injured on the job.

My First Beat: Skid Row

Being in excellent health, we were then assigned to ride with a patrol or traffic division officer. I was assigned to ride with Officer Bob Richards on downtown Beat 4, which ranged from 5th Avenue west to the bay and Ash Street south to the bay. It included the west half of skid row.

After Bob asked me a few questions about myself, he offered his brief summary of police work. He said, "It's much better to talk people into jail than to fight them. And if you bring in too many fighting drunks, the jail crew will start slamming the solid steel door in your face to send you a message. They get tired of fighting prisoners."

I let him know I agreed with that concept and understood why the jailers would get tired of skirmishes.

Bob then added, "This work gets in your blood real fast and spoils you for any other kind of work. And if you don't have a good sense of humor, this job can be hell, and you probably won't last very long."

I again let him know I fully understood and agreed.

Bob was over six feet tall with a light complexion and straight sandy hair, and he had a smooth stride like a big cat. He also had a subtle, dry sense of humor. He told me his brother was Sergeant Brad Richards, but I knew Sergeant Richards was a tall African/American detective, so I laughed.

Slowly patrolling west on Broadway in front of the Pickwick Hotel, Bob pulled to the curb and said, "I want to talk to him," looking at a tall 30ish man walking like he was lost.

Thinking he knew the man, I just sat in the car while he talked to him. But I quickly realized he was interrogating the man as a possible wanted subject, so I got out of the car. That was my first introduction to one of the most important parts of police work, seeking out suspicious and wanted subjects.

In San Diego, it was especially important because being a Navy and border town, it also was known as a "hot town," a fact that had never occurred to me. This was not only because of the potential criminal element, but also because the SDPD made it hot for vagrants and wanted subjects. Military towns are like a large magnet for all kinds of people who hope to prey on servicemen, who like to throw their money around and "let the good times roll" like there's no tomorrow.

Bob then explained to me that the FBI estimated about ten percent of transients were wanted for felonies somewhere in the United States. He said the police department tried to jail as many as possible to positively identify them by fingerprinting them and checking for any wants and also to deter them from coming to San Diego as the word spread throughout the hobo jungles. If transients were booked and found guilty of vagrancy, Judge Brennan sentenced them to six months in jail, which was suspended if they were out of San Diego by 1:00 p.m., never to return. If they did return, they would have to serve the six months.

That sentence was known as a "floater," and, sadly, was deemed to be unconstitutional by the U.S. Supreme Court along with vagrancy laws in 1955. The court ruled that the vagrancy laws specified conditions, not actual criminal actions, so they violated the freedom of individuals. With that concept, "floaters" were as much or more in violation of civil rights. But they were very effective as crime-fighting weapons for San Diego as long as they lasted.

At about noon, Bob told me we had better have lunch, because I had to be back at the station to start Recruit Training School at one o'clock. That was the first I knew of it, and I was having so much fun with Bob, it didn't sound so hot. As it turned out, the Recruit Training School was 1:00 to 5:00 p.m., Monday through Friday for eight weeks and was very valuable.

When we stopped to have lunch at the Pickwick Hotel lunch counter, which was in a very large room that doubled as the Greyhound Bus Depot, Bob told me to always take the car keys whenever leaving the patrol car unmanned. He said a few years before, an officer left keys in a car and a drunken sailor drove away in the car. He said it caused more than one problem, and mostly for the officer who left the keys in the car. Another being that the drunk could hear radio reports that the police were after him.

Meals for police officers at the Pickwick Hotel lunch counter, like many other restaurants and hotels, were half price, or in some cases, even free. It was the proprietors' way of getting extra police protection and security at a bargain price, even if free. And the Greyhound Bus Depot was always a potential hotspot for snagging vagrants or even wanted subjects.

We had just returned to the patrol car when a police detective walked over to the car and spoke to Bob through the open window on my side. I knew he was a detective long before he got to the car, because he was wearing a fedora hat. SDPD regulations required detectives to wear fedoras as part of the official uniform. I always thought it was a stupid rule, because the only people who usually wore fedoras in San Diego were the Mafia, SDPD detectives and old men — usually the bald ones. So "Dicks," as they were called in the police department, may as well have worn uniforms, because they could be spotted from a block away.

The detective spoke over me to Bob and tried to be funny with some corny remarks equivalent to junior high school humor. By the time he left, laughing at his own corn, I wondered about a few things.

In that Bob and I had hit it off really well so far, I risked asking him some questions. First, who was that? Bob answered "Sergeant Gerald Dorn, a vice officer." My spontaneous next question was, "How did he ever make sergeant?"

Bob's reaction to the detective told me he viewed him in the same light as I did, and with much more reason — that exposure to him was like a very bad sunburn or a case of poison oak.

Showing his disgust, he said, "When he was a patrolman, he threw thousands in jail in hopes they were wanted somewhere. With a ten percent potential, he made some good arrests, but he threw thousands of completely innocent people in jail for nothing. He couldn't detect guilty or wanted ones from the others, so they all went to jail. And that got him promoted."

Bob was an excellent officer and used his intelligence and interrogation skills to detect the people who should go to jail to be checked for possible wants. And he had a very strong dislike for officers he thought made anything less than good, reasonable, responsible arrests.

Accordingly, he did not like Officer Glen Langley., who was also on Captain Stark's squad, and was permanently assigned to Beat 5, which abutted Beat 4 at 5th Avenue. If a veteran officer liked you, he would openly evaluate other officers to warn of the less than desirable ones to avoid if possible. Bob was certain Glen Langley was arrest happy and made many bad arrests.

Recruit Training School

While imparting his best tips to me for the time being, Bob drove me back to the station to start my classroom training. At the station I learned I was scheduled to be off the next two days, Tuesday and Wednesday. I would have to attend Recruit Training School, but not work. I was so absorbed by the job and riding with Bob, I didn't want to be off. I hadn't had so much fun working since I was 14, when I lied about my age and joined the California Division of Forestry in June 1945, two months before the end of World War II. The forestry was desperate.

The training officer was Lieutenant Robert King, and he conducted most of our recruit training. He was well educated but appeared to be somewhat short on what could be called street savvy. In addition to the 26 of us in my group, there were two other SDPD recruits who had been hired some time earlier. One had reportedly been secretly hired months before and assigned to work undercover on a very big, important case. Only the chiefs and a few supervisors reportedly knew who he was and what he was doing until the case was successfully closed. There were also two El Cajon and two La Mesa police officers and one San Diego City reservoir patrolman.

The reservoir patrolman was assigned to the El Capitan Reservoir, which was off limits to the public. We were very nice to the young patrolman, hoping he would let us fish there, but he made it clear that wouldn't happen. Although not happy with him, we actually respected him for his firm stand. Also, if he had let one big mouth in to spread the word, the entire San Diego Police Department would have been at his door. Or, knowing cops, some would have probably just gone up there and put their lines in the water without knocking.

We learned that half of our group of 26 would be assigned to the 7:00 a.m. to 3:00 p.m. day shift, and the other half would be assigned to the 8:00 p.m. to 4:00 a.m. Fourth Watch. Then, after four weeks we would swap shifts. The Fourth Watch was primarily walking foot beats and was a manpower pool for special details.

The Manual No One Read

In the class, we were issued a manual of departmental orders, policies and procedures. I eagerly read mine on my following days off. I was somewhat baffled by one order that required the permission of a supervisor for an officer to enter a house of prostitution. The Navy had reportedly demanded the closure of the Stingaree bordellos in 1940, and they had been gone since then. I thought, does anybody else read this thing?

It was obvious nobody had seriously read the manual for 12 years, since before some time in 1940. But then, in due time during my cop career, I learned that getting cops to read much of anything of substance was like trying to sell ice cubes to Eskimos by mail order.

About a week later, a departmental order was issued to all officers to remove the house of prostitution order from their manual. It brought much laughter, because it broadcast the confession that nobody, including the chief, two deputy chiefs or any of their aides had read the manual for about 12 years. But then why should they? It had a terrible plot and could put one to sleep.

I was assigned to the 7:00 a.m. to 3:00 p.m. shift for the first four weeks, and it was Captain Stark's squad. He was the senior captain and enjoyed the reputation of being the shrewdest horse trader of the three patrol division captains. He knew how to pair compatible officers and get the best results. He also had mostly senior sergeants who were more patient, wise, understanding and helpful.

My first day back from the two days off, I again rode with Bob Richards. From the garage, he went directly to a sidewalk coffee stand at the edge of a pay-by-the-hour, off-street parking lot a half block south of Horton Plaza. Almost immediately, a rotund parking lot attendant bounced out to report to Bob.

His report to Bob was that he didn't have anything to report. It was obvious he was a very dedicated police informant, and the most enthusiastic one I saw in my over 31 years in the cop business.

In that the main police station was on Bob's Beat 4, the unit had to do some of the unexciting chores, such as transporting prisoners to the county jail. About mid-morning, we received a call to 10-19 the jail (return to the station.) We picked up a prisoner, and I rode in the right rear seat with him to the county jail about a mile away.

We just reached the rear exterior door of the jail when it opened and out walked my county deputy marshal cousin, George Chase. With my joining the police department, he and I were the only law enforcement officers in our San Diego family of over 60 kin. One of our cousins had been a California Highway Patrolman in the 1920s during what was known as "Dual Control," when the state and counties shared control of the CHP, but he got tired of crashing on his motorcycle and quit to work at the Caliente Race Track in Tijuana. The only other Wood family member on the edge of police work was Papa's brother George, who had been a Pinkerton detective in San Francisco.

When my cousin George Chase passed the Bar and became an attorney and San Diego City deputy prosecutor, I became the only cop in our extended family for nearly 50 years, until about 2000 when my eldest grandson became a city police officer, despite my efforts to dissuade him.

Bob's first day off was Saturday, and I rode with Jack Fowler on Beat 4. Before we left the station, the shift sergeant gave Jack a note with a vehicle description and license number to look for. The sergeant said the owner of the 1948 Ford sedan couldn't locate the car and thought it might have been stolen.

As Jack drove east on G Street toward the sidewalk coffee stand and the enthusiastic, rotund police informant's parking lot, I spotted a 1948 Ford sedan on a cross street. The license plate matched, and it was where the owner had most likely parked it while drunk the night before — and staggered away into the darkness. Jack radioed the location to dispatch and headed for coffee.

Before we could get to the sidewalk, the informant bounced out and said "A hot one just went by toward the Plaza." He then quickly added the wino was drunk and annoying others, trying to hit them up for money.

We got back in the car and drove north the half block to Horton Plaza. We immediately spotted the wino standing backed up to the curb at the east end of the small Plaza block.

Jack circled the block clockwise and stopped within three feet of the drunk. With his half empty wine bottle sticking out of his ragged suit coat pocket, he was so busy trying to bum money from all the passersby, he didn't see us pull up.

Even with only four full days on the police department, I knew he was going to jail. So, I stepped out of the car, pulled the wine bottle out of his coat pocket, opened the right rear door and guided him into the left rear seat. With that, his only reaction was concern for his wine bottle.

Jack didn't even get out from behind the wheel, and we were on our way to jail in less than one minute. Before we had gone a hundred feet, the wino moaned, "They told me all the way down the coast not to come here 'cause it's the hottest town this side of Berkeley Hills." Jack barked, "Shut up or I'll knock your head off."

Jack's bark surprised me so much I think it scared me more than it did the wino. Regardless, the wino didn't utter another word all the way to jail and through the jail door. He didn't even ask what was going to happen to his cherished half-empty bottle of wine, even though I later learned most winos usually did. Sadly, the bottle was all they had to keep them going in life.

The Sad Nose Story

When we left the jail, Jack explained why he had barked at the wino. He said it went back to a bad experience he had when he was a brand new rookie.

He said he took a prisoner in tow at the Santa Fe Railroad Depot, one who had been citizen-arrested by the railroad police. Being only four blocks from the police station and jail on Kettner Boulevard, he decided to walk the prisoner to jail. But immediately after crossing Broadway, the prisoner punched Jack in the nose — and Jack had somewhat of a large nose to begin with. So Jack got a bloody nose, and the blood dripped on his uniform shirt.

Dramatically, Jack squeezed his nose and said he was proud of his nose, and that prisoner was really going to pay dearly for punching it. So he said he briskly marched the prisoner the four blocks down Kettner Boulevard to the station and into the captain's office. The watch commander captain had to approve and sign all booking slips, except for common drunk arrests.

Jack said he had to get the captain's approval and signature on the booking slip, because he had San Quentin in mind for his assailant. But to Jack's dismay, the captain wasn't that much impressed with the situation. He told Jack to book the man for the original charge and no more.

Jack said he took the prisoner to the jail and went directly back to the captain's office to plead his case. He said that was a very big mistake. The captain yawned while Jack presented his case, and then said incidents such as that were why officers had handcuffs, and they should have sense enough to use them. And, Jack had not used them. He also said drunks and other lawbreakers like to punch an officer, that's what they do. So, let it be a valuable lesson to you, and good luck.

Although Jack related the story in a humorous manner and I laughed a lot, it was obvious that Jack was still bent out of shape over his sore nose and the captain's lack of sympathy and understanding about the idea of San Quentin.

In my more than two years on the San Diego Police Department and the hundreds of resisting and combative prisoners arrested during that time, I never heard of one of them being charged with the Penal Code Section 148, resisting arrest. It just wasn't done on the SDPD.

With Jack's sad nose story and other bits I was picking up in the classroom and from others, it quickly became obvious that the San Diego Police Department did not overreact to situations. The attitude of most officers and supervisors was to maintain or restore peace and order with the least amount of arrest activity. There was a strong belief that time was on our side, and we would be around forever. So, if we let them get away with it with a warning and that didn't work, we would get them the next time. It worked very well, and I liked it that way.

There was also a very strong feeling among most officers that it was much better to let a guilty person go than put an innocent one in jail. With that belief, it followed that if people were guilty they would break the law again and we would be waiting to arrest them. This worked very well.

We rarely used our handcuffs unless all else failed and there was no other way. I don't recall ever using my cuffs while I was in the police department.

The Very Large Butcher Knife

The next week I was assigned to ride with Officer George Miller on Beat 20 in East San Diego, where I grew up. About 9:00 a.m. we received a disturbing the peace call at a location bordering on the edge of a canyon near 40th Street. We approached two young African/American women standing in front of their cabins, along with a few small children standing close to them. I recognized one of the women as a girl I went to school with. We had gone to Woodrow Wilson Junior High School and Herbert Hoover High School together, and she had been one year ahead of me. It disturbed me to see her living on the edge of a canyon in that shabby environment, because her brother was a successful musician with a very popular band, and it seemed to me that he could have helped her. ·

At the same time, we saw and heard a large African/American woman standing about 30 feet away to our right. She was yelling and waving a very, very large butcher knife in the air like Errol Flynn with a sword in Robin Hood. I estimated the blade to be about a foot

16

long and two inches wide, and it was truly one of the largest knives I had ever seen.

George spoke to the younger women. They said the older, larger woman who was yelling had just been released about a month earlier from Patton State Hospital and was upset because she thought the younger women's small children were picking on her small children.

Hearing that, I thought, "What's the big deal? All kids do that." But to a mother just out of a state mental hospital it can be a big thing.

George then casually walked over to the yelling woman, and I followed. Standing about two feet to the left of George, I watched as the woman proceeded to beat George on the chest with the flat of the blade, yelling about those mean children.

George had been in the Marines in World War II, and he told me he had volunteered to be a paratrooper. But the first time he practice-jumped off the drill tower he broke a leg when he hit the ground. With that, he said he was pretty sure he may have set a record for the shortest paratrooper career in U.S. Marine Corps history. His active paratrooper career spanned from when he jumped until he hit the ground.

In the way he related that once-in-a-lifetime experience, George had a droll sense of humor and was definitely unflappable. So, watching him almost yawn while being beaten on the chest with a very large butcher knife amused me.

While beating George, the woman also said she was going to go to her mother-in-law's house to get away from those mean children. With that, George asked me to call for a sergeant, so I radioed a request from the patrol car.

Sergeant Cody Ingram must have been nearby, as he arrived in about five minutes. George quickly apprised Ingram of the situation, and the sergeant said it would be best if the woman took her children and went to her mother-in-law's house. The woman said she would go as soon as she could get ready.

With all apparently under control and agreed upon, the two young women went into one of their cabins with their "mean" children, and we returned to the patrol car. As soon as we got into the car, George said, "I was more concerned about what you might do than what she might do." Knowing his droll sense of humor, I replied, "It

didn't bother me. It was your chest she was beating on, not mine."
We both laughed.

George then said, "I don't like to call a sergeant to make decisions for me, but that situation was so shaky. I just didn't want to take the responsibility for what might happen after we left." "I agree," I said, and we soon became good friends and later worked as partners for two eight-week shift assignments.

With the San Diego Police Department environment as it was in those days and with George Miller's always cool head, that tense event turned out the way it should have. But I hate to think of what would happen to that poor, upset woman in today's sometimes trigger-happy police world.

Training Days in the Jail

On the first of my three training days at the jail, there was a mild panic. The San Diego County Grand Jury was scheduled to inspect the jail the next day and did not know about the candy and cigarette cart.

The candy and cigarette cart was the only source for the prisoners to buy their goodies, and the net profits were equally shared by the jailers, which was the only perk for working in that undesirable environment. I didn't ask, but it must have been fairly profitable for each of them, because there were some excellent officers on the jail crew. And, it would have had to be a real gold mine for me to want to work in the jail. However, in a timely manner the cart disappeared after making its rounds for a last purchase before being iced away in some secret cave.

The most interesting chore the jail crew had me do was to escort two young heroin addicts to the crime lab for the "criminalist," Lieutenant Walter Smith, to take photos of the numerous needle marks on their arms as evidence.

When the photos had been taken, I walked the two men back to their cell. They were in horrible shape, perspiring and shaking uncontrollably from withdrawal. It was about lunch time, so I asked them if they wanted anything to eat. As I expected, they were not at all interested in any food, and most likely, not even interested in living. It was a very sad scene.

When I told the jailers the heroin addicts were in bad shape and didn't want any lunch, the street-wise sergeant took the time to explain to me the evolution of narcotics addiction. He said the heroin addicts start by smoking marijuana. But, after getting high on pot for a length of time, its "happy" effect grows less and less as they acquire a tolerance for its influence. He said they then graduate to heroin to get their kicks and start peddling marijuana to support their expensive heroin habit. Then they end up like the two men in the tank.

The sergeant concluded by telling me not to feel sorry for the two men, because they were no doubt drug pushers and had probably got many younger kids hooked on drugs.

After serving my time in the jail, I was again assigned to ride with George Miller for two days. As was the very wise and effective practice of the police department, he, like most other competent, experienced officers, was permanently assigned to a beat with a permanent partner. His partner was Bob Long when they were teamed up on evening and graveyard shifts.

Contrary to some over-educated fools who suffer from "ivory tower" brainstorming and attempts to reinvent the wheel, the San Diego Police Department's permanent beat and partner system was by far the most effective. Beat officers could get to know who the good and bad guys are and develop confidential informants.

Like Bob Richards and most of the other officers I rode with during and after my first year in the police, Miller told me of some of his experiences. Some were educational and others were humorous, or both. They also told stories about other officers.

The Swede

In his droll way, he told me of his being partnered with a large, blond officer I'll call "Swede," because he looked exactly like a big Swedish lumberjack. All the time I was in the police department Swede was a big, affable, smiling juvenile officer. After George told me his story about Swede, I could easily see why he was a "juvie" officer. He could "B.S." the best of them, and no juvenile delinquent was going to verbally sneak up on him or lead him down a dead end.

George said he and Swede were working the beat in the area of the Midway Federal Housing Project just north of the Marine Corps Recruit Depot when they arrested a very belligerent drunk. Swede drove and George rode in the rear with the drunk. Just after Swede radioed they were on their way to jail, he released the mike "on" button and spoke into the dead mike. He loudly requested a records and wants check on the drunk — loud enough to be heard over the drunk's bellowing.

George said Swede waited until just after a call had been broadcast to another unit, and he stuck the transmitter on his right ear for several seconds. He then loudly said, "Just as I suspected, you're wanted for murder in Detroit." George said the drunk immediately went silent for a few seconds, then bellowed, "I've never been to Detroit and don't even know where it is."

"They all say that," Swede replied, then added, "but if you're really nice to the jailers, they will double check to clear your name or send you to Detroit. Now be a good boy and we 'll put in a good word for you with the jailers."

George said he had extreme difficulty to keep from laughing, and it worked perfectly. The drunk suddenly became a model prisoner all the way to and into the jail.

When the drunk anxiously asked the jailers to check for a want on him, one of the jailers looked at Swede and asked, "Detroit?" Swede nodded and said, "Yep." The jailer smiled and said, "Thanks."

I laughed and thought of Bob Richard's telling me it was much better to talk people into jail than to fight them. And I thought they should have Swede teach his sure-fire system to us rookies in Recruit Training. But then I thought the chief probably didn't know about it and may not have thought it was very professional. It didn't take long for me to discover that chiefs are funny that way. They hadn't been on the streets for years.

During my four weeks assigned to Captain Stark's squad I rode with three other officers: Judson, Stanley and Hall. They all treated me like a kid brother and bent over backwards to teach me what they could. Hall told me he was from Louisiana and thought we should knock heads like the cops did back home. He weighed about 240 pounds and liked his booze, but he treated me like a little brother and had a great sense of humor.

It was about half way through my four weeks and I was riding with Hall when we got a call to meet the sergeant at Texas Street and El Cajon Boulevard.

Sergeant Paul Sears got into the back of the patrol car and handed us our monthly paychecks. It was August 1, and mine was only for the two weeks from July 14 to the end of July. Sergeant Sears laughed and told me not to spend it all in one place.

The sergeant then reached up and handed Hall and me pledge cards to have a one-dollar deduction each month for the Community Chest charity. I explained to Sergeant Sears that my wife was expected to deliver our first child that month; she was on maternity leave from the phone company, and I didn't want her to go back to work until after our hoped-for two children were in school. And thanks to Blue Cross and Blue Shield splitting apart a few months before, we had lost half of our medical coverage to pay for her doctor. I also mentioned the cost of buying my police uniforms and equipment.

Brotherly Hall said, "George, Chief Jansen is very proud of the department's 100 percent donation participation. The last officer who refused to donate had to walk the graveyard foot beat in Balboa Park for a whole year, and he couldn't wait to sign up to donate the next year." Sergeant Sears still remained silent.

Then after a few seconds, Hall added, "And, George, you're on probation, and the chief can fire probationary officers without any cause at all. He has the last and final word, and there is no right of appeal."

Without hesitation, I signed the damn pledge card, even though I had to take a part-time job at my friend's sand plant to make ends meet. A dollar was worth much more in those days.

The chief's absolute firing right, which I hadn't been told of before, made me think of the second day of my business office/communications center orientation training.

The First Encounter

Just before noon, the deputy chief of field personnel stepped into the business office and asked if I was ready to go to lunch.

With that friendly invitation, I quickly replied yes. As we started walking across the large, drive-through patio toward the jail and adjacent employees' coffee shop, the deputy chief asked me if I planned to attend the two-week National Guard training camp the next summer.

Not knowing the chief hated military reserves and the loss of officers to summer training camps, I ignorantly answered, "Yes, sir."

"That's nice. Everybody has to make choices in their lives, and yours just happens to be if you want to be a policeman or a National Guardsman," he curtly exclaimed. He then instantly increased his pace and left me in the dust, with no free lunch — and we were where nobody else heard him say it.

Like thousands of other Americans aged 18 to 35, I had joined the National Guard to avoid the "Compulsory Military Training" draft. It was a very unpopular draft for one year in the Army as a "dogface" soldier with basic training only. And probably a year of being the lowest form of life in the Army, picking up cigarette butts and peeling potatoes, and receiving slave's wages. We envisioned it as being sentenced to a year in the sheriff's honor farm, or worse — maybe in some hell hole in Arkansas or some snake-infested swampland in the Deep South.

So, like nearly all the others, I was not a dedicated soldier. I was in the National Guard so I could go on with my life and start building a career of my choice.

But the deputy chief's snide remark that I must choose being in the National Guard or being a policeman was not his first sneak attack on me. The day before, he had me drive him home for no other reason than to ask me why I had joined the police department instead of the fire department. It wasn't until months later that I learned from my closest cousin that one of the many cousins I had never met had been married to the deputy chief's daughter for many years.

He had probably heard Grandpa Wood's outspoken opinion that "When firemen do their job, they make a friend, but when policemen do their job, they make an enemy." Solely from that, he no doubt thought I had joined the police department to make friends with law breakers, not arrest them.

All the pieces of the puzzle of why he was bird-dogging me didn't come together until months later, and only after he pulled another sneak attack on me the next month when I was on the Fourth Watch, 8:00 p.m. to 4:00 a.m.

He obviously knew only enough to be dangerous and didn't know I had been nearly raised by my surrogate father and role model — an honest, dedicated veteran San Diego police officer, who taught me firearms safety and all he could about law enforcement starting when I was about five years old.

With the kindly help of more than one sergeant and many officers I was able to survive the deputy chief's sneak attacks.

CHAPTER 3

"Bull" and More "Bull"

"We have information that 'Bull' Johnson, the leader of a Los Angeles armed robbery gang, is holed up in a lower end unit in Midway Housing. We're going to post you hidden near the rear door with a shotgun. Then we're going to turn on some large floodlights and order 'Bull' Johnson to come out with a bull horn. If anybody comes out the back door after we have used the bull horn, don't say a word, just blast them."

In the fifth week of training half of our group was switched from the day shift to the Fourth Watch, 8:00 p.m. to 4:00. The first night we were called into formation by Sergeant Art McCloud for roll call and assignments. He introduced Officer Ted Donovan, who would be an acting sergeant.

I had never seen either of them before, but they looked harmless enough, especially Donovan, because he appeared to be on the verge of bursting into laughter at any time.

We rookies were assigned to walk beats with more experienced officers. Not necessarily top notch officers, but experienced. Otherwise, they would have been assigned to the always beefed-up graveyard shift. In other words, they were sort of "leftovers," not the pick of the litter.

I was assigned to walk the El Cajon Boulevard foot beat with Officer Floyd Bean. He was the minimum San Diego Police Department size of five feet nine and one-half inches, weighed about 150, was baby-faced and the son of a lieutenant. As it turned out I quickly learned he was hell-bent on covering the beat as rapidly as humanly possible, without slowing to observe anything or anybody. I kept up with him, but anybody could have carried the beat away, and we would never have seen any of it. It was like a blurry race.

Both Sergeant McCloud and Officer Donovan quickly tried to set the stage for eight hours of fun every shift, starting with roll call, except on Saturday nights. That was the night when the deputy chief of field personnel always sat in his reserved chair next to the window overlooking the drive-through patio. From there he scrutinized everyone with his icy, steely eyes, and nobody was safe. He always wore a fedora and overcoat and could have passed for a Mafia hit man, but he was only the San Diego Police Department hit man, as I learned in due time.

It didn't take long for Ted Donovan and me to hit it off in a big way. It was probably because I laughed at him and his side-splitting antics louder than anyone else. But that wasn't difficult, because I quickly noticed that Bob Richards was not exactly correct about a great sense of humor being essential for enduring police work. Of course, the less-than-blue-ribbon officers on Fourth Watch were no competition in the "funny" department. Some obviously had no sense of humor, personality or social skills, and most of them took themselves so seriously, they thought they were super cops.

Apparently because I laughed at his almost non-stop humor binge, Ted Donovan had me ride with him some nights. The first night, he couldn't wait to tell me how he got booted out of the auto theft unit, and how much fun it was doing it.

As soon as he had dropped off the last officer at his walking beat, he told me he was on the Fourth Watch for the first time in his police career, which dated back about 12 years to before World War II. He said he was on the Fourth Watch because he had just been booted out of the auto theft unit. He laughed and said he wanted out, because he couldn't stomach the lieutenant in charge of the unit any more, and never could.

I immediately laughed, because I had seen that lieutenant several times during my four weeks on day shift and I had formed the opinion that he was very strange. He drove a big black Cadillac sedan with wide white sidewalls like movie stars drove. He dressed colorfully like a carnival barker, smoked with a very long cigarette holder and instantly reminded me of slicked-down movie actor Adolph Menjou. I also got the impression that he or his wife had inherited a fortune, and she dressed him every morning and sent him on his way to browbeat his riffraff inferiors in rank — with final instructions as she shoved him out the door.

The Staple Caper

Barely holding back another belly laugh, Ted said the most hated lieutenant had issued strict orders that all new reports were to be placed at the left top of his desk blotter in an absolutely neat pile for him every morning. Ted said each morning the lieutenant burst in the office door puffing on his cigarette holder, and without slowing, grabbed the pile and briskly out the opposite door to the coffee room without acknowledging anyone.

Ted said he wanted out so badly he volunteered to do the dirty work, as his partner was married, had children, and enjoyed working week days so he could be with them as much as possible. So, Ted said he stapled all the reports together then stapled the pile to the desk blotter.

Ted and his partner made it a point to be at their desks at the appointed time when the lieutenant always busted through the office door. He said in his anticipation of seeing the event, he could hardly keep himself from laughing.

Ted said the lieutenant stormed in as always, grabbed the pile of reports, and upon pulling on the pile, everything on the lieutenant's desk flew in all directions as he dragged the pile and the blotter behind him for several feet.

Ted said he laughed so loud that it was equivalent to signing a full typed confession. He had waited until a few days before the next eight-week shift rotation and transfer deadline so he could get out without the lieutenant assigning him some garbage detail, like a graveyard stakeout at the city dump.

From the beginning, my training officers confided in me about where some bones were buried and who had skeletons in their closets. And there were many hidden bones in some people's pasts.

One of my eager informants told me the well-known fact that Ted's father was a retired SDPD chief of detectives. I thought, "What a contradiction!" His father was in such an important, powerful position, and Ted's greatest ambition in life was to find police department foul-ups and relate them in his humorous way as Keystone Kop capers.

What was interesting to me about Ted's auto theft escape story was that he was assigned to the Fourth Watch as an acting sergeant with Sergeant McCloud, another police department clown. Those who earned the wrath of Chief Jansen or the deputy chief of field personnel usually ended up walking graveyard shift in Balboa Park. In that those two chiefs did show a glimmer of a sense of humor on rare occasions, I had to believe they may have thought Ted's staple job was funny and that the weird lieutenant got what he had coming. But nobody outside the exclusive inner circle of the corner chiefs' offices would ever know.

I laughed so hard at Ted's staple caper that it spurred him on with more of his comedy collection. He really enjoyed telling me about how fouled-up and disorganized the police department was when Clifford E. Peterson was chief from 1940 to 1947. He said they did not have any personnel inspections or much shooting practice at the range. So when Jansen became chief, he initiated both as routine, but it posed a problem for Officer Tom Horton.

The Moldy Service Revolver

Tom Horton was six feet six inches tall, trim and gray-haired with a gray pencil mustache. He was always impeccable and as distinguished looking as a superior court judge or southern colonel.

Ted said it was crazy that Tom had not fired or cleaned his service revolver in the seven years Clifford E. Peterson was chief, but thanks to Chief Jansen, that changed. Laughing, Ted said it was only then that the condition of Tom's department-issue gun became apparent. The handle had broken, so it was wrapped with a thick layer of friction tape to keep it together. Then when the sergeant tried to unload it, the .38 caliber cartridges wouldn't come out of the cylinder. The cartridge casings were brass, and they had turned green like mold in the salty San Diego air. Laughing loudly, Ted said they had to issue Tom another service revolver and put his moldy one in a bucket of solvent to soak for days before they could pry the cartridges out of the gun.

With me still laughing, Ted started on his next story of police department folly. He said one of the all-black 1940 patrol cars they had to drive during the war had been crashed so many times the body and frame were out of whack and had become flexible. When they turned to the right at higher speeds, the left rear door flew open. They hit the brakes hard to shut it.

As I laughed at that Keystone Kop scene in my mind, I wondered if that was the same black 1940 Ford sedan police car that had chased my friends and me for 10:00 p.m. curfew violations during the war.

The Nickel-Snatcher Gambling Raid

The second Thursday night of Fourth Watch, Sergeant McCloud told us in lineup that they had received word that the gamblers would be on the "Nickel-snatchers" the next afternoon. Those were the launches that ferried North Island Naval Air Station sailors and civilian workers to and from North Island. The fare was a nickel, thus the slang name.

Sergeant McCloud named about 10 or 12 senior officers to work undercover in work clothes with a lunch pail, if they had one, to pose as North Island workers. One he named was Floyd Bean, the extra speedy walking beat officer, who could also talk as fast as he could walk.

The North Island civilian workers were paid on Fridays, and I had read in the Union Tribune one or two years before that the police department had conducted a raid and arrested many for gambling on the Nickel-snatchers.

At the lineup on Saturday, Sergeant McCloud said the gambling raid went very well on Friday, and he asked Floyd Bean if he would like to tell everybody how it went for him. We all listened in anticipation of a successful arrest story.

Speaking very deliberately and slowly as though testifying in court, Floyd Bean said he sat next to a North Island civilian worker, and they had a very pleasant conversation. Having a fine gift of gab, we all figured he did well to blend in with anybody.

He said as soon as they cleared the North Island docks, the gamblers made their move to get the dice rolling. With that, the worker he had been talking to got up and started laying down bets.

Floyd Bean said as they started the approach to the docks on the San Diego side of the bay, where several police department undercover officers were waiting to take the gamblers into custody, he stood up with his badge in his hand and said, "San Diego Police Department, you're all under arrest."

Instantly the worker he had been talking to jumped up and yelled, "You son of a bitch, I thought you were my friend," grabbed Floyd and threw him overboard into the murky, not-too-blue Pacific Bay.

As we all roared with laughter, Floyd Bean just stood there stone-faced. Clearly recalling the captain not going along with Jack Fowler's desire to send his assailant to San Quentin, I figured Floyd Bean had similar wishes for the worker who so rudely put him in the bay — and without asking him if he could swim. Floyd's coolness may have been an act, but it worked.

The Unlocked Door

The next Saturday night I was assigned to walk the Hillcrest foot beat alone. There were rows of business offices and stores on both 5th and University Avenues. It was part of our job to check the front doors to ensure they were locked and secured. After grabbing and trying to turn door handles and push about 50 doors to be sure they were secure, it got to be routine and boring.

That was until the door handle turned on one on 5th Avenue, and I half stumbled through the door into a large dark room. Startled, I quickly backed out and drew my revolver, as we had been instructed to do whenever entering or checking an open or unsecured business.

I then reached through the door, found the light switch and turned on the lights, still standing outside the room. The room had row after row of desks with little on them other than a phone on each desk.

I checked the business name on the front door and the address and used the nearest phone to call the station to report the unlocked door. It took only a few minutes for the police department operator to tell me the owner said there was nothing of value in the office, so just lock the door for him.

The quickness of contacting the business owner was due to the department's very shrewd service to all business owners.

The police department had an annual policemen's ball. So, every year about a month before the ball, the police department mailed ten ball tickets to every business owner, along with a three by five filing card the owner was requested to fill out with information needed for emergency notifications. Without any duress, the tickets could be returned with the completed three by five information card or with a check for the purchase of tickets not returned.

As in my case of discovering the unlocked door, this system worked great for all concerned. But then, the policemen's ball left something to be desired with respect to a few issues that ended the gala bash years later.

Walking officers had to call in on a regular or Police "Gamewell" phone once every hour at a designated time after the hour. This call was to let the station know we were still alive, and sometimes to be told to stand by to be picked up for a special detail.

I called in about 15 minutes after locating the unlocked door and was told to stand by at 5th and University to be picked up for a special detail. I had called in on a "Gamewell" phone at 5th and University, so I just waited.

The Special Detail

About five minutes later, Ted Donovan drove up. I eagerly got in hoping to hear more of his hysterical Keystone Kop historical events, but he wasn't his usual jovial self.

After going down 5th Avenue about a block, Ted solemnly said Sergeant McCloud had a special detail for me. That was all he said. The rest of the ride was pretty much like being in a funeral procession with the grieving family.

When we arrived at the station, I walked from the garage through the locker room and into the squad room. Sergeant McCloud was standing almost in the open doorway to the drive-through patio, and next to another officer. The other officer was one of the two hired a few months before my group, was 27 years old and an ex-marine.

Sergeant McCloud immediately told me they had a detail for me in the Midway Federal Housing Project. He explained, "We have information that 'Bull' Johnson, the leader of a Los Angeles armed robbery gang, is holed up in a lower end unit in Midway Housing. We're going to post you hidden near the rear door with a shotgun. Then we're going to turn on some large floodlights and order 'Bull' Johnson to come out with a bull horn. If anybody comes out the back door after we have used the bull horn, don't say a word, just blast them."

After a brief pause, Sergeant McCloud said, "Go leave your cap in your locker, put on your leather jacket, and leave your badge on your shirt under your jacket." I said, "Okay," and went directly to my locker, but I thought something was fishy. First of all, I had just turned 22 years of age, was not a veteran, had not had shotgun training, and they didn't know if I had ever fired a shotgun. Conversely, the other officer standing next to Sergeant McCloud and silently observing the scene was 27 years old, had been on the police department longer than I had and was a marine veteran, so I wondered why they chose me.

When I returned to the squad room about five minutes later outfitted as directed, Sergeant McCloud was still standing in exactly the same place. He immediately told me they had just learned "Bull" Johnson was not where they thought he was and the detail was cancelled. He then told me I could walk the Ocean Beach beat with the silent observer officer.

That turned out to be another form of punishment. He got the car keys and drove to and from Ocean Beach like a crazy man — at about 60 miles per hour both ways in speed zones of no more than 35 miles per hour. I didn't scare easily because of another person's driving, but he put me over the edge in that department that night. Thankfully, we were never on the same patrol division squad and never worked together again.

It took me some time before I put all the pieces together to the "Bull" Johnson and "bull horn" mystery. First of all, the deputy chief was mysteriously absent that Saturday night. At least I didn't see him in his reserved seat at the window overlooking the patio. He was always there on Saturday nights and rode with a sergeant for hours after Fourth Watch lineup.

Along with his not being seen that night, Sergeant McCloud stood almost in the open doorway to the patio. Although it was summer and that door was usually left open when it was warm, it was also only several feet from the sergeants' office window. I also learned in due time that the deputy chief used that office for his dirty work or interviews. With Sergeant McCloud standing where he had, everything he said and I said could be heard in the sergeants' office through that window.

The Question

I also recalled that during my pre-employment interview with Chief Jansen and the two deputy chiefs, that this deputy chief had asked me a very specific and unusual question. He had asked me what I would do if a sergeant ordered me to do something illegal during an emergency situation.

Of course, you never completely tell the truth during an employment interview. You tell them what you think they want to hear. And most interview questions are so vague that you just have to take your best shot.

So I had said I would follow the sergeant's orders. Then, after the emergency was over, I would ask him why he had given me that order. I silently thought it depends on the order.

Then a few months later, I had a conversation with my deputy marshal cousin, George Chase. He told me Sergeant Art McCloud was his best friend and had been the best man at his wedding. He also casually mentioned McCloud was one of the deputy chief's pet sergeants. Bingo! That put most of the pieces together, but I wondered why the deputy chief was chomping at the bit to get something on me when he had the whole probationary year period to get rid of me if I didn't perform satisfactorily. And looking around on the job, I could sure see some others that he should be dogging instead of me. I've been getting along with everybody, so why me?

Really digging for some logical or even sick answer, I thought of what mother told me Papa said so many times about firemen making friends and policemen making enemies. I thought, did he hear what Papa said so many times and think I'm in a popularity contest to try to make friends with a police badge? Or is he just nuts and loves to fire officers to exercise his power and feed his sagging ego?

Actually, in due time I decided it was the latter. And I figured he didn't trust the sergeants, lieutenants and captains to do their jobs, so he had to be the one-man show to run the San Diego Police Department like the Lone Ranger. He later proved me right.

I also wondered why the silent observing officer I had to walk with in Ocean Beach was at the station over an hour after the rest of us had gone to our assigned beats. Did the deputy chief have me walk with him to find out if I would say anything about the concocted shotgun assignment? I would never know, but I started looking over my shoulder more often for sneak attacks. With that in mind, it came to me that a person should be able to keep his eye on the ball, not the umpire, but as long as he was the umpire, to hell with the ball.

But I couldn't blame Sergeant McCloud or the observing officer. McCloud had done everything possible to warn me it was a sneaky trap with his excessive use of "Bull" Johnson and "bullhorn." He did everything he could to tell me it was a bunch of "BULL." And like Sergeant McCloud, the other officer had no choice, if he was in on it as I had every reason to suspect.

The fact was if that deputy chief told you to do something, you had better do it with a smile. I learned this from Gary Gray, my partner starting four months later. If you displeased that deputy chief in any way, you would pay for it for a long time. So, Sergeant McCloud and the other officer had no choices in that sleazy matter.

As far as I knew, that was the last of the deputy chief's games to nail me for doing absolutely nothing wrong. I had to believe he would stalk some other poor soul. And he did!

CHAPTER 4

School Days

All in all, the Recruit Training School was very valuable, but we had to learn true police work on the streets in the years to come. And we learned in due time it was almost a never ending process.

The Recruit Training School was very demanding on the days we had to work on the Fourth Watch. With Mondays and Tuesdays off, Wednesdays, Thursdays and Fridays seemed like a marathon. We would work from 8:00 p.m. to 4:00 a.m., go to school from 1:00 p.m. to 5:00 p.m., then go back to work at 8:00 p.m. for Fourth Watch. We didn't get much sleep at one stretch, and walking eight-hour shifts was tiring.

That was only for four weeks, so life did go on. It was worth it, because we gained so much valuable information about police department operations, unwritten policies, personal tips and firearms training. However, we learned little about the Vehicle Code.

A motorcycle sergeant coached us on traffic law enforcement. We did not receive much if any Vehicle Code training, but we were issued 1951 California Vehicle Codes. And the sergeant advised us if we saw drivers do something we thought was illegal, but were not sure of it, we should not stop them and make a bumbling fool of ourselves. Instead, we should go down a side street, park and try to find the section in the Vehicle Code. That was it.

He also said we should never issue a traffic citation unless we would be willing to accept it if we were on the receiving end. And he said if we were in Judge Brennan's court too often with not guilty pleas, he would start dismissing our cases.

That was comforting to me, because George Miller was the first to tell me it was common police department practice not to stop or cite anyone for speeding unless they were going at least 15 miles per hour over the speed limit. And when for many years I knew of, Oceanside and San Clemente had bad names for writing wholesale tickets. U.S. Highway 101 went through those cities and the speed limit was an unreasonably low 25 miles per hour, even in the south end of San Clemente, which was undeveloped open space. At one time in the late 1940s, the National Auto Club reported one or both of those cities for being speed traps. So, I was pleased to hear the San Diego Police Department did not as a general rule write tickets primarily for revenue. I wanted to issue traffic tickets solely to prevent traffic accidents, a policy which the California Highway Patrol was noted for.

One of our instructors was a large vice officer named Rod Taylor, who was built like a pro football lineman. I immediately got the impression he had played football in college, and maybe in the pros.

Corruption in the Board of Equalization

He gave us an overview of the vice squad operations. He then emphasized not to make any alcoholic beverage (ABC) arrests. He made it very clear that ABC arrests only gave the enforcing agency, the Board of Equalization, the chance to extort a payoff from the liquor licensee to wipe it off the books. He said to ignore all violations, such as serving booze to a minor.

It shocked me to hear that blatant corruption still existed, because my brother Ed told me of it in 1946. Two of his friends' fathers owned bars, and they had both been extorted that year. One had a beer and wine license bar in East San Diego, not far from the police department substation. The other had a full liquor license bar in Hillcrest. Their bartenders had been cited by Board of Equalization agents for serving liquor to a minor. Thereafter, the fathers both received anonymous phone calls telling them to put old bills in a paper bag and give it to a man in front of a closed downtown store at a specific time and day. They were to say a code word to the man, and he would reply with a code word. They were not to look at the man and were to immediately leave.

They did what they were told, and a few nights later they received a second anonymous call. They were told the problem had been taken care of. The beer and wine bar owner had to give $1,500 and the full liquor license bar owner had to pay $3,000. That was when a new Ford or Chevrolet cost less than $2,000.

Taylor told us that the problem was being taken care of, and we would know all about it when it was corrected.

The Range Master

We spent one session at the police pistol range near Home Avenue and Federal Boulevard, only a few blocks from the future World Light Heavyweight Boxing Champion Archie Moore's "Chicken Shack" restaurant.

Sergeant James was the range master, and he knew his stuff. Most impressive was his demonstration of the penetration capabilities of different caliber firearms. He had some short lengths of utility poles he used to show which caliber firearms would completely penetrate them.

Just before he fired a high-powered rifle into a pole, he said, "If the gunman has his daddy's deer rifle, don't rely on a telephone or power pole to protect you." He then fired into the pole. The bullet came out the opposite side.

Three years later when I was on the California Highway Patrol in San Bernardino, a CHP officer was at a shootout in Alturas and used a utility pole for cover. The gunman was an escapee from an Oregon state prison and was armed with a deer rifle. He shot through the pole and killed the officer. The CHP did not have any firearms penetration training at that time.

All in all, the Recruit Training School was very valuable, but we had to learn true police work on the streets in the years to come. And we learned in due time it was almost a never ending process.

We soon learned there was no other work like police work, and as Bob Richards said, "This work gets in your blood real fast and spoils you for any other kind of work." He was so right. But his sense of humor thing was still not for sure.

We were also told during a class that Chief Jansen's position was protected by civil service, so he did not have to play political favors. Also, that in years past an officer had arrested and jailed a mayor for felony hit-and-run. In addition, that same officer had towed in the mayor's limousine because it was parked blocking a driveway. Despite those two bold actions, that officer was a lieutenant at the time.

With these assurances of objective, unbiased enforcement without political interference, influence or corruption, we felt good that we could do the job without fear or favor.

But in due time, that proved to be a myth.

CHAPTER 5

Strange Ducks

If it looks like a duck, walks like a duck, and quacks like a duck, it's a duck.

Our Recruit Training School ended on Friday, September 9th, and I had the following Monday, the 12th, and Tuesday, the 13th, as days off. They were my first complete days off without going to the police station for work or school in eight weeks.

My wife was pregnant with the first of our two children, and her obstetrician was certain she would give birth in the middle of August. He was sure she was a month overdue. I walked a beat on Sunday night, and I had just got into bed at about 4:30 a.m. when she told me it was time to go to the hospital. So we got up and headed for Mercy Hospital in Hillcrest. On the way I saw a Daisy air rifle in the middle of the street, so I had to stop and grab it.

> Years after retiring from the CHP, I looked back on my life and career and recognized several incidents that I had to identify as divine interventions, and our son being born on my first complete day off in eight weeks struck me as being one of them, as well as finding an air rifle for him.

With two full days off and no school homework, I finally had time to visit my surrogate father Nanno, and I told him I was disappointed in some of the officers who had been hired in our group of 26. Nanno chuckled and replied, "There have always been some strange ducks who wanted to be policemen." It was after he expressed that observation that he told me he had to give a City Councilman fifty dollars to get on the police department in 1908.

Being only one of the few in my group of 26 to be assigned to Captain Stark's patrol division squad, I was extremely fortunate. The others were assigned to the other two squads, or stuck on the painful walking-beat Fourth Watch indefinitely.

Not long after we graduated from the classroom training, one member of our group of 26 was fired for indecently exposing himself to some young girls at a school on his way home from work.

We were allowed to wear our uniforms to and from work, but we had to wear a coat or jacket to conceal our badge. And about the only men who wore black ties were cops, Navy chiefs and commissioned officers who weren't normally on the streets during business hours on weekdays, so it probably didn't take much to identify that "sicko" rookie cop.

That "weenie waver" was immediately fired but not criminally prosecuted, because a criminal charge would become a public court record and would probably be on page one of the next edition of the San Diego Union Tribune. Then every San Diego police officer would have to take cheap shots from the city's lowlifes or what we called "Shitbirds" and "Gunsels" for about six months thereafter. So the officer, along with too many others, got away with the crime, but will never again be a cop, since they were red flagged in police files.

I strongly disagreed with letting them go free of criminal prosecution. They were twice as guilty as John Doe citizen, because in addition to committing a crime, they violated a sacred oath and trust to uphold the law. I also felt that prosecuting and publicizing their firing and prosecution would tell the public that the department got rid of its bad apples and busted their own the same as John Doe. I also felt it would serve as a deterrent for weaker, borderline officers to think about before wandering off the straight and narrow path. As far as taking cheap shots from the lowlifes, we had to do that every day anyway. Furthermore, we didn't listen to them.

The gracious captains allowed us rookies to select Christmas Eve or New Years Eve off to celebrate one of them. One officer I really liked apparently had the same mentality he had while going to San Diego State College, where he had been in the same fraternity as my two older brothers, Don and Ed. He picked Christmas Eve, as I did. Then on New Years Eve, he called in sick and went to the fraternity New Years Eve party. That was too obvious, and with some witnesses, he was fired on New Years Day. Happy New Year!

Although those two officers were the most obvious in the crazy department, others weren't far behind. At the end of our probationary period, only 14 out of the 26 were remaining. Nanno had some humorous terms for describing unusual or strange people and "ducks" fit perfectly, because most of those fired could also be appropriately classified as "quacks."

CHAPTER 6

Street Thug with a Badge

Red was not only a "sterilized" whiskey and two-bit screwdriver thief he was a full-blown thief — of anything.

For the first four weeks after graduating from Recruit Training School, I was assigned to newly created Beat 13 on graveyard shift with Officers "Woody" Wallace and Terry Leach. Beat 13 was east of the cemeteries along Imperial Avenue and included the small, somewhat countrified 4-H community of Encanto.

Woody had been one of the original Junior Patrol officer supervisors and was well known by people my age and those years older. He smoked with a cigarette holder, was quite intelligent and sort of a country boy and plodding philosopher. He was enjoyable to work with, but in sleepy Encanto, there wasn't much if any police work to do. It was like a cemetery and an ideal beat for Woody.

Terry Leach was also well suited for Beat 13. Almost from the start, he let me know he didn't want to do any more than he had to. He said he got the same pay as the officers who work hard, so he was happy doing as little as possible. Somewhere along the way in our many hours together, he also said he didn't like Officer Gary Gray. He said Gray was brutal and was arrest happy. Somehow I found out Leach was one of the emergency wartime temporary hires and had gained permanent status after the war.

The only activity during those four weeks was the arrest of one very intoxicated DUI driver, and on one of my nights off, a two-car, major injury collision at the four-way-stop intersection of 47th Street and Imperial Avenue — and at about 2:30 a.m. on a week night.

Although 47th Street was a back way track to Tijuana, it amazed me that probably the only two vehicles on the road within miles of each other that time of the night could both run stop signs at the same time and crash into each other. It almost seemed like divine intervention in reverse.

Officer Speedy

The only other experience that could be classified as an event during those four weeks was the night Woody was off for some reason. Lo and behold, his one-night replacement was Floyd Bean from the Fourth Watch. I drove the first four hours, then he flew low for the last four hours. He went from one end of the beat to the other end again at the same speed.

At one point I said he was going so fast I couldn't see anything clearly enough to make out if anybody was out there who wasn't supposed to be. Actually, as usual, there was nobody out there, but if there had been, they would have been only a faint blur for an instant. He quickly replied that we had to cover the beat, then like walking on El Cajon Boulevard, off to the races.

By the time we pulled into the garage, I was worn to a frazzle. I thought it would be a great idea to pair him up with the other speed maniac I had to walk Ocean Beach with on the night of Sergeant McCloud's "Bull" fantasy.

The next eight weeks I was assigned to work with Glen Langley and "Red" Younger on Beat 5 from Ash Street south to the bay and 5th Avenue east to 16th Street, including the east part of skid row. It was on the 3:00 p.m. to 11:00 p.m. shift, which I liked.

From the beginning, Glen Langley and I hit it off and had much fun. Also, he almost immediately warned me to look out for Red Younger, because he was certain Red was a straight pipeline snitch for the deputy chief of field personnel. In that I had more than my share of experiences with that deputy chief, I took notice.

Glen's sole interest was making arrests. He hated ambulance calls and anything else that took him away from making arrests. I really liked him and Bob Richards, and contrary to Bob's opinion of Glen's arrests, I never saw him make an arrest that I thought was not completely justified. Somehow, Bob had got a false impression. I quickly learned Glen like to egg Bob on, so I had to believe that he had led Bob on just to jerk him around. The only thing Glen and I didn't agree on was taking well-behaved drunken sailors and marines to the Shore Patrol.

Sometime earlier in Glen's career, he had taken a drunken sailor to the Shore Patrol. The sailor had been well behaved until after he

41

got into the Shore Patrol station. Then he turned on Glen, cursing at him and generally giving him hell. So, Glen told me since then they have all gone to jail.

Red was sort of a walking time bomb. He was stocky, had a cocky swagger and a scary look in his eyes like he was anxious to brutalize anyone he could.

It was shortly after the start of the shift one afternoon when Red and I received a call to recover an abandoned stolen car at the foot of Pershing Drive.

It was a 1947 Chevrolet convertible, and the top was down. As soon as we got there, Red went directly to the glove box and opened it. All that was in it was an old screwdriver and a half-empty pint of whiskey. Red grabbed both of them and went directly back to our patrol car. Both surprised and concerned, I asked Red what he was going to do with them. When he replied he would drink the whiskey because the alcohol sterilized it, I almost gagged.

But my concern was if this was another of the deputy chief's sneaky traps. If Red was a snitch for the deputy chief and I didn't report his theft to a sergeant, would I be fired for failing to report an officer's theft that I had witnessed?

Glen was very observant, analytical and never missed much. So I had every reason to believe he knew Red was a pipeline snitch for the deputy chief. Also, Red was such a street thug, I had my own opinion that his being a snitch for the deputy chief was the only reason he was hired and was still around.

All of the sergeants had been so kind and caring to me, I could only hope that one of them would cover for me if Red was part of the deputy chief's traps and told the chief he had caught me. It would be easy enough for a sergeant to say I told him, but it would be my word against Red's.

So, we had the recovered stolen car towed in for safe keeping, Red enjoyed his "sterilized" whiskey, and it was over with no problems — other than I knew for certain I had a stupid petty thief for a partner.

For some mysterious reason, I had Saturdays and Sundays off. Glen no doubt wanted to work weekends, because he could make more arrests on those nights. I had no idea why Red worked weekends, possibly because the wonderful sergeants were trying to be good to me. Who knows?

It was shortly before 4:00 p.m. when Glen and I received an "11-40, Code 3" (Notify if ambulance is needed, emergency) call at the Arms apartment at 12th Avenue and A Street.

Our regularly assigned patrol car was a 1947 Plymouth that had been a detective division car for about four years before it was dumped on the patrol division to completely wear out or total. It was already tired and barely got out of its own tracks.

We were at 6th and Island, one block south of Market, when we received the call, and I was driving. Convair Aircraft shift change had been at 3:30 p.m., so traffic on Market Street was heavy. I put it in second gear to be able to maintain a decent speed and headed east on Island, red lights flashing and sirens blaring — much to Glen's discomfort. Losing valuable potential arrest time on some injured or sick person was one thing, but being exposed to a screaming siren was too much for him, so he sulked.

The Tired Patrol Car

I turned from Island onto 12th, blowing the siren long and loud for Glen's sake. We went through 12th and C Street, past Oscar's Drive-In with all eyes on us. Then about half a block north of Oscar's, our old car crapped out.

With his wad of snuff bulging in his cheek, Glen said, "Now look what you've done. You broke it."

Looking back, I saw that the car stopped directly behind us was a Plymouth just like ours. I set the parking brake, sized up our bumpers to see if they matched, then asked the nice driver if he would push us for a block and a half.

He readily agreed. I got back in our car, and away we went. I couldn't help myself. It was a once-in-a-lifetime opportunity, so I blew the siren all the way to A Street.

Simultaneously, Glen scooted down in his seat, pulled his cap down over his eyes like he was trying to hide and moaned, "Oh my God. What next?"

We coasted into a diagonal parking space and went up to the 2nd floor where there was an elderly lady lying on the floor in the hallway. I went back to the car and radioed for an ambulance.

When the ambulance departed, we got into the old, tired Plymouth, and it started. I drove it to the station. The police mechanic told us the same thing had happened to the graveyard shift officers the night before.

I wondered, then why didn't they fix it instead of just sticking it back out on the beat? The next day the mechanic told us it had been a defective ignition coil. When it got overworked and hot, it just took a rest.

Working with Red one night, we had to take a mental patient to the County Hospital psychiatric ward known as the "East Wing." Red had been driving, but he had me drive to the hospital.

After we had placed the poor man in the psycho ward, Red got behind the wheel again. We hadn't gone a block when Red waved a ten-dollar bill in the air and said he found it on the rear floorboards. He asked me if I wanted half of it.

I replied, "No, you found it so it's yours." I knew he somehow got it from the poor mentally disturbed man. Although I wouldn't have anything to do with any "dirty" money, I also had to wonder if this could be another one of the deputy chief's tricks. By then, I was not only extremely cautious, I was somewhat paranoid about that deputy chief.

I also realized if it was not one of the deputy chief's traps, Red was not only a "sterilized" whiskey and two-bit screwdriver thief he was a full-blown thief — of anything.

Wino Psychology

It was about 5:00 p.m. when Glen and I received a call of a disturbance on the west side of 5th Avenue, a block and a half north of Market Street. Glen was driving, and it took only a couple of minutes for us to get there.

The disturbance was an average-sized white male wino verbally cursing an African/American man, calling him every derogatory name and word known to the Ku Klux Klan. The black man, who was at least six feet four inches tall, just stood there taking the abuse without any visible reaction.

The white male wino was so busy berating the black man he didn't notice us drive up and park. I got out of the car, walked over to the foul-mouth wino and took the half-empty wine bottle from his coat pocket. I grabbed his left arm and told him he was under arrest.

As I guided him through the right rear door, I turned to the African/American victim and said, "Thanks for not killing him. That would take a whole lot of paperwork, and we don't get paid overtime." He smiled slightly and said, "You're welcome," and walked north on 5th Avenue like nothing had happened.

Strangely enough, the wino didn't ask what was going to happen to his half-empty wine bottle like the others routinely did. When we told winos we were going to pour the wine out, they usually would almost cry and beg for it. We would then tell them they could have it if they would drink all of it before we got to jail.

It worked like a charm. They always downed it all, went in the jail as happy as could be, behaved themselves and slept like babies. But no way was this one going to get his wine, even if he cried and begged, because he had been a very bad boy.

In that our beat was only about a mile from the station and jail, we usually typed arrest reports before going back to the beat to get them out of the way, and so they wouldn't pile up on us, like the night when we made 11 arrests for drunkenness.

That night was like an early Christmas for Glen. It was like somebody was giving free Muscatel or Port wine to every wino on our beat. Whatever caused it, Glen didn't care, because he was in heaven.

After typing the arrest report on the nasty racist wino, we returned to Beat 5 with the half-empty wine bottle rattling around on the rear floorboards. There were no rubber floorboard mats in the rear, as they had gone to their final resting place long ago. There was just bare metal.

The Popular Jail Trustee

A car blew the red light southbound on 5th at Market Street and Glen had it stopped in about a half block. As I wrote the ticket, I noticed Johnnie Flores, one of our most popular jail residents and trustees, talking to Glen through the open right front window.

When I completed the ticket and returned to the car, I asked Glen what Johnnie wanted. With a devilish smirk, he said Johnnie wanted to borrow 50 cents. Then he said, "But he's about half shot already, so I gave him the bottle of wine. When he downs that, he'll be ready for the bucket, and we'll nab him." Then he laughed like a mad man.

About a half hour later, we saw Johnnie getting his shoes shined at a shoeshine stand at 5th and G streets. We wondered, where in hell did he get the money to get a shoe shine? He was a case.

Glen was still driving at about 8:20 p.m. when he turned north on to 5th Avenue from Island, a block south of Market. We barely turned the corner when we saw a police department car stop eastbound on Market at 5th and drop off a Fourth Watch officer. The signal light turned green for 5th Avenue, and the walking officer crossed Market Street to the corner in front of the 24-hour Ferris and Ferris Pharmacy.

The signal turned red for 5th Avenue before we reached the intersection. As we sat there helplessly, we watched as the walking officer arrested Johnnie who was by then good and drunk on Glen's investment of wine.

I thought it was funny, but Glen didn't. After he had invested in an arrest, he lost it then had to transport his intended prey to jail. That was like salt in the wound.

Johnnie Flores was one of the regulars in the city jail, served as a reliable trustee, and was much like a member of the police department family. Like some others, he was in jail about half of the time. It saved him and others from drinking themselves to death and probably added 10 to 20 years to their miserable lives.

Because of his so-called seniority, Johnnie was always assigned to trustee duty in the garage. It was the best trustee job. At the end of the shift, we just parked the car at the gas pumps and left it for Johnnie to gas up and check the oil. Included in Johnnie's servicing was pulling out the rear seat and checking for loose change or contraband. That's why it was the best trustee job. All of the police department cars had leather seats for ease of cleaning, which helped any loose change slide behind and under the seat. It was like tips for Johnnie.

I was told that a couple of years before I went on the police department, one of the trustees found a loaded .32 caliber automatic pistol behind a rear seat. Finding something like that was also a big plus. Trustees took great joy in delivering such an item to the patrol division captain to get a pat on the head.

Not long after I went on the police department, one eager trustee peeked into officers' unlocked lockers to see if they were empty. Lo and behold, more than once he found the officer's off-duty snub-nosed revolver. When it was delivered to the captain, he wasn't very happy that an officer would leave a loaded firearm for a trustee to get his hands on. The officer then had to retrieve his handgun from a very unhappy captain. A notice was immediately forthcoming warning of severe punishment for leaving lockers unlocked when containing firearms.

Johnnie also drove and parked the patrol cars in their designated parking spaces after servicing them. That was until about a year after I went on the police department, when he backed a car into the field personnel deputy chief's car. We thought it was hilarious, but the deputy chief reacted quite differently.

The deputy chief again proved that chiefs don't always have a sense of humor when he grounded Johnnie for life. This incident and another one years later clearly showed that the deputy chief had a personal policy of "One strike and you're out." He didn't believe in warnings.

More than ever, I realized I had dodged a fatal bullet the night of Sergeant McCloud's "Bull" illegal assignment. To shoot a fleeing person without identifying myself as a police officer and warning that person to stop or be shot would be illegal.

There were three reputed Mafia members in San Diego. They were Frank "Bompo" Bompensiero, Frank Matranga and Tony Mirable. Tony Mirable owned the bar on the southeast corner of 4th Avenue and G Street. When we drove past Mirable's bar, he was often standing at the curb of G Street wearing a fedora and with his hands in the pockets of a top coat. The top coat was probably to conceal the illegal snub-nosed revolver he reportedly carried.

Being one of the old Mafia members, he showed respect for honest cops, so he would always nod to us as we passed. Glen was never impressed, but Red appeared to me to react with some show of respect and even admiration. Later in the 1950s, Tony Mirable was fatally shot in his security apartment. There were two opinions about the motive, and it was never resolved for certain.

For about the last two weeks I was assigned on Beat 5 with Glen and Red, Glen urged me several times to ask a sergeant or Captain Stark not to assign me to work with Red again. With only five months on the job, I was reluctant to ask. Also, if Red was a snitch for the deputy chief, it may not set well with the deputy chief. It was a dilemma.

Also, knowing Glen was very observant, analytical and shrewd and was looking out for me, I figured he wanted others to complain about Red so he might be able to get rid of him as a Beat 5 partner. With the high arrest activity on Beat 5, Glen was in heaven and would not want to give it up even to get rid of Red.

Near the end of the eight-week Beat 5 assignment, the first shift back to work after two days off, Glen told me the jail crew was extremely angry with Red. Glen said Red had slammed the jail door on Betty Hicks' hand. Betty was a pathetic, harmless skid row alcoholic and one of many that the kindly jail crew tried to protect from any harm. Considering my early assessment of Red and the scary look in his squinted eyes, there was no doubt in my mind that he had done it on purpose. With that, I decided to risk asking to get away from Red when the time was right, but I wasn't sure it was necessary.

First of all, kindly, fatherly, 25-year-veteran Sergeant George Mason had told me that during my one-year probationary training period, I would be assigned to work with as many different officers as possible. He said all officers had some good work habits and practices and maybe some bad ones. He said to try to adopt the good ones and disregard the bad ones.

Also Captain Stark's squad was rotating to the day shift, and I would be loaned out to Captain Bernard's squad on graveyard shift or assigned to the Fourth Watch. Day shift was one-man units, and probationary officers were not normally allowed to work a patrol division beat without a senior partner.

Of course there are always exceptions to every rule. Two African/American officers were hired in my group of 26, and upon graduation from Recruit Training School, they were assigned to work the black area of Logan Heights with a veteran black officer. Two nights a week they worked the beat together, and one worked alone on days during that first year. With their being hired, that boosted the number of black San Diego Police Department officers to seven. Although the first African/American San Diego police officer was hired around 1920, racial discrimination on the San Diego Police Department was quite evident.

When the assignments were posted for the next eight weeks, I was assigned to work with brutal, arrest-happy Gary Gray, as he was described to me by wartime hire Officer Terry Leach.

CHAPTER 7

Blind and Blinder

Fortunately, we did not encounter any similar cases thereafter, so sanity ruled. But it quickly proved it was the blind leading the blinder, and I wasn't sure which of us was which, but I had a good idea.

We did not wear name plates in those days, so I didn't know many officers assigned to other squads. Gary Gray was on Captain Bernard's squad with partner Bob Anders, and we would be working graveyard shift on Beat 8 — the Mexican/American and African/American district of San Diego.

Many times at shift change I had seen an officer about six feet three inches tall, and it seemed he was always laughing about something. He was like a tall Ted Donovan. On the first night of graveyard shift on Bernard's squad, I met Gary Gray for the first time, and lo and behold, he was the tall, laughing officer.

It didn't take any time at all to find out that Gary Gray was nothing like Terry Leach had described him. Gary had been a lifeguard before joining the police department in 1941, and he was not happy about his hiring date. He and two other lifeguards, Henry Gates and George Whitmore, had been hired only days after the San Diego fire and police department retirement plans were changed to make retirement possible after 25 years rather than 20 years.

Gary was a very devout Catholic, and it was my impression that he never had to go to confession. He also had a full-blown sense of humor. Accordingly, he appreciated all humor.

As many of my other training officers had done, Gary gave me his opinion of many other officers. He rated them on their abilities and skills as policemen then added, "But I don't like to work with them because they don't have a good sense of humor."

So much for Bob Richard's mandatory sense of humor. I had already seen enough officers without a sense of humor, so I knew what Gary was talking about.

I soon learned that Bob Anders was also somewhat short in the sense of humor department. In fact, I soon formed the opinion that Bob was assigned to work with Gary so that Gary could keep him from getting lost.

My impression of Bob's decision-making problems surfaced at about 2:30 a.m. one shift on Harbor Drive. Bob was driving and we stopped to check out a car that was parked on the southbound shoulder.

I walked over to the car and saw a Navy chief lying on the front seat. Wanting to know if he was all right, I opened the driver-side door. When I spoke to him, he sat up. Without hesitation, he told me he had been drinking at a bar and didn't realize until he had reached that location that he was in no condition to drive, so he stopped to sleep it off.

I told the chief he was not in the best neighborhood in town, so he should lock all the doors. He acknowledged that advice and pushed the lock buttons down on the two right-side doors. I reached in and locked the left rear door, then locked the driver's door as I closed it.

As I got back in the patrol car, Bob asked me what the chief's problem was. When I told him what the chief had told me, Bob asked, "Aren't you going to arrest him?"

I could hardly believe my ears — arrest a man who honestly admitted to me what he did? Furthermore, he didn't really appear to me to be under the influence enough to arrest even if we had stopped him driving. With that, I feared I may have a very, very long eight weeks with Bob. Fortunately, we did not encounter any similar cases thereafter, so sanity ruled. But it quickly proved it was the blind leading the blinder, and I wasn't sure which of us was which, but I had a good idea.

Bribery in the Vice Squad

At the earliest opportunity, Gary Gray related to me that he had been assigned to the vice squad. He said he very diplomatically requested to be transferred back to the patrol division after he personally observed a large wad of money change hands from a bookie to a vice squad sergeant. He said he did not want to be a part of or a witness to bribery or graft. He also named a big-time bookie who was the son of a former fire chief who had been my grandfather's best friend.

Gary said his request, although diplomatic and without any mention of any wrongdoing, earned him the wrath of the field personnel deputy chief. He said even though that had been a few years earlier, he had just recently got out of the chief's torture chamber. He said he was given every crappy detail the deputy chief could find, including walking a lot of foot beats.

With that coming from Gary, I figured I had found a true ally and friend. He got in deep crap with the deputy chief for asking to get out of the vice squad, and all I did was join the police department instead of the fire department. Regardless of cause, we both ended up in the same target shoot as bull's eyes, and I was still on probation.

Beat 8 and Logan Heights in general were minority areas of the city, but contrary to false beliefs of most San Diegans, they were fairly free of crime. I knew of only one burglary during my eight weeks on the beat. It was a forced entry of a commercial building on Logan Avenue. The burglars were such bunglers Bob and I had them in custody within an hour. I marveled, how's that amazing work for blind and blinder? Obviously, they left some very noticeable clues behind. Not much to my surprise, they were in my same National Guard unit.

Liquor License Extortion

With so much dead time particularly after 3:00 a.m. every shift, Gary told me of some of his more interesting experiences. One was his part in the liquor licensee extortion investigation.

He said California Attorney General Edmund G. "Pat" Brown had initiated the investigation. The attorney general's investigators went to SDPD Chief Jansen and asked for a knowledgeable officer to assist them in their investigation of the liquor licensee extortions.

Gary said when Chief Jansen offered them the sergeant in charge of the vice squad the attorney general's investigators rejected him and said they wanted an officer named Gary Gray. They had obviously done some advanced spy work to clearly identify an honest cop and one who was a Mafia expert, as Gary was.

Gary said they also recruited a deputy sheriff named Bob Norris, but he said nearly all the extortions took place in the city of San Diego, not in the sheriff's unincorporated areas, so Norris couldn't give much help.

In conclusion, Gary said he gave the attorney general's investigators more than enough evidence to prosecute a few people. He said if there weren't any grand jury indictments and arrests in the next six months, then Attorney General Pat Brown had to be in on it and be corrupt.

Six months later in June 1953, Mafia bagman Frank "Bompo" Bompensiero and some others were arrested, but the secret grand jury indictments were not all that secret, because elected Board of Equalization Director William G. Bonelli beat it for Mexico. Bonelli had obviously been tipped off well in advance for him to flee to Mexico in enough time to grease the palms of the right Mexican authorities to block his extradition back to the United States. Many years later, Gary told me Bonelli made visits to the United States, but nobody ever grabbed him to bring him to justice.

The one result of that Board of Equalization scandal was the reform of the Alcoholic Beverage Control (ABC) enforcement unit.

I could not help but be suspicious of why it took about seven years to clean up that very lucrative racket, also, why the California attorney general had to do it instead of the San Diego Police Department. If Gary Gray could give the attorney general's people enough to indict, it was impossible to believe that the SDPD vice squad and chief didn't know about it many years before. I knew it, and I wasn't even a cop then, so why didn't they?

I told Gary about losing a suspicious male on 5th Avenue about a half-block south of Market Street one night when I was walking the foot beat. I said he looked extremely suspicious and was walking south as I was walking north. He spotted me just as I saw him and started toward him. He quickly ducked into a café with a very long counter that was full of cop-hating patrons.

Knowing of near cop stabbings in the back in similar skid row dives, I was very leery, but I went in after him. I walked the long distance to the rear of the bar looking for him and looking over my shoulder for a knife. I checked the restrooms and tried to open a rear door at the end of the hall. The rear door handle would turn, but the door wouldn't open, so I cautiously walked out of the café wondering where in the hell he had gone to.

Without hesitation, Gary told me the center of the block between 5th and 6th and Market and Island was a vacant lot. He said the suspect probably held the door shut with his body, then crossed the vacant lot to the rear door of another dive and went in.

The Secret Tunnel

Gary then told me when he was on the vice squad he discovered a tunnel between 4th and 5th between Market and Island. He said it had been dug by the Chinese around the turn of the century. He said he had removed his coat, fedora and tie and explored the buildings and when he found a suspicious door, he opened it. There was a staircase down into the tunnel, so he followed it to where it came up on the other end.

Of all the officers I worked with, Gary was the only one who ever mentioned the vacant lot and tunnel. As the sharp lieutenant had told us during our first-day orientation, to be a good officer, we had to be naturally curious. It was obvious that Gary had more than his share of curiosity and the desire to satisfy that curiosity.

At about 2:30 a.m. one weekend night in the last part of the eight-week assignment, Bob was driving and stopped at the stop sign on Crosby at National. It was right next to Fire Station Number 7 where Daddy had been assigned when he died.

Sailor Dummies

Bob waited for one southbound car to pass, as we were in no hurry to get anywhere. It was a 1948 Mercury convertible with a sailor driving and a second sailor standing on the right front seat guiding the convertible top down. This case was easier to solve than the burglary. We knew before we even stopped it that it was stolen — and the idiots were headed for Tijuana, which would make it a federal FBI Dyer Act felony case the instant they crossed the Mexican border.

First of all, the idiots were putting the top down in January, and it was colder than hell. It didn't take much to get them to admit they had just stolen the car downtown. They were assigned to a submarine, and on the way to jail, one of them said to the other, "Boy, the skipper is really going to be mad about this." I thought what about the superior court judge and the Navy court martial?

But talk about divine intervention, the owner of the stolen car was from Long Beach, California, and because we recovered her car before she knew it was stolen, she refused to prosecute.

We never knew what happened to the two dummies, but Dwight D. "Ike" Eisenhower had been elected president in November and military discipline was about to change radically.

Shortly after Eisenhower moved into the White House, sailors started calling us "Sir" instead of "Chicken Shit." One of my closer cousins was married to a career Navy chief warrant officer. About a year later, he told me of the fate of a commander on Admiral Dyer's staff.

I already knew about the Navy commander being cited for making an illegal turn and his telling the officer he couldn't cite him because he was on Admiral Dyer's staff. The citing officer had also told me the commander was a borderline DUI, and his fly was hanging open. About two weeks later, the same Navy commander was arrested for DUI by La Jolla Substation Sergeant Cannon, who reported that the commander had also told him he couldn't be arrested because he was on Admiral Dyer's staff.

Ted, my cousin's husband, told me Admiral Dyer's reaction to the commander was well reported throughout the Navy circles as a warning. Admiral Dyer called the commander into his office and directed him to go straight to the Police Court and settle his affairs with the court, then return to his office with proof of settlement. When the commander returned, Admiral Dyer curtly handed him his 30-day transfer orders to Japan.

The Korean "Police Action" War had been dragging on for about two and one-half years. An unofficial report cited one reason for President Eisenhower's crackdown on discipline of military personnel was because of the outrageous number of them being injured or killed in traffic accidents on U.S. highways throughout the 48 states.

Gary was driving the second half of a weeknight shift, and, being the cop he was, he started toward the station a little early near the end of the shift to survey skid row on the way to the station.

Our Beat 8 abutted skid row Beat 5 to the east, so it was right on the way in.

Gary stopped on G Street at 4th Avenue directly across the street from Tony Mirable's bar. The front door was open, and we could see only one customer sitting at the bar talking to the bartender. Gary identified the customer to me as a San Diego Police Department detective.

"That pisses me off to see one of our people in a Mafia bar," I said with disgust. "I know how you feel," Gary replied, "but he's the only one in there at this hour, and he can get more valuable information from that bartender in an hour than he can get in a week or a month on the street." Then chuckling, Gary added, "While he drinks free Mafia booze."

Glen was in the squad room a few mornings a week when we got there at the end of our shift. He repeatedly urged me to ask not to be assigned to work with Red again. It was only a little over two weeks before the eight-week shift rotation that I finally built up the courage to ask.

I didn't see a sergeant around, so I walked into the captain's office. Captain Stark was sitting at the desk, alert and ready to start his day shift. I said, "Captain, I would like to request not to work with Red again." Smiling, he asked, "Personality?" "Yes, sir," I replied, thinking how tactful and diplomatic Captain Stark was to put it that way.

Captain Stark said, "Okay, fine." "Thank you," I said and walked out the door directly into the squad room. Glen was standing next to the door in front of the shift schedule bulletin board, and he asked if I had done it. I replied, "Yep," and walked across the squad room and into the locker room.

The next morning Glen said he had something to tell me. He waved for me to get over where nobody could hear and said, "As you walked out the door to the locker room, Sergeant Mason walked out of the captain's office and said to me, 'There goes number seven who asked not to work with Red.'"

Glen was delighted that so many had joined him in his hatred for and distrust of Red. I was also pleased to hear that at least six others had made the same request, so the captain and sergeants would see that Red was a problem, not me.

After I left the police department and joined the CHP, I had plenty of unhappy police department informants to keep me up on the latest at the San Diego police asylum.

About five years later, I was told Red had finally been fired and had become a bartender. Then several years later, I was told he drank himself to death at age 42.

One time during a conversation while patrolling, Red expressed his hatred for the CHP, because they had rejected him based on his background check. They had obviously discovered something in his past that disqualified him according to CHP standards. I don't like to think of all the damage he did on the San Diego Police Department in his eight to ten years of stealing and injuring people — even with no proof he was a deputy chief's spy and snitch.

CHAPTER 8

Shoot, Don't Shoot

Some officers had seen violent deaths right next to them in battle and were not quick on the trigger, not wanting to have a death or injury on their conscience. This is not to say they wouldn't use deadly force if absolutely necessary, but not at the drop of a hat.

Enacted in 1872, California Penal Code Section 196 provided for justifiable homicide by public officers for several reasons including in the discharge of any other legal duty. One specific condition also listed was against a fleeing felon, and auto theft was a felony. So, deadly force could be used against any auto thief who attempted to resist arrest by fleeing.

One of my early training officers told me about a San Diego Police Department officer who had fatally shot a young sailor who fled from a stolen car during World War II and was still on the job. My training officer was extremely critical of the shooting officer for killing the young sailor only because he had stolen a car, because he said auto theft by military personnel during the war was quite common due to limited transportation and overwhelming demand.

That same shooter officer was also highly suspected of shooting his partner in the buttocks while they were both searching a residential neighborhood for a reported prowler, but that suspicion was discounted when the victim officer years later accidentally shot himself in the buttocks.

I had the displeasure of working partners with the buttock-shooting victim after I transferred to the traffic division. I quickly concluded he shot himself in the buttocks both times. Much like Lieutenant King, the classroom training officer, the shooting victim officer was very scholarly and well read but very short on human relations and street smarts. In fact, he was not a joy to work with as he had so sense of humor or personality.

Like all adult Americans at that time, San Diego police officers had suffered through the Great Depression, and most had served in the military during World War II. With those extremely difficult hardship experiences, the majority were very compassionate and empathetic in their dealing with the public, including minorities and unfortunate people. They knew what it was like to be without and to endure the disgrace of being at the bottom of the social heap. But, as in every group, some were not so kind and caring.

Accordingly, some had seen violent deaths right next to them in battle and were not quick on the trigger, not wanting to have a death or injury on their conscience. This is not to say they wouldn't use deadly force if absolutely necessary, but not at the drop of a hat. However, there were some like Red, and there were others even scarier.

The immediate emotional reaction to shooting a fleeing felon played out in classic form starting one night while I was working graveyard shift with Gary Gray on Beat 8. We heard the radio call of a possible burglary, but that was all.

One of the officers responding was Dick Malone who lived a block from me. We sometimes commuted to work, and he told me what happened in detail on the way home that night.

The janitor of an upscale steakhouse restaurant heard strange noises in the independently-owned grocery store next door and called the police. One of the first units to arrive was a traffic division "crash car," as we called them. One officer was Billy Malone, the older brother of Dick Malone, and the other officer was Bob Reed. They drove up the alley and saw the rear door of the grocery store damaged and open.

The Safe Burglar

They entered and saw the burglar intently drilling open the safe. Guns drawn, they ordered the burglar to raise his hands and stand up. As he started to stand up, he quickly swung his drill around, hitting both officers and knocking them off balance and backwards. He then ran for the glass front door.

Knowing the front door was key-locked from the inside, Billy and Bob thought for sure they had cornered him. To their surprise, the burglar raised his arms up in front of his face and crashed right through the glass door without getting injured.

By then, other units were covering the area out in front. Sergeant Paul and three officers started firing at the fleeing burglar as he ran south on the sidewalk next to a high brick retaining wall. Nineteen shots were fired and luckily spent most of their velocity when they bounced off the wall. Amid the firing, most shots were loud reports, punctuated by some sickly "poofs".

Dick Malone was around the corner going to or from the alley. He said he didn't know all that the burglar had done but with all the shooting, he thought shooting the burglar would be clearly justified. He said as the burglar ran around the corner and across the street at an angle, he fired three times and on firing the third shot, the burglar went down in the street.

Thinking he had hit and maybe killed the burglar, Dick said his spontaneous impulse was to throw his revolver down and vomit on it. He said he ran to the burglar lying flat and motionless and asked him where he had been hit. The burglar said he hadn't been hit but he had wet his pants and then collapsed from the overwhelming fear of being shot.

Dick said he was so happy he hadn't injured or killed the burglar, he felt like he wanted to hug him, but he didn't think it would be a good idea, especially with the wet pants.

Dick and Billy Malone, like most San Diego police officers, were excellent, competent, dedicated officers and had great senses of humor. Billy was the older and was more reserved. Dick was more expressive and sometimes acted out his stories to add humor by mimicking the star performers in the true-life comedies.

Dick's account of his shooting at the frightened fleeing burglar gave me the clear impression that if Dick had hit and killed the safe burglar, he would have never forgiven himself and would have had to live with guilt for the rest of his life. My impression was supported in later years upon hearing some first-hand accounts from cops and World War II veterans alike.

Haunting Wartime Traumas

One incident was years later when I was a CHP Big Bear Lake resident officer. The suspect was a retired mustang Navy officer lieutenant who had been temporarily promoted to a Naval Reserve commander during the war and was a submarine commander.

I arrested him two times for common drunkenness, although he had been driving as a DUI, but I didn't witness him driving. And my intention in arresting him the second time was to prevent him from driving away from where I discovered him parked about 20 miles from his home in Big Bear Valley.

Although I found him in the Highland Judicial District area, the law allowed me to take him before another local court. Like most Big Bear residents, he knew Judge Jack Matthews, the magistrate of the Big Bear Judicial District. When I gave him a choice of courts, he chose the Big Bear court.

In that it was about a 30-minute drive to the Big Bear jail, we had time to talk about his drinking problem. Apparently from my showing interest in that issue, he opened up and told me about his still haunting trauma of the war.

He said he roamed the South Pacific for months searching for Japanese ships. Then one night he spotted a Japanese tanker and sunk it with one torpedo. He said the torpedo hit a most vital area of the ship, and it exploded in a ball of flame.

He said he and the entire crew celebrated loud and long, and then he retired to his stateroom in a mood of achievement and satisfaction. He said about 15 minutes later his mood instantly changed to depression upon realizing the truth that he had just killed about 200 Japanese sailors with two words, "Fire one."

He said when he was later relieved of command of the boat, the crew gave him an expensive suitcase full of quarts of whiskey. He stayed in a motel the first night and got drunk. When he left the room, he abandoned the suitcase and whiskey in an attempt to erase all memory of his sinking the tanker and the war in general.

He then said he thought if his wife would listen to his traumatic story and understand, and if she would tell him whatever she could to let him know it wasn't his fault, that he would be able to live with it in peace of mind. However, his wife was a simple person from the Deep South and whenever he tried to approach the subject, she would say, "The war's over, so forget it."

Whether his wife's approval would have made any difference or not, who knows, but it was obvious the war would never be over for Bill until he was laid to rest in peace.

A few years later when I was a duty officer and instructor at the CHP Academy I was having a discussion with four in-service officers about various subjects in the PX. Something said by one of them prompted me to relate the story about the submarine commander.

Immediately, one of the in-service officers in a salty response said, "That's just an excuse for being an alcoholic." Another younger officer I knew very well from San Bernardino said, "No, I believe it, because I had a similar problem when I returned from the Korean War."

He then went on to relate that he had come face-to-face with a Chinese soldier and while looking eye-to-eye with him, shot and killed him, and he was afraid to tell his wife about it. The fine young officer said when he returned from Korea, he thought his wife would think he was some kind of evil person for killing the Chinese soldier face-to-face. He said he did not get any completely restful sleep for six months after returning home. Out of desperation, he went to a doctor for advice or treatment. The doctor said he couldn't continue as described, so he must tell his wife and see what would happen.

He said when he anxiously told his wife, she calmly and quickly responded, "Well, I'm glad it was him and not you."

He said that was it. He had suffered for six months in fear for nothing.

While I was studying for promotions on the CHP, I read several police management and supervision books and management test preparation books. These were usually written by college or university professors or some other "ivory tower" mental giants who had never worn a badge or gun, but their years of superior education made them experts in every field known to mankind.

One of these experts was the genius who wrote that policemen should leave their job at work and not discuss any aspect of it with their spouses or other family members. What a load of crap! Wives in particular should be very interested in their husbands' work, because they should be their best friends and confidantes.

This is only one blatant example of self-proclaimed, over-educated experts meddling in police work and practices, about which they know nothing. Again, the only place true, effective police work can be learned is on the street. Even in police circles it is said, "Those who can, do and those who can't, teach." In other words, the police academies are full of those who couldn't make it on the street, so they got a college degree as a free pass to get on an academy staff as a teacher. And I should know, because I was one, but without a college degree. In lieu of a college degree, my hard-earned academy pass was ten and a half years working the streets and highways and working alone for eight and a half of those years.

Even without the later stories of those who had killed, I knew Dick would have had serious trouble if he had killed the burglar — mostly because he told me the burglar was really a nice guy and showed a hint of fondness for him. Dick told me how the burglar had made himself at home and had a picnic lunch while drilling the safe and that he was a two-time loser with two prior convictions and prison terms for burglary. As such, he could have been classified as a "habitual criminal" and sentenced to life in prison with certain provisions for the possibility of parole after so many years. The critical act that made his crime burglary of the first degree was his assaulting Billy and Bob with his drill. The assault during a burglary was one of the habitual criminal elements.

Another fatal shooting incident and lifetime trauma was related to me by a veteran officer when I was a CHP Academy instructor in methods of arrest, riot control and baton use in the late 1960s.

Upon my recommendation, the CHP commissioner had approved the adoption of the Los Angeles Police Department Koga physical arrest, riot control and baton methods. While demonstrating the baton method of disarming a person with a knife or other smaller deadly weapon to an in-service class, a five-year veteran officer popped off with "it was a bunch of crap" or some other very negative comment. He obviously had not been listening to my prior explanation, as he made a comment about a baseball bat, which I had earlier clarified that the baton was no match for a softball or baseball bat.

When I asked him what he would do to disarm an assailant with a knife or small weapon, he responded he would shoot them.

I asked, "A fourteen-year-old boy?" He had committed himself so strongly to being antagonistic that he replied, "Yes."

I said, "I am showing you what the commissioner has approved in such a case, so if you want to use force beyond what he has approved, you are on your own. Good luck on your new job."

I clearly recalled that officer and his contrary attitude when he was a cadet and I was a CHP Academy duty officer in the early 1960s. I was curt with him because I knew he had a strong tendency to try to be the unofficial class leader.

Also, I wanted to make it clear to the entire class that California civil law mandated that peace officers comply with their department's policies or they could be solely, civilly liable for their unapproved, independent, unruly actions.

Lingering Guilt about Justifiable Homicide

Immediately after the completion of my instruction that day, a veteran officer contacted me and said that the pop-off officer didn't know what he was talking about. He said he had fatally shot a serial armed robber years before and never got over it, even though it was absolutely and completely justifiable homicide.

He said there was an urgent All Points Bulletin (APB) on the serial, armed robber who had in rapid succession robbed several service stations and pistol-whipped the attendants. There was an excellent description of the robber and his getaway car, which was a coupe, a rare body style.

He said he saw the robber's car drive into a service station, but it then started to speed away when he got close. With that, he fired several shots at the fleeing coupe. Not long after, the car was found abandoned on a side street. The car was stolen, and the robber was found dead in the passenger seat next to the right door with the window down. There had been three people in the car when it fled.

In those days before the riotous 1960s it was not unusual for officers to have listed phone numbers. He said he received crank and threatening phone calls for about two weeks, and he couldn't get much sleep for nearly a month. He said it was still on his conscience and he knew it would bother him for the rest of his life.

Robber Kills CHP Officer

Although he didn't directly kill anyone, another officer confided in me that he felt responsible for the fatal shooting of another CHP officer. As it happened, a San Quentin escapee named Jimmie Kendricks robbed the manager of a grocery store in Grand Terrace, south of Colton and San Bernardino. An APB was broadcast describing the getaway car and saying the robber was armed. This officer was working alone on Route 66 in Cajon Pass and clearly heard the APB. Patrolling 66, he saw a car parked on a dirt road off the main highway, so he drove down to check it out for the robber's vehicle. He said he was off Route 66 for several minutes and then returned to the highway to observe all northbound cars.

After Victorville CHP Officer Richard Duvall was fatally shot, he realized Kendricks had passed while he was off Route 66.

It was a weeknight, February 23, 1960, and as usual in "Berdoo," traffic was extremely light on winter weeknights. With the usual light traffic the officer said he was able to observe every northbound car going toward Victorville, Barstow and Las Vegas. He was a former San Bernardino deputy sheriff and was a good, alert officer. So, as he related his account to me, I was as certain as he was that Kendricks had slipped by during those several minutes he was away from the highway.

The investigation of Officer Duvall's slaying revealed that he had radioed Barstow that he was stopping a "hot one" as he stopped Kendricks. That was somewhat of a mystery in itself, because calling in routine stops wasn't done as a norm, so that remained a big question. The most obvious evidence that Duvall hadn't heard the APB on Kendricks and his 1950 Chevrolet getaway car and didn't know who he was stopping was that he had his citation book and flashlight with him as he approached on the driver's side.

Also, if Duvall had heard the broadcast and even suspected it was Kendricks, he would have certainly called for backup to help with the stop, or if no backup, he certainly would not have approached the vehicle. As it happened, Duvall was about half way up to the driver's door when Kendricks shot him, then shot him again as he was lying on Route 66.

I tried to console the officer by telling him he was doing his best to spot Kendricks and not goofing off, but it didn't help. He later resigned from the CHP.

Within a few days, Kendricks was captured in a Shell Beach, California, motel in his home territory. As usual in those days, justice was swift and he was convicted and sentenced to death.

An extra deputy sheriff assigned to Big Bear Lake for a later holiday weekend made it a point to tell me of his experiences with Kendricks. He had been assigned to guard him during his trial and trip back to San Quentin for his execution. The deputy was amazed at Kendricks' bragging about being in his glory with a dead CHP officer to his credit and no visible concern for his death sentence.

The rather humorous ending to the 21 shots fired at the safe burglar Dick Malone thought he had killed was the issuance of new, fresh ammunition to all police officers. The "poofs" punctuating the loud reports during the initial 19 shots fired were from Sergeant Paul's revolver. His gun was still loaded with ammunition issued to him when he joined the police department many years before. Much like the 12-year-old obsolete order to get permission from a supervisor to enter a house of prostitution, it proved that the top brass didn't pay much attention to basic operational details.

At the next eight-week shift rotation, Dick Malone and my partner, Gary Gray, moved to the 3:00 p.m. shift on Captain Bernard's squad and I went back to Captain Stark's squad for another miserable eight weeks of 11:00 p.m. graveyard shift.

The Shooting Marinette

Dick Malone was on his regular Beat 4, west of 5th Avenue. A large former Marinette who had received an undesirable discharge from the Marine Corps, believed to be a psycho discharge known as a "Section Eight" during World War II, commandeered a shooting gallery on West Broadway by grabbing a .22 caliber gun and chasing the attendant from the gallery.

She then announced she was going to shoot the biggest cop to arrive, and Dick Malone was about six feet three inches tall and weighed 200 pounds. As passenger officer, Dick and his partner were the first to arrive. When Dick was about halfway out of the patrol car door, she shot him in the waist. Although shooting gallery .22 bullets are even shorter than .22 shorts, the impact knocked Dick back onto the car seat. He quickly scrambled across the seat and out the driver's door.

With a few shots, Dick and his partner hit the shooter in the leg and groin and she went down. She survived, but that ended the incident in short order. Dick told me it was completely different than the safe burglar shooting incident because she had tried to kill him.

CHAPTER 9

Shootout at Linda Vista

From the muffled shotgun blasts, we could tell the gunman was moving from one window to another and taking shots at any cops he could spot or randomly shooting at police cars parked on Linda Vista Road.

I had been a San Diego Police Department motor officer for exactly four weeks and was on El Cajon Boulevard at Fairmont Avenue when the "All units, 11-99 (Officer needs help) officer shot and down, Code 3 (Emergency)" was aired. It was about 3:00 p.m. shift break time for the patrol division, so only 2:00 p.m. shift overlap traffic division and a few 8:00 a.m. shift detective division units were in the field. The location was on Linda Vista Road in the World War II Linda Vista Federal Housing Project north of Mission Valley.

Fairmont Avenue was a direct link to Mission Valley, so I had a clear road down to Mission Valley and west in light traffic on the expressway. I screamed with red light and siren and arrived at the ongoing shootout in less than ten minutes.

Hearing gunfire, I parked my motor south of the shooting and started across the wide lawn area toward the rear of the involved unit. Within seconds, my old high school friend Deputy Sheriff Warren "Swede" Larson hailed me and offered me his shotgun. Pretty certain the shootout would end with tear gas and not wanting to risk injuring an innocent person with wild, unnecessary gunfire, I politely declined.

Swede had quickly responded because at that time the police department, sheriff, CHP, county marshal and fire department were all on the same radio frequency. He had no doubt been nearby when he heard the emergency broadcast.

As I reached the front of the unit to the south of the gunman's, two women stopped me. They had four small children with them, and one immediately pointed to a small boy and told me he was the son of the gunman and his wife.

68

I picked up the boy, cradled him in my arms to make him feel protected and told the women to follow me. I led them across the wide lawn to a group of about 30 spectators about 50 feet to the south. I was certain they would be safe there, because the police firing was crazy crossfire to the east and west, and they were shielded from the gunman's shotgun firing by one of the units where they had contacted me.

I then quickly left them and continued to the rear of the gunman's unit and took cover around the corner of the woman's unit to the south of the gunman's. On the way, I drew my revolver to protect myself or anyone else in the event the crazed gunman ran out of the unit and started firing in the open. I had no intention of wildly firing at him while he was concealed inside the unit.

There was no communication between officers on the east side and west side of the units, so although I knew the gunman's son was not there, I did not know if any other innocent people were in the gunman's unit. And, if there were others in there, he might use one as a shield when he fired at us, hidden behind the curtain-covered east window.

Also, knowing how Dick Malone felt about thinking he may have killed the safe burglar and my early teachings from Nanno, I wasn't inclined to try to kill the gunman when I was certain tear gas would be used to flush him out and end the madness. Furthermore, I didn't want to kill him and leave his cute little son without a father the rest of his life. I grew up without a father, so I knew what it was like.

In addition, Nanno had taught me to never pull the trigger without knowing for sure where the bullet would come to a stop. If I fired into the window and it went out another window, it might hit another officer on Linda Vista Road or an innocent person blocks away.

When I arrived at the corner of the unit to the south for protection, I saw a veteran motor officer and a veteran traffic officer kneeling behind a box trailer for cover. They had made the major mistake of advancing to that location, and the trailer was little protection. Another veteran motor officer was about 20 feet further to the north of them behind a pine tree about one-fourth the width of his body. Having also made a big mistake of advancing to that location with next-to-nothing cover, that officer was firing wildly at the east window every time the gunman blasted a shot out of the curtain-covered window.

In sort of a panic, the motor officer behind the trailer yelled at the one exposed behind the tree to stop shooting, but the officer vainly trying to hide behind the undersized tree responded with, "Throw me some more ammo."

My God, I thought, he has already fired 20 rounds, and he had.

If it hadn't been such a critical situation I would have laughed. About 20 years of combined police experience to their credit and they had done everything wrong — and they were all pinned down with almost no protective cover.

Within minutes, I was joined safely hiding behind the unit corner by my old Junior Traffic Patrol supervisor, Bill Ward. Then shortly thereafter by Sergeant Cody Ingram, who was then a detective. In all, there were six of us to the east of the gunman's unit.

From the muffled shotgun blasts, we could tell the gunman was moving from one window to another and taking shots at any cops he could spot or randomly shooting at police cars parked on Linda Vista Road.

We heard the siren of a patrol car and then it stopped on Linda Vista Road. We could tell it stopped directly in front of the gunman's unit. Instantly, there was a muffled shotgun blast followed by six sharp revolver shots. We later learned the officer in the car was traffic car officer Waldo Allen, who was always good for laughs. He had definitely stopped in the wrong place.

We also learned from Waldo Allen that before he could get out of his car, the gunman blasted the right side of his patrol car, so he emptied his gun into the window of the gunman's unit.

Several minutes later, there was a loud blast. It startled me because it sounded like the gunman was outside of his unit and firing. Then a split second later there was another very loud blast, which caused me to raise my revolver because it came from a very short distance. Instantly, a cloud of smoke spewed from the corner of the closest unit to the east, about 40 feet away.

Our new range master, Bill Sams, also a comic of sorts, had obviously never before fired a tear gas gun, and he had fired that first grenade completely over the gunman's unit into the one nearby.

Without reservation, I openly admit it scared the hell out of me. I thought the gunman was on top of us until I saw the smoke spewing in all directions, and then I did laugh.

To Bill's credit, the second grenade was a bulls-eye right through the window. Within minutes, the gunman staggered out the north door, unarmed and with his arms high in the air. Seconds later, his poor wife crawled out the door. He had shot her in a leg, which was severely injured.

Some expressed the wish he had come out armed.

Upon examination, it was discovered that both the gunman and his wife had suffered minor, superficial graze wounds to their necks from police bullets.

We soon learned all the details of this event. It started with the gunman, Barney Davis, buying the shotgun from a private party through a newspaper ad. We were all grateful he hadn't bought a high-powered rifle, as there could have been some dead cops if he had.

Neighbors saw Barney Davis shoot his wife as he approached her unit, and they called the police department. The officer who took the call in the business office failed to note on the radio dispatch slip that a gun was involved. That officer was suspended for five days without pay for that gigantic blunder.

Deputy Marshal Elwin "Bunny" Bunnell, a former San Diego Police Department officer in Linda Vista to serve some civil papers, and San Diego bicycle theft and licensing juvenile officer John Zemcik, who took a lot of ribbing for that soft job, in Linda Vista to deliver some bicycle licenses to a school, heard the call and teamed up to investigate.

As they approached the unit, they heard the wife scream, "Don't shoot them too," but it was too late. Immediately, the gunman blasted Bunnell in the stomach and sprayed Zemcik, who quickly dragged Bunnell to safety behind another unit.

A fire department battalion chief arrived to aid Bunnell and Zemcik. He parked his car at an angle at the curb headed toward the gunman's unit, and the gunman immediately blasted the radiator of the chief's car.

When I returned to my beat, I happened to see an old high school friend who was the wife of another Hoover High School friend who was a deputy sheriff. TV reports of the shootout had already been aired, and she was very anxious to hear what I knew about it.

As I sat on my motor at the curb telling her, I glanced down and was amazed to see the front of my highly polished motor boots to be pockmarked by shotgun birdshots. I was so completely concealed behind the corner of the adjacent unit I could only guess that the birdshot had ricocheted off a protrusion on the box trailer. I thanked God they hadn't hit higher and into my eyes.

The next day, my brother-in-law phoned to tell me he had worked with the shooter at Convair Aircraft. He said Barney Davis was definitely crazy and really scary, but of course that was already obvious to me.

Also that day, the San Diego Union-Tribune reported the wounded wife of Barney Davis, who had filed for divorce, was scheduled to appear in divorce court the day after the shootout. The paper also reported that Barney's son was four years old.

At the end of the shift the day of the shootings, I was in the squad room typing reports when I heard a loud argument behind me. It was four traffic car officers all claiming credit for grazing the gunman's neck.

Disgusted, I turned around and asked, "Which one of you sharpshooters shot the wife?" Like a barbershop quartet, they all replied in unison, "Not me." "Oh, I guess the one who hit the wife isn't here yet," I sarcastically replied. They then quietly dispersed.

It was easy to deduct that if the bullet had hit the wife a few inches further into her neck, it could have severed her spinal cord or one or both of her carotid arteries. If the spinal cord had been hit, it could have left her a quadriplegic or if one or both carotid arteries had been severed, she would have quickly bled to death.

Despite the many tactical errors that were made during that "O.K. Corral" shootout, everything went on like nothing had gone wrong. It wasn't until I had been on the CHP for a while that I learned what corrective action had to be taken and was taken.

On the CHP, all uniformed officers were issued a manual of Headquarters General Orders (HGOs) and it was called the Blue Book because of its blue cover. Even after decades of being a state agency, new unpredictable events occurred which mandated detailed reports of the incident by the commander of the squad office where it took place. If any corrective policies or procedures appeared necessary, they were established and every officer received a copy of the new order for inclusion in the Blue Book.

But in that it had appeared nobody had read the San Diego Police Department manual of policies and procedures for 12 years since the houses of prostitution had been shut down, who would read it if corrective measures were written and published?

It was estimated that 50 police shots had been fired at the Linda Vista shootout, which was much like a free-for-all turkey shoot. Even though the police department officers were armed only with six-shooters, the police department shotguns and 30.40 Krag rifles remained safely locked up in cabinets in the sergeants' office. If nothing else, a change should have been made for sergeants to have one of each of those weapons in the trunks of their cars.

Another Shootout

Then in 1965, the San Diego Police Department had another shootout at a downtown pawn shop with a lone gunman. It was estimated that 900 police department shots were fired, including numerous shots by one officer firing a Thompson submachine gun into the pawn shop. When all else failed, the police department asked the Navy to assist with concussion grenades to stun the gunman or cause him to surrender. Bad idea! All the grenades did was to blow out all the large pawn shop plate glass windows onto the sidewalk in small pieces, and the gunman continued to shoot. Being in a pawn shop, the gunman had a very large arsenal of firearms and ammunition at his disposal.

The long shootout finally ended when Sergeant A.D. Brown, a World War II paratrooper lieutenant and a man's man and a cop's cop, with a few reluctant cops trailing at a distance climbed the stairs to the second floor where the gunman had retreated. Alone, A.D. cornered the gunman and put him down with a shotgun blast. However, the gunman survived.

Not long after that second major shootout melee, Sergeant Brown was instrumental in initiating and forming the first San Diego Police Department Anti-Sniper Platoon (ASP), similar to the Los Angeles Police Department's Special Weapons and Tactics (SWAT) teams.

A.D. retired from the San Diego Police Department at the rank of lieutenant and passed away in 2007 at the age of 87.

The Judicious Judge

When the Linda Vista gunman Barney Davis went to court, he had the misfortune of going before Judge John Hewicker, a true judge's judge. His decisions and sentences were so judicious that he was a news figure.

A previous noted case was an example of his fairness. It happened when a lonely 18-year-old sailor went to town on leave and was taken in tow by an ex-con who got him drunk. The ex-con then told him the manager of a locker club was an old man and would be a pushover to rob. He gave the very drunk sailor a handgun and sent him on his way. What the ex-con did not know was that the old manager was a former deputy sheriff from the Midwest and also an ordained minister.

Knowing how to deal with criminals with experience and able to preach the gospel, the old manager preached a sermon to the drunk armed sailor about repentance and forgiveness.

With that, the drunken sailor surrendered himself and the ex-con's gun to the old manager and waited for the cops to take him away. When the sailor told his story to the cops, they were able to identify the ex-con, and he was quickly arrested.

After the sailor pled guilty, Judge Hewicker sentenced him to ten years in prison, then immediately suspended the sentence with the condition that he serve out the remainder of his enlistment with good behavior. He fined him $11 and had the Shore Patrol escort him away.

That was a far-reaching sentence and suspension arrangement. It was a legal court mandate ordering the Navy to give the sailor a second chance so he could fulfill Judge Hewicker's condition of sentence suspension to earn "Good Conduct" ribbons. To do otherwise could be contempt of court on the part of any Navy brass that deprived the sailor of that opportunity.

With the sailor out of the way, Judge Hewicker then addressed the ex-con and said, "And now for you, sir," and sentenced him to the maximum. After Barney Davis pled guilty, Judge Hewicker acknowledged his plea, then told him he had added up all the maximum sentences for two assaults with intent to commit murder and five assaults with a deadly weapon — for a total of 77 years in prison.

Then Judge Hewicker added, "As long as I'm around and have anything to say about it, you will serve 77 years."

It was reported that Barney Davis had physically abused his wife and four-year-old son. We could only hope the two would be able to go on with their lives and enjoy some happiness, knowing they would never have to fear Barney Davis again, thanks to the amazing Judge Hewicker.

CHAPTER 10

Giant

Max Palmer was eight feet four inches tall, weighed 410 pounds and had appeared on at least two TV variety shows as a sort of side show attraction. He suffered from acromegaly, a very rare disorder of the pituitary gland that causes excessive production of growth hormone and physical overgrowth. I have heard of only three such cases in my life. Two were from foreign countries, and one came to the U.S. and became a professional TV wrestler. It is a very painful disorder and the victims have a life span of only 40 to 50 years.

Somehow, Max ended up in San Diego in November 1952 and got drunk. In that it takes six beers or six ounces of whiskey for a 150-pound person to have a 0.15 blood-alcohol level, which was the presumptive level for driving under the influence but not staggering drunk, Max had to have about 16 beers or ounces of whiskey in his system when the trouble started.

At about 2:30 a.m. Officers Lloyd Draper and Robert Shipley were dispatched to a restaurant at 2nd and Broadway when the manager complained that Max wouldn't pay his meal bill. Max had a large following of supporters, mostly sailors, who had probably paid his large booze bills.

Max was belligerent and told the officers, "My middle name is Trouble, and I'll give you plenty." The officers eventually talked Max into paying his bill then walked him out front, where Draper attempted to talk Max into returning to his hotel room — but no go.

Draper and Shipley were both over six feet tall and weighed 200 pounds, but they were no match for Max in a one-on-one tussle.

A crowd of about 150 people had gathered in front of the restaurant when Sergeant Art McCloud arrived and Max threatened him and tried to grab his necktie. Not being able to reach Max's neck, Draper stood on the bumper of a car and grabbed his neck to apply a carotid-sleeper hold. With that, Draper and Max fell to the ground with Max landing on top of Draper, who was later treated for injuries to his left knee, right hip and lower back.

But Max stayed down. Either Draper had put him out with the carotid-sleeper hold that cuts off the blood to the brain or Max just crapped out on his own.

Then the problem was with Max passed out, they couldn't get his limp body into the rear of a patrol car. He just wouldn't fit, so they had to use the paddy wagon with an eight-foot bed and bend his knees to close the door. His wrists were too large for handcuffs, so they cuffed him with the leg shackles attached to the front bulkhead.

Sadly Max, who was only 25 at the time of the incident, died a few years later of the painful acromegaly disorder.

The Body Builder

When I was working skid row Beat 5 with Glen Langley, we had an experience with a former universal body-beautiful champion, although he was not even close to being a giant like Max.

I was driving when we received a call about a disturbance at a hotel. As soon as we arrived in front of the hotel, Glen bailed out and entered the lobby. Not wanting to double park, it took me a couple of minutes to park in a space at the curb.

When I entered the lobby, a lady told me Glen, the hotel manager and the female victim had gone upstairs to the second floor. I got on the elevator to the second floor, and I had barely stepped out of the elevator when I heard a loud thundering of footsteps coming down the stairs — and Glen was nowhere in sight.

Within seconds, a wild-eyed, crazy-looking man stopped at the bottom of the stairs and stared at me. He was six feet three inches tall and 235 pounds of bulging muscle, wearing only a pair of trousers with the fly hanging wide open.

I thought, "Oh, shit, where are you, Glen?"

So I said, "Hi, where are you going?" trying to act calm. Within seconds that seemed like an hour with the wild-eyed man silently staring at me, Glen, the manager and female assault victim appeared at the west corner of the hallway in front of the man's room.

I said, "Let's go," and amazingly, he walked to his room. Inside the room there was a discussion about what had happened and Glen or I told him to get dressed, but Glen was standing between the wild man and the large open window over 5th Avenue. So I slowly walked over and got Glen by the arm and pulled him away from the window. With just one quick push Glen would have been on the 5th Avenue sidewalk.

As we put it all together, it turned out that the wild man had consumed a quart of whiskey then thrown the empty bottle out the window, breaking a neon sign below. Then only in trousers with the fly open, he kicked in the door of the female victim's room, which was directly across the hall from the elevator. He then threw her on the bed to assault her, but she screamed bloody murder as loud as she could, and he ran out of the room and all over the hotel until he and I met. He was definitely not one you would invite to dinner.

Glen was noble enough to ride in the right rear with the crazy in the left rear, which was standard positioning. The man started ranting loudly that he could be a policeman too. Because he was so bizarre and unpredictable, I had initially planned to use my handcuffs for the first time to cuff him, but that thought died when I took a good look at his wrists. His massive weight-lifting wrists were clearly too large for cuffs to get around — the same problem as with Max.

So with him directly behind me, I sort of sat sidesaddle, steered and shifted gears with my left arm and kept my right arm free to poke him in the eyes with my fingers if he made a move on me.

He was still raving when we got to the jail. The jailers were A.D. Brown and Al Dobson, both about six feet three inches tall and over 200 pounds. A.D. was behind the encaged booking desk with a looped opening for prisoners to put their heads through while being searched. A.D. was to type the booking sheet while Dobson searched the still raving wild man.

Dobson just started to search the raving man when he pulled his head out of the loop. Dobson pushed him back and told him sternly to stay in the loop, but he instantly pulled his head out a second time, raving about how he could be a policeman.

Dobson quickly put his arm around the man's neck to apply the carotid-sleeper hold, and A.D. ran around the cage and punched the wild prisoner a good one in the stomach. With that, the prisoner ended up sitting on the floor.

Immediately, the prisoner started to pop back up, but Dobson kept him down as A.D. cocked his right fist back and barked, "You want some more of that?" The raving man replied, "No," and instantly turned into a completely cooperative gentleman.

Glen and I stuck around to see what would happen when it all went down. We knew very well that both A.D. and Dobson were patient to a point but they had a limit, and we enjoyed the show.

A few weeks later when I was working Beat 8 with Gary Gray, there was a rape at about 5:00 a.m., not far from where the wild man lived. In that he had attempted to rape the young woman in the skid row hotel, I told Gary I thought it might be the same crazy man.

Gary told me to tell Lieutenant Gene Mullen, who worked sex cases. Gary put me in touch with Mullen, and I explained Glen's and my experience with the strange man.

Unlike some detectives, Mullen was great about getting back to informant officers and always gave them credit for their help in solving cases — rare qualities for sure. A few days later, Mullen got back to me. He said he interviewed the wild man and his stepfather in private. The stepfather gave his crazy stepson an alibi because he knew for certain he was at home for a long time before and after the rape. Then Mullen smiled and said, "But the stepfather said if he didn't know for certain where his stepson was at that time, he would suspect him too, because he wouldn't put it past him."

CHAPTER 11

Crap Shoot

I had joined the police department when I was 21 years old, three weeks before I became 22. In that there was no written pension formula that I knew about, I asked Sergeant Anderson how much I would get at 55 with over 33 years service. His answer was very brief. He said, "It depends on how much is in the pot when you get there."

Motorcycle Sergeant Dave Anderson was the president of the San Diego Police Department Relief Association. Although without any real clout, it was the bargaining unit for all police department officers, including Chief Jansen and the two deputy chiefs.

As such, Sergeant Anderson had been sent to San Francisco and Los Angeles to compare our pay and benefits with the police departments of those two cities. Not long after that trip, some of us cornered him in the squad room to ask him many questions, and he was very willing to answer them.

We had already been told that the San Diego Police Department had been classified as the tenth most efficient police department of cities of its size, but it was never disclosed who or what group had come up with that crystal-ball number. Without mentioning that amazing number, Sergeant Anderson told us that the San Diego Police Department had .9 officers per thousand people, the Los Angeles Police Department had 2.2 officers per thousand citizens, and the nationwide recommendation was one officer per thousand persons.

We were amazed and wondered what all of those LAPD officers were doing. We thought many must be behind desks.

In that graveyard was the most undesirable and even hated shift, Sergeant Anderson apparently tried to cheer us up by telling us about the San Francisco shift schedule system. He said new officers had to work graveyard shift for about their first seven years. Then they could work the afternoon shift until they had about 15 years service, at which time they could finally work the day shift.

We couldn't in our wildest dreams understand why anyone would want to be a San Francisco cop, and we wondered how many officers survived seven years of that torture.

In 1941, the San Diego Police Department and San Diego Fire Department requirement had increased from 20 to 25 years of service before retirement. Then in 1947, it was increased to a minimum of 30 years with a required minimum age of 55 years.

I had joined the police department when I was 21 years old, three weeks before I became 22. In that there was no written pension formula that I knew about, I asked Sergeant Anderson how much I would get at 55 with over 33 years service. His answer was very brief. He said, "It depends on how much is in the pot when you get there."

Talk about a crap shoot, I thought. For at least a few months after I went on the police force, I was the youngest on the job. When my group of 26 was hired, the San Diego Union-Tribune reported our group increased the officer strength of the police department to 407 officers. It also listed our names, ages, home addresses and previous employment. There were a few who were 22 or 23, but I was the only one who was 21 years old.

It didn't take a math major to figure out that there were at least 406 officers ahead of me to retire with more on the way.

Also, an insurance broker city councilman was reportedly working very hard to get the city council to dump the public City Retirement System and replace it with employees investing in insurance annuities. I was not well versed in the concept of conflict of interest at that time, but when I did become familiar with it, that scam smelled like it to me.

Considering all these facts, my interest in taking the California Highway Patrol and deputy sheriff tests shot to the top of my agenda for an escape route.

After waiting two years and four months for a CHP test, it finally came about in February 1953.

I was still only halfway through my probation, and it was well known that the chief and deputy chief hated the CHP. I was working my second eight-week torture of graveyard shift when the test was given on a Saturday at the San Diego High School cafeteria. I did not dare to ask for the night off before the 8:00 a.m. test for fear the ever vigilant deputy chief would know why and fire me. He didn't miss anything.

So, I had to rush home, change out of my uniform, eat and rush back to the San Diego High School — and not in the most wide awake and alert state.

When I walked into the cafeteria, I immediately spotted four other San Diego Police Department officers who were there to find an escape route out of the department. We sat together at the end of a table, and we were all hoping for a miracle.

There were more than 200 questions on the test, and there was a time limit of four hours. Unlike the specialized SDPD test on laws, the CHP test was about general knowledge and was a sort of IQ test.

About a month later, I took the deputy sheriff exam. It was unique in that the physical agility test was the first part, unlike the San Diego Police Department and CHP tests. It was conducted at the downtown YMCA and included swimming two lengths of the 60-foot indoor pool. It was the only swimming test I had to take and the only swimming instruction received in police training. The later written test was much like the SDPD test as it was mostly based on laws and police-related subjects. Upon completion of all testing, I came out number four on the list.

Several months later, I received notice that I had passed the CHP written test and was given the date, time and location of the agility and oral interview tests. Lucky for me, I had my oral interview prior to the exhausting agility test. I must have received a very good interview score, because I came out 249 on the CHP list without the ten veterans' preference points. If there had been no veterans' points or if I had them, I would have been about 25 on the list.

We were told by the sergeant who conducted the agility tests that nearly 6,000 had taken the written test and about 1,500 passed.

About three days before the CHP exam, it had been reported that CHP Commissioner Clifford E. Peterson had died from a massive heart attack, and his funeral was to take place on the Saturday of the test. Not long after his death, Governor Goodwin Knight, a true friend and admirer of the CHP, appointed retired LAPD Deputy Chief Bernard Caldwell as CHP commissioner.

After I received my notice of being 249 on the list, my good CHP officer friend Russ Tanner told me the legislature had told Caldwell they would not give the CHP any additional officers until they saw how he ran the department, and he was ordered to get the CHP out of cities, including Pasadena for traffic control and direction at the Rose Parade. For decades, the CHP had sent a small army of CHP officers to Pasadena to assist the police department with its big traffic problems.

Parade Traffic Directions

When I was assigned to the CHP San Bernardino area in 1954, one of the many comic officers, Walt Cook, told me of the traffic directing technique he had used when the Rose Parade crowd was leaving after the parade. He said many motorists asked him directions to their destinations. When they asked how to get to San Diego, he would say, "Two blocks and turn right." When they asked how to get to Ventura, he would say, "Two blocks and turn right."

Walt concluded that he had no idea how to get out of there to go anywhere but he just wanted to get them out of his hair.

Although my getting on the CHP was delayed for one year by the legislature's order to Commissioner Caldwell, after hearing Walt's traffic directing technique, I figured the lawmakers had done many Rose Bowl viewers a great big favor.

That order also proved that Clifford E. Peterson hadn't managed the CHP any better than he did the San Diego Police Department, letting it go to pot.

Just after receiving the CHP notice of my position on that list, the sheriff's office offered me a position, but with the hope of getting on the CHP I waived the offer. If I hadn't been on the CHP list, I would have jumped at the offer, not only to get away from the San Diego Police Department and its administrative confusion, but also because the sheriff's office had a very fine reputation.

So, I stuck it out on the police department and applied for motors that next fall. The motor training couldn't have been better, and it served me very well when I became a CHP Academy motor instructor in 1960.

But for the following ten months on the police department, I sadly watched morale, general working conditions and environment sink lower and lower.

CHAPTER 12

Screwy Sex

I immediately said, "You're under arrest for lewd and lascivious conduct." Those two words were straight out of the Penal Code, so I thought they would sound clear and official enough, and I felt like adding "You sick bastard."

Based on my limited experiences walking downtown beats on Fourth Watch my second month on the police department, I had at that time estimated that about 90 percent of police problems were alcohol-related. Then when I was assigned to beat cars, I started finding out what the other ten percent included — and one problem or activity of police interest was strange or screwy sex.

One of the first eye-openers was when I was working the North Park beat with Frank Foster. Between the east end of Balboa Park and the Municipal Golf Course next to Pershing Drive was an undeveloped brush-covered canyon, and there was a dirt road into the area on our side of the canyon.

We were on the 3:00 p.m. shift and Frank was driving down the dirt road for the first and only time he did so in those 16 afternoon shifts I worked with him. About a quarter mile into the canyon, we saw a large sedan parked to the west of the dirt road, and we could see a large man behind the wheel and a young boy in the passenger's seat next to him.

Frank stopped and I got out and walked over to check the situation out. At the driver's door, I saw him masturbating. The boy had a bewildered look on his face and the fat pervert was so engrossed in his sick activity he hadn't heard or seen us drive up or noticed me walking toward his car.

I immediately said, "You're under arrest for lewd and lascivious conduct." Those two words were straight out of the Penal Code, so I thought they would sound clear and official enough, and I felt like adding "You sick bastard."

After the man was booked in jail, the boy, who was about 12 years old, told us how he got there. He said he lived in the Midway

Federal Housing Project, and that's where the pervert offered him a good time and other goodies to entice him to get into his car.

Where we found them was miles from Midway Housing, which was north of the Marine Corps Recruit Depot and not far from Old Town. Living in Midway Housing, the kid most likely came from a lower income family and was very vulnerable to offers of anything his family couldn't afford. That really made me happy that we had nailed the pervert, because he was obviously preying on underprivileged kids.

The most important part of the apprehension and arrest was that sex criminals are very unpredictable. There was no way of knowing what he would do to that boy after he had an orgasm. Sex perverts can escalate their sexual desires.

We then asked some detectives to take the boy home to attract less attention from nosy neighbors and avert a lot of prying questions.

Peeping Tom

Frank Foster and I were on graveyard shift and still in North Park when about midnight on a Saturday night we received a Peeping Tom call. It was in the neighborhood where Baseball-Hall-of-Fame star Ted Williams and tennis champion Maureen "Little Mo" Connelly grew up and perfected their athletic skills.

We walked up to the front door and Frank rang the doorbell. A woman in her 60s opened the door and as she and Frank spoke, she pointed to the south where the peeper had been.

It was winter and the lawns were covered with silvery dew. I walked around to the south side of the house on the concrete walkway to a window that was exposed. There were no shades or curtains to conceal the interior of the room. I thought, "How stupid. No wonder she had a peeper."

I started to return to the front porch where Frank was conversing with the woman to tell her to pull her shades on that window. As I walked toward the front of the house, the street lights made the dew glisten and I saw footprints. There were two sets, one to and the other from her walkway.

The woman's concrete walkway was exposed to sunlight and was dry, but the walkway of the house to the south that led to the rear yard apparently did not receive sunlight and was slightly damp.

I followed the footprints across the grass onto the damp walkway. They were crystal clear. They went to the rear of the house and up the concrete stairway to the rear door. It was conclusive proof that the Peeping Tom had entered the rear door of the house to the south.

Quite proud of my detective work, I returned to the front porch where Frank and the woman were still conversing. At the first pause in their conversation, I proudly divulged my amazing findings.

That's when it hit the fan. The woman exploded. In so many words, she chewed me out for falsely accusing Mr. so and so, that sweet old man, of such a thing. He and Mrs. so and so had lived there for 20 years, were good Christians and he was one of the finest men she had ever known — and blah, blah, blah.

With that tirade and case closed, Frank was just as anxious as I to get out of there without delay. There was more promising police work to do, and since I hadn't had a chance to tell her to pull her shades, Mr. so and so could peep at will.

As soon as Frank and I had settled in our freezing car with no heater, thanks to Chief Jansen, I asked Frank, "Do you know of any cure for stupidity?"

"Nope, if there was, we'd be out of a job," he replied with one of his trademark chuckles.

As Frank pulled away from the curb I thought, "If that old motor mouth can't keep her yap shut, she just might tell Mr. so and so about the crazy cop who insanely accused him of peeping in her window."

With that wishful thought, I hoped he would know the cops had him fingered and take up another hobby, like maybe fishing or shuffleboard. His past neighborhood resident Ted Williams was a died-in-the-wool fisherman, so maybe he would emulate the great slugger and follow suit, I dreamed.

On the next graveyard shift, my regular partner was Chuck Osborn, a five-year veteran San Diego police officer and a joy to work with. We were completely compatible and could almost read each other's minds. That's the way it's supposed to be in police work.

Sexual Pervert in Little Italy

We were on Beat 2 adjacent to and north of downtown Beat 4, and our beat included "Little Italy" and India Street that ran through it. We received a call to take a burglary report in that Italian neighborhood about midnight on a Sunday night.

We were met out front by the extremely concerned and anxious father of two teenage daughters. He led us to the rear bedroom where his wife and two daughters were nervously waiting.

The mystery of the burglary was that the only thing taken was a piggy bank containing just a few dollars in change, and it had been on a dresser next to where a rather expensive camera remained. In addition, the father told us of other more expensive items in the house that had not been taken.

As we all pondered for an answer to the mysterious event, I remembered the sex-crimes detective who told us during Recruit Classroom Training of female bedroom sex perverts. He had told us they were so twisted they got their jollies from being in a female's bedroom and usually defecated and ejaculated sperm in the middle of the bed.

With that sudden brainstorm, I quietly walked out the connecting door into the rear yard. With the rear porch light on, I saw a concrete stairway leading down to a landing in front of a cellar or basement door, and it was well lit.

There it was — defecation and a small wet spot in front of it. The pervert burglar had apparently squatted, leaning against the concrete wall and enjoyed his sexual gratification. It pleased me that the pervert had not done his thing on the bed where the two pretty daughters would have seen it.

I quietly returned to the bedroom, tapped the father on the shoulder and nodded my head toward the rear door for him to follow me. At the top of the stairway, I pointed to the defecation and wet spot and told him what I had been told about the female bedroom sex perverts.

In that it would probably seriously disturb his daughters and perhaps his wife, I told him it was up to him to tell them what he thought would be best. He agreed but did not indicate what he would do. It was obvious to me that he would have to think it over.

I then told him I was certain the weird culprit lived within a block of them and he probably saw his pretty daughters coming and going and knew they lived there. And with the piggy bank and other teenage decorations in their bedroom, he had no problem identifying which room was theirs. I also told him we would pass the information on to the sex-crimes detectives and they might be able to readily identify a prime candidate.

With all of that, the father expressed his gratitude and Chuck and I went back to patrolling side streets.

Later in my cop career, I learned more about sex criminals. One of the jewels I learned about sex criminals, rapists and serial rapist-killers was that some took personal items from their victims as trophies. They would keep them to later relive the excitement of their sexual gratification and possibly to experience an orgasm. With that later realization, I was certain the "Little Italy" pervert had experienced much enjoyment from that piggy bank, if the sex detectives didn't nail him.

In that many criminals are pathological and some are just plain stupid, those who collect trophies have no idea that those items found in their possession or living quarters can be crucial evidence to prove their guilt. With that on the side of the good guys, we could only thank them for their cooperation.

Parks are generally a magnet for sexual activities, along with 24/7 public restrooms. Chuck and I had both on our Beat 2, most of all gigantic Balboa Park and a restroom in the parking lot of the world-famous San Diego zoo.

There was a walking officer around the clock in Balboa Park. This was mandated by the insurance carrier that insured the many large buildings and the organ pavilion. The sole purpose of that mandate was for the officer to serve as a fire watchdog. Because of the size of Balboa Park, it was next to impossible for an officer to cover all of it with any degree of efficiency. Prior to Chief Jansen's rise to power, there had been mounted patrols, but like so many other things, he ended the horse patrols.

The Fishing Expedition

Chuck, our relief partner, "The Dunce", and I didn't pay much attention to Balboa Park because of the walking officer being there, except to snooze for about an hour after dining at the El Cortez Hotel. The only time I recall that we went up Park Boulevard to the zoo parking lot, Chuck was driving. We saw a man standing by the door of the men's restroom. I got out and asked the man what he was doing there, since there was a city ordinance making it a misdemeanor to loiter in or around a public restroom.

"I'm waiting for someone," he replied. Suspecting he was a homosexual on a fishing expedition I asked, "Anyone in particular?" His "no" answer made it clear that I was right.

Knowing I knew what he was up to, he opened up and told me his sad story. He had just got off work from Convair Aircraft and had the urge. He said he had been married for many years, had two children and had only recently lost interest in his wife and had become attracted to men.

I told him he was committing a crime by loitering there, which he obviously didn't know or he wouldn't have told me his number one secret. He was also no doubt ignorant of the fact that homosexual activities were a felony as sodomy and oral copulation were both felonies as stated in the California Penal Code — even if committed by married couples in the privacy of their bedrooms — and remained as such until after Governor Jerry Brown took office in 1975.

Not wanting to be the one to destroy his marriage and shame his two children, I told him he was committing a crime and to leave and never come back.

The Gold Gulch Incident

The only time Chuck and I went down the dirt road to what was called "Gold Gulch" during the 1935-1936 International Exposition in Balboa Park Chuck was again driving.

A couple of blocks into the "Gulch" there was a car parked just off the road to the west on my side of the patrol car. Nobody was visible, so I was concerned that it might be a suicide situation as was sometimes the case on rare occasions. I hoped it was not.

Daylight had just broken, so I could see everything very well. When I got to the left rear window I was relieved to see a man and a woman soundly sleeping and stark naked. I almost laughed, because it was obvious to me that they had enjoyed much fun and fell asleep after the main event. So I beat on the window and yelled, "Time to get up."

I then hustled back to the car, slid into my seat and slammed the door. I could see all kinds of hurried movement and commotion inside the car and I said to Chuck, "Let's get out of here."

It was a Monday morning, so I couldn't help but think one or both of them may have to be at work by eight, so we may have saved one or both of their jobs or at least saved them a lot of explaining.

Stopping a Pedophile

About a year later on motors, I was assigned to a beat that covered Logan Heights and Encanto in the east end of the city. As I passed an elementary school, I saw an occupied car parked in the parking lot across the street from the school. It was parked at the end of a row of parked cars, where the man behind the wheel had a clear view of the school playgrounds. It was a crime for unauthorized persons to be on school grounds and the parking lot was included as part of school grounds.

I made a U-turn, went into the parking lot and parked to the rear of the car. I asked the 20-year-old man what he was doing there, because I thought he might be there to pick up a student or school staff member, and school was almost out.

When he replied that he was just there to take a rest, I automatically considered he could be a pedophile and may have an arrest or conviction record for such offenses.

I got his driver license and radioed for a record check of arrests, convictions and wants. The files had to be hand searched, and it could take 25 to 45 minutes, depending on how busy the records staff was.

After about 30 minutes, the man said he worked on a hog farm and it was time to feed the hogs, so could he leave. It sounded like hogwash to me, but I was also tired of waiting, so I said he could. I told him I would follow him until I received a reply, and if I turned off, he was clear, but if I turned my red lights on, he was to pull over and stop. Then I returned his license to him.

We had gone about a block when I got the reply. He had seven outstanding Failure to Appear (FTA) warrants, but no other arrest records. That was the most FTA warrants I had ever made arrests for. FTAs are issued when a violator signs a promise to appear on a traffic citation and fails to appear.

I turned on my red lights and he pulled over and stopped. I radioed for a beat car to transport him to jail. Within minutes, a patrol division unit arrived. The officer was the number one self-imagined super cop on the police department with absolutely no sense of humor or personality, and he had a brand new recruit with him.

I readily noticed Officer Super Cop and his trainee had curious looks on their faces. Super Cop quickly came straight to me and asked me where I had located the FTA violator. When I told him on the school parking lot, he blurted out, "I just checked him out about 45 minutes ago. How did you get wise to him?"

I could not believe my ears. I thought this is too good to be true — a "Stupid Motor Monkey" like me had outdone the king of all "Super Cops" and the strange look on his trainee's face made it even more joyful for me.

Gloatingly, I calmly replied, "It was obvious to me that he wasn't right and had something to hide," but I sure didn't tell him I was fishing for a sex-crimes record and was almost knocked over by the seven FTAs.

That was only about an hour into my shift, and I couldn't wait to get to the squad room at quitting time and spread the word to all of the regular guys. It was a very, very long shift. When I told the other motor cops, it was like I had hit a grand slam homer in the World Series for the "Motor Monkeys," and it was the entertainment hour of all entertainment hours.

Despite his not having a sex-crimes record, there was never any doubt in my mind that he was a pedophile. I always suspected he was there to ogle at and size up the little girls as they left school, and it was less than an hour before the end of the school day when I first contacted him.

But that's police work. You may never know for sure until it is too late, and making it hot for them can be a lifesaver.

The Modest Prostitute

At a later end-of-shift entertainment hour, two Beat 4 skid row officers came into the squad room to type an arrest report before going back to their busy beat. Laughing, they shared their experience with us. As they told it, two vice squad officers spotted a well-known prostitute pick up a sailor and take him to a hotel room. The vice officers followed, then stood in the hall at the door waiting to catch the two in the act. By the time they busted into the room, the prostitute was stark naked and they arrested her.

The vice officers then called for the two telling the story to transport her to jail. The vice officers told them they would take the sailor to the Shore Patrol. The two beat officers remained in the room to keep a watch on the prostitute so she didn't make a break for it. It was normal procedure to keep an arrestee in sight at all times.

They said the veteran prostitute put her hands on her hips, glared at them and snarled, "It's just like you rotten bastards. You don't even have the decency to leave a lady's room while she gets dressed!" And this was after she had disrobed for probably thousands of "Johns" of all kinds while plying her "oldest profession" trade.

CHAPTER 13

Nighty Night

So, after intently beating the bushes on side streets with great success, Chuck and I would eat our free gourmet lunch at the El Cortez Hotel, then go to our special spot to snooze for an hour or a little bit more, but we only napped and popped up completely awake whenever the radio squawked anything.

About two years before I joined the San Diego Police Department, the San Diego Union-Tribune published a letter from an apparent cop hater about a motor officer who regularly sat a particularly busy intersection. He expressed his sentiment that the officer should be doing something better, like catching murderers — a very old, tired violator's complaint.

A few days later, the Union-Tribune published a letter from a San Diego police motor sergeant defending the motor officer's reasons for "sitting in."

The sergeant wrote that the particular signal-lighted intersection was a high accident location and the officer's presence was a deterrent to discourage drivers from trying to beat or run the red light and causing a crash and that the officer's job was primarily to enforce traffic laws, not search for unknown murderers. That was primarily the detectives' job.

Then the sergeant also wrote that riding a motorcycle in heavy traffic for eight hours could be very tiring and could diminish an officer's necessary alertness. Therefore, as a motor officer for many years, he believed that riding for six hours in heavy traffic was an honest day's work. He also wrote that the motor officer had a two-way radio and could quickly respond to any emergency.

The sergeant concluded by thanking the complainant for writing so he could explain some inside details of police work to him and all other readers. Being intensely interested in police work, I never forgot that sergeant's eloquent, tactful and diplomatic letter of response.

After being assigned to graveyard shifts for six months of my first year on the police force, the very first partner I had who offered the idea of taking a snooze for an hour or so about 4:00 a.m. was Chuck Osborn. Remembering the motor sergeant's Union-Tribune letter, I thought it was a dandy idea. Also, any graveyard burglar with an ounce of sense should be in bed anyway, I rationalized. I had just completed my probation, so I was almost bulletproof.

So, after intently beating the bushes on side streets with great success, Chuck and I would eat our free gourmet lunch at the El Cortez Hotel, then go to our special spot to snooze for an hour or a little bit more, but we only napped and popped up completely awake whenever the radio squawked anything.

In that our five-year veteran relief partner was a dunce and addicted poker player in legal poker parlors, he jumped at the snooze idea, and without beating the bushes.

Secret Snooze Spot

What we thought was our secret snooze spot was south of Laurel Street that split Balboa Park in the middle. The location was at a wide clearing for park gardeners, and there was a gardener's shed for their tools at the east edge of the clearing.

With Balboa Park being hundreds or thousands of acres, surely it was only our find, we thought.

Then one Sunday night when Chuck and I were walking to the garage through the locker room, he asked me if I would drive the entire shift. He said he had partied in Tijuana that day and hadn't been to bed since our Saturday night shift. I immediately agreed to do so, and away we went.

At about midnight, we responded to a trash barrel fire on B Street to assist the fire department with any traffic control needed. Of course, there was no traffic, and the fire was doused in less than a minute.

As we were there watching the sleepy firemen finish up, good old Sergeant Paul Sears drove up. We had a brief conversation with the sergeant then we all departed. I noticed the sergeant was driving an unusual marked car. It had just been switched from the detective division, was lime green with white front doors and had chrome

Utility-make overhead lights. It was definitely different. All other patrol cars were black and white with cheaper black overhead lights.

Luckily, it was a very dead Sunday night. Even though I searched the side streets, nothing was stirring.

With an almost blank Daily Activity Report, except for the trash barrel fire, I drove onto the circular drive in front of the El Cortez Hotel at 3:00 a.m. and parked. Chuck then told me he was too beat and tired to eat, so he would lie down on the rear seat and sleep.

After I finished another delicious gourmet dinner that had been in the food warmer oven, I returned to the patrol car. Chuck was sound asleep, so I didn't disturb him. I just drove less than a mile to our exclusive snooze spot.

It was a pitch-black night, and I made a circular turn to back onto the pedestrian path that was about eight-feet wide. About halfway up the slight incline, I barely touched the brake pedal. All of a sudden the brake lights revealed two chrome Utility-make red lights. I instantly knew it was Sergeant Sears' car. I started laughing and quickly turned off our car's lights and slowly headed out of the clearing.

My laughter woke Chuck. He popped up, groggy with his cap slightly cocked to the right and asked, "What happened?"

"I just almost backed into Sergeant Sears' car," I replied, holding back laughter just long enough to tell him. "Did he see us?" Chuck asked with a touch of fear in his almost-alert voice.

"Hell, I don't know," I replied, already trying to think up an alibi if Sergeant Sears had the sneaky deputy chief with him.

I quickly concocted the lie that we were only there to make a security check of the gardener's tool shed, as we routinely did every shift, but the only problem was that Chuck was still in the back seat. So I got out of there as speedily as I could, got some distance and stopped for Chuck to get into the front seat — and nobody followed us.

At the end of the shift, Chuck was sitting next to me in a slight daze as I completed our Daily Activity Report by hand, as always, when Sergeant Sears walked in.

His cap was slightly cocked to the right, he looked like he had just got out of bed and was sort of plodding along, looking at the floor as if he was trying not to trip over something.

As soon as he was out of earshot, I turned to Chuck and said, "He didn't see us. Hell, he just woke up." And we sadly learned for the first time that our exclusive secret snooze spot was neither of those things. We didn't snooze there again when Sergeant Sears was on duty. We went elsewhere.

About a year after I had happily left the San Diego Police Department and joined the CHP, I learned that Chuck and I had dodged a very big bullet. One of my SDPD pal officers still stuck in the madness told me the deputy chief had taken one of the few weasel sergeants with him on a graveyard shift and caught two officers sleeping in our snooze spot.

One officer was a five-year veteran, and his partner was a newer probationary officer. The veteran officer was suspended for five days without pay, and the probationary officer was fired.

"What a stupid boner," I thought. Probation officers are in training, and the training officer/partner is in charge, so the probationary officer wouldn't have a say in what his partner decided to do. But the deputy chief had clearly proven to me that he loved to find ways to fire officers, especially probationary officers that didn't have the right to appeal. I had to conclude that there was something seriously wrong with that deputy chief. As it has been said, "Power corrupts, and absolute power corrupts absolutely." So true in some cases!

I could only thank God that His many gifts to me had allowed me to qualify for the CHP.

CHAPTER 14

Detective Dopes

A few hours later, Sergeant Mason met us and told us the detectives had interviewed our armed robber and his friend Smith, and from what Smith told them, they concluded that our suspect was not the Chinese-owned grocery store robber.

The eight weeks I worked with Chuck Osborn was the most successful crime-fighting experience of my police department career. We concentrated on side streets, because they were not as well lighted as the main arteries, and we knew burglars, rapists and other sneak criminals preferred darkness.

On the first day on the police department, my group was told we were to always report 15 minutes before shift start time to get a "hot sheet" and update it by hand. Hot sheets were published every day at noon, and the radio log from the business office with crimes and other incidents was placed on the hot sheet counter for officers to add information that developed after the hot sheet was published. The hot sheet listed all of the vehicles reported stolen in the past 30 days, as well as other major thefts and crimes.

One Sunday night, the radio log contained an APB for a double-fatal pedestrian felony manslaughter vehicle. The deceased victims were illegal Mexican immigrants and they had been struck and killed on the Montgomery Freeway between San Diego and Tijuana. Like some officers would do before line-up when there was a hot vehicle or suspect on the radio log, Chuck and I loudly announced we would find the hit-and-run vehicle.

Chuck drove first up Kettner Boulevard next to the Santa Fe Depot. On C Street one block north of Broadway I saw one lonely sedan parked on the south side of the street. It was the only vehicle parked in that block east of Kettner.

I told Chuck what I had seen, and he made a U-turn and went back to the sedan. Within a minute, we confirmed it was the fatal hit-and-run vehicle.

The right front headlight was broken and the right front fender had contact abrasion marks obviously made by clothing. On the right front floorboard was a smashed taco and wrapper spread around as though someone had dropped it after the surprise and shock of the collision. With all of that, we knew for certain it was the hit-and-run vehicle.

In that it was a CHP case, we radioed for a CHP unit to meet us at our location. The CHP was on the same radio frequency as the police department so it only took a few minutes to get a reply, but the reply was a surprise. The CHP had only one unit on duty in the county, and we were asked to impound the vehicle with a hold on it for the CHP.

I had known since I was a teenager that the CHP had resident officers on 24-hour call throughout the county, but only one on the road on a Sunday night?

I was sort of shocked, because some of the most gruesome accidents occurred in CHP areas on U.S. Highway 101, Pacific Coast Highway, north of San Diego to the Orange County line — especially through Camp Pendleton, which was widely known as "Blood Alley." Most accidents involved sailors or marines speeding to get back to their ship or base before return time, many having been in Los Angeles on a weekend drunken spree. Others were Los Angeles residents returning from Tijuana after a weekend of drinking.

In fact, two CHP officers had been hit by those types north of Oceanside and had to retire on disability. The drivers were both hung over, fell asleep at the wheel, ran off the road and hit the officers who were on the shoulder writing citations.

So we had no choice but to call for a tow truck and impound the hit-and-run car with a hold for the CHP for evidence.

The Roaring Chevy

Another Sunday night, Chuck and I were standing in a service station at the southeast corner of 11th Avenue and A Street at the foot of the Cabrillo Freeway that went through Balboa Park to Mission Valley. I saw four sailors hitchhiking. There was almost no traffic, so I wondered if they would make it back to their base in time.

Within minutes, a 1950 Chevrolet club coupe stopped, and they all jumped in. When the car took off, it sounded like a large airplane. The modified exhaust had dual "Smitty" mufflers.

Although illegal, "Smitty" mufflers were made in California and amplified the exhaust noise to extreme levels. They were loud on Fords, but almost unbearable on Chevrolets.

As a teenager, I thought they were great, but when I was working graveyard shifts and they woke me up when I was trying to sleep in the day time, my attitude dramatically changed.

Chuck was driving, so we jumped in our car and took out after the roaring Chevy. We caught up with it north of Balboa Park near University Avenue. To our surprise, the car had Baja California, Mexico license plates on it. Then when I got to the driver's open window, I immediately smelled the familiar odor associated with illegal Mexican immigrants or "Wetbacks" as we called them.

Almost certain it was a stolen car I asked the Caucasian driver, "Where did you get the car?"

Without hesitation he replied, "I stole it in Tijuana." He said he was an Air Force airman and stationed at March Air Force Base in Riverside County. His buddies had left him behind in Tijuana, and he was desperate to get back to the base in time, so he borrowed the car.

I thought, "You poor idiot, you just committed the federal Dyer Act felony of taking a stolen car across a state line." What made it worse was he was a nice, honest guy. When I told him he was under arrest, he immediately said the sailor passengers had nothing to do with it, as he had picked them up hitchhiking.

I told him we knew, because we saw them hitchhiking and saw him pick them up. When I told the sailors they had to get out of the car, they started moaning about losing their ride and being dumped in the middle of nowhere, even though they were only a few blocks from University Avenue. With that, the airman spoke up and told them they were lucky we had seen him pick them up and were turning them loose.

With that and many other stupid incidents I experienced with military servicemen, I often wondered how we won World War II.

Deadbeat Dad

Another Sunday night, Chuck and I saw a lone hitchhiker at 11th and A Streets, where the sailors had hitched the Baja California stolen car ride. When we questioned him, his answers were all over the place and didn't track, so we decided to take him to the station to check the criminal arrest, conviction and wanted files.

Chuck drove, parked in the drive-through patio at the station and went to the records bureau. When he returned in about 15 minutes, he said to the bad liar, "You're wanted in Arizona." The extradition subject quickly replied, "No, I took that car back." Chuck then said, "No, you're wanted for failure to provide for your minor children."

In addition to apparently slipping by an auto theft count, he was a deadbeat dad, so back to Arizona.

Although we spent most of our shifts patrolling the darker side streets, Chuck and I never fell into a routine pattern of cruising. Keep them guessing. Bob Richards and Jack Fowler routinely started their shifts by going to the sidewalk coffee shop, but that was to see if the rotund parking attendant informant had any hot poop for them, and it sometimes bore fruit.

Also one of our regular duties was to visually check safes in commercial offices and other buildings. They were all lighted with a lamp, so if the light was out, we had to radio for the owner to be notified and check the building for any break-ins. All of those safes were in buildings on main arteries.

There was a concentration of medical and dental offices on 4th Avenue. Many of them had been converted from old residences and remodeled. In that 4th Avenue was on a hill, it was called "Pill Hill."

After checking all the safes on "Pill Hill" one week night, I randomly drove to the north end of our beat on 4th Avenue at Upas Street for variety. I then made a U-turn and headed back down 4th. After going several blocks, we saw a single light abruptly weaving back and forth in the center of the street. I moved to the right and slowed to get out of its path and to see what it was.

The Wild Motorcycle Ride

When it got close enough, we could clearly see it was a motorcycle with a female passenger hanging on behind the operator.

It was going about 35 miles per hour and weaving to go between the white center lines and through the unpainted spaces.

I made a quick U-turn, turned on the red lights and siren and floored it. We were only about six blocks south of Walnut Avenue where 4th jogged to the left for about 30 to 40 feet at the offset intersection.

We were able to overtake and stop the motorcycle just half a block south of the offset intersection, and just in time. As soon as the motorcycle stopped, the female passenger jumped off and ran back to us. She was almost hysterical. The operator slowly got off the motorcycle on the left side and held onto the handlebars to keep from falling down. There was no need to give him a sobriety test. He was drunk.

After we had him secure in the rear seat, the shaking female told us how it all came about. She said a large group of her friends had been to a beach party. Then they went to one of their homes about a mile south of where we first saw the weaving light. She said the motor operator had ridden from the beach to the home, so she thought he was sober. After they had been at the home for a while, the motor rider asked her if she would like a ride. She said he looked sober enough, so she agreed. But she didn't notice he was still drinking and getting more inebriated by the minute.

She then said she didn't realize how drunk he was until it was too late, after he started weaving and speeding. She said she panicked and told him to stop and let her off, but he just kept going.

If we had not seen them and stopped them, the motorcycle would have run over the curb, across the sidewalk and about 15 feet of lawn and crashed into the side of the corner house at about 35 miles per hour.

On the way to jail, we dropped the woman off at the home where the crazy ride started, and she thanked us for everything.

Much like when Frank Foster and I caught the masturbating pervert in the canyon east of Balboa Park — an experience that could have harmed the enticed boy, our intervention in this situation saved the woman from injury or death, causing me to believe it could be divine intervention. We had stopped the motorcycle about two or three seconds before it would have jumped the curb and crashed into the house.

101

The thing that clinched this belief was although our beat spanned from the Balboa Park Naval Hospital over five miles west to Rosecrans and the Naval Training Center and from Ash Street north to Upas Street, a total of ten square miles, and where we got the motorcycle stopped was a block and a half north of the north end of our beat. Why were we there?

Also, traffic accident statistics showed that passengers on motorcycles were usually injured much more severely than operators, because passengers didn't have handlebars to hold on to and would be propelled over the backs of the operators. They would fly and bounce farther than the operators and sometimes slam into a fixed object.

With that history, it was very likely Chuck and I had prevented the woman from being crippled or killed. In any event, it was a very satisfying feeling for us.

The Barefoot Escapee

Another night patrolling the darker side streets, Chuck and I saw a young man walking north on the sidewalk to the west and across the street from the CHP and DMV offices at 3rd and Cedar. It was about 5:00 a.m., not long after our snooze in the park.

When we approached the man, we immediately noticed he was in stocking feet with no shoes. Chuck instantly decided he was a burglar looking for an opportunity.

After briefly interrogating him, we took him to his rented room to get his shoes. He said he didn't have a key to the door, which raised some other serious questions. There was a transom over the locked door, and he said he could get into the room through the transom.

We told him to go ahead and do it, but not to try anything funny. We said we would be at a distance when he came out of the door and would shoot him down if he came out with a weapon. Letting a suspect out of our sight was risky, but we knew we could deal with it if he armed himself.

He came out empty-handed, wearing shoes.

Chuck was hell bent on booking him for suspicion of burglary, so we took him to the captain's office for approval. On the way, he openly confessed to escaping from the Camp Pendleton prison barracks a few weeks before.

When we got to the captain's office, Chuck's suspect poured out his sad story to the captain and added that he had an advanced case of "Bullhead Clap," which he hadn't told Chuck and me.

With that news, the captain immediately told us to take him to the Shore Patrol. He did not want him in our jail.

In those days, there was a standing reward of $25 for the capture and delivery of AWOL and deserter servicemen, and when we turned him over to the Shore Patrol at their headquarters, they gave Chuck a receipt.

The $25 reward was normally deducted from the AWOL or deserter's next paycheck, but our boy wasn't going to get another paycheck. He was headed for a dishonorable discharge.

A couple of weeks later, a request from the Marine Corps to explain our arrest of the escapee/deserter was sent to me. We never submitted an arrest report when we turned prisoners over to the Shore Patrol, so they had just one question for me to answer: Did he voluntarily surrender himself to my partner and me of his own free will, or did we apprehend him and learn of his escape and desertion after he was in custody. The answer would make the difference between his being AWOL or a deserter. My honest answer made him a deserter.

In that the U.S. government was going to have to pay the $25, that measly sum apparently had to be approved at the White House or the Pentagon, because it took about three months. In the interim, Chuck was promoted to sergeant and assigned to the jail. I was then on the 3:00 p.m. shift and received a radio call to return to the station and go to the jail. Chuck was waiting for me at the jail door and handed me $12.50 for my half of the reward money. I had almost forgotten about it, and I thanked him. In many ways, he had been one of my best partners.

More Escapees

Another Sunday night, we had just left the station, Chuck was driving and he went north on Pacific Coast Highway to get back to our beat as soon as possible. Just north of Broadway, we saw two

103

sailors in civilian clothes walking north on the east side of PCH. Even in "civvies," sailors and marines could be recognized as such from a block away. Their haircuts, shoes and sometimes their swagger gave them away.

It was well after the time that servicemen normally had to be back to their ship or base, so I asked Chuck to stop. When I asked them for their IDs and Liberty Cards, they couldn't produce Liberty Cards, so I asked them why.

They offered a story full of holes, so I suggested to Chuck that we take them to the Shore Patrol to let them figure it out. Chuck was in sort of a rare Father Flanagan mood and shrugged his shoulders, so I told him if they were clean, the Shore Patrol would just kick them loose, and the Shore Patrol was less than a mile away. With that, Chuck agreed with a sigh.

I got in the rear seat with the two sailors. Before Chuck pulled away from the curb, one of them said, "We just escaped from the 32nd Street landing prison barracks."

Just as we turned down the front corridor into the Shore Patrol, a communications enlisted man ran out of the radio room and yelled, "Four prisoners just escaped from the 32nd Street landing prison barracks." As he slowly walked back toward the radio room, we were at the end of the corridor about ten feet from him. I said, "Here're two of them." With that, he looked at me as though he had just heard from God.

Almost immediately, the tall lieutenant-in-charge appeared and curtly asked them, "Where are the other two?" One of them answered, "We don't know." The lieutenant, who was about six feet three inches tall, quickly snapped, "Come in here. I want to talk to you."

Hearing that, I said to Chuck, "Let's go." I did not want to be a witness to that potential blood bath that I was certain would evolve if the two didn't come clean. For their sake, I could only hope they could give some very, very good answers.

Armed Robber in Logan Heights

On another Sunday night, there was a red-hot APB for an armed robber who had hit two Chinese-run mom and pop grocery stores in

Logan Heights — one on Friday night and the other on Saturday night of that weekend.

The descriptions of the robber and his car were very complete, even with a partial license number of the car. He was African/American, 5' 8", 165 pounds, left-handed, wearing a Marine Corps fatigue jacket and a woman's stocking mask and carrying a .45 automatic weapon. And somehow it had become known that he had a friend named "Smitty." A witness had described the getaway car as a Chevrolet with a partial license number of C737.

As we had done before with the CHP double fatality hit-and-run car APB that we had located so easily, Chuck and I loudly announced before line-up that we would nail him. Ho, ho, ho.

I drove first, going up Kettner, east on Ash and north on 4th to get to the middle of our beat as quickly as possible. I turned west on Laurel then turned south on Front Street to start patrolling the side streets.

We had gone about three and a half blocks when a big black Lincoln sped west across an intersection about a half-block ahead of us going about 35 miles per hour in the 25-mile zone, or 15 miles per hour if it was a blind intersection.

I immediately put the car in second gear, turned the corner and floored it. By the time we had turned the corner the Lincoln was almost to Kettner, ran the stop sign and turned right onto Kettner.

When we got to Kettner, the Lincoln had about a three-block lead on us. The Lincoln made it through Laurel on a green light, but it changed to amber and red before we could get there, so I had to turn on the red lights and siren to run the red, and it was the last thing I wanted to do.

As expected, the Lincoln took off at over 90 miles per hour in the 25-mile per hour speed zone. I got our 1950 Ford up to its top speed of 90 miles per hour, but the Lincoln's tail lights just kept getting closer and closer to each other.

The Lincoln went out of sight at the sweeping S-curve at the north end of Kettner where it ended at Washington. I stopped at Washington and we looked both ways, but no car of any description was in sight in either direction.

There was a large building supply complex to the west of Kettner and behind us south of Washington. It had a wide concrete street with high buildings on both sides, about 150 feet long. South of the buildings, there were many tall stacks of lumber well-spaced apart, and immediately south of the building backed up to Kettner, there was an unpaved driveway into the area of the stacks of lumber.

I quickly made a U-turn and drove down the wide street to the stacks of lumber. Between the first and second stacks of lumber was the abandoned Lincoln.

As had become a habit of mine, I first took a look at the license plate. It was 4F3737. I joyously told Chuck, "We got him." Of course we didn't have the Chinese grocery armed robber, but if it was his car, it would no doubt lead our detectives to him without much trouble.

We radioed for a tow truck to impound it as evidence for the detectives.

Within a short time, Henry's Tow arrived. With more good fortune as it turned out, the owner, Henry, was driving. He was about 40 years old and very astute. Being the owner, he could readily order his employees to do whatever we requested.

As Henry hooked up the Lincoln, Chuck and I discussed the car being a Lincoln, not a Chevrolet as described by the witness who provided the partial plate number. Based on our experience, we agreed it didn't matter, because many vehicle descriptions provided by citizens included an incorrect make.

Also, the license mounting on the rear bumper of the Lincoln was deep set between two vertical bars that obscured the view of the entire plate from both sides, so what the witness reported as a "C" was no doubt the first of the two 3s.

When Henry had the Lincoln hooked up, he pulled the car about halfway up the wide concrete street and stopped. We told him to be sure to put a hold on the car for our detectives and if the owner showed up to reclaim it, stall him and call the police department.

He assured us he would order all of his employees to do just that, and we departed. We had gone only about a block down Kettner when we received an urgent call to return to the location where we had left Henry. The call said the owner of the car had returned.

I made a speedy U-turn, drove north on Kettner to north of the large buildings and turned south on the wide street. The instant we saw the owner he was standing by the right side door of the tow truck, pulling on the door handle and trying to talk to Henry through the closed window. Henry had locked both doors.

When the owner saw us coming at him, he stiffened and jerked his head to the left, looking for an escape route to the south, but there was none. If he had tried to run, we could have quickly overtaken him and run him down, and I'm not too sure that I wouldn't have done that in desperation. He then sagged and waited to meet us and say hello.

I always thought that after we told Henry to put a hold on the car and call us if the owner showed up to reclaim it, he set a trap for the owner. There was really no reason for him to stay after we left. He had locked both doors and hung around. He must have had his radio microphone in his hand ready to use it, because we got the call to return in less than two minutes after we left him.

Unfortunately, in all the activity in handcuffing the owner and the excitement of finally having him in custody after our wild chase, I never had a chance to thank Henry for his marvelous "posse comitatus" work, but I think he knew, because he departed soon after we had the owner cuffed, and he probably had a huge smile on his face all the way to his tow yard.

Chuck and I were overjoyed when we saw the owner was African/American, 5' 8", 165 pounds, left-handed and was wearing a Marine Corps fatigue jacket.

Soon after Henry left, fatherly Sergeant George Mason arrived. When our robbery suspect said he had come there to get his paycheck at nearby Convair Aircraft but it was closed, Sergeant Mason called him a liar. Sergeant Mason was very familiar with Convair's work days and hours. At that time, Convair was designing and constructing a prototype of the first F-102 fighter-planes on a cost-plus contract with the U.S. government and Sergeant Mason knew it very well.

And I learned of it less than two years later when I was on the CHP and led the low boy trailer carrying the prototype from the Riverside County line to the Los Angeles County line on a motor with two CHP car officers, including Rose Bowl traffic director Walt Cook protecting the rear.

For some reason, Chuck drove to jail and I rode in the rear with our already-convicted armed robber. I interrogated him and he was very cocky, but not overly bright. He proudly said his best friend was named Smith. Then when I asked him about his beautiful Lincoln, he said the monthly payments were $163. With that figure, I asked him how much he made at Convair. Then he freely replied that he made $185 a month as a janitor.

We first took our robber to the captain's office for his booking approval. Without delay, the captain quickly gave his okay, and he said he would notify the graveyard detectives.

A few hours later, Sergeant Mason met us and told us the detectives had interviewed our armed robber and his friend Smith, and from what Smith told them, they concluded that our suspect was not the Chinese-owned grocery store robber.

Our shocking disappointment almost instantly turned to red-hot anger. They hadn't even talked to us to get the whole story. Who were these detectives?

I had heard two versions how detectives were selected. The official front-office version was that they were selected by their well-proven skill to write outstanding quality reports for many years. The other version from the street cops was they got to be detectives by playing poker with the right people.

Chuck and I had to conclude that we had got stuck with two poker players, and two loser poker players at that.

Most interesting was that a few years after I left the police department, one of my old friends told me the police department gods had all of a sudden discovered that experienced traffic-accident investigators were the most qualified to be detectives — after more than 40 years of the police department investigating crashes. They had much more experience investigating and collecting evidence.

Proof that Chuck and I were right and the brainless detectives were dead wrong surfaced in the year to follow. The first indication was that the armed robberies of Chinese-owned grocery stores abruptly stopped, along with Logan Heights armed robberies for months to follow.

Then the year later, also in the summer, two La Jolla Substation beat officers caught our armed robber red-handed in the act of robbing a liquor store in Pacific Beach. As they slowly cruised by the front of the liquor store, the passenger officer clearly saw "Mr. Big Lincoln Sedan" pointing his .45 automatic over the counter at the store clerk, and they quickly captured him without resistance or incident.

Although deflated by the detectives dumping our sure-fire case, Chuck and I were elated that he had finally been nailed, and we could only hope the two bungling detectives would realize their gigantic mistake. We didn't count on it though, because they obviously couldn't put two and two together or connect the dots.

With the way it turned out for Chuck and me, we regretted relying on the detectives to search the Lincoln for the .45 automatic, stocking mask and any other incriminating evidence. If we had searched it and found the gun and mask, we could have had it all wrapped up and the specialized robbery detail detectives would have taken over the next morning.

Any search of the Lincoln would have been legal, because it was two years before the "Exclusionary Rule" was put into effect by the California Supreme Court in the Los Angeles Police Department Cahan search case. With that restriction, searches of persons and property required search warrants or other conditions, such as exigent/emergency situations or by consent of the owner. "Happy hunting" was over. Then the U.S. Supreme Court followed suit in about 1960 with an Ohio case.

At about 2:30 a.m. on a later night, Chuck was driving north on 6th Avenue when I saw a sailor lying still on the Balboa Park lawn about 50 feet from the curb. I told him to stop and we both got out and walked over to see if the sailor was all right. He was obviously drunk, so we each took an arm, lifted him up and started half dragging him to the car. We were about halfway to the car when another police department patrol car went by on 6th Avenue. The drunk instantly stooped down trying to hide and said, "Look out, there's the cops."

I said, "It's okay. We know those cops real good."

He slept all the way to the Shore Patrol. When the tall lieutenant routinely asked if there were any charges, we said, "No, just get him back to his ship."

CHAPTER 15

Shakedown Slips

The San Diego Police Department had a small form entitled Shakedown Slip. From the first time I heard that label I thought it was tacky, because one definition of that word is extortion. However, the Shakedown Slip was a very valuable crime-detection tool and was the same as what other police agencies called Field Interrogation Cards.

Shakedown slips were completed by street cops to report all field contacts with suspicious persons that might be connected with a crime, especially crimes that had not yet been reported. The completed forms were submitted to the detective division for matching with the location, time and date of crimes reported, both old and new, but especially crimes reported the following day.

The most famous Shakedown Slip completed and submitted involved a serial medical and dental offices burglar who always hit on Sunday nights.

After he had burglarized a few offices, there was a traffic accident late one Sunday night on a side street just off 4th Avenue in the middle of the "Pill Hill" area. After the accident scene was cleaned up, a remaining traffic investigator noticed a man get into a parked car. The man couldn't get the car started, so the officer approached him and asked if he could help. The man accepted the offer, and as soon as the officer hit the starter the engine started.

That aroused the officer's suspicions, so he obtained the man's driver license and completed a Shakedown Slip without any extensive questioning of the man.

It could only be later assumed that the man would have used an excuse of his car breaking down earlier for his being in that area of medical and dental offices at that late hour on a Sunday night, and he had just come back to again try to start it.

The next morning the burglary of a "Pill Hill" medical office was reported. Detective Sergeant Paul Weber connected the Shakedown Slip and burglary report. The young man's name was George

Shockley, but he did not have a criminal record. Quite certain he was the burglar, Sergeant Weber and his partner staked out George Shockley at his home the next Sunday night. George Shockley departed from his home and drove to a church. After late services, they followed him to El Cajon Boulevard and Illinois Street where there was a two-story building on the southwest corner.

They watched him park his car then go up the exterior staircase in the middle of the building. Sergeant Weber and his partner were at a distance to stay out of sight, so George Shockley had a good head start on them. They got to the top of the stairs just in time to see the door of a medical office close.

Sergeant Weber tried to open the door, but it wouldn't budge. He pulled his revolver and fired a shot into the door lock like they do in the movies. The door opened and George Shockley ran from the door, across the office, out an exit door on the opposite side of the office and down an exterior staircase. Sergeant Weber used an office phone to call the station to request help to search for him.

George Miller, who told me of this event, was in the first unit to arrive, and they parked in the alley behind the building. He said he walked to a wooden gate on the same side of the building as the exit staircase, unlatched the gate and tried to open it. It wouldn't move so he looked over the gate to see what was stopping it. Lying on the walkway against the gate was the body of George Shockley. He was dead.

It was then learned that George Shockley had held the office door closed in sort of a football lineman's stance with his left shoulder against the door at doorknob level. When Sergeant Weber fired to try to break the lock he thought was holding the door closed, the bullet hit George Shockley in the left upper back.

Years later, the most infamous Shakedown Slip was submitted by a veteran patrol division officer who was dying to become a detective and almost died trying to be one.

Like some officers permanently assigned to the same beat for years, he kept copies of all the Shakedown Slips he had submitted in a personal file for future reference. He had been on a Logan Heights beat long enough to have a fairly thick file. There was an armed robbery one night on his beat, and a good description of the robber was aired, so to make points with the detective supervisors he got a bright idea. He searched through his Shakedown Slip file and found one with an almost identical physical description as the armed robber at large, so he made out a Shakedown Slip using the name, address and description of the hot suspect.

It was such a good match two detectives went to the address given and rang the bell. An older man answered the door and when the detectives asked to speak to the hot suspect by name, the older man identified himself as the father. When the detectives told the father why they wanted to talk to his son, he said his son hadn't been there for six months because that was how long he had been in state prison. The submitting officer was suspended for five days without pay and probably retired as a patrol division officer.

The effectiveness of Shakedown Slips was proven by Captain Stark and his well-horse-traded sergeants and officers. Although he never did it while I was in line-up, one of my partners told me Captain Stark on at least one occasion stepped out of his office and said, "We could use more Shakedown Slips." That was all he had to say. The officers quickly increased the numbers.

Its impact was reported by a burglary detective. He told a group of officers that about two weeks after Captain Stark's squad rotated onto graveyard, the burglaries started decreasing, and they continued to decrease until they bottomed out six weeks into the eight-week assignment. They stayed at the lowest point ever until Stark's squad rotated to the afternoon shift. About two weeks later, the burglaries started increasing and six weeks later had again topped out. This sterling record proved that when intended burglars were stopped by officers and the suspected burglar saw the officer record his name and other personal information, he decided it was best to do something legal.

CHAPTER 16

Nowhere to Hide

"Where's the dead guy?" Although it was about 3:00 a.m. a small group of about 15 spectators were still there. In response to his stupid question, a young man replied, "You're standing on him."

The relief partner Chuck and I had was a five-year veteran and a real dunce. He was also something of a compulsive gambler who played poker in the legal poker parlors. I had only been in the police department one year and was assigned as a regular partner — something I had reason to believe didn't set well with him. As relief, he had to walk a beat one night a week, which was kind of a slap in the face for him, but I wasn't sure he knew it.

It didn't take long for me to see why he was only a relief after five years service. At the start of every one of the 16 nights I had to work with him, he had to go see his informant bartender at a swingers' bar on 5th Avenue close to the north end of our beat. Then after about 15 to 20 minutes, he would come out of the bar in a cloud of smoke puffing madly on a cigarette, obviously trying to mask the odor of the booze he had downed.

In the entire 16 nights together we accomplished absolutely nothing on our own. Unlike Chuck and me, he spent most of his driving time on main arteries where there were no crooks.

In addition to writing in newer information on my Hot Sheet, I also read the crime and stolen reports posted on an arch board. After returning to work after two nights off one week, I saw that three cars had been stolen in three nights. All three had been stolen from the same block on the cross street directly across 5th Avenue from the Dunce's boozing bar.

As he drove out of the garage, I mentioned it to him. He was still driving south on 5th Avenue at about 1:00 a.m. when we went by the block where the cars had been stolen. I looked down that street and saw a man squatting down working on the door handle or lock of a car. "Stop," I said. "Why?" he replied, and he didn't so much as slow down.

The cars had been stolen from in front of a large apartment building. "There's a guy tampering with a car," I abruptly responded. "Oh, he probably lives in the apartments," he replied. "Go around the block," I snapped. With that, he slowly drove around the block clockwise. When we finally made the full circle, there was nobody in sight. He probably did live in the apartments, I thought, but he's also our auto thief, I also thought.

We usually had some meaningless conversations to pass the time, but I went totally silent. I was pissed. It was bad enough to have to endure his stupidity but not his stupid kid's games.

After about an hour of silence, he said, "You're mad about my not stopping, aren't you? "You're damn right," I said. "When your partner says to stop, don't ask stupid questions, just stop." "Well I didn't know why you wanted to stop," the idiot tried to rationalize. I didn't even respond to that stupid excuse and kept my mouth shut the rest of the shift.

I was certain he refused to stop because he resented my being the regular officer with only one year on the job when he was the relief officer with five years. It was a mystery to me how he knew that apartment building was on that cross street when he never saw anything, even on main arteries that he nearly always stuck to. I could only conclude that he frequented the swingers' bar on his off time and parked in front of the apartment in broad daylight when there were empty spaces and he might see something big.

Another night he was driving down 5th Avenue late in the shift and as in every other shift so far, we had done absolutely nothing. As we passed a closed service station with a phone booth out front, he slowed and looked at the phone booth. He said, "We could get some names out of the phone book and make out some Shakedown Slips." I looked at him like he was nuts and curtly replied, "Not while I'm in this car." I knew he was stupid, but with that comment I knew he was also crazy. He didn't respond.

About 5:00 a.m. on a later weekday shift, there wasn't a car in sight. Then a car with two men about 25 years old in it came up 5th Avenue. As we met it and it passed, Dunce made a quick U-turn and followed. A few blocks up 5th, it turned west on a cross street. He followed it. There was absolutely nothing wrong with the driver's driving and the car had no visible defects, but he turned on the red lights and it quickly pulled to the curb.

I wondered what the fool was up to now. Knowing it was another of his bizarre antics, I stayed in the car to watch the fireworks from a distance. I routinely got out on stops and stood behind the front door when my partner made the contact. I also wanted to be near the radio to call for backup if he turned it into a full-blown donnybrook.

It took him only about 30 seconds to inflame the two occupants and turn it into a screaming match. When that erupted, I got out and stood behind the right door, but I was thinking, "You started it, so you can finish it, big boy."

After about a minute of the loud three-way screaming and yelling, he slowly retreated to the car, yelling at the two men over his left shoulder. When he got back into the car, I didn't say a word.

About halfway through our snooze hour in Balboa Park one week night, we got a call of a suspicious man with a dog just off of 6th Avenue, the west border of the park. I immediately said, "It's the park gardener." Dunce looked at me and said, "How do you know?" "Because I've seen him several times pulling sprinkler hoses with his big German Shepherd at his side," I replied. At the same time I thought, "How many burglars, rapists or other sneak criminals do you know of who take a dog with them to commit their crimes?"

He drove to 6th Avenue and I was certain he was hoping I was dead wrong. When we arrived there in less than five minutes, the night gardener was pulling hoses with his German shepherd at his side.

Just after dawn one morning, Dunce drove down Laurel Street onto Harbor Drive past Lindbergh Field and floored it. The 1950 Ford quickly got up to 90 miles per hour, and he held it at its top speed for miles, all the way to Rosecrans Street. After about a half mile, I looked at him. He had a "Look at me, look what I can do" glow on his face.

I didn't mind going 90 miles an hour in that old Ford to chase big Lincolns, but this was insane. There were no seat belts and if a tire blew, we would be all over the road, off the road or flipping end over end. I had to conclude that he was a major mental case.

The Fatal Accident

About 2:15 a.m. on another mid-week night, Dunce and I got an "11-80 (major injury accident) Code 3 (Emergency, red lights and siren)" call at the foot of Washington at Kettner.

Fortunately, I was driving or it may have given him an excuse to again go 90 miles an hour. When we arrived, I parked at the right edge of Washington. Without a word, he grabbed the car keys, opened the trunk, grabbed some flares and threw the keys on the front seat. Then he went up Washington and set up a flare pattern.

We were the first unit to arrive, so I went to the wreckage. The Studebaker Starlight sports club coupe was on its left side against a debris-catching fence in the natural dirt runoff channel parallel to Washington. The topsoil was soft and covered with tall weeds with burrs that stick to socks.

As soon as I left the roadway, I saw a dead body about 30 feet east of the car. It was sunken at least two inches into the ground, and the car had obviously landed on it when it rolled off the roadway and the man had been ejected from the car. There was a woman sitting next to the rear of the car and a young man was next to her trying to comfort her. She was covered with a white bedspread, and she said her leg was broken.

Wanting to cover the body, I went back to the patrol car, got the car keys, opened the trunk and grabbed the Army blanket that was standard in all San Diego Police Department cars. I returned to the injured woman, removed the bedspread and covered her with the blanket. I then quickly went to the body to cover it with the bedspread, but before I could cover it the injured woman screamed, "Oh my God, Daniel's dead." In her pain and shock, she hadn't noticed him in the darkness until I stood over him.

I then asked the young man and injured woman how many people had been in the car. They said four, and the other person was a woman. She was nowhere in sight and just as I started to look for her, Sergeant George Mason arrived.

I told him about the missing woman. He walked around the car to the fence, got on top of it and almost immediately said, "Here she is." I got on the fence behind him and saw the woman lying motionless on the ground between the car and the fence.

Just about then, the traffic car and ambulance arrived at the same time. We quickly put the woman with the broken leg in the ambulance and rolled the car onto its wheels away from the unconscious woman. We carefully put her on a stretcher and into the ambulance, and it left with siren howling, but she died on the way to the Naval Hospital.

The young man, the only one not injured, stayed behind at the scene to tell the traffic investigators what happened. He said all four were in the Marine Corps and had spent hours drinking at a 5th Avenue bar in Hillcrest. Daniel, the driver, downed six orange juice and vodka screwdrivers in the 30 minutes before the bar had to close at 2:00 a.m.

As they were going down the slight downgrade on Washington, Daniel weaved to the left and the left wheels went over the raised center divider of the four-lane highway. Taking a deep breath, the fairly cool but shaken marine hesitated then continued. He explained that Daniel didn't slow down to get off the raised divider, but started jerking the steering wheel to the right to get back to the right side of the highway, and when the car jumped the divider, it went out of control and rolled. He said he and the woman with the broken leg were in the rear seat, and the two in the front seat were thrown out of the car when it rolled.

About that time with the ambulance out of earshot, my partner came down to the scene. It made me wonder if he couldn't stand the sight of blood or guts and thought one or both might be there.

He sauntered off the paved road onto the high weeds and stood on the bedspread to get away from the burrs. Standing and looking around he asked, "Where's the dead guy?" Although it was about 3:00 a.m. a small group of about 15 spectators were still there. In response to his stupid question, a young man replied, "You're standing on him."

I was talking to Sergeant Mason and hadn't noticed Dunce get on the bedspread. Hearing the young man's reply, I quickly turned and looked, and sure enough, he was standing right in the middle of the bedspread, directly on top of dead Daniel. There was nowhere to hide.

The End of Dunce's Career

About two years after I left the police department, one of my old friends told me of the end of Dunce's illustrious police career.

He called in sick one afternoon shift and went to a poker parlor in La Mesa, a small city bordering San Diego to the east. When he had lost all his money, he asked the female parlor manager if she would cash a check for him. She did after he showed her his driver license and police department ID for good measure — and apparently to impress her.

She got suspicious about a policeman playing poker and losing a large sum of money, so she phoned the San Diego Police Department office to confirm that he was actually a policeman. The officer who took her call transferred it to Dunce's patrol division captain. When the captain heard the manager's story, he sent a sergeant to the poker parlor. The sergeant found Dunce very involved in playing poker, so he retrieved Dunce's police department ID card, and he was no longer a cop.

Then some time later, my old police department friend told me Dunce wrote bad checks to cover his gambling losses and ended up in San Quentin — not a very nice place for cops.

CHAPTER 17

Sore Losers

I reached into his pocket and pulled out an old, loose, ratty-hinged break-open Iver Johnson revolver. I almost laughed again, because if he had made it back to the poker game and pulled the trigger of that junky gun, I thought everybody in the room may have ended up in the County Hospital ER.

I was certain Captain Stark and his sergeants had really done me a great big favor by assigning me as the regular officer on popular Beat 2 with Chuck as my regular partner, but Chuck was number one on the sergeant list and I never wanted to work with drinking, poker playing, stupid Dunce ever again and we were going to rotate to the 3:00 p.m. shift.

So a couple of weeks before the eight-week shift rotation I asked Sergeant Mason if I could be assigned as relief with Seward and Castillo on Logan Heights Beat 9. Those two permanent partners were enjoyable to be around in the squad room and they were very obviously compatible as a team.

Sergeant Mason assigned me to Beat 9 and I never regretted making my request. They were both a joy to work with, but all the big things happened when I was with "Cass" Castillo.

The bigger one took place on a Friday, which was payday for most blue-collar workers. It was about 5:30 p.m. and Cass was driving when we got the unusual radio call. Nearly all calls were extremely brief, using only 10-11 codes, but this was urgent and was like a brief telephone call explaining the details and the urgency.

The call said a man had lost all of his week's paycheck in a poker game. He was certain the other players had cheated him and he had gone home to get his gun to go back and kill all of them. The location was a federal housing project and all or nearly all of the tenants were African/American.

Amazingly, and like divine intervention, we were only about two blocks away from the location and headed that way. As we rounded a short sweeping curve at the address given, we saw a man slightly staggering across a wide lawn and he had his right hand in his trouser pocket.

I immediately told Cass to stop, and when he did I jumped out and half ran in a wide arc to stay behind the man so he could not readily see me in his peripheral vision. When I got directly behind him, I could see he was staggering worse than it first appeared. As soon as I knew I had him, I had to keep from laughing. I had been half running on my tiptoes on the grass to circle him without his hearing. It struck me funny because I had tiptoed on thick, soft grass.

I got to him and grabbed his left shoulder with my left hand and his right wrist with my right hand. "Police, don't move," I said. He complied so I then said, "Open your right hand and remove it from your pocket very slowly." I had a death grip on his right wrist and once I knew his hand was open, I actually removed his hand from his pocket.

I reached into the pocket and pulled out an old, loose, ratty-hinged break-open Iver Johnson revolver. I almost laughed again, because if he had made it back to the poker game and pulled the trigger of that junky gun, I thought everybody in the room may have ended up in the County Hospital ER. Or, if he had made it back and by some miracle the gun had fired properly, we could have had about three dead or wounded people to deal with. And one or the other of these scenarios was only about 30 seconds to a minute from becoming a reality.

The Super Marine

One Sunday night as Cass was slowly driving west on Market Street at the end of our shift, he was looking at something that interested him on the south side of the street.

As we cleared 4th Avenue I saw a sailor in the street near the curb on top of a marine lying on his back, and the sailor was pounding the daylights out of him. Being on the north side of Market, Cass hadn't seen them. "Stop," I told Cass. Unlike Dunce, Cass stopped so quickly he almost put me into the windshield. I jumped out, ran over and put a loose, relaxed carotid sleeper hold on the sailor's neck. He instantly looked up and saw my cap piece and said, "I didn't want any trouble, I give up," and stood up.

120

I walked him about 20 feet to the rear of a car and told him to stay there. He was completely cooperative. I'd seen the sailor land at least a dozen blows on the downed marine, so I thought he was probably dazed or no longer interested in the battle. Wrong! As I started to turn to the right to go see if the marine was all right, he was running toward the sailor with his arm pulled back and his fist clenched for another round, and it appeared he was also heading for me.

All I could do was spin left to make a 360 degree turn to grab him from the rear when he got to the sailor. Just as I completed my turn, I saw Cass jump on the marine and get him under control. With everything stabilized, I said to Cass, "I want that marine," meaning he was going to jail.

Sheepishly Cass said, "I already gave him to the Shore Patrol." "You what?" I barked. "I'll tell you what happened in a minute," Cass solemnly said, like he was going to make a full confession.

A pint-sized Shore Patrolman joined us, brushing off his uniform, and we put the marine in the back seat of our car, all alone. As Cass explained it, by the time he got around our car, the marine was on his feet and heading for the sailor and me. He did not recognize the Shore Patrolman as being one, so when the Shore Patrolman jumped on the marine's back, he thought it was part of the donnybrook and pulled the Shore Patrolman off the marine and bounced him off the ground.

Visualizing that comic cop caper, I almost laughed out loud, but I held back because the poor Shore Patrolman didn't look happy. It also explained why the Shore Patrolman was still brushing himself off when he joined us, and I had to agree with Cass that the Shore Patrolman had earned the right to the marine as first prize.

The Shore Patrolman sat in the rear seat between the sailor and the marine. With that seating arrangement, we went to the Shore Patrol with no more trouble. When the tall lieutenant routinely asked if there were any charges, I pointed to the small Shore Patrolman and said, "I think he has plenty."

The Shore Patrol had only a skeleton crew of full-time permanent personnel. Like the one we had been involved with on that shift, nearly all were involuntary one-shift patrolmen — not a good system because they were expected to arrest their own shipmates who got out of control.

At that time, the Shore Patrolmen wore only their white uniform hats, a web waist belt and a "S. P." arm band on their left arm. Not long after our very confused melee, the walking Shore Patrolmen wore white helmet liners to better distinguish themselves as such.

When they started wearing the helmet liners, I thought, "You gobs can thank Officer Castillo for that improvement."

The police department actually had two overlapping watches for every patrol division shift. A-watch went on duty at the shift start hour, and a B-watch started a half hour later. Cass and I were on the B-watch. The next day, an A-watch walking officer stuck around to tell Cass and me what he saw.

He said when he got off duty half an hour before we did, he walked up the north side of Market Street, not too far behind our marine. He said there were many sailors walking west, apparently returning to their ships or bases.

Apparently from the marine's big mouth, he had heard that the marine had just graduated from boot camp at the Marine Corps Recruit Depot and was on his first leave. His drill instructors had told his group that one marine could easily whip the entire Navy at one time, and he believed it. So he tried to pick a fight with every sailor who came his way. The officer said they all laughed at him and brushed him off. Tired of this treatment, when our sailor brushed him off, our marine took a swing at him. Our sailor quickly decked him and pounced on him where we found them with our sailor pounding on him.

In that we did not submit arrest reports when we took sailors and marines to the Shore Patrol, about two weeks later I received a request from the 11th Naval District to submit a report to that office about the entire event, and like the one I received for the Camp Pendleton escapee and deserter, there were some specific questions.

I started with telling them about the A-watch walking officer who could answer most of their questions in complete detail. I typed a full report of what I had witnessed then concluded with my own expert recommendations of what actions I believed were most appropriate and just.

I first recommended that the sailor be awarded the highest commendation possible for his complete cooperation with my partner, me and the Shore Patrolman. I then concluded by saying he should be put on their boxing team. As for the marine, I recommended he be scheduled for a second boot camp of training, and with only rational, sane instructors, if they had any.

But it was not all fun and games with Cass and me. One afternoon we received a call to pick up a found stolen bicycle at a residence near the east end of our beat.

Cass was driving and when we got to the address, he took the car keys to open the trunk to store the bicycle. Cass enjoyed doing crazy things to entertain me. A few minutes later, he came out of the garage and down the sloped driveway riding a small bicycle built for about an eight-year-old, his legs sticking out to the sides and his legs too long to apply the pedal brakes.

We had a good time laughing about his very short bike ride, but the laughter did not last for very long. We had gone only about six blocks headed for the station to unload the bike when we got a call to take the report of a suicide. The address was on a street that we had just passed two blocks before, and we were there in less than two minutes.

The Suicide

We were met by a middle-aged man waiting out in front for us. He led us down a sloped driveway and in a door to a dirt-floored cellar of sorts. Hanging from a floor joist was a man. It first surprised me, because the joist was only about five feet from the floor and his legs were bent at the knees. Without thinking clearly about it, I mistakenly thought his natural reaction would be to stand up and save himself before choking to death, but our further investigation clearly proved he was determined to kill himself.

I reached out and felt his arm to see if he was cold and stiff. He was, and it was obvious he had been dead for hours. Cass and his regular partner, Bernie Seward, were proven first aid providers. When I let go of the man's arm, Cass asked, "Shall we give him artificial respiration?" Before I could say no, the middle-aged man, who was the suicide victim's brother-in-law, quickly said "No."

The brother-in-law took us into the house to meet the victim's wife. The couple had a nine-year-old daughter and she was next door at the brother-in-law's house.

The widow told Cass and me the sad story of her husband's life. He was an Army medic during World War II. After about two years of seeing hundreds or thousands of severely injured soldiers, some with limbs blown off, he had a complete mental breakdown. He was hospitalized for a while but it didn't help. In 1944, he received a medical discharge and returned home. Hoping he would eventually recover, they had their daughter.

As sad as it was, it was apparent that the wife was not surprised or shocked by his suicide and was sort of relieved that the nine-year nightmare was over.

Police department policy was that a sergeant must respond to all death cases. Veteran Sergeant Chapman arrived, puffing on his pipe like Sherlock Holmes. He had been a major during World War II and a provost marshal and was an expert investigator.

We told him what the wife had told us and he silently started looking about. There was a restaurant-type booth in the kitchen. On it there was a large empty ashtray and about 30 cigarette butts scattered across the table top and some on the benches and floor.

Sergeant Chapman said, "This is where he decided to commit suicide, blew up and smashed the ashtray."

Cass and I then followed Sergeant Chapman into the bathroom. There was blood in the wash basin and the shower curtain and supporting rail were in the bathtub. Sergeant Chapman said, "He tried to sever his carotid arteries but couldn't so he tried to hang himself on the shower curtain rail." He had lost touch with reality by that time, because the rail could obviously not support more than about 50 pounds.

We then went down to where he was hanging. There was a single strand of clothesline rope on the dirt floor, and it had blood on it, and one end was frayed. The victim was hanging by a double strand of clothesline rope.

Sergeant Chapman said, "He tried to hang himself with the single strand of rope and it broke, so he doubled it and it held him."

Sergeant Chapman said he would wait for the coroner, so we could leave and complete the report at the station. We also had to get rid of the bike, so we started to leave.

As Cass and I walked up the driveway the wife stopped me and asked, "Can you in any way keep this out of the papers?" She added, "If it's in the papers, our daughter's classmates could hear about it, and children can be cruel."

I told her I agreed with her and would do everything possible to keep it out of the papers, but I couldn't promise it. I would explain it to the police reporter at the station and hope that he would cooperate.

As Cass took the bike to the Property/Evidence Room, I went directly to the San Diego Union-Tribune reporter's office. His nickname was also Cass, short for Castanien. He was a small, very pleasant sort. After I explained the very sad event and about the daughter, he said he was required to report it, but would do his best to hide it as well as possible.

I left hating the newspaper managers more than ever, and I already hated them for their slanted or partial reporting that made the police department look bad. I quickly looked through the paper the next morning and found the brief article buried among some whiskey and coke ads in the sports section.

It was a very enjoyable eight weeks with Cass and Seward, and I learned more about investigation from Sergeant Chapman.

CHAPTER 18

Mexico

At that time, we called illegal immigrants "Wets," short for "Wetbacks," and that name came from Texas where they would get wet crossing the Rio Grande River that was the international border with Mexico.

Illegal immigrant border crossings were so common in the San Diego area it was sort of a joke on the police department. Often times when we left the station and started up Market Street, we had to stop at the San Diego and Arizona Eastern Railway tracks when freight trains pulling empty boxcars and gondolas passed to the north. They were returning from Arizona and had to slowly chug up the eastern side of the Laguna Mountains between Imperial County and San Diego, and the Wets jumped on the crawling trains.

Every time we had to sit and watch them, there were about a hundred Wets standing and looking out of the open boxcar doors, looking over the side of a gondola or sitting between cars on a connector, but most police department officers weren't interested and wouldn't bother them wherever they were.

There was also a nasty story that the Mexican Customs agents robbed those deported by the U.S. Border Patrol at the San Ysidro Port of Entry. Many of the Wets wore two or three layers of clothing to avoid carrying clothes and making it obvious they were on the road — and probably for warmth when they slept in open brush land areas without blankets.

It was reported that the Mexican Customs agents would strip them down to their last layer of clothing and steal their clothes, their valuables and, of course, their hard-earned money.

Only officers who couldn't make any arrests other than drunks were inclined to arrest the Wets as a big thing, and some were even desperate enough to arrest Wets who were headed south to go back to Mexico on their own with a wad of hard-earned money in their pockets for the Mexican Customs agents.

The Sewing Machine

One very noble action was fairly well known by most police department officers. It reportedly started with two officers arresting a 40-year-old Wet on his way back home to Mexico carrying a portable sewing machine for his wife.

When the jailers searched him, he had $1,500 in his pocket. That amount was equivalent to about two to three years of hard work. With that, the jail sergeant who was aware of the robberies by Mexican Customs agents told the man to stand by the public telephone the prisoners used.

The sergeant phoned the radio dispatcher and told him to send the detective unit to the jail. When they arrived, he told them to take the man to San Ysidro and let him loose. San Ysidro is a small community on the U.S. side of the border, and there were reportedly holes in the border fence out of sight of the Mexican Customs agents.

Adios Amigos

One afternoon shift when I was again working with George Miller, we received a call to go to an address in very affluent Kensington Heights. A woman resident called to complain about four men who used her garden hose to get a drink of water.

We knew they were Wets because they didn't walk on main streets or drink from service station drinking fountains. Instead, they used side streets to be less conspicuous. George was driving, so I went to the door and spoke to the complaining woman. When she described the four men, I knew for sure they were Wets.

I told George they were Wets, and he headed north toward the Mission Valley area bordering Kensington Heights. We had gone about four blocks when we overtook them. I got out, patted them down and put them in the rear seat. They were wide-eyed because they didn't trust Mexican policemen and obviously weren't too sure about us.

When I sat down, I looked at George and asked him, "Are you thinking what I'm thinking?" In his impassive way he said, "I think so." Without another word, George drove back to Adams Avenue, circled a couple of blocks to Ward Road, down Ward Road to

Mission Valley, across Mission Valley and about a mile up Murphy Canyon and stopped on a wide turnout west of the roadway.

I got out, opened the right rear door and said, "Adios amigos" and pointed north. Four great big smiles blossomed and "Gracias" flowed like cheap wine.

George and I were not overwhelmed with the idea of taking them to jail. First of all, if we did, they would be back that far again within 48 hours, and we didn't want to make them walk that far again. We felt sorry for them and if we took them to jail we would be off our beat for about an hour.

Before I left the police department, Chief Jansen campaigned to annex the land all the way to the border as part of San Diego City. His excuse was so the police department could establish a border checkpoint to prevent juveniles under 18 years of age from crossing the Mexican border, and he was not a soul saver.

The only problem was that National City and Chula Vista were between San Diego and the border and annexed land must be contiguous to the city annexing it.

About two years later, somebody dreamed up the idea that the city could annex to the border by connecting the two lands with a strip of land on the bottom of San Diego Bay. That proposal was battled by the opponents in court but, in the end, Chief Jansen won, and his empire expanded to the border.

Apparently like many orders or guidelines on the San Diego Police Department, the police department brass apparently did not inform the officers they could not cross the border into Mexico in pursuit.

Armed Invasion of Mexico

Traffic car officer Denny Hayes was a jovial, amiable, always smiling lovable blond. Working the South Bay beat to the Mexican border one shift, he went in pursuit of a serious violator. When the violator busted across the border, Hayes stayed in hot pursuit and did the same.

Without any wasted time, Hayes arrested for "Armed Invasion of Mexico" with his loaded six-shooter. After much legal wrangling between Mexico and the United States, Hayes was released with no charges.

Not long after I left the police department, they started an in-house newsletter. The next headline was "HAYES INVADES MEXICO."

CHAPTER 19

The Do-Nothing Partner

I told the sergeant that Leach didn't want to do anything except respond to radio calls, and then did nothing to resolve the callers' reported problems. I had to do everything while he just stood around.

One afternoon shift, I was assigned to Beat 19 as the relief officer with Officers Hall and Leach. The beat ran from Fairmont Avenue east to the La Mesa city limits and was sort of an "Elephant Graveyard" beat. In the eight-week shift assignment, we received only about four radio calls while I was working.

Leach was driving east on El Cajon Boulevard one early afternoon and we were talking about this and that. When there was a pause in the meaningless conversation, he asked me where I was from. "East San Diego," I responded. He immediately said, "You were probably one of those little bastards I had to chase after for curfew violation."

Not too crazy about him to begin with, especially with his calling me a bastard, I grinned and said, "And you never caught me, either," to piss him off.

My reply worked. He instantly went silent, his jaw muscles protruded and he got a death grip on the steering wheel like he was going to try to pull it from the steering column. All I could do was look out the right door window and smile.

Code 3 in Rolando Village

Leach was again driving on an early afternoon when we received a Code 3 (Emergency) call to cover a major injury accident for the CHP. We were on El Cajon Boulevard east of College Avenue. The accident was just north of University Avenue at the south end of Rolando Village and about two miles away.

I turned on the red lights and switched the siren to the horn button. Leach went into a panic and speeded up to about 60 miles per hour in the 35 miles per hour zone. At that speed, he jerked the steering wheel back and forth and we went all over the two eastbound lanes like he was the worst drunk driver in recorded DUI history.

I had ridden with some of my crazy high school friends who could have killed me and with Dunce at 90 miles per hour for no reason, but that was the scariest ride I had ever experienced. I thought for certain he would put us out of control and into a power pole or some other deadly fixed object.

When we miraculously arrived, I immediately saw a young man lying unconscious about 40 feet up the street. The crashed car had hit a parked car and turned on its side with the gas spout on the ground side. Gas was slowly spewing and running down the gutter only about six feet from the unconscious teen's feet. I quickly grabbed the First Aid kit out of the trunk of our car and ran to the injured teen.

He was bleeding profusely from his left forearm and blood had flowed to the gutter and mixed with the gas. It was arterial bleeding and was pulsating and spurting. I compressed the artery on the inside of his upper arm then firmly held a six-by-six gauze compress on the bleeding artery. Those oversized compresses were made by jail trustees.

I held the upper artery and compress tightly for about five minutes and when I released both the bleeding had stopped.

Looking at the stream of blood on the street and the unknown amount mixed with the gas, my best estimate was that he had lost over two pints of blood and maybe three, and I later learned that a loss of three or four pints could be fatal to a person his size. With that I felt very good and figured I had earned my pay that day.

The Fake FBI Agents

Again with Leach, we received a call to meet the owner of a classier steak house and bar on the north side of El Cajon Boulevard, just east of Euclid Avenue, and to meet him at the kitchen door next to the alley.

We arrived shortly and the owner was waiting at the door. The owner was a 50ish Italian gentleman impeccably dressed in an expensive suit. He led us into the kitchen and stopped us to the side of the door to the dining room and bar. There were two men about 25-years old sitting at the bar, and they were the only ones at the bar.

He said the two had flashed ID cards at the bartender and told him they were FBI agents. They said they were investigating counterfeiting and wanted to inspect every currency bill he took in.

Leach and I knew counterfeiting was investigated by the Secret Service, not the FBI, so I went straight to the car and radioed a request for the FBI to meet us there. Much like the owner, Leach and I thought the two men might be trying to find out how much was in the till before they pulled their robbery.

Two FBI special agents arrived within 20 minutes — one was wearing a bow tie. I met them in front at the curb and told them what was going on and without hesitation they openly walked to the front door of the restaurant, went over to the two men, identified themselves as FBI special agents and asked them for their IDs. The two quickly produced their U.S. Army IDs.

With the two soldiers in the rear seat of the FBI car, the special agent who was wearing a bow tie got me out of earshot of the prisoners and said he wasn't sure the U.S. Attorney would prosecute them. He then said, "Even if he doesn't, two days in jail might teach them a lasting lesson."

The fine restaurant owner was so pleased with our "Dragnet, Jack Webb" speed in the case, he openly invited us to come back for dinner any time, but for some reason, we never did.

The Bogus Investigation

About two weeks later, Leach was driving west on Montezuma Road about 8:30 p.m. It was very dark and we saw a car pulling a box trailer with no rear lights. I told Leach to stop the car and I would tell the driver his trailer lights were out and give him a verbal warning.

Before I could even get to the trailer, the driver quickly got out of his car and met me between our car and the trailer. Although he looked like he had been put through the wringer, he looked familiar to me. I then almost instantly recognized him as being the FBI special agent wearing the bow tie.

When I told him we had stopped him only to tell him his trailer lights were not working, he threw up his hands and exclaimed, "What next?"

Then he told me his sad story. He said he had been directly ordered by J. Edgar Hoover to conduct an investigation of a San Diego resident, bypassing all levels of management. He said Hoover told him to personally deliver the completed file to him in his Washington, D.C. office en route to his new field office assignment on the East Coast.

He said he sold his house and was to be moved at government expense to his new assignment. The movers were to arrive that morning to pack all of his furniture and family belongings so he could vacate the house. But in the late afternoon the day before the move, he was told that Director Hoover no longer wanted the investigation file, so his transfer was cancelled and he was to remain in the San Diego field office.

He said early that morning he had to rent a house, borrow the old box trailer from a friend and move in about 14 hours.

That was the first I knew of J. Edgar Hoover's secret files — and how he treated his special agents in such an indifferent, cold-hearted manner without regard for them or their families. It disgusted me and made me understand why two of the three San Diego boys who had joined the FBI a few years earlier had resigned in less than two years.

It was about eight years later when I was assigned to the CHP Academy as a duty officer and instructor that I learned more about Hoover. There was an FBI special agent who had instructed a course at the CHP Academy for many years and, unlike most FBI agents, enjoyed telling FBI stories.

The Closet Door

One day in the dining room he told of a special agent who was coasting into retirement when he was given one of Hoover's bypass-management direct orders to investigate someone who might get in Hoover's way to greater power, but the order strangely enough did not include a transfer to a new office.

When the special agent completed his dirt-digging investigation, he flew to Washington, D.C. and to Hoover's office in a very nervous state. When he was told Director Hoover would finally see him, he went into Hoover's office, hoping to leave as soon as possible. When Hoover cordially greeted him, the agent walked straight to his desk and handed him his report.

Hoover briefly flipped through the folder, thanked the agent, dismissed him and told him he could leave. When the agent turned around to leave, he was shocked to see there were two doors exactly alike side by side. As the agent learned too late, one was the exit door and the other was a closet door.

In his panicked state, he opened the closet door, stepped in and closed the door before he realized what he was doing. Since Hoover had been reading his investigation report, the agent didn't think he had seen him enter the closet, so he decided he would wait the hours until quitting time and sneak out undetected after Hoover had left the office. But after several minutes had passed, Mr. Hoover politely said, "Agent So and So, you're in the closet."

He immediately opened the door, headed for the exit door and said, "Thank you, Mr. Hoover," and quickly departed. After we had all stopped laughing, we concluded that Hoover most likely had the twin doors installed in that manner for that very reason and may have had many laughs at the expense of nervous wrecks such as the star in that drama.

The Deficient Partner

I was driving one afternoon when I saw a motorist commit a minor traffic violation. With nothing else to do, I told Leach I was going to stop him, but do-nothing Leach balked and told me not to, saying the violation wasn't bad enough to bother with.

Remembering Leach telling me when I worked with him on rural Beat 13 the year before that he got the same pay as the hard-working officers and didn't want to do any more than he had to, I stopped the minor violator anyway. When I told the driver I stopped him to give him a warning and routinely asked to see his driver license, he confessed that he didn't have one.

As I walked back to the patrol car to get the citation book, Leach obviously knew what I was going to do and held the citation book out the right window for me. When I had completed the citation and got back in the car, Leach never uttered a word about my getting our only citation of the shift.

Hall and I repeatedly complained about Leach not wanting to do anything except respond to radio calls, then let us do all the work necessary to resolve the complainants' problems — and much like with the FBI impersonators at the fine steak house, all Leach did was stay out of my way.

Hall also angrily told me of the prior shift when he and Leach were assigned a traffic car with an external loudspeaker because our regularly assigned beat car was down for repairs. He said he was driving south on College Avenue when they saw two very cute teenage girls walking down the west sidewalk. He said Leach grabbed the loudspeaker microphone and made some extremely inappropriate remarks to the very innocent-looking girls. He said the comments were borderline vulgar and that Leach had been drinking before he came to work. This incident happened in College Park, which was a rather affluent section of the city.

He said not long after this incident, they received a call to meet a sergeant at a specified location. Sergeant Paul Sears got in the rear seat and told them the captain had received a complaint from the father of a teenage girl about a remark one of them had made to his daughter and her friend. Hall said Leach claimed he didn't know what it was all about.

Being the tolerant sergeant he was, Sears said, "Well, all I can say is that where there's so much smoke, there has to be some fire." With that warning, Hall said good old Sergeant Sears got out of the car and left, and not in a good mood. Hall then told me that had happened the day before on the second of my two days off.

Later that day we got a call to meet a sergeant. Hall immediately said, "That's Sergeant Mason, and he wants to talk to you."

I knew it was going to be about Leach, but I wasn't concerned because Sergeant Mason had always treated me like a favorite son. Mother had told me the double funeral for my father and grandfather was the largest in San Diego at that time, and the news clippings she saved for my brothers and me reported it was so large that it had to be held in the Elk's Hall, and even then the massive crowd of firemen, policemen, the mayor and other elected officials had overflowed into the street. And since Sergeant Mason had just completed 27 years on the SDPD when I joined, he no doubt had attended the funeral and knew all about my family.

We were to meet him at El Cajon and Euclid and Sergeant Mason was already parked on Euclid a short distance north of El Cajon. I got out of the car and got into the front seat of his car.

After a friendly greeting, he said, "Nuttall, I need your help. I heard you don't like to work with Leach and I need to know why, because nobody wants to work with him." In that I had previously asked not to work with Red again, it made me feel better about telling Sergeant Mason all of the reasons. I knew Sergeant Mason was absolutely honest and trustworthy, so I felt what I told him would help him and all the officers who might get stuck with Leach as a partner in the future.

I started by telling him about Leach not wanting me to stop the minor traffic violator that ended with a citation for the violator not having a driver license and that Leach didn't want to do anything except respond to radio calls, then he did nothing to resolve the callers' reported problems. I had to do everything while he just stood around.

Then I told Sergeant Mason about the wild, death-defying ride Leach took me on going to the CHP accident. I said it was one of the scariest rides of my life and I was too young to die.

We were in the sixth week of our eight-week shift rotation assignment and Sergeant Mason asked me if I could endure two more weeks with Leach until the end of the shift assignment.

I was really taken by Sergeant Mason's kind consideration to get me away from Leach so I said, "Oh, sure, it's not that I want you to juggle the schedule for me. I can stick it out."

Even though I had applied for motors just the week before, I wasn't certain I would get one or even be transferred to the traffic division, so I said, "I just wanted to tell you so you would know I prefer not to ever work with him again."

Sergeant Mason smiled and assured me I would never have to work with Leach again, thanked me, and that was it. When I got back in the car with Hall, he asked, "How did it go?" Jokingly I said, "It went very well for me, but I don't know about you," even though I knew Hall had already told Sergeant Mason what he thought about Leach and had arranged my meeting with Sergeant Mason to back up his wild tales. Chuckling in his usual 240-pound jovial way, he said, "Thanks a lot, old buddy."

I readily determined that it was Leach's loudspeaker antic the day before that put Hall over the edge. And in that Sergeant Sears had let it slide, his comment about smoke and fire indicated to Hall that he and Leach just might come under the gun and receive much more future supervisory attention than would be comfortable, so he wanted to get Leach out of his Beat 19.

Despite Leach, Hall and I had two more weeks of fun.

At the end of that eight-week rotation assignment, I was transferred to the traffic division for motor training, so there was no way I would ever again have to work with Leach, Dunce or Red.

Then about two years after I left the police department and joined the CHP, one of my loyal police department informants told me Leach had been put on three-wheel motors to write one-dollar meter parking tickets to help pay for those 50 additional officers hired in 1953.

CHAPTER 20

Tickets, Tickets, Tickets

Chief Jansen made a deal with the City Council. The agreement was if they would give him 50 additional officers, he would assign 25 to the traffic division and would increase the number of traffic citations issued to offset the cost of the 50 additional officers.

About a dozen of us were assigned to take the two-week motorcycle training course and two weeks of accident investigation and Vehicle Code training with other officers to be assigned to traffic cars.

Officer Stan Boland was our motor instructor and was an outstanding one. After some basic safety and motor operation instructions in the police garage, we risked our lives and rode to the Organ Pavilion in Balboa Park. Whether by prior arrangement or not, the seats had all been removed from the large Pavilion audience area where we practiced trying to kill ourselves.

After a week of that drill, Officer Boland took us on a long ride into the Laguna Mountains that didn't go very well.

The Close Call

I was behind "Smoky" Wheeler, a classic comic who had been a San Diego fireman, thus the nickname. As we approached a sharp, tricky uphill curve, the rider in front of Smoky hit the dirt shoulder and went down on his back in the roadway and didn't move. I watched in horror as Wheeler very skillfully swerved to the left to miss the downed rider and barely missed his head by about a foot.

Initially, the downed officer didn't move. By the time I quickly put my motor on its stand, got off and reached the officer, he was in major convulsions. I instantly thought, "My God, he's dead," and knowing from a fatal motorcycle accident several months before that basal skull fractures caused by striking the back of the head on the pavement were the deadliest of skull fractures, and I had seen the back of his head bounce off the pavement when he landed on his back.

Very shortly Officer Boland ran down the road and upon seeing the officer in violent convulsions said, "Oh my God, he's dead." We all stood in shocked silence for several minutes then the officer's convulsions stopped and he slowly got to his feet.

As Officer Boland asked him how he felt, the officer kept backing up toward the edge of the roadway and a shallow canyon with a steep drop-off slope. He stopped and stood on the raised dirt berm, slightly weaving back and forth, saying nothing.

I quickly went to him, took hold of his left arm and slowly led him away from the drop-off and canyon. Smoky wishfully said to me, "He looks like he's okay and will be all right."

I had already seen the glassy stare in his eyes and it continued, so I said to Smoky, "I hope so, but he doesn't know where he is or why." Smoky replied, "I think you're right."

Officer Boland radioed for an ambulance on the amazing motor radio built by city radio technicians. We were about 50 miles from the station, but being high in the mountains probably helped his request get through. His request was acknowledged by the station and all we could do was wait about 45 minutes for the ambulance coming from San Diego.

While waiting, CHP Officer Lou Downey arrived on a motor to investigate the accident. Lou was the nephew of legendary CHP Officer George Downey, who was the long-term Alpine resident officer. And Lou was the son of a San Diego City fireman who had worked with my father and grandfather.

San Diego was a small world for my family in those days. My mother knew just about everybody who had been around for decades and knew where some of their skeletons were buried.

But with her near paranoia about death and deadly fear of motorcycles, she did not like the idea of my being a motor cop, mostly because Papa had a motor just after they were invented and someone ran him off the road and he ended up on the sidewalk. He quickly sold the damn thing.

When the ambulance arrived, the comatose officer refused to get on the gurney and demanded to ride in the right front seat of the ambulance. The ambulance quietly departed for Mercy Hospital without using its siren.

The week after we completed our motor, accident investigation and Vehicle Code training, the traffic division captain and lieutenant interviewed the dozen motor trainees for assignment to motors.

For decades, San Diego was reportedly the only California city that had a "Motorcycle Officer" civil service position. It paid $20 per month in skill pay and if one with that position was removed from motors, the police department had to continue to pay the $20 a month.

Chief Jansen did not like motors or the $20 skill pay, and there were 40 police department motors he didn't like, so he got the city fathers to do away with that special classification. Then he could remove officers from motors as he wished without paying $20 a month thereafter.

As in most work environments, people like to talk, so there were no secrets in the police department. By the time we went for our motor interviews, the word of Chief Jansen's secret agreement with the City Council had spread like wildfire.

In that California law provided that 50 percent of traffic fines went to the city or county where the violation was committed and Chief Jansen had disposed of the Motorcycle Officer position and $20 a month, he made a deal with the City Council. The agreement was if they would give him 50 additional officers, he would assign 25 to the traffic division and would increase the number of traffic citations issued to offset the cost of the 50 additional officers.

With that bold agreement, all San Diego police officers were under the gun to lower their traffic enforcement standards to a new low, even if they couldn't sleep nights suffering from guilt.

During my interview with the traffic division captain and lieutenant, I was asked if I could disregard general police work and direct my undivided efforts to traffic enforcement.

I knew all too well that those loaded questions demanded an answer they wanted to hear, but that one rubbed me wrong. I was hired as a "Police Patrolman," and I took a sworn oath to uphold the laws of the State of California, and I also had busted my butt learning about all street police work.

So, I gave them my honest answer. I said I would do my best to enforce all traffic laws, but I couldn't ignore crimes committed in my presence — and most criminals drove cars.

There were three motor openings and three losers junior to me in seniority were assigned to motors. One was a former Marine Corps drill instructor who wrote as many as 35 traffic citations a shift and years later resigned because all other officers hated him, and he couldn't figure out why. Another was an insignificant short, dumpy officer who walked as though he had a severe crotch rash. And believe it or not, the third was the former comatose officer who went on his ass in the mountains and in the years after went down again so many times he rightfully earned the nickname of "Horizontal George."

When their appointment to motors was announced, Officer Boland contacted me. He knew why they had gotten motor assignments instead of me and he did not want me to think he had anything to do with it.

All he could say was, "Nuttall, I told the captain and lieutenant that you were a very good and safe rider." I said, "Thank you, Stan, but you and I both know why I didn't get a motor." He didn't say anything, but I knew it made him feel better, and I wanted him to because he was a great cop and great person.

I knew I had been passed over for tickets, tickets, tickets, and it made me wonder if the police department had any objective, rational, constructive merit system. Obviously not!

The Typing Test

I thought back to the stupid hoop I had to jump through to pass probation. It was a typing test, and I was hired as a police patrolman, not a typist.

Although police department policy prohibited probationary officers from working alone on day shifts on patrol division beats, I was put on the day shift a month before my probationary year ended. Furthermore, I was assigned a rookie to train.

About two weeks before the end of my probation, 13 other survivors of our group of 26 and I had to take typing tests. We had to type 25 words per minute. I barely squeaked by with 26, with one error deducted. Not bad for a hunt and pecker.

About a week after my probation ended, Sergeant Mason gave me my final probationary appraisal. It was so good that the San Diego City Personnel director wrote "Excellent report" on it and signed his name below it. But even with that appraisal report and being assigned days to work alone with a rookie to train, if I had flunked the typing test, I would have been fired just like the 12 others in my hired group, so it made me wonder who dreamed up that bizarre crackpot idea, probably Lieutenant King and the deputy chief.

But as it turned out fate or God had to be on my side. Those three losers started on motors on December 1, 1953 and had to ride from December to March in those cold, damp winter months. Then effective April 1, Officer Boland transferred to the Junior Traffic Patrol unit and I got his motor.

Although all Harley-Davidson motorcycles apparently come off the same assembly line, some ride like silk and others are what we called "Shakers." Shakers can quickly wear the rider down. Maybe that was what the SDPD sergeant had in mind when he sent the letter of response to the San Diego Union-Tribune to say riding a motor six hours a shift was a day's work.

The motor I rode during motor training was okay, but the motor I inherited from Boland was like a Rolls Royce. It was a dream to ride. So, I had a joy of a motor and rode out my final six months on the SDPD in the best months of the year, from April to September. What could be better?

In the interim, from December to April, I was assigned to traffic cars. I had a few pretty lousy partners, but I hit the jackpot when I was assigned to work with Officer Bob Reed. He was a joy to work with, and he was an expert traffic accident investigator. He was one of the officers hit by the safecracker.

But before I was assigned to graveyard with partners, I was put on the 2:00 p.m. shift and worked alone. I hadn't investigated any traffic accidents while in patrol division, but I started studying the Vehicle Code three years before, which helped.

Starting the first of December was a real sink-or-swim drill because of the increased traffic, including pedestrians, due to

Christmas shopping, parties or whatever else they were doing out there to get into accidents.

One shift, I was dispatched to four car-versus-car traffic accidents, one after the other. I finished the last one just prior to the end of my scheduled shift at 10:00 p.m. I then spent four hours typing the reports. I finished at 2:00 a.m. With absolutely no police department overtime, I involuntarily donated four sleepy hours to Chief Jansen's pot to pay for those 50 additional officers.

The Rowing Club Member

Then after dark on New Year's Day, I was dispatched to a property damage accident at 32nd and Market. It involved a black driver who made a turn from westbound Market to southbound 32nd and was hit by a Cadillac eastbound in the right lane of the two lanes, and the driver of the Cadillac was obviously intoxicated. Regardless of who was a fault in the accident, the Cadillac driver was guilty of driving under the influence.

Before I could ask him how much he had to drink that day, he quickly told me he was a member of the San Diego Rowing Club and had a few drinks there. I thought, "A few, you liar."

I knew the Rowing Club was one of San Diego's upper crust organizations because I also knew Fire Chief Courser was a member. I knew this because he had told my mother about the time he and a young man were swimming in the bay at the Rowing Club and the young man was bitten on the hand by a sea lion.

The Vehicle Code provides that after a driver stops at a stop sign or signals his intention to make a left turn he must yield to all vehicles that pose an immediate hazard. Then after allowing those vehicles to pass, the driver has the right-of-way over all other traffic that follows.

In interviewing the turning driver and a driver who had stopped in the eastbound center lane to yield to the turning driver, I concluded that the DUI driver had violated the turning driver's right-of-way. I also concluded that if the driver of the Cadillac hadn't been so drunk, he would have most likely stopped and yielded.

In that the Cadillac driver was drunk and at fault in causing the collision, I radioed for a car to transport him to jail, and I typed the accident report and arrest report to clearly state both violations.

Remembering we were told during our Recruit Training Class that Chief Jansen had a protected civil service position, and about the time the then-lieutenant had arrested a past mayor and towed his city-owned limousine, the Rowing Club didn't influence my arresting the DUI member. The next day was a court day. About 9:00 a.m., a deputy city prosecutor phoned me at home and said Chief Jansen had phoned the city prosecutor about my Rowing Club DUI arrest.

As tactfully as possible, he said the DUI had the steel doors slam behind him and spent six hours in a drunk-tank cell, and he and the city prosecutor thought that was punishment enough to teach him a lesson, so they wanted to dismiss the DUI charge. He also questioned my charging the DUI as being at fault in the accident.

Knowing I couldn't fight City Hall and didn't want Chief Jansen to sic the deputy chief on me again, I said, "Do whatever you want to do. I did my job according to the Vehicle Code and that's all I'm paid to do, so it's your decision." He thanked me and hung up, and I thought, "For what?"

It was my first real life experience with how rotten politics can be and how it discourages good cops and undermines honest law enforcement, but I never told any other officers about it. I figured things were bad enough on the police department as it was.

CHAPTER 21

Double Headers

Upon arrival, we were shocked and amused that it was the same 1940 Ford from the previous accident at El Cajon and Park Boulevards.

Reed and I had just left the garage on a 10:00 p.m. graveyard shift when we received a call of a property damage accident at El Cajon Boulevard and Park Boulevard.

It was a two-car collision involving a westbound car carrying two middle-aged couples on El Cajon and a northbound 1940 Ford sedan on Park Boulevard with only the 25ish driver inside. Reed and I quickly concluded that the 1940 Ford had run a red light, so Reed issued the driver a citation.

A couple of hours later, we received a call of another property damage accident on U.S. 395 at an intersection that connected the 395 and Linda Vista.

Reed was driving and before I could get out of the car at the scene, a young man rushed up and told me he wanted to show me something. He led me to his car and showed me a broken quart of whiskey on the right front floorboard and whiskey all over the floorboard.

"See, the seal isn't broken," he said, "the bottle broke when I hit the other car, and I wanted you to see I hadn't been drinking it." The young man was obviously shaken by the accident and fear that we would think he had been drinking, so I decided to try to lighten up the situation with some Ted Donovan humor.

"I can see you weren't drinking it unless you were lapping it up off the floor," I said. He looked a little taken back by that thought, then smiled and said he had not lapped any up. I wrote the other driver a citation for violation of right-of-way at a stop-signed intersection, and we left.

Reed drove down to Mission Valley where we saw a speeder going east on Mission Valley Road Expressway. He chased it down and turned on the red lights. As the car was slowing to stop, the right

145

front passenger threw a quart bottle of beer out the window out of sight over the side of the roadway.

As Reed talked to the driver, I asked the right front passenger to step out of the car. After he got out, I directed my flashlight at the broken bottle spread over the old two-lane highway that was then the frontage road.

"I didn't know that was there," he said, referring to the frontage road. I could tell he was telling the truth from the surprised look on his face. Luckily, the quart bottle had broken into large pieces, so I got his driver license and told him to go pick up the pieces and bring them back.

In that he was such a nice, honest kid, I wrote his citation excluding the beer part. It was only an empty quart bottle. In those days, cited juvenile offenders like him had to appear before a SDPD juvenile officer for hearing and any appropriate punishment. I wondered if the juvenile officer would contact me for further details about what kind of bottle it was, but it never happened. The "Juvies" were all great guys and smart enough to read between the lines, so I was sure he figured it out but let it slide. Only beer came in quarts.

Shortly after 2:00 a.m., we received a call of a property damage accident on Park Boulevard at the sweeping "S" curve at the north end of the zoo. Upon arrival, we were shocked and amused that it was the same 1940 Ford from the previous accident at El Cajon and Park Boulevards.

It had left 75 to 100 feet of arced skid back to the right, jumped the curb and wrapped around a street light pole. It was obviously a total in that it had a Blue Book value of no more than $500 at best, even though it had been in showroom condition — but not any more.

We alternated investigating accidents. The investigator recorded information about the vehicle, driver, witnesses and injuries and interviewed those who could talk. The other officer drew the diagram of the street and any skids or debris.

On this one, Reed investigated while I got the width measurement of the street and paced off the length of the long arced skid, and its length clearly showed the car had been going well over the safe speed for that curve.

This time there had been one male passenger in the car. As I finished pacing off the skid and was at the curb next to the car, I saw

Reed looking at the left side of the previous accident driver's head and moving his hair back and forth. Reed dropped his hand and said, "You were driving. You have glass in your hair, and the driver's window is the only one smashed and broken."

Obviously the two-time loser driver had conned his new passenger into saying he had been driving. With Reed's accusation, the guilty one reluctantly confessed.

When the tow truck left, the almost innocent passenger departed in the tow truck — almost innocent because he had also lied to Reed, but it wasn't a crime until 12 years later.

We told the one-time lying driver we would give him a ride to 12th and Market where he could catch a bus — 12th was the extension of Park Boulevard. As we passed the Naval Hospital, he said, "That's my sister's car, and you guys really screwed me up tonight."

I could hardly believe what I had heard. When my head cleared, I asked, "Who crashed your sister's car two times tonight? We sure didn't." He didn't say another word all the way to Market Street. We dropped him off at Market on our way to the station to type the three accident reports.

After he was out of the car, Reed and I had a good laugh. We screwed him up? And we didn't have any lunch because of his second crash, and we might have to donate overtime to type his two accident reports. Foster said there was no cure for stupidity.

Another Double Header

Another double header we had was not two crashes by one driver. It was a double header for the Navy because both cars involved in the direct head-on collision were loaded with sailors.

The head-on collision occurred at 10th Avenue and Market Street. The eastbound sedan was completely on the wrong side of Market in the westbound center lane, and there had been four sailors in each car. About half of them had suffered injuries of some sort and one was unconscious. We were quickly told the unconscious sailor had been in the right rear seat of the guilty wrong-way car, and the impact launched him forward over the back of the right front passenger and into the windshield. That was easy to believe because there was a head-sized hole in the windshield.

The Shore Patrol arrived shortly after we did. Two permanently assigned chiefs always manned the Navy gray 1947 Plymouth sedan that was known as the "Gray Ghost," and because the car was equipped with a radio that monitored police calls, they would quietly show up like ghosts and never get involved unless asked to or if they clearly saw the need.

One chief was "Woody" Woodward, an African/American about six feet tall weighing about 250 pounds. Woody was truly an officer and a gentleman, and we all knew him. I had never seen his partner before. He was about 6'3", over 200 pounds of solid-looking beef and had a deep southern accent.

The accident was only a stone's throw from the California Garage on Market Street, so we had the crashed cars out of there about 15 minutes after the Navy ambulance had departed. I was investigating the accident, so I rode in the rear with the wrong-way driver to the Naval Hospital. With the needed information, I issued him a citation for his obvious violation.

When we arrived at the Naval Hospital, Woody and his tall southern partner pulled in at the same time, and the partner followed the errant driver, Reed and me into the receiving/waiting room. Reed continued into the medical treatment rooms to get the extent of the injuries information for our report, and especially of the unconscious one to see if he was going to make it or not. We had to report if there were any fatalities.

The guilty driver took a seat in the far corner of the room at the end of the receiving nurse's desk. Before I could start interviewing the less seriously injured sailors, the guilty driver held his wallet in his hand and said, "What happened to my ten dollars?"

One of the first things I learned on the police department was officers were never to touch a person's wallet or purse unless it was a lost and found, especially not a dead person's. Only the coroner could touch them, because the coroner was also the public administrator to release personal property to the rightful heirs.

Obviously the driver was strongly implying that I had taken his ten dollars in retaliation for my citing him for reckless driving, so I said, "I don't know, but you and I can go look in the back of our car to see if it's there." He quickly snarled, "No, I know where it is."

Another precaution I learned early in my police department career was that officers should never carry more money on the job than was necessary for meals and goodies — and in the event they were accused of a Red's type sleight-of-hand magic to lift money from anyone. So, I didn't have but a few dollars in my wallet, but that was all I had to my name anyway.

The tall Shore Patrol chief immediately said, "I'll go with you." He and I looked in the rear seat area of our car, and as we already knew, there was nothing. As we walked back to the receiving/waiting room door, I said to him, "I never saw a ten dollar bill of his on the way up here." The chief responded, "I know where that ten dollar bill is, it's in a till in some sleazy bar, if there was one."

As soon as the chief and I came into sight of the guilty driver, he snarled, "You didn't find it did you?" With that, the chief said, "No, and if you don't shut your big mouth, you're going to need this hospital a lot more than you do now." That was a clear enough promise, so big mouth didn't utter another word all the time we were there.

Seconds later, Reed came out of the treatment area and said, "It looks like the unconscious one is going to make it."

Due to big mouth, I hadn't had time to interview the slightly injured sailors, but it wasn't necessary anyway because it was an open-and-shut case from the beginning. So I said, "Let's go." As soon as we got outside with the southern chief quietly following, he asked me where we were going. "We have to go to the tow yard to complete storage reports on the cars," I replied. "Would it be okay if we followed you there," he asked. "Certainly, you're always welcome," I responded.

Stolen Navy Property

When we got to the tow yard I got the keys out of the ignition of the wrong-way car and opened the trunk. The first thing that caught my eye was a police-type sap. The Penal Code classified it as a deadly weapon, along with several other such assault-type weapons, and it was a felony for anyone other than a peace officer to own or possess them.

But before I could tell the chief of that great find, he said, "Just what I was hoping for. Look at those tool boxes. They have U.S.N. stamped on them." With that, I opened one of the tool boxes and pulled out a wrench. Clearly stamped on it was U.S.N. I then shined my flashlight into the tool box and every tool I could see was stamped the same.

"Can I take those?" the chief asked. "They obviously belong to the Navy, and you are the Navy, so they're yours," I gladly answered, "but if you don't mind, I'd like it if you would sign a receipt to cover our butts," I added. "Gladly," he said with a smile, and it was his first smile. I worded a brief receipt on the reverse of the storage report, and the chief gleefully signed it like it was for a free gold mine.

With that precious find, it also turned out to be a double header for the big mouth guilty driver. The least of his worries now had to be the $50 reckless driving citation I issued to him. With the determined chief now in possession of his stolen government property, big mouth was no doubt headed for a dishonorable discharge and about five to ten years in Leavenworth Federal Prison for military and other convicted felons, and it couldn't have happened to a nicer "Swabby" as we in the police department called wayward sailors.

It was obvious to me that the southern chief was as astute a cop as almost any police department officer. He had no doubt sized up the guilty driver at the accident scene and followed us to the hospital to confirm his profile of the arrogant ass, and when big mouth spouted off about the phantom ten dollars, his suspicions were confirmed.

I never knew if it was the ten dollar issue that caused him to go to the tow yard with us, but I suspected it was, and I like to think that it was.

The fact that Woody stayed out of the picture was in no way an indication of his reluctance to get involved in heavy-duty stuff, and even though Woody was quiet and reserved and always had a big smile for everyone, look out, bad boys.

Woody the Hero

One of my first partner training officers told me of Woody's saving a police department officer from getting a knife in his back. It happened next to the front door of "The Shadows," a bar on 6th Avenue between Island and Market. The Shadows abutted "The Cobra," which was on the corner of 6th and Island, and its front door faced the corner and intersection of those streets. The Cobra and The Shadows were reputed to be the two sleaziest bars in skid row, or even in San Diego, and they were black hangouts, including black sailors. The only lights in The Shadows were candles, and the window covers were burlap sacks.

When a call went out of a brawl in The Shadows, Woody no doubt knew their reputation and that it was a hangout for black sailors. Woody and his partner just happened to be the first to arrive and parked the Gray Ghost out of the way. There was a black man standing next to the front door of The Shadows, and Woody didn't like the looks of him, so Woody got out of the car and positioned himself on the other side of the door.

A SDPD unit arrived within minutes, and the passenger jumped out, leaving the right front door open, and headed for the front door of The Shadows. Just as he passed Woody and the black man on the other side of the door, the black man raised his arm high with a large knife in his hand to stab the officer in the back. Lightning fast, Woody lunged over and grabbed his knife-bearing arm, swung him around, grabbed him by the collar, and with his 250 pound delivery, threw him across the sidewalk into the end of the open police car door.

The attempted cop-stabber's head hit the end of the door, splitting his head open. He fell to the sidewalk face down, unconscious and bleeding profusely on the dirty sidewalk. And the potential stab victim cop didn't see any of it as he rushed into The Shadows' candle-lit near darkness.

When it was all over and with the attempted cop-stabber still bleeding on the sidewalk, Woody quietly returned to the Gray Ghost with his big trademark smile and departed without any fanfare.

With those incidents, and much more, the Shore Patrol was like a police department enforcement division in itself, so if at all possible,

I always took well-behaved drunk sailors to the Shore Patrol with no charges, just wanting to get them back to their base or ship.

And to the credit of the Marine Corps, with the exception of that one crazy marine who wanted to whip the entire Navy at one time, I do not recall ever arresting a marine for anything in my more than two years on the police department — dozens of sailors, but only one marine, and he would have gone to jail if Cass hadn't bounced the pint-sized Shore Patrolman off the dirty Market Street blacktop.

There was also the Marine Corps deserter who had escaped from the Camp Pendleton prison barracks, but he was what could be classified as an ex-marine by the time we caught him.

CHAPTER 22

The La Jolla Iron Curtain

"Motors don't go into La Jolla unless they get a call to go there," he warned. I thanked him and couldn't wait to tell Cooper the good news. I overtook Cooper in the garage and told him. "Is that so?" he responded with a smirk. With his devilish response, I knew it was like waving a big red flag at two ground-pawing bulls.

When I got my motorcycle on April 1, 1954, I was assigned to the day shift for the next eight weeks. The scheduling sergeant obviously wanted me to get the hang of it before putting me on the 2:00 p.m. shift, which included a 7:00 p.m. to 3:00 a.m. shift on Friday and Saturday nights.

On a Saturday, I was assigned to Pacific Beach, which included U.S. 101 through Rose Canyon and north to the city limit at Torrey Pines Beach. There was a rear-end accident at the bottom of Rose Canyon about a hundred yards north of signal-lighted Balboa Avenue that led into Pacific Beach. There was a wide dirt divider and when a tow truck pulled the rear-ending car into the center divider I could see much broken glass in the southbound center lane.

The traffic was backed up out of sight into Rose Canyon in the southbound center lane. To prevent any more rear-end accidents, I went over and got the push broom off the tow truck and quickly swept the glass onto the dirt center divider.

As I started back to return the broom, I heard a man say, "Officer." I turned around and saw a sedan stopped in the center lane where I had just cleared the glass. The driver and the woman sitting behind him were about 50 and a young man about 25 was sitting in the right front and a woman about the same age was sitting behind him.

The driver smiled and said, "Officer, we just drove all the way from Chicago and it was worth it just to see a police officer actually do some work." We all laughed and I said, "Sir, you're in California now, and you could see a lot of things that might surprise you." We all laughed again and he drove away with a friendly wave.

I knew what he was talking about because the Chicago Police Department had been widely reputed to be corrupt since the days of prohibition or before. The most common reports were that a ten dollar bill in a driver license holder saved you from a traffic ticket.

These rumors were confirmed when I was a CHP cadet. One of our classmates was from Chicago and he told some of us about two incidents with money-seeking Chicago cops. The second was when he was a soap salesman and took orders from stores and other outlets. One day a customer returned some cases of bad laundry soap that had turned rock hard, so he took them, gave the retailer credit for them and put them in the trunk of his car.

On his way home on a major thoroughfare, he was stopped by a Chicago cop. With no ten dollar bill with his license, he asked the cop if he would like a case of laundry soap. He said the cop readily agreed, so he opened the trunk and gave the cop a case of the rock-hard laundry soap. The cop was overjoyed, because it was worth more than ten dollars and let him go with a smile. With that, he said he never used that thoroughfare again. He found another route to avoid ever again going through that cop's beat.

Also, in June 1955 on the CHP I stopped a speeder on the U.S. 99 Expressway for going 18 miles an hour over the speed limit. He had a California driver license and in those days it showed the driver's last state of licensing. As soon as I saw "Illinois," I turned the license over and there was a ten dollar bill in the DMV-issued transparent holder. I handed the loaded license back to him and said, "Only the license, please."

With that he became hostile. By the time I completed the citation, he was livid. He was bigger than I was, and I was pretty sure we were going to go to the ground over it, but he scribbled his signature on the citation and departed saying some very nasty things.

A few years later, I told another CHP officer about that confrontation. He said, "Being from Chicago, he probably got pissed because he thought that ten dollars wasn't enough and your price was twenty more. Chicagoans think all cops are crooks."

On my first Friday night on the 7:00 p.m. shift, I was very pleased to have a three-year veteran partner named Bob Cooper, who was a ball of fun. The sergeant assigned us to Beat 232, which included Mission Beach, Pacific Beach and La Jolla. As soon as we were dismissed from line-up, a veteran motor officer walked over to me and asked, "Do you know about the unwritten rule?" There were so many unwritten rules that I asked, "Which one?"

"Motors don't go into La Jolla unless they get a call to go there," he warned. I thanked him and couldn't wait to tell Cooper the good news. I overtook Cooper in the garage and told him. "Is that so?" he responded with a smirk. With his devilish response, I knew it was like waving a big red flag at two ground-pawing bulls.

George C. Nuttall on San Diego Police Department duty in 1954, two years before motorcycle helmets became standard equipment.

We knew that entertaining Jack Fowler was the desk officer at the La Jolla Substation, so we headed straight for La Jolla. Jack Fowler was the comic who told me about getting punched in the nose when he was a rookie and wanted to send the puncher to San Quentin.

We parked in front of the substation, turned our radios off and went in for something to drink and some laughs. I didn't drink much coffee in those days, so Jack made some cocoa for me and Cooper had coffee.

After about 20 minutes of laughs, Cooper and I went back through Pacific Beach to Mission Beach. We sat in on a side street next to an elementary school to watch for speeders northbound on

Mission Boulevard. That location was diagonally across the intersection from the roller coaster that was in the amusement park then called "New Mission Beach" and later was called "Belmont Park." Going back to the 1930s, the rickety old roller coaster had been condemned more than once, but they put some more nails and bolts in it and put it back into death-defying operation.

We were there for several minutes when a car went north on Mission Boulevard at about 40 in the 25-mile zone. We stopped it just north of Old Mission Beach and as I walked up to the driver's door, I saw a man lying in the rear seat. The driver excitedly told me his brother-in-law had suffered a heart attack and he was rushing him to Scripps Hospital in La Jolla.

I took a closer look at the man on the rear seat. He was perspiring and didn't look too good. I told Cooper and we agreed to request permission to escort the car to Scripps Code 3 (red lights and siren). I radioed for permission and we were given the okay. We screamed the few miles to Scripps and the car stopped at the curb directly in front of the main entrance.

As soon as it stopped with Cooper and me behind the car, the right rear door opened and the dying heart-attack victim stepped out and casually strolled up the wide concrete walkway toward the front door. He sure didn't look sick to us. Cooper looked at me with a blank look and said, "Let's get the hell out of here."

I sure wasn't a doctor and had never seen a heart-attack victim up close, but he looked bad to me. For all we knew, he could have fallen over dead before a doctor saw him, but we weren't going to stick around to find out, so we left in a hurry.

A week later on Saturday night, we decided to try our luck again, so we went to the La Jolla Substation to see Jack Fowler for coffee, cocoa and more laughs. We were about halfway through our drinks when Sergeant Cannon stormed in and said, "One of you left your radio on." I remembered I hadn't turned mine off, so I said, "That's mine, sergeant, I'm sorry." I then went out and turned it off. Sergeant Cannon was a really nice man, so I was truly sorry.

When I returned, Sergeant Cannon had already gone into the sergeants' office and closed the door, maybe to call our sergeant, I thought. Cooper and I soon departed and returned to our spot next to the school across from the roller coaster. We were there only a few minutes when Sergeant Anderson went speeding by northbound on Mission Boulevard.

I looked at Cooper and said, "There it goes. Sergeant Cannon squealed on us, and the unwritten rule is going to become an official written rule." Cooper laughed and said, "And no more free coffee and cocoa."

About a minute later, a call about a major traffic accident on Pacific Coast Highway just north of Convair Aircraft was aired. The call was to a traffic car and the patrol division beat car and Sergeant Anderson. It was the first time in my two years on the police department that I had heard a sergeant dispatched to a traffic accident of any kind. If it was a major accident, they automatically responded to the scene.

About a minute later, Sergeant Anderson went speeding southbound without red lights or siren. "We just got a reprieve," I said to Cooper." "And maybe long enough for more free coffee and cocoa," he said laughing.

In that Cooper and I had never heard a sergeant dispatched to a traffic accident, we talked it over. The only thing we could imagine was that when the sergeant called the main station, his call went to the business office and he told the answering officer why he wanted to talk to Anderson.

We figured Sergeant Anderson then took Sergeant Cannon's call and headed for La Jolla. Knowing why he was going there, and with the strong resentment about the pampered treatment the residents of La Jolla got from most officers, when the accident call came in, one of our friends and an enemy of La Jolla decided to head Anderson off at the pass, so they dispatched him to keep him out of our hair. After much deep discussion, that was the only conclusion Cooper and I could come to. As much as we hated to give up waving the red flag at sergeants, we came up with an amazing idea, and we carried it out for the first time the following weekend at about 2:15 a.m. on Sunday morning.

When everything was quiet on our beats, we rode up U.S. 101 through Rose Canyon to the signal-lighted intersection at Torrey Pines Road. We turned west onto Torrey Pines Road that curved back and forth downhill through La Jolla to the level downtown section.

We put our motors in second gear, retarded the sparks, turned down the volume on our radios and coasted all the way to downtown with our motors loudly popping and banging, sounding like a wild shootout.

When we got to downtown, I said, "Let's get out of here." We turned up our radios and took off for Pacific Beach to get out of the sovereign state of La Jolla, and listened for any calls of a shooting or other disturbance in north La Jolla, but there was none.

Cooper and I figured it was a message from many police department officers and minorities in Logan Heights who got rough treatment from the bully and racist cops that were assigned there by design.

We repeated our popping and banging ride again the next Sunday morning with the same disappointing results, so we gave up.

Early in the shift on a following Saturday night, Cooper had just completed writing a citation on the northbound shoulder of U.S. 101 not far south of Balboa when Chief Jansen pulled up in his big city-owned Buick sedan. He greeted us in a friendly manner, and we talked with him for about 20 minutes. As he drove away, Cooper stood watching him go out of sight southbound on 101.

"I wonder if he found what he was looking for," Cooper said in a sarcastic manner. I said, "If he found out anything from us that he didn't already know, he sure doesn't know very much about anything."

With La Jolla games in the past, Cooper found other ways to amuse me. For example, one night when I was writing a citation, he rode off out of sight. When I followed his trail, I couldn't find him. Then I spotted him crossing an intersection a block south of the main street I was on. It was obvious to me he was going nowhere in particular. This went on for about ten minutes until I finally met him at a side street intersection. Just to break the monotony, he was playing hide-and-seek.

We actually kept our beats clean while we had lots of fun. Then tragedy struck in Mission Beach.

CHAPTER 23

Money in the Pot

"Great work, Nuttall, but you're going to get your ass chewed out for not writing any tickets." Jokingly I said, "I wrote one." "Not nearly enough," he seriously replied, "you're going to get your ass chewed out."

On the Sunday three weeks before I was to leave the police department for the CHP Academy, I bounced back from the 3:00 a.m. end of the Saturday shift and back to the 2:00 p.m. shift.

As I turned north on Pacific Coast Highway from Market Street, I saw a small motorcycle parked at the west curb of PCH between some parked cars. It looked suspicious to me, because motorcycles are so easy to steal. Even Harley-Davidson 74s were easy targets because the same ignition key fit every Harley-Davidson 74 in the entire U.S. The location was one where a sailor would have dumped it on the way back to his ship.

I made note of it and continued to my beach beats, because a traffic car and I were the one-hour overlap units for the La Jolla Substation units. As I approached Rosecrans, a stolen vehicle report was aired by our station. It was a motorcycle the same make and model as the one I had seen. I immediately radioed the location of the possible stolen motorcycle to our station. The radio operator acknowledged my information and dispatched the Beat 3 patrol division unit to check it out.

As I turned from U.S. 101 onto Balboa towards Pacific Beach, radio confirmed to the Beat 3 unit that it was the stolen motorcycle. I felt good. I had at least done something worthwhile on a normally quiet and dead Sunday.

I headed for Old Mission Beach to write some parking citations in the alley that was posted in a staggered manner on both sides to provide room for fire trucks to get through.

I had just completed two parking citations when I received a call of "11-40 (Notify if ambulance needed) C (Child) Code 3 (emergency, red lights and siren)" Radio dispatched the traffic car to

159

transport the injured child to Scripps. The location was only two blocks to the east on the other side of Mission Boulevard. Without red lights and siren in less than two minutes, I parked to the west of the address on Mission Boulevard.

Four-Year-Old Shooting Victim

There were two rows of cottages facing each other at 90 degrees from Mission Boulevard, with a grassy area between them. The address ended in an even number, so I knew it was on the north side.

I ran down the concrete walkway to the address. There was a screen door and the front door was open. I stepped in and saw two men kneeling over a small boy lying on his back. The four-year-old child had a white towel around his neck, was unconscious and was slightly gurgling.

Although I knew he was drowning in his own blood and dying, I saw a surfboard about four feet long on the west wall, so I grabbed it to serve as a stretcher. The two men kneeling beside the boy and I slipped it under him.

I heard the traffic car's siren, so the two men and I took the boy to the alley toward Mission Bay. The traffic car arrived in a few minutes. The two men got in the rear seat with the boy and departed with siren screaming.

I had recognized the younger of the two men as one I had cited for driving 40 miles per hour in the 15-miles-per-hour zone in that same alley the night before. I had seen a Smith & Wesson .44 Magnum on the couch below where the surfboard was hanging and wondered if he was the shooter. His driving the night before had been so reckless that I thought he could be the nut who pulled the trigger. He definitely fit the profile of a complete crazy.

Soon after the traffic car departed Detective Sergeant Cody Ingram arrived. I stepped outside and he asked me what had happened. I told him what little I knew at that time. Sergeant Ingram told me to investigate the scene and report it all in a memo. He then said he would go after the shooter and quickly departed.

With the worst part over, I first asked a woman who was sitting in a chair beyond where the boy had been lying next to a small table with a TV on it what she had seen. She was very traumatized and said she wanted to see her doctor for a sedative prescription. She asked if I would phone her doctor to explain to him what she had experienced. I said I would and she gave me his phone number.

I went into the kitchen and used the wall phone. The doctor answered and when I explained the horrible experience she had, he let me know that he wasn't the least bit interested. I hung up and thought, "You rotten bastard."

I returned and told the poor woman what he had said. I then told her she should go to the County Hospital emergency room and they would take care of her, but I wanted her to tell me what she saw before she and her husband left. Her husband was sitting silently on the couch.

She said right after her husband left to get something out of their car, the older man who lived there got the gun and pointed it at the front door. Then he said he was going to shoot the first person who walked in the door, and that was going to be her husband, but before her husband returned, the gun went off and hit the boy sitting in front of the TV table.

With that, the husband wasn't a witness to any of it. I thanked the woman and her husband and told them they could leave. I knew I was wrong about the younger man being the shooter, but birds of a feather flock together, so I figured he was probably as crazy as the shooter.

There was a hole in the front of the TV table drawer. I pulled it out, and the only thing in it was the fatal bullet. As I put it in my pocket, it amazed me that the reputed most powerful handgun in the world had only penetrated the boy's neck and the wood less than an inch thick.

I drew a diagram of the room, picked up the gun, returned to my motor and headed for the station. I knew it would take the rest of the shift to type the full memorandum report in triplicate.

For some reason, I went south on Kettner to the station rather than PCH. When I was about a hundred feet from G Street, a car blew through the stop sign at about 25 miles an hour. I chased him down and wrote him a citation.

All on-duty officers had heard the call, so every one who came into the squad room asked me what had happened. I had completed the first page of three when a veteran motor officer came in. He picked up page one and read it carefully for a few minutes. He laid it down and said, "Great work, Nuttall, but you're going to get your ass chewed out for not writing any tickets." Jokingly I said, "I wrote one." "Not nearly enough," he seriously replied, "you're going to get your ass chewed out."

I completed the three pages just before the 10:00 p.m. shift ending time.

At the end of the next 7:00 p.m. to 3:00 a.m. Saturday shift, Sergeant Anderson called me aside. He said I had written only 22 citations in 11 days, and motor officer Bob Warren had written 88. I said, "Of all people, please don't compare me with Warren."

Warren worked the downtown beats and was well known for writing five-dollar citations for no mirrors on motorcycles, a 1953 legislated law, and two-dollar citations for double parking and for pedestrian violators. He would also beat patrol division units to their drunk calls and take credit for their arrests. Nobody ever compared traffic division and patrol division Daily Activity Reports, so he had reportedly gotten away with padding his reports for years.

I asked Sergeant Anderson, "What do they want?" He raised his right hand, rubbed his thumb over his four fingers and said, "They want money in the pot."

Being only two weeks from leaving to go on the CHP I bravely said, "Fuck 'em. I'm not going to pick the pockets of people to fill their pot, and if you compare my fifteen-dollar or more speeding tickets with Warren's measly two-dollar and five-dollar tickets, I'm putting more in their pot than he is."

He didn't respond. He certainly knew Warren much better than I did, and knew his slippery ways, so he just walked away without another word said, and probably knowing he had made a big mistake using Warren as a model. And to think the Sunday before I had been instrumental in quickly recovering a stolen motorcycle, written two parking citations, nearly single-handedly investigated a homicide and written one stop sign citation.

More than ever, it proved to me that the SDPD was a grossly mismanaged department with absolutely no method or system for objectively measuring the performance or overall production of its officers, and in years thereafter, the officers they promoted to the rank of captain or above further proved their slipshod way of managing a police department.

CHAPTER 24

Point Loma or Logan Heights?

With that bargain basement arrangement, when the ambulance company had only one ambulance available and received a police department call to the west edge of minority area Logan Heights and a private party call from affluent Point Loma, it didn't take a genius to figure out which one they rolled to first.

On a weekday I was assigned to Beats 5 and 8 on the 2:00 p.m. shift. Just after the start of the shift, I stopped a northbound speeder on 16th Street for going over 40 in the 25-mile zone. As I walked up to the driver's door, I saw a beautiful Mexican woman lying in the rear seat. She had a white towel between her legs up against her crotch.

Before I could say anything, the driver excitedly said his sister in the rear seat had had a miscarriage, had been bleeding badly and he was trying to get her to the County Hospital as soon as he could. The woman in the rear seat quickly said she was on welfare and the county would not pay for an ambulance.

With that, I radioed for a beat car to my location to take her to County Hospital Code 3. The radio dispatcher asked what kind of emergency it was. I responded, "O.B" (Childbirth or related treatment). The operator responded they would dispatch an ambulance with no further information or explanation.

Several minutes later, patrol division Officer Alan Wiseman pulled up and parked behind my motor. He was one of the 26 officers hired in my group and was a delightful person. He was very outgoing, always smiling and very smart.

He walked up smiling and asked what I had. I was very irritated, so I told him what had happened. He said he didn't know why he couldn't take her in his car and readily agreed with me that something was amiss. Alan stayed there until the ambulance finally arrived about 45 minutes later. By that time, I was livid.

As soon as the ambulance departed with the woman, I radioed that I was 10-19 (Return to the station). I wanted to know why somebody sitting behind a desk would overrule an officer at the scene and do something so stupid.

When I rode into the garage angry as hell, Sergeant Anderson was waiting there to head me off at the pass. He said, "Now cool down. Don't do something you'll be sorry for."

As I walked past him to the locker room, I said, "I want to find out what in the hell is going on now. Since when did the radio operator make critical decisions for officers at the scene who know what the situation is?"

The police department radio was communication from field units to station and station to field units, not field units to field units. So with Sergeant Anderson knowing I had something to get angry about, everybody hearing the many radio monitors in the station must have known.

As I burst into the business office/communications center sergeants' office, a sergeant I had not had any past contact with sat behind his desk looking uncomfortable.

"Why didn't you dispatch a beat car as I requested?" I blurted. "Because a new order prohibits transporting O.B. cases in our cars," he replied sheepishly. "And if you want to, you can talk to the patrol captain. He's the one who told us to dispatch the ambulance."

I knew he was telling me the truth, so I thanked him and went out the door. I didn't bother to see the captain, because I knew very well that the stupid order had come from the chief's office, and it would be an exercise in futility, and just another unwritten order like so many others we were not told about in advance.

All police department cars had leather interiors for ease of cleaning. Drunks could vomit, pee or whatever in the cars, but no O.B. cases were permitted.

Furthermore, any number of jail trustees would have jumped at the chance to clean blood from the rear seat, including Johnnie Flores. They could pull out the rear seat to hose it down and search for loose change, or even a .32 automatic to give to the captain for a pat on the head.

This fiasco all started when Chief Jansen discontinued the police ambulance service in 1947 and the police department contracted with private ambulance services. I had heard the low bidder for city compensation when the patient or the patient's responsible party couldn't pay their fare got the contract, and I heard the low bids were $3.50 and $4.

With that bargain basement arrangement, when the ambulance company had only one ambulance available and received a police department call to the west edge of minority area Logan Heights and a private party call from affluent Point Loma, it didn't take a genius to figure out which one they rolled to first. And it was not likely the ambulance dispatcher would tell the police department caller about the Point Loma call.

It may not have been Point Loma, but any private party call would most certainly take first place over a police department case, and that's exactly what I figured happened in my case. So, I decided in the future I would request permission to escort any such cases to the hospital, Code 3 or not.

With that arrangement, there were two levels of ambulance service — one for those who could probably pay and one for those who probably couldn't pay. Since the ambulance service risked settling for $3.50 or $4 for transporting police department cases, they most likely put them on hold, even if the patient bled to death.

It wasn't until about ten years later that this shameful Chief Jansen deal was corrected. In the mid or late 1960s, the police department converted 17 station wagons into ambulances and spread them throughout the city as patrol division beat cars.

In the early 1970s when the new chief added paramedic officers to the small ambulances, the City Council went back to private paramedic ambulance services. So what goes around finally comes around, especially when it involves the almighty dollar, even if it means the lower class gets second-rate emergency services.

Several years after I left the police department, I ran into Alan Wiseman at a flea market near my in-laws' home in El Cajon. He was smiling more than ever. He had quit the police department not long after I did and opened a very lucrative private investigation business. That proved to me that he was even more brilliant than I had originally thought. We had a nice talk and laughingly agreed we were fortunate to be out of the San Diego Police Department.

CHAPTER 25

The Great Escape

*Seeing the light at the end of the tunnel, I decided to
coast for my final days in hell, but even coasting proved to
be hazardous to my health and well being, so I decided to
go into very early retirement on the job.*

My last Friday night on the 7:00 p.m. shift, Sergeant Anderson
told me the deputy chief wanted to talk to me the next night. Of
course, I knew what it was about, so I dreamed up a good story for
him so I wouldn't burn my bridges, and I knew the CHP had been
conducting my background check.

The next night the deputy chief wasn't in sight anywhere, so
Cooper and I headed for our beach beats. As we approached
Rosecrans, I got a call to 10-19 (Return to the station.)

I made a U-turn and headed south on PCH. I saw a police patrol
division car parked at the west curb in an open area about halfway
between Old Town and Convair Aircraft. An officer was standing
next to the car in the street. As I approached his location, I saw him
cup his hands on the sides of his mouth like a megaphone and as I
passed, he yelled, "Don't let him talk you out of it."

I nodded my head and waved to him. He was a veteran officer I
had never worked with or been on the same squad with. It told me
that not only the word of my leaving for the CHP was known
throughout most of the police department, but also the deputy chief's
plot to try to talk me into staying.

When I arrived at the station, I was told to go into the
sergeants' office and as I walked in, the deputy chief told me to
close the door and take a seat. Without hesitation, he asked me
why I wanted to leave, he said the CHP was not nearly as efficient

as the police department and that I had a very bright future on the police department.

I actually told him the truth, even though it was only one of the many reasons for my wanting to leave. If I had told him all of my reasons, we could have been there all night.

Up until that time and for a few years after, all city employees were required to reside within the city limits of San Diego, so I told the deputy chief I had lived in San Diego City all my life and my wife and I wanted to find a new place to live. And on the CHP with enough seniority, we could live in any part of California we so desired.

That appeared to stop him, so I didn't bother to tell him that the cold, damp weather caused my wife to have dull headaches and I suffered from sinus problems in the winter.

It probably damaged his ego as an expert manipulator, because shortly after I joined the police department, I was told how he conned an officer into not going on the CHP with a false promise, and the officer fell for it.

The officer involved was at the bottom of the CHP list before the 1953 list I was on. Even though the eligible candidates on a State Personnel Board employment list could waive job offers two times before being dropped from the list, when a list was replaced by a new list, the older list died — except for military personnel who were on active duty, who stayed on the list until discharged from duty. With his list dying, he had only one chance to accept.

The deputy chief probably knew he had only one chance to go on the CHP, so he gave him whatever the officer asked for. When the officer said he wanted to be a detective, the deputy chief promised him he would be a detective, and the deputy chief immediately transferred him to the detective division. Then as soon as the CHP list he was on died, he was sent right back to the patrol division.

About 20 years later, that officer was the captain in charge of the traffic division. One Sunday he phoned the business office and told the answering officer he was resigning from the police department and would be in the next day to sign his resignation papers. That's how bad it got in the years after I escaped.

Seeing the light at the end of the tunnel, I decided to coast for my final days in hell, but even coasting proved to be hazardous to my health and well being, so I decided to go into very early retirement on the job.

The frightening event that quickly changed my plans occurred on my last Sunday night on the police department. It was dark and I stopped for a red light southbound on 16th at Market. Traffic was very light, and I was the only one southbound. I had just stopped and the handlebars felt like they were loose. I wiggled them back and forth like they weren't even in touch with the road.

I looked down at the pavement and saw my front tire was in the middle of a large puddle of motor oil. A car that had earlier stopped there was losing all of its crankcase oil and had created the large puddle. As I cautiously pushed my motor back and to the curb, I saw a small line of oil leading up to the puddle. I radioed the hazard to the station for the street department to sand it.

It was only a line of leaked oil like that in the center lane of University Avenue that had put the motorcyclist down and caused his death with a basal skull fracture. This was a very large puddle, and I was wearing a soft uniform cap, not a motor helmet. With that, the next shift I stopped to visit my saintly grandmother and found other safe ways to stay alive.

On my last shift on the police department, the motor officer who had the locker next to mine gave me hell for leaving the motor squad. He had a dapper pencil mustache and was sort of a dandy. He tried to glorify the SDPD motor squad like it was equal to or better than the Navy's Blue Angels, and he was a friend of my partner Bob Cooper. I thought I was the first motor officer to quit and go on the CHP, and it wasn't until decades later that I learned that CHP Sergeant Les Ford had done the same thing in the early 1930s.

Cooper and I became very close friends, and he followed me into the CHP two years later in 1956. In about 1958, Cooper told me the dapper motor cop who had given me hell had cried the blues to him because he was too old to take the CHP test. All I could do was laugh.

It was about a half hour after shift change on my last police department day when I walked into the squad room to go out under the arches to my car in the parking lot for the very last time, carrying a few of the things I could use on the CHP.

The only one in the squad room was Motorcycle Sergeant Jimmie Gilbert. He was sitting on a table swinging his boots back and forth. As I entered the room, he extended his hand out to me and said, "Good luck, Nuttall, if I could, I'd be going with you," and I could easily see he meant it. "Thank you, sergeant," I said as I shook his hand, "I can only wish that you could." As I turned to walk out, I said, "And the best of luck to you, sergeant."

As I walked to my car, I realized that things had to be much worse than I even knew. There was a motor sergeant with about 15 years of service and with a 20-year retirement plan, he could retire in about five years, and he wanted out so much he would openly tell me so. I knew he must be right in the direct line of fire to pressure officers to write more and more tickets. Like the one who had yelled at me to not let the deputy chief talk me out of it, I had never worked with or for Sergeant Gilbert. And both of them were about ten years over the maximum age to take the CHP test.

All I could think of was how in just two years the police department had gone from a happy, enjoyable place to work to a hell hole, and I thanked God I could leave.

CHAPTER 26

Den Mothers

Most of all, the two duty officers' primary duties were to assist and counsel cadets with any personal problems, keep us in line after hours and answer all of our training-related questions they could. They were also our first line of contact with the rest of the staff in the front offices. Therefore, they had for years been nicknamed "Den Mothers".

Cliff Dennis, who had been hired on the SDPD in our group of 26, was going to the CHP Academy with me. He was a tall Texan, a graduate of Hardin Simmons, and like most Texans had a great sense of humor. Although also like most Texans, he was still ticked off about losing the Civil War or "War Between the States" or "War of Northern Aggression," as they insisted on calling that event. We went to Sacramento together by train.

Our class of 80 cadets was nearly all additional expansion officers, except for at least one vacancy resulting from the shooting death of a Siskiyou County Happy Camp resident officer. He was Officer Bill Chansler, who was fatally shot by a husband with a rifle who had tried to kill his wife in a restaurant where she worked. In his dying moments, Chansler fired one shot and killed the gunman.

Much like the SDPD Recruit Training Class and field training officers, we were treated like new brothers or sons, or at least that was the way I was treated on the police department by all except the deputy chief. The CHP Academy treated us with the utmost courtesy, respect and care. They had all gone through the same experience as cadets and knew what it was like.

The academy commander was Captain Leonard Overhouse. He had a great sense of humor and put on a gruff show, but had a heart of gold — so much so that he was soon called "Captain Outhouse," without any fear of his kicking back. He instructed two or three short classes and told some clean jokes.

The second in command was Lieutenant Reece Brainard, a large man who had been the state heavyweight wrestling champion in college. He instructed the 40-hour Vehicle Code class and did an outstanding job of teaching us all of the code, in addition to all of the case laws and legislative intents of the statutes.

Most impressive to me was after he had completed the course, he added some good old CHP enforcement advice. He told us he had covered all sections of the Vehicle Code, but he hoped we would use the important accident preventing ones and kind of ignore the nit-picking ones that the public didn't know existed.

That pleased me and made me think about SDPD motor officer Bob Warren and his motorcycle mirror citations with that new Vehicle Code law that was hot off the presses from the state legislature.

There were four other academy staff instructors, including straight-faced comic Sergeant Jim Booth, who instructed a few classes with many laughs. Two of the other staff members were Officer Orville "O.P." Johnson and Officer John Pedri. They had been duty officers together for six years that I knew of from my old CHP friend Officer Russ Tanner, who had been a cadet in 1948.

They both had a great sense of humor and O.P. loved to play practical jokes, mostly on Pedri, who was more reserved, played the straight man and ignored the tricks O.P played to keep from getting bored with the same routine over and over for at least six years.

As duty officers, one or the other was always there when the other staff members were off nights and weekends. And O.P. sort of instructed motorcycle training with Sergeant Booth, and Pedri instructed firearms training. I say "sort of" for the motorcycle training, as will become obvious later.

Most of all, the two duty officers' primary duties were to assist and counsel cadets with any personal problems, keep us in line after hours and answer all of our training-related questions they could. They were also our first-line of contact with the rest of the staff in the front offices. Therefore, they had for years been nicknamed "Den Mothers."

At any time during classes, we were free to raise our hands to ask a question or speak. When recognized by the instructor, we would rise to our feet and speak freely.

During our Related Laws class, the instructor told us that arrest warrants were not valid if not personally signed by the issuing judge. I had seen so many San Diego Police Court parking meter warrants with Judge John J. Brennan's name rubber-stamped on them, I raised my hand.

I told the instructor of the rubber-stamped warrants. He said that was no surprise because judges could not be sued for any reason. Then he said that the serving police officer's department could probably be sued for serving the invalid warrants and unlawfully jailing the persons named in the warrants.

I thought if I knew a good attorney, I would tip him off to Judge Brennan's rubber-stamped warrants. Then he could have someone get a meter citation, let it go to a failure to appear warrant and provoke the serving officer into arresting and jailing him, then sue the hell out of the police department, Chief Jansen and the deputy chief.

I say "provoke" because of the dozen or more I was given to serve, I never arrested any named in the warrant because they were the legally-registered owner of the vehicle. Some had loaned their car to their brother-in-law the day of the parking violation or whatever. Regardless, I told them to hustle down to the court and pay it before it was given to another officer to serve who didn't listen to sad stories.

One I was given to serve on was an old Hoover classmate of mine. I told him to get his butt down to the court to pay it before it was given to "Super Cop" to serve.

Then I served the funniest two warrants on my father-in-law. At about the time I first started dating my wife in 1947, he and I had seen a SDPD officer writing a meter parking citation. He worked at Convair Aircraft, and like most blue-collar work places, there were more than enough "locker room attorneys" to go around.

So he told me that nothing was ever done if you didn't pay the fifty-cent fine, and he had been told that by one of his fellow workers who had got away with it. At that time, I hadn't met any of his fellow workers, but when I did, I could understand the misinformation. It was probably the drunk who didn't bother to register his old, worn out 1928 Buick in his name. He was too cheap to pay the transfer fee.

Knowing what he had told me five years before, I had a hard time controlling myself as I logged the two warrants on our Daily Activity Reports. I then told my partner what he had told me five years earlier about not paying them and how much fun it was going to be when I told him he was under arrest.

He opened the door and I said, "You're under arrest for not paying your parking tickets that you don't have to pay." As required by law, I handed him the two warrants to read. Parking citation warrants did not have a copy of the citation with them as signed failure-to-appear warrants did, but when he looked at the dates of the violations, he said, "That was after we sold Pete's '35 Ford."

Pete was my brother-in-law and was not 18 so was not old enough to register a vehicle in his name, so it had been registered in my father-in-law's name. They had traded it in on a 1941 Ford at an "Honest John's" used car lot, one of many in San Diego at that time.

With the fun over, I retrieved the warrants. I then wrote on the warrants that I, SDPD Officer George Nuttall, personally knew the car cited had been sold by the registered owner prior to the citations being issued, and that was the end of that, but it was fun while it lasted.

The first week at the academy, the uniform vendors set up in the gym to sell us our uniforms and service revolvers. When I left the police department, my retirement contribution of about $500 was refunded. With the price of the motorcycle breeches and Star leather jacket, it was all gone, plus more. My monthly salary on the police department was $427, including motor pay, and my starting monthly salary on the CHP was $358, with a four-year progression scale to top pay.

The dorms and bathrooms were in two wings like a squared "U" about 30 feet apart. The cadets in the north wing were Platoon A and my side on the south was Platoon B. One platoon had motorcycle training while the other had firearms training, and every other Saturday we switched.

Motorcycle Training

The first Saturday my Platoon B had motor training, O.P. brought a motor from the motor carport that was backed up to and attached to the covered firing range. The 40 of us, O.P. and Sergeant Booth were at the north end of the asphalt road that extended almost to the fence that surrounded all but the front of the Academy building.

O.P. asked who had riding experience, and about ten of us raised our hands. He then told us to demonstrate by riding a Harley 74 Hydro-glide about 100 yards down the road and return. He was satisfied, so he sent us over to get motors.

When we returned, he assigned each of us to train three other cadets. I parked the motor on the road and explained the hand shift lever, the left foot clutch, the hand and foot brakes, the hand accelerator, the spark and choke lever. I then showed them how to start a cold engine by lowering the choke lever four clicks, then raising it to two clicks for a few seconds until the engine was running smoothly. I showed them how to retard the spark and emphasized to always retard the spark when kicking the kick starter or it would violently kick back.

That was the entire extent of the mechanics of motorcycling. Then all they had to do was practice riding. In about 20 minutes I did what motorcycle training officer Boland took two weeks to do, except for the practice riding — the hard part.

O.P. then sent all of the new motor riders to the carport to get a motor. They were like a bunch of kids shopping for their first bicycle. Then away they went. In ten minutes, motors were going in all directions on the long paved road and all over the 275 acres of weed-covered fields. When I saw that, I rode over and parked in front of the carport. I couldn't bear to watch the inevitable mayhem.

Amazingly, the only accident was on a road trip in a small burg off the River Road miles south of the academy. We were bunched up and one motor rear-ended another motor, but the damage was slight. It didn't matter because all training motors were over mileage and ready to be sold by sealed bid.

Sergeant Booth strolled back to see what had happened, then in usual straight-faced humor, he said he had the cause figured out. He said the rear-ender had already been at the academy too long and had developed an amorous attraction for the rear-ended motor and just wanted to get his special attention.

LAPD High-Stress Training

About the third week, I was so pleased with the academy and the wonderful treatment the staff officers gave us, I thought about the LAPD high-stress cadet training. It all started in about 1949 when about ten Mexican pachucos were beaten until they were bloody in the jail after they had injured two LAPD officers. It was Christmas Eve and the jailers had reportedly been drinking. It was later reported that there was blood splattered on the walls and ceiling. The L.A. Times found out about it and called it "The Christmas Eve Massacre," but the LAPD had a more palatable title for the unfortunate incident.

The result was the chief was fired and replaced by a retired Marine Corps general to discipline the LAPD. The new Marine Corps chief quickly turned the LAPD Academy cadet training into a Marine Corps Boot Camp with the same high-stress training environment.

At the same time, one of the pre-employment physical requirements was that applicants could not have so much as one tooth missing. It was truly a "Super Race" standard. The tooth requirement made me wonder if the LAPD had a physical arrest tactic of biting resisting arrestees, but of course they didn't.

About four weeks before graduation, the openings and number of vacancies in each CHP office were listed on the blackboard, and we were given a "Wish List" form to list our preference of assignment in the field. There were openings in Riverside and San Bernardino Counties, including three in San Bernardino. Because I liked Big Bear Lake since going there to summer camp in 1940 with my brother and cousin with the Hollywood Boy's Club, I put my first choice as San Bernardino, and I wrote my reason was to make it my permanent assignment.

One cadet from El Centro had driven us nuts asking if we were going to request that location. He was dying to go back to El Centro and he didn't shut up until the assignments came out and he was assigned to El Centro. We were all so happy because none of us were going with him.

We were scheduled to graduate on December 24th, but Commissioner Caldwell changed it to December 23rd so we wouldn't have to fight Christmas Eve traffic and drunk drivers, and we were given five extra days off for travel and relocation.

Although we were treated like royalty by the academy staff, it was wonderful to be free again and free at last.

CHAPTER 27

Drama King

Like the beautiful accident report, he was overly dramatic in many ways. For example, he smoked like a social queen. When he took a drag on a cigarette, he leaned his head back and blew the smoke up at the headliner, and he would dramatically raise his right leg and cross it over his left thigh. So I privately called him "Drama King."

The San Bernardino Area Commander was Captain Frank Freeman. He had started his traffic law enforcement career as one of the first two San Bernardino motor cops in 1915. His birthday was October 15th and on every birthday he said he would retire on his next birthday. Many hoped, but when he bought new uniforms, their hopes were dashed.

I was the only one of the three who were assigned to San Bernardino who wasn't from that county, so I had a lot to learn about its culture and police politics, and it was very different. The sheriff's office and San Bernardino Police Department were political.

Our first day, Captain Freeman and Lieutenant Marion Fitch had the three of us sit across a squad room table from them for a brief orientation. Captain Freeman started by saying, "Forget everything they taught you at the CHP Academy, because we'll teach you how to be real highway patrolmen." He then told us to get our motorcycle gear, because we would soon be assigned to motors, and that was about it.

I was assigned to ride along with Officer Pern Nielsen. He had been on the Chula Vista Police Department, so we hit it off. The city of Chula Vista is between the city of San Diego and the Mexican border, so Nielsen and I soon identified some cops that we both knew. We discussed the ones we liked, didn't like and the ones we hated.

Like most of my SDPD training officers had done, Nielsen told me about some of the other officers, which ones to be wary of and to

177

avoid if at all possible. The most important one he warned me of was Officer Burdette Shidler. He said Shidler loved to drive at high speeds and took great delight in scaring his partners with his fast driving. He was 55 years old and had owned and operated an auto repair shop before joining the CHP at age 42 in 1942 when the maximum age was relaxed during World War II.

Just as it was on the SDPD and at the CHP Academy, Nielsen made me feel very much at home in "Berdoo," as it was called by the natives and outsiders alike.

My first night on the road was New Year's Eve, and I worked the graveyard shift with three-year veteran Officer Dick Mark. He was a native of Berdoo and knew much of the history of the CHP in that county. We started the busy weekend with a DUI accident on Valley Boulevard, which had been U.S. Highway 99 before the expressway was built.

Valley Boulevard was an old three-lane highway with a center lane for passing and left turns. The center lane was called "The Suicide Lane," because drivers going in both directions would see it was empty, then both enter it to pass at the same time and hit head-on. Expressways were divided highways like freeways, but they had intersections at major cross streets, which were officially called "Crossings at grade."

Dick Mark and I packed our lunches. The Monday following New Year's weekend, Mark drove into a brush-covered area for lunchtime. On winter weeknights, Berdoo was like an abandoned cemetery. It was nearly always dead. As soon as we finished our baloney sandwiches, Mark scooted down in the driver's seat and said, "I like to rest my eyes for a little while after eating so I don't fall asleep driving." So we sat in the front seat together trying to get comfortable to rest our eyes. After about five minutes of that discomfort I said, "You know Dick, there is a back seat."

I could tell he was trying to test me to see how I would respond to his "resting my eyes" alibi, and he immediately agreed with me that there was indeed a back seat. So I got into the back seat and made myself comfortable. In that it was cold and an exceptionally wet winter, I always took my raincoat and Star motor jacket to work on that shift, just in case, so I folded my raincoat and put my motor jacket on top of it with the large fur collar on top. Also, unlike on the

SDPD, the CHP cars had very good heaters, so that became our routine for the rest of January just like Balboa Park on the SDPD, and it was almost like home.

After about a one-hour doze, Mark drove to the U.S. 99 Expressway and headed east from Sierra Avenue, the main north-south street in the City of Fontana, the home of Kaiser Steel west.

As Mark was cruising at about 50 miles per hour, a motorcycle slowly passed us at the 55 speed limit. The driver was wearing a denim Levi jacket with "Hell's Angels" in large letters and a logo on the back. The rider had long, scraggly hair and looked like something I'd never seen before.

"What in hell is that?" I exclaimed. I had never seen or heard of the Hell's Angels in San Diego. Mark explained that the Hell's Angels were an outlaw motorcycle club started in Berdoo by San Quentin ex-cons who organized it while still in "Q" as San Quentin was called. I later had contact with some of those animals in Big Bear and Sacramento, and some of it was humorous.

During another dead night, Mark told me one of the funnier stories in the history of the Berdoo CHP. San Bernardino County is the largest county in the United States and one of the poorest. It includes thousands of square miles of Mojave Desert and other desert wastelands that stretch to the Colorado River and state line to the east. It was on those wastelands that General George S. Patton trained his tank troops during World War II and while doing so, he acted in his usual blustery manner and generated a couple of interesting stories.

Armed Robbery in Colton

Being a poor and very political county, the sheriff had hundreds or thousands of untrained volunteer unpaid special and reserve deputies, and some actually manned beat cars in pairs. Many sheriffs give out special and reserve deputy badges because each of those badges equals at least one sure vote, and Berdoo county had more than its share of those badges floating around. So, one night there was an armed robbery in Colton, which is directly south of the city of San Bernardino. Two CHP officers just happened to be at Valley Boulevard and Riverside Avenue, which is the main north and south streets through the city of Rialto, and they were driving a 1947 Pontiac.

When the APB of the armed robbery was aired, the robbers' car was described as a Pontiac exactly like their CHP car, and the broadcast said that the robbers' car was westbound on Valley Boulevard with a sheriff's car in pursuit. Between Colton and Riverside, Valley Boulevard had several rises and dips, and some of the dips were so long that when in them, the view of the roadway ahead was lost and out of sight. When the robbers' Pontiac passed the CHP officers' location, it was going at least 80 miles an hour, so they gave pursuit.

By the time the CHP officers got their Pontiac with its straight-eight engine up to top speed like the robbers' car, the robbers had at least a quarter-mile lead on them. It was a standoff, and the CHP officers pursued them for about 16 miles into the city of Ontario, where the robbers turned south onto a main street in that city. The officers pursued them for about a mile when the robbers' car went out of control, ran off the roadway and crashed into something.

The officers immediately ordered the robbers out of their car at gunpoint, and the robbers exited their car with hands high. Before the officers could handcuff them, a sheriff's car arrived with siren howling. As the CHP officers handcuffed the two robbers and put them in the back seat of their car, they noticed the two reserve deputies closely inspecting the rear of the robbers' car. Then one said, "I reloaded once, and I know I couldn't have missed it 12 times."

With that, one of the CHP officers walked back and looked at the rear of the CHP car and saw 12 bullet holes in the trunk lid. Mark didn't say what happened after that, but I could easily imagine that there was a lot of profanity in the air.

I later worked with one of those officers and he confirmed the story almost exactly as Mark had told it. And after five and one-half years of dealing with Berdoo County deputies, I knew the story was so true it could have been etched in stone.

Memories of General Patton

On one later shift, Mark told me a couple of General Patton stories. When Patton was training his tank troops on the Mojave Desert, several CHP officers were assigned to the desert to stop what little traffic there was when the tanks crossed highways. There was a lot of dead time, so one officer decided to go fishing in the Colorado River during a lull. While sitting in uniform with his line in the water, the officer heard a booming voice bark, "What in the hell do you think you're doing?"

Without turning around, the officer responded, "What in hell does it look like I'm doing?" There was no response so the officer finally turned and looked up at the top of the river bank, and standing there was General Patton.

When I went on the CHP that officer was then a CHP captain, so I had to assume Patton may have appreciated the officer's brassy response.

The other second-hand Patton story Mark told me was when about 50 of his tank troops didn't return to camp on a Monday after their weekend leave. Patton's aides quickly tracked them down and discovered all 50 were in the San Bernardino County Jail. With that bad news, Patton dispatched a bus to the jail and personally phoned the jail and asked to speak with the deputy in charge. When he got him on the phone he barked, "I have a bus on its way to your jail to pick up my troops, and if my troops are not back here on that bus by noon, I'll bring my tanks in there and level your '*&#$@*+#' jail," so the 50 wayward troops were put on the bus without delay.

My other graveyard partner was nothing like Mark. He didn't suggest resting our eyes and he was very different in every way. During our first shift together, he announced that he would investigate all accidents and show me how to do it right. As it turned out, we investigated only about two.

Technicolor Accident Reports

At that time, CHP field accident reports were three-fold cardboard forms. From those, the radio dispatcher clerks typed the final reports onto 8½ by 11-inch accident report forms. Right after he had completed the first accident report, he proudly showed it to me.

On the one-page diagram of the accident scene, he had used colored pencils to color it in to make it a beautiful Technicolor work of art.

I thought he was crazy. After the final report was typed, his drawing would go into the file and nobody would ever see it again. I could only figure he did it to impress the sergeants, because he sucked up to them, even helping one build a new home free of charge. And he liked to tell everybody about it.

Like the beautiful accident report, he was overly dramatic in many ways. For example, he smoked like a social queen. When he took a drag on a cigarette, he leaned his head back and blew the smoke up at the headliner, and he would dramatically raise his right leg and cross it over his left thigh. So I privately called him "Drama King."

The late CHP Commissioner Clifford E. Peterson's claim to fame was that he had attended the FBI National Academy in Washington, D.C. and the Northwestern Traffic Institute at Northwestern University in Chicago, but to my knowledge he never boasted of his amazing misplaced political pull, wherever that was well concealed.

Probably at Northwestern Traffic Institute he learned of and was impressed with the idea of in-view patrol to deter potential traffic law violators. I used it and quickly learned that it works. So, with that in mind and the fact the CHP could buy about 100 more gutless Chevrolets and Fords for about the same amount that 75 to 80 Oldsmobile's would cost, Peterson went crazy buying the cheaper, slower cars.

When I went on the CHP, there were far too many of those "bargain basement" dogs around, and they were all assigned to sergeants and above to eventually run out at 100,000 miles.

One night when I was driving southbound on Alabama, which was at the very west end of the city of Redlands and approaching U.S. 99, we received a car-to-car call from Sergeant Kingsley that an Oldsmobile going over 80 had just passed them traveling eastbound on 99 just east of Waterman. Sergeant Haley was with him.

Sergeant Kingsley was a well-known comic, and I knew they were in a Chevrolet, so I beat Drama King to the radio mike and told Kingsley where we were, which was in perfect position, and I innocently asked, "Are you gaining on it?" "No. Its damn tail lights just keep getting closer and closer together," he responded in his usual droll manner.

From my experiences on the SDPD I was somewhat concerned about this high-speed Oldsmobile. When speeders come into view of or pass a black-and-white police car, they usually hit the brakes and slow down, but this one didn't. This made me think that this one could be fleeing from an armed robbery or other felonious act that had not yet been reported, or it could be a stolen car, or both.

I quickly drove across U.S. 99, made a U-turn and parked far enough south of the intersection so the speeding car's occupants couldn't see us until entering the intersection. Then when the Oldsmobile reached Alabama, it slowed and turned north instead of going straight on 99 into the city of Redlands.

That increased my concern, because Alabama was an open road for miles, unlike 99 through Redlands where the speed limit was 25 miles per hour and there were signal lights — and the Redlands Police Department might get involved.

More concerned than before, I crossed 99 and turned on the red spotlight and siren. The Oldsmobile had initially rapidly increased its speed, so it took about a quarter of a mile to get it stopped. We were in a high-mileage, two-year-old 1953 Oldsmobile Rocket 88. With much use, the radio mike spring-coiled cord was stretched and hung down to the hump in the middle of the front floorboard.

I quickly put the car in neutral and set the parking brake, and before I could step out of the car, Drama King dramatically bailed out and fell flat on his face onto the damp dirt shoulder. He still had his legs crossed with his right thigh on top of his left thigh, and the sagging and stretched mike cord was around his right ankle.

I was about halfway out the door when I saw that hilarious act. I started laughing so hard, I wouldn't have been able to defend myself if the occupants of the Oldsmobile had started shooting at us or chase them if they had made a run for it. Fortunately, neither of those things happened; the three people in the Oldsmobile just sat still.

Before the sergeants were close enough to see Drama King unravel the mike cord from his right ankle, stand up and brush himself off, he was standing as if nothing had happened.

Sergeant Kingsley wrote the speed ticket and all departed. The sergeants were not on duty. Sergeant Kingsley was starting his days off the next day, so Sergeant Haley was taking him to his home at the east end of Redlands. After Drama King and I left the scene, neither of us said a word about his tumbling act. I thought he must have taken a big blow to his high-and-mighty position, and even his great Technicolor accident reports couldn't save his injured ego.

During my cadet class, one of the academy staff told us that our expansion class increased the number of CHP officers of all ranks to about 1,750. Even with those numbers, the California Highway Patrol, or "California Haywire Patrol" as Sergeant Booth called it at the academy, was still spread pretty thin. There were two 11:00 p.m. graveyard units — one east of Riverside at Rialto and the second west of Riverside. We were the east unit. Then on the 3:00 p.m. afternoon/evening shift, a third unit was assigned to U.S. Route 66 up to the Cajon Pass Summit and many square miles of open and residential areas to the east of Route 66.

Tragic Accident

About an hour after Drama King's command performance, the mood abruptly changed from humorous to tragic when we received a call about a major injury accident involving a fatality. The location was on U.S. 99 a few hundred yards east of Riverside, so it was on our beat. We were still in the Redlands area, so it took us about 15 minutes to get to the scene with red spotlight and siren. The west-end unit was already there when we arrived on the scene.

It was a horrible scene — the most terrible traffic accident I experienced in over ten years on the streets and highways. A truck tractor with a semi trailer was blocking the eastbound lanes, and the volunteer driver of that big rig was chaining his truck tractor to the rear of another big rig of the same combination. The truck tractor he was hooking to was over the south shoulder and was about halfway through a 1947 Chevrolet "Woody" station wagon.

One of the west unit officers told me there were seven people in the station wagon, and they were all crushed up against the front seat or the dashboard. Four were already dead, including a baby.

The other west-end unit partner was Moses Delgado, a seven-year veteran officer. He was the only Mexican/American officer in the San Bernardino squad and spoke Spanish. Since the seven occupants of the crushed station wagon were of Mexican descent, he investigated the accident.

About the time the big rig was pulled out of the station wagon, two ambulances arrived. The critically injured were loaded into the ambulances, and they sped away with sirens wailing. The four dead had to remain there for the coroner to handle.

The only blessing was the assisting big rig driver had stopped and volunteered to pull the other big rig out of the station wagon. If he or another big rig driver had not done so, we would have had to wait up to an hour for Continental Tow to roll their heavy-duty tow rig from Ontario.

With Officer Delgado volunteering to investigate our accident, all there was to do was wait for the coroner, so Drama King and I departed, but we stayed on the west end of our beat to cover both beats in the event of another accident on either beat. Luckily, there were none.

I had seen enough deaths of different kinds, and like all others, I consoled myself with my beliefs that they were then safe in the hands of God. The only one that had a lasting effect on me was the four-year-old boy who was fatally shot in Mission Beach when I was on the San Diego Police Department. My son was two years old at that time, and I never again walked into his bedroom wearing a handgun — maybe senseless, but I just could never take any chances, regardless.

It wasn't until the start of the graveyard shift the next night that we were able to get the details about the cause of the accident from Delgado. It was absolutely incredible. Delgado said the driver of the station wagon got sleepy, so he parked on the eastbound shoulder to get some sleep, instead of exiting U.S. 99 at Riverside and parking on a side street. Then the driver of the truck tractor pulling a semi trailer fell asleep, drifted off to the right, plowed into the rear of the station wagon and pushed it over the side into a drainage ditch.

It was beyond me how that could have happened. That big rig driver had probably loaded his cargo in Los Angeles about 50 miles to the west and fell asleep within 50 feet of going safely past the parked station wagon. It was such an unbelievable horror story the worst screen writer in Hollywood wouldn't touch it with a ten-foot pole, but in police work, nothing should surprise us.

CHAPTER 28

Officer Slow

I told him to kick it up to 90 or we would lose them if we couldn't overtake them before they got to Devore. It was like talking to the windshield. He puttered along at his top speed of about 75 and we lost the speeder in traffic at Devore.

In February, I was assigned to the west end on the 3:00 p.m. shift with two officers who were seven-year veterans. One officer was very excitable, which kept things going in the wrong direction much of the time. The other was a spit-and-polish, neat and clean freak. When we gassed up at the full-service contract stations, he would spend about five minutes washing the windshield until it was invisible.

After that up and down month, I was happy to be assigned to work with speedy Officer Burdette Shidler and an officer who had graduated from the academy in the class before mine — and it didn't take long for me to privately name the other one "Officer Slow."

So I spent the month of March working with "Officer Speedy" and "Officer Slow" on U.S. Route 66 through Cajon Pass on the 3:00 p.m. shift. On the first shift of March, Officer Slow drove first. Our first assignment of every weekday was to direct traffic at an intersection where Norton Air Force Base employees exited the base. The traffic was so backed up by the time we got there it took about 30 minutes to clear it out.

We had gone only a block or two from the office when Officer Slow asked me if I liked to direct traffic. I replied that I didn't mind it, and I told him if he would do it that day, I would do it the next day. He was sort of sheepish, so he reluctantly agreed. I didn't want to be pushy, but it was obvious to me that he had never directed traffic before, so I thought he should get his feet wet as soon as possible.

After about 30 minutes of doing a good job of flagging the long line of backed-up traffic out, he got back in the driver's seat. He sat for a few seconds, then took a deep breath and slowly exhaled it. He then said, "That wasn't so bad. Cramer told me they would try to drive over our toes, but nobody tried to."

I laughed. Officer Bill Cramer was a former San Bernardino Police Department officer, had been on the CHP for about four years, was well known to be a harmless practical joker, and was a bundle of fun. If he thought he could B.S. anyone, he always did his best to give it a try, and in this case, he hit gold.

On the way to Cajon Pass, Officer Slow proudly told me he had driven 18-wheel big rigs before joining the CHP and soon I could clearly see that he drove CHP cars the same as he had driven 18-wheelers.

The first time Officer Slow was driving and I saw a speeder going in the opposite direction on Cajon Pass, I said, "Let's get him." "Get who?" he replied. I couldn't help but think he either had tunnel vision or he didn't want to chase speeders at high speeds. Before long I decided it was the high speed that he was afraid of, and on Cajon Pass of all places.

I quickly told him about the speeder and to turn around and go after him. At the first break in the six-inch-high raised divider, he started to make a U-turn. As if he were driving an 18-wheeler, he cranked the steering wheel to the left about a quarter of a turn with both hands, and again and again. What should have taken less than five seconds to do took almost fifteen seconds. Needless to say, I never saw that speeder again.

On the first shift with Burdette Shidler, he told me to drive, and he would direct traffic at Norton. Shidler smoked and chewed on cigars, and I later realized he wanted to see how I drove. After the traffic direction was over, I headed straight for Cajon Pass. As soon as we got there, I spotted a speeder who was going northbound from Verdemont Junction near the south end of our beat.

Working with Officer Slow, we had never chased a speeder northbound on Cajon Pass. We always tried to work the southbound from Highway 138, because many of those speeders had driven at high speeds across the desert from Las Vegas, and when they hit our downhill Cajon Pass, they were so mentally adjusted to very high speeds, they would have felt like they were parked at 55 miles an hour.

I floored it and went after the sedan going more than 70 miles an hour. Luckily, when I started into the Blue Cut Curve, the tightest curve on Cajon Pass, I started into it at the extreme right edge of the right lane of the two northbound lanes. To my sad surprise, the damn curve just kept getting tighter and tighter, and the car kept slowly drifting into the middle lane. By the time we came out of the curve, the left wheels were about six inches from the raised center divider. I was scared breathless. Sitting calmly puffing on his cigar, Shidler said, "Damn good driving, kid. You just broke my record. I've never been able to make it at over 85." Still shaken, I asked, "How fast was I going?" "Ninety," he replied.

Convinced he was crazy as hell, I asked, "Why didn't you tell me about that curve?" "I just wanted to see if you could break my record," he calmly answered. With that, Shidler and I went on to try to scare the hell out of Officer Slow, and it was like taking candy from a baby.

The only restaurant on Cajon Pass was at Verdemont Junction. It was a great family-cooking eating place and was half price for the CHP. On the second stretch of shifts with Officer Slow, something strange happened. When I drove first, Slow became starved at about 5:00 p.m., about two hours into our shift. Then when he drove first, he didn't even start to get hungry until after 8:00 p.m.

Knowing that he was cutting my driving time to a minimum, I sort of went along with it and with a plan. My next first shift with Shidler, I told him about Slow's very irregular dining hours, and I told Shidler I was convinced Slow was scared to death of our driving. It was like I had given him a million dollars. He beamed and said, "You really think so?"

In addition to the lunch hour adjustments, one other event proved to me that Officer Slow was afraid of any speed over 75 miles per hour even when he was driving. An earlier shift, we were sitting on Highway 138, which was nearer to the north end of our beat, watching for southbound speeders. Slow was driving when a speeder went south at about 75 miles per hour. Slow slowly went after it, but when we went onto Highway 66, he topped out at about 75 miles per hour, about the same speed as the speeder.

From 138 to where the highway narrowed to two lanes at Devore Cutoff was not many miles, and if we didn't catch them before we got to the two lanes, they could mix with other traffic and we would lose them. I told him to kick it up to 90 or we would lose them if we couldn't overtake them before they got to Devore. It was like talking to the windshield. He puttered along at his top speed of about 75 and we lost the speeder in traffic at Devore.

So to answer Shidler's question, I told him about that maddening defeat. With that Shidler beamed again. It was obvious he was ready for the kill. I was off the next two days, and at the start of my next shift with Shidler, he couldn't wait to tell me all about his torture of Slow.

He said he was driving when they received a major injury accident call to the east of 66 in a residential area. He said they were at 138, so he headed south at 90 miles per hour. At Verdemont Junction, there were stop signs for both northbound 66 and the road that went south into an open area, then to the residential area a couple of miles farther south. He said there were no vehicles at the 66 stop sign, so he went through Verdemont Junction at 90 miles an hour.

He said when they had completed and cleared the accident scene he headed back for Cajon Pass. He said they hadn't gone very far when Slow said, "Burdette, you drive too fast." Shidler said he told Slow, "When people are in a major injury accident, they expect us to get there as soon as possible, and where did I go too fast?"

Slow sort of stammered and said, "Well, like at Verdemont Junction." Shidler said he loudly said, "At Verdemont Junction? Don't you know it's safer to go though intersections at higher speeds, because the quicker you get through an intersection, the less chance there is of somebody getting in your way and crashing?" Laughing, Shidler said Slow threw his head back, threw his arms up and cried, "Oh, no!" Shidler and I had a good, long laugh. Poor Slow!

Speeder in a Cadillac

I was behind the wheel with Slow sitting in at Highway 138 when a Chevrolet and a Cadillac went south at about 75 miles an hour. I gave chase and had them stopped well before the Devore Cutoff. I took the Cadillac, and as I walked past the Chevrolet up to the Cadillac, I noticed two Navy sailors inside. The driver of the

Cadillac was about 50 years old and his very attractive female passenger was about 25 or 30. He was a blustery type and told me that 75 miles an hour was not safe for a Chevrolet, but was safe for a Cadillac.

He must have thought I was an idiot, because the stopping distance for all passenger cars is the same. So I ignored that bit of bragging about his being a big Cadillac driver and issued him a citation, and without telling him he was full of crap, which I wanted to do.

The next morning I had to go to the Fontana Justice Court to testify in a February DUI accident I had investigated. In that the Fontana Court was miles west of the office and I lived east of the office, I stopped at the office to get a patrol car. I had just entered the squad room when Barney Shell, the senior sergeant, promptly came after me. He was widely known in the squad to be an opportunistic cheap politician of sorts left over from the 1930s CHP.

He immediately told me that the Cadillac driver I had cited the night before on Cajon Pass had started phoning him about midnight about my citation. It was absolutely obvious that Barney was more than hinting that he wanted me to allow him to fix the ticket, but I played dumb to that and went over and got some car keys.

Before I could get out of the office, Officer "Millie" Minder, the staff accident follow-up investigator, told me that the Cadillac driver had called him at about 2:00 a.m. to plead his case, but Millie in no way hinted anything about fixing the ticket. In fact, after retiring from the CHP years later, he became the Justice of the Peace of the Fontana Court.

Before I arrived at the court, the defendant had changed his plea to guilty, so I went back to the office. When I arrived, Millie told me of the latest event in the case of the obnoxious recipient of my citation. Millie said shortly after I left the office, my Cadillac speeder had frantically called the office demanding a Code 3 (Red lights and siren) escort to Orange County. His teenage son had ditched school with some others to go to the beach, and his son had crashed head-on into a concrete mixer truck and had been killed. Of course, he was denied an escort of any kind.

Millie then told me about the escort-demanding big shot: He was an attorney and had either been disbarred or nearly disbarred for unscrupulous and illegal misconduct, and he was a disgrace to the community because he had abandoned his wife of decades for a younger, flashy woman. Millie said his large family had a very lucrative business in San Bernardino, and he was the disgrace of the otherwise fine family.

With that, I was very pleased that I had cited him instead of Slow doing it. Knowing Slow as I did by then, I knew he would have caved in to Sergeant Barney Shell and let him fix the crumby $15 ticket. Based on all that had happened in less than 12 hours, it was clear to me that the Cadillac driver had taught his son to totally disregard the law, and it had caused his son's tragic death.

The story spread like wildfire throughout the office. The next shift I worked with Shidler, and he told me he had cited the son of the big shot for driving 90 miles an hour about a year before. Then the first time I saw benevolent seven-year veteran Officer Ray West, he told me he had also cited the kid for 90 miles an hour. He said after he cited the kid, he had him sit in the patrol car and gave him a long lecture on the death-threatening risks of high speed, and he was very sorry that his lecture had not done any good.

One contributing problem may have been that juveniles such as the son were cited to appear before county probation officers, and several months later when I cited a juvenile violator for the second time, I asked him what had happened when I cited him the first time. He laughed and said nothing. He said the probation officer just laughed it off. He then said he had received nine traffic citations in a couple of years, and probation officers never penalized him in any way.

He didn't realize he had turned 18 the month before and was no longer a juvenile. When I told him he was not going to a probation officer but he was going to see Judge Rodick in the Highland Court, he didn't think that was so funny. I told him he was a big boy now, so he had better get a good-paying job to pay for his tickets.

Also, it wasn't until years later that the law was enacted to require that juvenile traffic law convictions be reported to the DMV. If convicted of four or more in 12 months, six or more in 24 months, or eight or more in 36 months, juvenile violators would be classified as "Negligent Drivers" and lose their driver's licenses.

So with an attorney father who had no respect for the law, a derelict probation department and the failure of the state legislature to require reporting juvenile violations to the DMV, it was no wonder that the teenager sped his way to an early death.

Fatal Pedestrian Accident

I was driving on a Saturday night when Shidler and I received a call of a fatal pedestrian accident in the Fontana area. The radio report also said the west unit was tied up with a fiery crash, so we had to handle it. After using three highways to get to a wide north-south concrete roadway that also served as a flood channel, I pushed it up to 80 miles an hour, with red light and siren. We were about 300 yards from Foothill Boulevard when Shidler said, "Be sure to stop for the stop sign." "Aw, to hell with it," I said.

I timed it perfectly to stop at the stop sign if there was any traffic in sight on Foothill, and I held it at 80 miles per hour. Out of the corner of my eye, I could see Shidler pressing the floorboard with both feet, so I waited until the precise split second to apply the brakes to stop if necessary. There was no traffic, so I turned right onto Foothill at about five miles an hour. As soon as I had turned the corner, I said, "Gotcha." Shidler laughed and said, "Good driving."

On the first shift I worked with Shidler, he told me he was tired of investigating accidents and wanted me to handle all of them, so I agreed. When we arrived at the scene, the deceased pedestrian had already been taken to Kaiser Hospital by ambulance.

It was a two-lane county road with no lighting. I closely inspected the dirt shoulder on the side of the highway where the pedestrian had been struck and killed. There were no tire tracks or footprints, so the collision had to be on the paved roadway. Also, there were no skid marks in the roadway.

When pedestrians are struck, the hard rubber or leather soles or heels of their shoes always leave a mark or gouge on the surface of the roadway, but I couldn't find either one. I did find a piece of the victim's shin bone about two feet from the dirt shoulder on the opposite side of the road. I then interviewed the shaken driver of the car involved.

He said he was going about 45 to 50 miles an hour and passed a slower moving car. Just as he pulled onto the left side of the road to pass, he saw the pedestrian in black clothing right in front of him. He said before he could even hit the brakes, he hit the pedestrian.

As soon as I finished interviewing him, we went to Kaiser Hospital. When we arrived, the ambulance was parked in front of the main entrance to the hospital. The right rear door was open, and the victim was in sight on the gurney. I immediately noticed that he was wearing new yellowish soft-gummed sole shoes. It was a new style of shoes that had just appeared on the market. That clearly proved to me why there had not been any marks or gouges on the roadway.

When we entered the receiving room, Deputy Coroner McCarthy was waiting for us. He said he had phoned the Fontana Police Department to see if they would make the death notification, but when he told them the name of the deceased, they said not a chance. They told him they had been to the deceased's home so many times, they didn't want to go back unless one of them killed the other, and they thought that was a possibility.

Deputy Coroner McCarthy was about 55 years old and had been on that job for many years. It was obvious that he was burned out on making death notifications, and Shidler was far senior to me, so I was the one at the bottom of the totem pole.

When we left to make the notification, McCarthy rode in the rear seat of our patrol car. I figured he didn't want us to split and leave him holding the bag, and after what the Fontana Police Department had told him, he wasn't taking any chances.

The victim's residence was in a complex of cottages scattered about with dirt areas between them. I always liked to learn what I could about the victim's family situation before making the big move. If they had been married for 20 years or more and had a bunch of children and grandchildren, it could be rough, but if they had been married for only a few years and had no children, it might be much easier.

I knocked on the door of the cottage to the rear of the victim's, and a 50ish woman answered the door. I told her about her neighbor being killed and asked her if she knew his wife very well. She said everybody knew them and nobody would have anything to do with them because they drank and fought and the wife had been in two mental institutions in Pittsburgh before they moved to California and he went to work at Kaiser Steel.

It was getting worse and worse, but I was stuck with it. I told McCarthy and Shidler what the neighbor had told me. When I walked up to the wooden porch to knock on the door, McCarthy and Shidler kept their distance behind me. I knocked and a thin woman opened the door. As soon as she saw me, she took two short steps backward, and I could see at least a dozen empty beer cans on a coffee table.

I always tried to get the survivors to the hospital before telling them the bad news, so if they became hysterical, a doctor could give them a shot to calm them or knock them out. I told the woman that her husband had been injured and she had to go to the hospital to sign the release forms for his treatment. She took one short step back and said, "No, my husband just went to get a Sunday paper, so if you'll leave, everything will be okay."

We went back and forth like that a couple more times and by then I was convinced she thought we were there to take her to another mental institution. I went back to McCarthy and Shidler and said we had better call for a sergeant to try to get her to go to the hospital. I radioed for a sergeant to meet us there and about 15 minutes later, Sergeant George Goodwin arrived.

Sergeant Goodwin was a Texan about six feet two inches tall and had been an Army medic in World War II. He also was a former L.A. County deputy sheriff and was very assertive. I told him what the problem was, including my belief that she thought we were there to take her to another mental institution.

With that, he knocked on the door and the wife opened it. Sergeant Goodwin told her if she refused to go to the hospital, he would arrest her for obstructing an officer in the performance of his duty. This was a lie, because legally, she didn't have to go anywhere. She believed him and agreed to go to the hospital, but only in an ambulance.

I radioed for an ambulance and it arrived in about 10 minutes. She then demanded to ride in the front passenger seat, not in the rear with the gurney, probably because she had been strapped down on a gurney in the past. By then, I didn't care if she rode on the roof or hood, so I told her she could ride on the right front seat. We followed the ambulance to the hospital and I quickly went in to tell a doctor about our problem with her. The first doctor I saw was a woman, and I told her the problem. The female doctor took the wife into her office and closed the door. About 15 minutes later, the doctor opened the door and stepped out. She looked at me and said, "She's not with us. She's in her own world, so I'm going to have her committed for a 72-hour observation." With that, it was all over except for my completing one of the most difficult accident reports of my career. It was a fatal, not a property damage accident with no skid marks, shoe marks or gouges, no footprints or tire tracks on the dirt shoulder and only a piece of shin bone on the other side of the road.

As it was, it was Shidler's last month on road patrol. The next month he was transferred to the commercial detail to work the Cajon Scales, weighing and inspecting large trucks until his retirement. I felt very lucky to have worked with him. He was a hard worker, never scared me with his high-speed driving, which was much the same as mine, and he was a barrel of fun, but I couldn't help but believe that Officer Slow was overjoyed to see him off the highways and out of his hair for good — no more 90 miles an hour through Verdemont Junction.

But the fatal pedestrian accident wasn't over. About a year later, I was a Big Bear resident officer and happened to be in the Berdoo office, and there was a civil subpoena in my pigeon-hole mail slot. It was for the pedestrian case, and coincidently, the insurance adjuster phoned the office to speak to me while I was looking at the subpoena. He asked me if there were any footprints or tire tracks on the dirt shoulder. I had clearly stated in my report that there were none, so I began to wonder what kind of a simpleton he could be. Then he volunteered that they were willing to pay the widow the full personal injury liability of their insured, which was $10,000.

I was surprised and told him I didn't know why, because the pedestrian had to have been in the main traveled portion of the roadway, was wearing black clothing and was probably intoxicated. He said their insured had killed the pedestrian, so they were going to pay to avoid going to court. I then asked him why I had been served with a subpoena. "Because the two brothers of the deceased came out from Pittsburgh and filed a law suit for a hundred thousand dollars, because they claim his death cased his wife to lose her mind," he said.

"Are you kidding?" I asked. "Don't you know she was in two mental institutions in Pittsburgh before they came out here?" "How did you find that out?" he excitedly asked. "I knocked on a neighbor's door and she told me," I replied. "You'd better get out there and talk to the neighbors, the Fontana police and the female doctor who was on duty at Kaiser Hospital the night of the accident," I volunteered. "Oh, okay," he said, then hung up. About two weeks later, my subpoena was cancelled, and that was finally the end of the most involved, complex accident I had to investigate in my entire cop career. And I figured the insurance adjuster probably took all the credit for the great discovery and probably got promoted — for sitting at his desk and disposing of major cases over the phone.

CHAPTER 29

Petersonmobile

*"Look at what I'm driving," I said with a laugh. I
wanted to say it was a "Petersonmobile," but for all I knew
he could have been the late Commissioner Peterson's
brother or cousin, so I let it go with that.*

In April, May and June I was assigned to a motor on the 7:00 a.m.
day shift. Day shifts were usually quiet, because Berdoo was a blue-
collar town and most residents were working. There were only two
incidents worth mentioning.

The first was escorting the Convair Aircraft F-102 prototype from
the Riverside County line to the Los Angeles County line on
Highway 138. I led the escort through the city of San Bernardino,
then up Route 66 Cajon Pass to two-lane Highway 138. All went
well up to 138, and Officers Herald and Walt Cook, the Rose Bowl
Parade traffic directing expert, followed to protect the rear.

As soon as we turned onto 138, they all stopped for me to go to
the top of the hill, which was called Mountain Top, to stop all traffic.
There was a small grocery store at Mountain Top, but as luck would
have it, it was the one day of the week that it was closed — and that
soon became an issue as I started stopping traffic onto a wide dirt
turnout shoulder.

It was anticipated that it would take about 20 minutes for the
parade to go from Route 66 to Mountain Top, but there were
telephone poles on one side of 138 and pine trees on both sides. So I
told several motorists it would be only about a 20-minute delay as
they started collecting on the turnout, and I told them the short wait
might be worth it, because they were going to get to see the first
prototype of the F-102 fighter airplane. They were all pleased about
that, so we waited.

After about 30 minutes of waiting, I radioed Herald and Cook and
asked them how much longer it would be. One of them replied that it
would be about 20 minutes more, so I told each motorist it would be

197

about 20 minutes more. Well, that exchange of radio calls was repeated about three more times, and they were still not in sight.

Although the grocery store was closed, it was getting very warm and there was no place to get something to drink, the motorists were very good-natured each time I told them it would be about another 20 minutes. Each one of them laughed and one said, "That's what you said the last time and the hundreds of times before, so will we die here?" and we all laughed.

After almost two hours of waiting in the hot sun, the big plane finally came into sight, and the good-natured motorists took long looks at it, then departed very contented. Cook and Herald told me the wingspan was too wide to go between the pine trees, so they had to cut a bunch of them down.

The interesting part of the event to me was that my father-in-law was the superintendent of transportation at Convair Aircraft. He oversaw everything with wheels, from wheelbarrows and pushcarts to lowboys, such as the one carrying that F-102. I had expected to see at least two CHP units waiting for us to escort it across the high-speed open desert, but when we got there, there was only one car unit manned by the 250 to 300-pound legendary Officer Wylie Gainsworth.

Like so many other interesting CHP character officers, there were many stories about Wylie, who was assigned to the Lancaster substation. One was that he was very wealthy, probably from a family inheritance. He lived in a large, expensive home, played his grand piano and had a defanged rattlesnake as his pet. Another was that his favorite hobby was driving his permanently-assigned patrol car across the open desert through the sagebrush exploring for whatever he could find. In doing this, both sides of his patrol car got very scratched up, so when it got too bad, he would have it painted at a paint and body shop on his days off and pay for it out of his own pocket.

He was only one of many amazing CHP officers, including Stockton Captain Ancona, who had been one of the original "Quiz Kids."

One morning when I went to work, the "Santana" winds (not "Santa Ana," as mispronounced by L.A. weather forecasters. Santana comes from the Spanish and translates to "Devil Wind.") were blowing with gusts up to 50 miles per hour.

I was assigned to the west end where the sand would blow across U.S. 99 from the miles of Cucamonga and Etiwanda wine grape vineyards. When I got to the office through the near gale on my motor, Sergeant Barney Shell told me not to take a 1954 Oldsmobile because it could get sandblasted. He said to take the district sergeant's 1953 Ford.

Never having driven one of the late Commissioner Peterson's bargain buys, I headed straight for Sierra to chase speeders westbound on U.S. 99. I had been sitting in for only a few minutes when a 1952 Oldsmobile went west at about 80 miles an hour. I gave chase, and the great Ford V-8 soon topped out at 79 miles an hour. The speeder was over a quarter of a mile ahead of me, and when wind gusts hit the front of the Ford, it would slow down to 75 to 77 miles an hour.

That went on up and down for about 16 miles until the speeder got into heavier, slower traffic in Ontario. With that in my favor, I was able to turn on the red spotlight and pull him over. I could see he was about 40 years old and nicely dressed in a suit. After a courteous greeting, I said, "I stopped you for going 80 miles an hour for the last 16 miles." "Oh, if I had known you were back there, I would have stopped much sooner," he apologized.

"Look at what I'm driving," I said with a laugh. I wanted to say it was a "Petersonmobile," but for all I knew he could have been the late Commissioner Peterson's brother or cousin, so I let it go with that.

He was such a fine gentleman, I cited him for 70 miles an hour, and he was happy with that as he departed. For the rest of that shift, I concentrated on stop sign violators and defective vehicle equipment violations.

CHAPTER 30

Wild West Cowboy Cops

Many years later, I bought a large framed portrait of a grizzly cowboy wearing a well-worn Stetson. The caption at the bottom said, "There were a helluva lot of things they didn't tell me when I hired on with this outfit."

In July, I was assigned to the east car with Officer Pern Nielsen and another officer who was one of the most obnoxious, antisocial, verbally abusive, black-racist creatures I ever had the misfortune of meeting in my life. He had been an attendant at Patton State Hospital mental institution before joining the CHP, and after working with him for one shift, I concluded the attendants at Patton wore distinctive uniforms so they could be identified as attendants, not patients. He was a real nut case.

I had worked with three worthless officers on the San Diego Police Department and had been able to tolerate them for six weeks, but this animal put me over the edge in one shift.

Then Commissioner Caldwell saved me the first week in July when he put out the order that all officers would work alone every shift around the clock, seven days a week, and that was to start a week later on July 15th. With that, I had to take only two weeks of the worst torture of my 31-year cop career.

Less than two months earlier, on May 27th, Officer James Maroney had been fatally shot helping the sheriff in a shootout in Alturas, a substation in the Susanville area.

In November 1954, while I was in cadet training at the academy, the Big Bear Lake and Crestline resident posts were increased from one-officer posts to two-officer posts, and the second officer assigned to the Big Bear resident post later submitted his transfer request for the Susanville area.

The second Big Bear Lake officer with the transfer request found out too late that he was going to be assigned to the Alturas substation to replace the slain officer, with whom he had been friends in the Marine Corps, but it was too late to cancel his transfer request.

Coincidentally, it was also in November 1954 that Sammy Davis Jr. was in a traffic accident on Cajon Pass and lost an eye. CHP Officer Bill Poole, a quiet, unassuming, enjoyable gentleman, investigated Davis' accident.

Davis was returning from Las Vegas and had many silver dollars in his car that spewed over the highway in the crash. When the scene was cleared, Poole collected all the silver dollars. With no container to put them in, he put them in his trouser pockets. Some do-gooder or cop hater saw Poole put them in his pockets so he went to the nearest phone, which was probably at the Verdemont Junction, and called the CHP office to report the theft of Davis' silver dollars by Officer Poole.

When Poole arrived at the hospital, it was very busy and Sammy Davis Jr. was on a gurney in the hallway. Poole immediately told Davis he had all the silver dollars he could find and asked him what to do with them. Davis was in bad shape, so he told Poole to just put them on the gurney next to him. As Poole was interviewing Davis about the crash, the sergeant walked in and immediately saw the silver dollars on the gurney. Case closed!

Poole had collected the silver dollars on very busy Route 66 in broad daylight with some spectators still around. What kind of fool would openly steal anything with an audience watching? I couldn't help but think the crime reporter was from Chicago or an outpatient from Patton State Hospital, or perhaps both.

I wanted to be a Big Bear Lake resident officer for more than one reason. One was that I wouldn't have to work graveyard shifts. Also, I enjoyed living in the mountains and wanted a safe and healthy environment for my two children. Our lieutenant and two sergeants had been resident officers, so I thought it would be a plus on the first sergeant exam I could take.

The second Big Bear Lake resident officer was transferred to the Susanville area and assigned to the Alturas substation to replace his slain Marine Corps buddy, so my first Big Bear Lake partner had been there for six years, was burned out and was then number one on the sergeant promotional list.

Old Miners' Days

My first day on duty there was Saturday, August 6th — my 25th birthday. It was also the last day of the seven-day, somewhat unruly, wild, drunken affair called the "Old Miners' Days." The last day was the height of the affair, ending with a typical hick-town parade through the village, and the CHP always led the parade. My partner had his fill of it, so he told me to do it.

The "Old Miners' Days" event started with dozens of young men with nothing else to do wrangling wild, freshly captured desert burros up the steep rear grade from Lucerne Valley.

The burro wrangling was an overnight event. A year or two later during that trek, word came up that one of the wranglers had been bitten by his not-too-happy burro, and on another occasion a wrangler was kicked by his burro. On the overnight stop, the wranglers had to eat and sleep with their burros, so that might explain the burros' bad attitudes.

With that event over, I tried to orient myself to what I'd gotten into. The sheriff's office was manned by two deputies, a captain and a deputy, who had been on the job for two years. The sheriff's department was non-civil-service and very political, and the deputies had no formal training. They were given a gun and a badge and then only on-the-job training.

One of the first things my partner, Gil Stokes, told me was that I had to be crazy to volunteer for that resident post, but I thought he said that because he was so burned out. It didn't take long after I met and became friendly with the deputies that the lowly deputy made a couple of cutting remarks about "City Cops," and how they were hard-nosed, and he knew I had been one.

On the first Monday after Old Miners' Day, I met the judge, who was a Justice of the Peace or "J.P." as we called them. J.P.s did not have to be attorneys; they just had to pass a written test to be eligible to run for the position.

Judge Jack Matthews was six feet six inches tall and was well known in Big Bear Valley to be a drunk. One of the first things he told me the first day that we met was he wanted me to be at court every Monday morning, so I got the impression he thought I knew more about the law than he did and wanted my moral support — and it didn't take long to prove that I was right.

There was an elected constable who had been the only law man in Bear Valley until after World War II. His name was Coy Brown, he was also about six feet six inches tall, and he was proud to be from "Nor' Car' liner." He had a big black and white retriever named "Rudy." Another local man ran against Coy for constable in November, but Coy won and even his dog Rudy got seven write-in votes. Coy was harmless but never did a thing in law enforcement. His office was in his favorite bar across from the "Emergency Hospital."

After I had made my rounds of the local law enforcement, I was beginning to believe my partner was right. I was crazy. Many years later, I bought a large framed portrait of a grizzly cowboy wearing a well-worn Stetson. The caption at the bottom said, "There were a helluva lot of things they didn't tell me when I hired on with this outfit."

Every time I look at that portrait on display in a conspicuous place in my living room, I think of Big Bear Lake and all the exciting events the sheriff's deputies dreamed up.

Free Pass for Drunks

That same week, the deputy told me that newly-elected Sheriff Frank Bland, a former FBI agent from a desert cattle family, told the captain and him that they were not to make any misdemeanor arrests. They could only make felony arrests or with a warrant of arrest. He obviously wanted all the Big Bear Valley votes he could get, and drinking was a favorite pastime in the valley.

In due time, I became aware that giving drunks that free pass contributed to the many DUI ran-off-the-road traffic accidents on the curvy roads — many crashing into pine trees. Although the deputies told me a few times in the years to follow that they had warned some drunks leaving Chad's Restaurant and Bar that if they drove the CHP might get them.

The second Saturday I worked the 6:00 p.m. to 2:30 a.m. night shift as a DUI watch. My partner offered to ride along and introduce me to some of the finer people in the valley. We made a few stops and I met some outstanding residents on the south shore of the lake. Then we went to the Fawn Lodge on the north shore in Fawnskin to meet the owners, Mr. and Mrs. Gene Watson.

They graciously offered us steak dinners, which we of course accepted and had a great meal and an enjoyable visit. Not long after we finished our meal the phone rang. The lodge was closed when we arrived, so I knew it was for me. It was the Berdoo CHP dispatcher. He said the sheriff was looking for a man who had tried to kill his wife by running over her, and the attempted killer had left and headed toward the dam.

Attempted Killer

Stokes and I were about halfway between Fawnskin and the dam when we got a call about a car in a ditch about a mile west of the dam in the Arctic Circle. The Arctic Circle as it was commonly called spanned from Big Bear Dam to the Lakeview State Division of Highways Maintenance Station, and there was about a 600-feet-deep canyon abutting the highway to the south. "That's him," I said to Stokes, and he agreed.

When we got to the car, the engine was roaring, the left rear tire was spinning at about 35 miles an hour, and smoke was billowing from the tire. If we had arrived 10 minutes later the tire next to the gas tank would have most certainly burst into flames and eventually set off the gas tank.

The driver was sitting and staring straight ahead as though he was cruising along on a freeway. He was in a trance, so I reached in and turned the engine off.

I got him out of the car to give him a field sobriety test. As I tried to explain the balance tests, he kept bending over and picking up small stones and putting them in his right pants pocket.

He was obviously drunk, so after he had picked up about half a dozen stones, I told him he was under arrest for driving under the influence. Even though I did not witness him driving, the law provides that if a person is parked behind the wheel with the engine running, they can be arrested for DUI.

When I reached to take hold of his right arm, he violently pulled away, so I twisted his right arm and stepped behind him. At the same time, Stokes grabbed his left arm, and I handcuffed both hands behind his back.

Stokes sat in the right rear and we put the prisoner in the right front. I had to drive about a hundred yards to a wide pull-out area where there was a spring-fed drinking fountain. I made a U-turn in the pullout area then had to stop for a car that was approaching from our rear.

The 1954 Oldsmobile's door handles had to be pulled upward to open the door, which was a safety feature. As soon as I stopped to wait for the approaching car to pass, the prisoner raised his right leg, opened the door and jumped out. Not expecting that bizarre antic, I had not seat-belted him in.

In a flash, Stokes jumped out and got him under control. As the approaching car passed, the prisoner yelled, "Help, police." Then when a second car passed, he yelled, "Help, police."

We put him back in the right front again, and I seat-belted him in. Stokes got in through the driver's door and again sat on the right rear seat behind the strangest prisoner I ever had to deal with in my cop career. He then remained silent all the way to jail and during the booking process.

When I arrived at the sheriff's office and court on the following Monday a little before 9:00 a.m., a man about 50 years old and a young, pretty, petite woman were standing in front of the sheriff's office. Before I could walk to the door, they quickly approached me.

The man introduced himself as the father of the wild DUI and introduced the young woman as the DUI's wife. The insides of her forearms were severely scratched as if she had been in a bad cat fight. She explained that her arms were scratched so badly when she hugged a large pine tree to keep her husband from throwing her to the ground to run over her, and when he pulled her from the tree, the tree bark scratched her arms.

The father then started telling me his son's history. He said his son was a fine young man until he returned from the Korean War. After that, when he drank he went crazy. He said his son had been arrested two times before, once in Orange County and once in San Bernardino County. He said both times he kicked a policeman in the face and acted so crazy they committed him to a psycho ward which precluded his being charged with drunk driving. I said, "We don't have a psycho ward in Big Bear," so he went to jail.

The father and wife agreed that was possibly the best solution. They said their only hope was if he had to spend about six months in jail that it might give him time to think it over and get straightened out, and it would give them a chance to visit him and talk to him when he was sober.

We all agreed that if the wife filed charges against him for battery or attempted murder, it would make matters worse and would end their marriage, and there would be no hope at all of his making a recovery. So I said I would talk to Judge Matthews and have him sentence her husband to six months in the county jail on my DUI charge. They agreed with that plan, so I told the judge.

Judge Matthews agreed and sentenced him to six months. About a month later I went to the county jail for some reason. The jail was on the second floor, and when I stepped onto the elevator, there he was operating the elevator. He looked at me in a way that I instantly knew he recognized me. "How are you?" I asked in a friendly tone. "Fine, thank you," he replied. He looked fine, so I said, "That's good."

I figured his father and wife had visited him and maybe talked some sense into him, so I could only hope. He was a nice looking young man, and his father and wife were such sweet, caring people, I wanted it to turn out for the best for all of them, and I didn't want to deal with him again.

Teenage Hoodlums

The next major event started on Highway 30 City Creek Road a mile or two miles west of Running Springs. A car occupied by three young hoods broke down on the south shoulder of the roadway. A U.S. Forest Service ranger stopped to see if he could help, but he got suspicious of their answer, so he quickly departed and radioed for his station to notify the sheriff of the suspicious situation.

Two sheriff's detectives responded. One was about 50 years old and had the nickname of "Tom Cat." When the detectives asked the one who claimed to be the driver and owner of the car for his driver license, he said it was in the trunk.

Any good "city cop" would have known that was a lie, because how many drivers carry their driver license in the trunk? This was as bad a lie as the dozens of violators who could not produce a driver license when I stopped them and claimed that it was in their other wallet — and the routine office follow-up check with DMV showed that they didn't have a driver license. In most cases, their license had been suspended or revoked.

Most of all, a good "city cop" knows not to believe a word that a suspicious subject utters. Being political, on-the-job-training cops, not "city cops," they let the lying suspect open the trunk, and he immediately reached into the trunk and grabbed a handgun.

He and his two accomplices quickly relieved the two shocked detectives of their service revolvers and unmarked sheriff's car and headed east in the direction of Running Springs to where Highways 18 and 30 merged all the way to Big Bear Dam.

At least one of them probably knew the mountains, because they went west on Highway 18 toward Lake Arrowhead. If they went toward Big Bear from Running Springs, they would no doubt run into a road block at Big Bear Dam where Highways 18 and 30 separated.

The detectives quickly hitched a ride to Running Springs to the nearest phones and spread the alarm. With a sheriff's radio in the stolen sheriff's car, the juvenile hoods most certainly heard the APB broadcast, so they turned off Highway 18 and holed up at Lake Arrowhead's Rim-of-the-World High School.

They were quickly discovered there and soon pinned down by numerous cops of all kinds. It didn't take long for them to realize it was over and give up. About an hour after it was all over, I stopped at the Big Bear sheriff's office to gloat. "City Cops," you say, deputy?

When I walked in, the deputy was sitting at his desk with a plastic grin on his face like he had just eaten a lemon. I didn't say a word about the hick-town cop bungle. I just smiled like I had just won first prize in a debating contest.

The Hare and Hound Race

The next big event was the Big Bear Hare and Hound Race, a motorcycle race originally started in Victorville in 1932. Some time later, the starting point was moved to Lucerne Valley at the bottom of Highway 18 Cushenberry Grade and up the north slope of the mountains and west on a dirt Forest Service road to Fawnskin.

It was always on the first Sunday after New Year's, and about 850 crazy motor riders started in Lucerne Valley, but only about half made it to Fawnskin. It was reported that the others were lying all over the road where the race course radically narrowed at the foot of the mountains.

The racers were no problem. It was the outlaw motor gangs of the Hell's Angels and Galloping Gooses that congregated in Fawnskin who were the problem — and they came looking for trouble, as usual.

For four years, the Berdoo CHP office sent about eight motor officers and a sergeant to reinforce my partner, me and the sheriff's deputies. The race was like a powder keg waiting to go off at the touch of a spark.

One year an overzealous CHP motor cop wrote one of the dirty outlaw club members a citation for equipment violations. The rider then stole some scotch tape somewhere and taped the ticket to his headlight, then paraded back and forth among the gangs trying to stir up trouble.

I was standing alone on the south shoulder of the road across from the Fawn Lodge when a dirty motor club member swaggered up to me. He said, "If any of our people get arrested, we'll all come over and tear that jail apart." "Do you know how to get there?" I calmly asked. He looked blank, so I pointed east and gave him directions how to get to the jail.

He looked at me like I was crazy for not begging for mercy. Then I said, "About half of the men in Big Bear are special or reserve deputy sheriffs, and at least a hundred of them and the rest of us will be waiting for you." With that, his mood became decidedly gloomier.

"Also," I said, "the doctor's office is right across the street from the sheriff's office, but he and the other doctor in town will not treat motor riders. They say motor riders are always dirty and never pay their bills, and the ambulance owner won't transport motor riders for the same reasons." His mood withered even more with all that bad news.

Then I said, "So, if you have your own private transportation to haul your injured to Berdoo, we'll see you at the jail." He jerked both arms up to raise his sagging shoulders and swaggered away.

In that my partner and I had to work alone, thanks to Commissioner Caldwell, I was on the 6:00 a.m. shift one of the following Hare and Hound Race Sundays. I left home about 6:00 a.m. and headed for the sheriff's office to find out how many regular deputy reinforcements they had.

About a mile east on Highway 30, I saw two motors without mufflers. In the cold, thin air of the higher elevation, they could most likely have been heard across the lake in Fawnskin. I was always extra tolerant of the actual racers, because they were usually good people, so I made a U-turn and stopped the two to give them a warning and tell them to go directly to Lucerne Valley.

I asked the first one for his driver license, which was routine even for a warning. He was bundled up around his face, but before he handed me his driver license, he looked familiar to me. When I looked at his driver license, it was movie star Keenan Wynn. I looked back at the other one and it was Lee Marvin, another movie star. I told them I would like them to leave Big Bear, and they thanked me and departed.

Somehow I learned that Wynn and Marvin stayed at Gerald Dooley's higher-class lodge on Highway 30 next to Moomjean's service station and tow. His lodge was composed mostly of large, three-bedroom, two-bath structures like family homes.

I happened to see Gerald near the front of his lodge the next day, so I stopped to mention stopping Wynn and Marvin, who, incidentally, never finished the race. They weren't crazy enough to get killed trying and they probably enjoyed the excitement but had better things to do than to lie in a hospital bed.

When I mentioned their names and told Gerald I had heard they stayed at his lodge, he quickly said, "But no more." He then went on to tell me they had stayed there for a few years but he was fed up with it. He said they would let about a half dozen other motor racers move in with them and when they left, the place was trashed. I suggested he double their rental fee to pay for cleaning up after them, but Gerald vetoed the idea, saying it was too much trouble that he didn't need.

In 1960 when I told our much-hated new lieutenant when the Hare and Hound race was to be, he said he wasn't interested in my "fucking motorcycle race," and said he would send two "motor monkeys" up to help — and he refused to allow my partner and me to work together that day.

One of the motor officers sent to help was an officer in charge or "OIC" as they were called. It was an unofficial title for acting sergeant. He had been in the cadet class just before my class and was definitely not OIC material.

Without consulting my partner or me, the crossing at Highway 18 was moved from Doble Dump Road to about a hundred yards west of that location. In that I had to work the 2:30 p.m. shift, I took my wife and two children out to the crossing to let them see part of the race and see how the crossing at that location was working.

I parked to the south of Highway 18 in a weeded area. We had been there about 30 minutes when I saw the OIC was allowing spectators to park on both sides of 18. Not wanting to get blocked in, I decided to leave. On the way out, I stopped and told the OIC he had better not let them park on both sides of the road because it would result in one-way traffic. He ignored me and continued to allow parking on both sides.

Not long before I went on duty at 2:30, my good friend Bob Lowry, a Berdoo motor officer, showed up at my house and said he hated the OIC.

As soon as Bob and I got into the patrol car when my partner came to pick me up, the OIC was yelling over the radio for me to get to the crossing right now. I knew what the problem was, so I didn't rush to get there. I dropped my partner off on the way at his home in Big Bear City.

When Bob and I got to the crossing, the OIC was in a state of rage. The westbound traffic was backed up out of sight around the top of Cushenberry Grade about a half mile to the east, and the second officer, Fred Ellis, wasn't in sight.

I interrupted the OIC's raving and asked him where Ellis was. Fred Ellis was a fine officer and a very pleasant gentleman, but the

OIC was in charge. The OIC said he had sent Ellis down Cushenberry Grade to find out how far the westbound traffic was backed up.

Bob Lowry laughed out loud because once Ellis got to the end of the long line of backed-up traffic, he couldn't get back. He was too smart to pass all the backed-up cars on blind curves, so he was just a part of the back-up. I again interrupted the OIC's ranting and told him to stop the few eastbound cars and I would flag all the westbound cars through. The race was over, and most of the spectators were in their cars trying to leave, but they couldn't because of the two-way traffic on the roadway.

As soon as the OIC stopped the eastbound traffic, I stopped the westbound traffic to let the parked cars leave. In about two minutes, all but a few of the parked cars were gone, so I flagged the westbound traffic through. In about ten minutes, all was back to normal, and Ellis was back with us, just as if the OIC-created mess had never happened.

It was so simple that a Boy Scout could have unraveled the chaos just as easily — but not that OIC. When all was settled other than the still-enraged OIC, he said he was going to write a memo explaining how the entire event had been mismanaged and what a traffic jam it had caused. Bob Lowry asked him why he was going to write a memo when he was the one who had created the entire mess from the start. That only added fuel to the fire, and the OIC was more determined than ever to write a scathing memo blaming everybody else.

I was off the next two days. When my partner came to turn the patrol car over to me Tuesday evening for his days off, he told me what the lieutenant had told him when he went to the office the day before. He said the lieutenant was going to file charges against him, me, the OIC and Fred Ellis for dereliction of duty.

I told my partner to forget it, because I had witnesses and other evidence to prove the OIC caused the mess from the start, and knowing his sneaky ways, I knew he was trying to cover his own butt in the event complaints were lodged by some of the motorists who had been stuck in the long line of stopped traffic.

The next morning I headed straight for the office. When I entered the rear door into the squad room, the lieutenant was walking toward his office. He barked, "Come into my office, Nuttall, I'm going to chew your ass out."

I stopped and said, "Lieutenant, be careful, because I have much to tell you about how you screwed it up." There were a few officers in the squad room, just as there had been when he told me he wasn't interested in my "fucking motorcycle race." I entered his office and left his office door open so all within earshot could hear what I had to say, and I remained standing while he sat at his desk. I knew it wouldn't take long to shoot him down, and I wanted to be able to look down at him while I stated my airtight case.

"To start with, the president of the Orange County Motorcycle Association that sponsors the race held a meeting before the race," I started, "and I wasn't told about it. The deputy sheriffs were invited and attended the meeting, but I didn't know about it until afterwards when the deputy told me about it," I said, "and he told me the crossing of Highway 18 was being moved from Doble Dump Road to about a hundred yards to the west. If I had been at that meeting, I would have refused to let them move it, and I'm not happy with the deputies for not telling me about the meeting beforehand."

The lieutenant just sat and listened with his arms folded. "And when I told you about the upcoming race, you said you were not interested in the race, and I have several willing witnesses who heard you say it," I emphasized. With that, the lieutenant didn't look so chipper.

"Also," I said, "this was the first year the office didn't send a sergeant and at least six motor officers or 'motor monkeys' as you called them to assist us with the outlaw motor gangs. At least one of those sergeants is still in this office, so why didn't you consult him before sending two motor officers including an OIC who wouldn't listen to me and screwed the crossing all up. In addition, I have an uninvolved officer who is a willing witness to how the OIC caused the whole mess, so if you want to file charges against any of us, consider that charges might be filed against you."

I then turned and walked back into the squad room without saying another word. There were still a few officers in the squad room who had hung around to hear my campaign speech. They all smiled and then went out the rear door to the parking lot.

As it was, the lieutenant had told my partner that he was going to file charges against the four of us to suspend us for five days without pay. Within a week, I was told that the president of the Orange County Motorcycle Association had heard about the lieutenant's wild charges and offered to pay the four of us our lost pay if we were in fact suspended for five days without pay.

As crazy as it was, it prompted two very favorable actions. Within a short period of time, the bungling OIC resigned from the CHP and was hired by the sheriff who had been his chief of police in a small Mojave Desert town. And the big one was that Captain Freeman had retired after about 44 years in traffic law enforcement about a year and a half before, and his second replacement who took command just after the motor race internal war that was still smoldering was Captain Robert Hollingsworth. As it happened, Captain Hollingsworth had an extensive law education, and he took rapid action to end the motor races.

Without delay, Captain Hollingsworth contacted the president of the Orange County Motorcycle Association and told him the race crossed a state highway and extended for miles on a U.S. Forest Service road, which was also a public highway because it belonged to and was maintained by a governmental agency — and it was a misdemeanor to race on a public highway.

Then Captain Hollingsworth told him that when two or more persons conspire to commit any crime, even a misdemeanor, they could be criminally charged with conspiracy to commit a crime, and the penalty could be up to one year in the county jail or up to three years in a state prison.

Captain Hollingsworth told the association president if they staged another motor race, he would charge him and all the others involved, including the hundreds of racers, with felony conspiracy as soon as they crossed Highway 18. That ended 29 years of that illegal racing on public highways.

Jail Trustee Steals Sheriff's Car

The granddaddy of all the Big Bear deputies' screw-ups occurred on April 21, 1956. There was always a county jail trustee at the Big Bear Jail. The trustee at the time of this caper was Art Roberts, a hardcore alcoholic who wrote bad checks to support his habit. He

213

and the sheriff's captain had something in common. They had both been at the Battle of the Bulge during World War II, the sheriff's captain as a captain and Roberts as a foot soldier. With that in common, the sheriff's captain became extra chummy with Roberts. I didn't think that was a good idea because I knew hardcore alcoholics could not be trusted. They will usually lie to get whatever they want, but it was none of my business, so I kept my mouth shut.

There was an unlocked gym locker in the small public office area, and there were about three six-packs of canned beer in it. I once asked the deputy why they were there, and he said they were evidence, but evidence of what? First of all, there must be a chain of possession of evidence to identify it in court, which requires it to be secured. Also, about the only cases where alcoholic beverages could be valuable evidence are when they are illegally in the possession of a minor. But that also was not my business, so I let it drop and the six-packs stayed there undisturbed until April 21, 1956.

Roberts was usually very quiet and sullen, so when I walked into the fire department garage from the sheriff's office and met him coming from the fire department front office, I was surprised to see him smiling. Also, I noticed his face was flushed, but I thought he may have heard a joke that amused him.

When I went into the front fire department office, they told me that the deputies had received a call of a shooting in Holcomb Valley, which was north of Fawnskin and was one of the most remote areas in Bear Valley.

As I walked to my car, I noticed the deputies' Ford sedan was parked there, and their four-wheel-drive Jeep station wagon was gone. I figured they took the station wagon because the roads in Holcomb Valley were all dirt and very bumpy.

I drove east to Big Bear City at the eastern end of the developed part of Bear Valley. As I was returning west back to the heart of Big Bear, I heard the CHP radio broadcast that Trustee Roberts had stolen the sheriff's Ford sedan and was seen driving west toward the dam.

I later learned that the service station and tow service operator, Ted Moomjean, had seen Roberts drive by his station and called the fire station to find out if he was supposed to be driving the sheriff's car. I was way out of position to intercept or pursue him, but I headed west toward the dam to do whatever I could.

About 15 minutes later as I crossed the dam, the ambulance owner and operator was returning from San Bernardino and radioed that he found the sheriff's car abandoned just west of the Division of Highways Maintenance Station. The ambulance was equipped with an unlicensed six-watt transmitter. The FCC would not license it, but it was very helpful to all, such as in cases like this one.

I knew the deputies had a 30.30 rifle, a shotgun, and a Thompson submachine gun, so as soon as I arrived at the abandoned sheriff's Ford, I checked for the weapons. The 30.30 was in the dashboard Electrolok, and there were no guns in the trunk.

Jim Stallcup, the ambulance owner was still there, so I used his illegal radio to ask the deputies how many firearms were in the Ford. They replied that only the 30.30 rifle was in the Ford. They also said they could not locate any shooting in Holcomb Valley, so it was obviously a false report.

I was relieved to learn that the 30.30 rifle was the only firearm in the Ford, and the false report amused me. It was probably Roberts who called it in to get his pursuers as far away as possible in Holcomb Valley so he could get a good head start on us.

I put the keys back in the ignition and radioed for Crestline resident CHP Officer Don Hooper to meet me at the Green Valley Lake Road about five miles west of where the sheriff's Ford was located.

Hooper arrived about the same time I did, and we set up a road block for westbound traffic. We started checking all cars to be sure Roberts hadn't hitched a ride with some unsuspecting motorist or stolen another car in Snow Valley.

The sheriff's inspector pulled up and stopped. He asked me if the keys were in the sheriff's stolen Ford. I lied and replied that I didn't know. He thanked Don and me and left, knowing I had lied.

After about another 30 minutes of our road block, it started to get dark so we folded up shop and headed off in different directions. I went straight to the sheriff's office to try to help. When I walked into the office, the deputy was sitting at his desk with another plastic smirk as though he had gas, but he quickly went somber.

The door to the captain's office was closed. Then about five minutes later, it opened and Inspector Axton walked out, greeted me with a smile, thanked me again and departed. The captain slowly walked out of his office and said, "The inspector told me that if we don't catch Roberts before he gets out of the mountains, he's going to transfer me to Amboy and you to Vidal Junction."

The thought of that even scared me. Amboy and Vidal were small wide spots in the road in the middle of the desert. "I'll get Moomjean and Al Bloss as observers and head to the area between Arrowbear and Running Springs," I said. The captain replied that he would meet me there, but first he was going to go home and have dinner.

I couldn't believe it. He was going home to have dinner when looking at the prospect of going to Amboy? No "city cop" worth his salt would even think of that for one second. I picked up Moomjean and his partner Al Bloss and we headed straight for the Running Springs area.

I needed observers so I could keep my eyes on the curvy roads or I might run off the road and crash into a large pine tree, especially at night. As I touched the brakes to slow at the curve in front of the "Irisher Bar and Restaurant" just north of Dry Creek, we saw Roberts quickly climb up the south bank of the highway.

"There he is," Al Bloss exclaimed from the rear seat. Roberts was instantly out of sight, but we knew where he was and I knew he hadn't stolen another car and left the mountains. I went to Running Springs to wait for the captain.

When he arrived about 30 minutes later, I told him where we had seen Roberts. Despite my telling him that, he insisted Roberts had to be west of Running Springs. He said he had phoned Bruce Holder, the owner and operator of the Running Springs Union Station and had him drive back and forth east of Running Springs, and Holder hadn't seen Roberts.

I thought that was dumb, because in the dark any headlights could be a cop car, so Roberts would duck from all of them. So the captain went west and I went east of Running Springs.

Like hundreds of others, Bruce Holder was a special deputy and was mentally sharper than most of the politically appointed regular deputies. One morning he had called me instead of the sheriff's office and told me a trucker had stopped at his station and told him he had picked up two teenage hitchhikers in his truck, and he was suspicious of the two teenagers. The trucker said he would take as much time as possible going down City Creek so the CHP could set up a road block at the bottom of the grade.

I radioed Bruce's information to Berdoo CHP as I was in Big Bear. Two CHP officers stopped the truck at the bottom of City Creek. In searching the two teenagers, the officers found that one had a loaded .22 automatic pistol in his front pants pocket.

After they were arrested, they told the CHP officers where they had dumped a stolen car in Big Bear. I located the stolen car and had it stored at Moomjean's for the owner.

Knowing it was senseless to drive looking for Roberts, I parked behind the school bus garage at the Running Springs Elementary School about a half mile east of Running Springs. I turned off the lights and engine, turned down the radio volume and we waited and watched the highway and school playgrounds. About ten minutes later, we saw Roberts trudging up the south shoulder of the highway.

I radioed Berdoo CHP and told them to tell the sheriff's dispatch that if the captain would hide behind the large rocks just to the east of the Forest Service Ranger Station that Roberts would walk right up to him. About five minutes later, Berdoo CHP dispatch radioed that the captain had Roberts in custody.

I drove to the captain's location where I had said to wait for Roberts, and Roberts was handcuffed in the right front seat looking more depressed than ever before.

The captain departed for the county jail, and I headed back to Big Bear. I didn't tell Moomjean and Al Bloss, but I was unhappy with the deputies. Now Roberts would probably be sent to state prison for auto theft, and it was the fault of the deputies for leaving six-packs of beer unsecured, leaving the keys in their patrol car, or both.

The captain later told me that Roberts said he had consumed the pint of whiskey that was always under the front seat of the fire chief's car. Roberts also said every time he washed the car, he asked the chief to take the whiskey out of the car, because it was too much of a temptation for him. The captain did not mention how much beer was missing from the open locker.

The next day on the front page of the San Bernardino newspaper was a glorifying article reporting the expert capture of Roberts by the captain. It told of his World War II Army training as an infantry captain and his amazing skills of tracking the enemy. There was no mention of any assistance from the CHP in the capture.

When I finished reading the article I was disgusted, but I knew the paper only reported what it was told by the sheriff's office, and that glorious report would probably get Sheriff Bland many votes when he ran for reelection two years later. Politics, politics, politics!

A few days later, I received a very nice letter of thanks from Inspector Axton, but it did not say anything that could detract from the "Lone Ranger" version in the news article.

Starting in April 1957, the front highway to Big Bear was closed from 6:00 a.m. to 6:00 p.m. on weekdays to widen about a quarter of a mile of the Arctic Circle from two lanes to four lanes. Being the off season for Big Bear and with the west end of my beat shut off to me, I went to the CHP office as much as possible. I had to go down Cushenberry Grade to Lucerne Valley, then west through Apple Valley to U.S. Route 66 and south to Berdoo. It gave me an opportunity to chase speeders.

Returning from the office up Route 66 Cajon Pass one day, I fell in behind a speeder over a half mile ahead of me. The Dodge I was driving wouldn't go over 85 miles an hour uphill, so it wasn't until after I passed over the Cajon Summit and started downhill that I could gain on the speeder.

Before I could get up to a good speed, the car slowed and turned off 66 onto U.S. 395. There were four men in suits in the car and as it slowed and turned, one or more of them spotted me and the driver slowed down to 55 miles an hour on Highway 395.

I followed it for a couple of miles and picked up the radio mike as though I was calling ahead to other units to watch out for the potential speeder. I had no way of knowing if it worked, but it was the best I could do. I had passed an abandoned car on the west shoulder of 395 during my scare performance, so I made a U-turn and went back to check it out.

Stolen Car from Barstow

The first suspicious thing that I saw was a cardboard box on the left rear seat with three one-gallon bottles of orange cocktail wine in it — and on the right rear floorboard was an empty gallon bottle. I knew nobody would buy four gallons of that sickening-sounding stuff, and if they were that crazy, they surely weren't crazy enough to leave it for the taking, so I radioed to check for a stolen report on the car.

A few minutes later, it came back that it was a car stolen in Barstow. I radioed for a deputy sheriff to meet me at that location to take the obviously stolen wine as evidence. A deputy arrived before long, and I quickly got the impression that he had to be the dumbest deputy in San Bernardino County, or the United States. He immediately asked me why I had checked the car out in the first place, and I told him the CHP checked out all abandoned vehicles.

That surprised him. Then when I told him the wine was obviously stolen, he was dumbfounded and asked me how I knew. I explained it to him in very simple terms like he was a 10-year-old kid. Then I completed a stolen recovery report.

At that time, the CHP Victorville office was no more than the sergeant's desk in the sheriff's substation, so I asked the deputy if he would take my report and put it on Sergeant McDonald's desk in their office. He was only too happy to do that, so I left before the tow truck arrived and headed back to Big Bear.

The next 4th of July, some extra deputies were assigned to help the two Big Bear deputies. One was a veteran deputy from Barstow who had a pet monkey. We were talking about this and that when I asked him if anything had developed from the recovery of the stolen orange cocktail wine. He looked at me as if surprised and asked me what I knew about that case.

I told him the whole story and said I had wondered since then if anything came from that recovery. He got an agitated look on his face and asked, "Did you ever get a letter of thanks from the sheriff for your help in that case?" I said, "No." "I'll be a son of a bitch," he angrily responded. "The sheriff always sends letters of thanks to officers who help in any way with our cases," he declared. I knew he was telling the truth, because of the one I had received from Inspector Axton.

He went on to tell me that the fingerprints on the empty wine bottle had solved the case, leading the sheriff's deputies to a gang of seven high school boys who were serial burglars and had been driving them nuts. He then angrily said the deputy I had turned the Barstow stolen car and wine over to had taken full credit for solving the case and was promoted to detective as a reward. Although he was just learning the truth of the case, he didn't indicate that I should take any action to let the sheriff know the truth, so I just let it drop.

Obviously, that self-serving deputy had disposed of my recovery report, completed one of his own and never mentioned my handing the case to him on a silver platter.

The Fake Suicide Attempt

In 1958 the Big Bear deputies outdid themselves. That was the year Judge Jack Matthews had to run for reelection as Justice of the Peace in the Bear Valley Judicial District Court. He faced a formidable opponent for the first time — a retired Marine Corps lieutenant colonel who was a fine family man with two small children, who was also very intelligent and did not have a drinking problem of any kind.

In the latter part of the campaign, I was returning to Big Bear from the Berdoo CHP office one afternoon when the CHP dispatcher gave me the news — that Judge Jack Matthews had attempted suicide. When I got to Big Bear, I went straight to the sheriff's office to learn what I could about it. I liked Jack, but he was not judge material like his very able opponent.

The deputies told me Judge Matthews had shot himself on a dirt road just east of Cushenberry Grade and was in the Apple Valley Hospital with a not-too-serious shoulder wound. Then the San Bernardino newspaper article the next day quoted investigating sheriff's deputies as saying the judge had accidentally shot himself while he was hunting coyotes, and the investigating deputies were from the Big Bear sheriff's substation.

The original sheriff's captain had been promoted the year before, and the original deputy was then the sergeant in charge of the Big Bear substation. The entire concocted report was a bad joke, because hunting coyotes, bobcats and cougars did not require a hunting license.

A few days later, I ran into my good buddy and confidant Doctor Bernie Goodson. He was comical and pretty much of a sideline spectator of the Big Bear antics, and years later he wrote a book about it called, "The Valley of the Wounded."

He told me that one of the doctors at the Apple Valley Hospital told him that Jack Matthews must have had extensive knowledge of human anatomy, because he shot himself in the shoulder in a place where it caused nothing other than a minor flesh wound. Doc and I laughed about it because it was just one more example of the circus of life in Big Bear. Anything could happen and always did, and that was where he got the material for his book.

After his speedy recovery, Judge Matthews attended church every Sunday until after he won the election, then went back to his second home at the Elks Lodge bar.

By 1960 I was burned out with the 24-hour calls out of bed and the out-of-control politics, so I started looking for a soft spot to land where I could work eight hours a day on a motor. Also, since I couldn't take vacations during the busy summer months, I wanted an easy motor riding job with summer vacations to take my family to Disneyland and Knott's Berry Farm in good weather.

CHAPTER 31

Berdoo Legends

As much as Big Bear and Berdoo were full of so many hardships, I always considered it an honor and privilege to have known those legendary CHP officers. They were one of a kind in their own individual ways and are gone forever.

The state of California established the State Personnel Board and merit system as a form of civil service for the hiring and promoting of state employees in the 1930s, replacing the political system that had been used for more than 80 years.

Most important in the merit system was that an employee could not be punished or terminated because his boss didn't like him or didn't like the way he did his job. It provided job security as long as an employee performed his or her assigned duties in a satisfactory manner.

There are about 19 government code sections that can be charged against employees to punish them or terminate their employment. They include inefficiency, incompetence, theft, dishonesty, insubordination, intemperance and some other offenses — but not differences between employees and supervisors or managers.

Consequently, many of the old CHP officers, supervisors and commanders were extremely independent in nature and didn't always go by the book — and some went to extremes to get the job done any way that they could.

During my five and a half years in San Bernardino County, I had the pleasure of meeting or learning of a few of them.

Sergeant Walt Terry

Probably the most well known and admired was Barstow Sergeant Walt Terry. He was originally from San Diego and he had a brother who was a San Diego County Superior Court judge. My mother knew Judge Terry and campaigned for the judge when he ran for reelection. With that relationship, she also knew of Walt Terry and told me about him before I joined the CHP.

Sergeant Terry sported a handsome handlebar mustache and retired before they were banned in the CHP. He was affectionately called the "Desert Rat." Sergeant Terry's first assignment in the 1930s was to the San Bernardino County Office, and that was when that office and squad covered the entire county. Officer Walt Terry was assigned as the only Barstow resident post officer and rode a motorcycle over his beat spanning two hundred miles to the east to the state line at Needles and the Colorado River.

I never saw it, but I was told by more than one officer who did see it that there was a photo of Officer Terry riding his motor into Barstow with four small children hanging onto him and his motor.

The children and their parents had been in an accident in the middle of the desert and the parents had been injured. By some miracle, the children were not injured, but the parents had to be taken away in an ambulance, so Officer Terry was stuck with them and did the only thing he could — and that photo became legendary.

Another believable legendary story illustrates Terry's sporting nature when he stopped character actor Wallace Beery, also a sporting sort, for speeding. When Terry told Beery he was speeding, Beery said in his gravelly voice that he had a deal for Terry. He said they should have a shooting match with Terry's service revolver. If Beery won, he wouldn't get a ticket; if Terry won, he would. Terry agreed and they gathered some bottles and cans, set them up in a line and each fired six shots. Terry won and wrote Beery a speeding citation. Thereafter, each time Beery drove through Barstow, he looked Terry up and they had a nice visit.

During World War II, Terry accumulated about 3,000 hours of overtime covering the Mojave Desert alone. It wasn't until 1961 when the CHP began paying overtime — then overtime had to be taken as compensating time off. So when the war was over and Terry had some assistance, he filed to recover his overtime.

Terry's claim sent CHP Sacramento headquarters into a frenzy. A year of work was about 2,000 hours. If they gave him compensating time off, he would be off for about a year and a half. The CHP hadn't yet recovered from the shortage caused by the many officers still in the military after the war, and there was no overtime pay, so they had to get special dispensation to pay Terry about $4,000.

To plug that hole after the fact, a maximum of 80 hours of overtime on the books was initiated for all officers, but that didn't help me in a couple of long, snowy winters in Big Bear because when I requested necessary help I was told "too many officers were maxed out on overtime, so do what you can." The first year after I transferred from Big Bear to the CHP Academy in 1961, paid overtime was initiated. All I could say was "Thanks a lot you *$#@&%$#s."

By the time I was assigned to the San Bernardino squad out of the academy, Barstow was a separate office and squad, included the Victorville substation and George Air Force Base just north of Victorville.

With the always helpful staff at the base, it was well reported that when Sergeant Terry had to respond to a major traffic accident in the middle of the Mojave Desert, they would send a helicopter to pick him up behind his house and fly him to the accident scene. But those days are gone forever, and so are the officers the caliber of Walt Terry.

Captain Floyd Yoder

When I arrived in Berdoo, Captain Floyd Yoder was the commander of the Barstow CHP squad. Like Walt Terry, he was a class act, but in some different ways. He was a rebel.

Captain Yoder had two hobbies. One was that he was a "rock hound" and scoured the desert for prizes. His other joy in life was actively taunting the headquarters brass. It was well reported that he would drive to Sacramento on some of his vacations. There he would make the rounds of CHP headquarters and tell selected members of the staff how they were screwing up. Needless to say, he was not liked in CHP headquarters.

Starting in 1929 when the CHP became a statewide agency, the originals of all traffic and parking citations were batched by every field office and sent to headquarters. There a unit gathered arrest and citation statistics for the annual report, accounted for all citations and checked for errors on citations.

To check the efficiency of that unit and the process, Captain Yoder completed a traffic citation with the offense of unlawfully passing a stopped streetcar in the small town of Needles at the Colorado River. As he suspected, it went through without the usual response when an error was detected. With that, he had more ammunition for his next vacation.

Captain Yoder retired in about 1957 and my wife and I went to his retirement dinner in San Bernardino. The large banquet room was filled with about 300 CHP officers, friends, admirers and some curious onlookers to see if he was really going to retire. Even the supervising inspector zone commander from Los Angeles came with great hopes.

After much hoopla, Captain Yoder gave his farewell speech. In his hilarious manner, he reorganized the CHP by firing many he thought were under-qualified for the job and told them so on his vacation trips to Sacramento.

For about an hour, he had the crowd roaring with laughter — all except the 300-pound zone commander who was seated next to him at the head table. As Captain Yoder jabbed the top CHP brass, the commander's face got redder and more bloated.

After it was all over, I couldn't help but thank God for the State Personnel Board and the merit system. If Captain Yoder or anybody like him had been on the San Diego Police Department then, they would have had a very short career or a miserable one, walking the graveyard shift in Balboa Park indefinitely.

And with his very able Sergeant Walt Terry at his side, the Barstow CHP squad was probably the happiest and most hard working on the CHP, and like Sergeant Terry, he was one of the last of the breed that built the CHP to what it was then.

Officer Baldy Calkins

Another colorful Berdoo legend was Crestline resident Officer "Baldy" Calkins, who had joined the CHP in the mid 1930s like Terry. One day on his way to the office, he stopped in Berdoo for a Foster Freeze and a man walked up to him and told Baldy he was wanted for murder in Los Angeles and wanted to turn himself in.

225

Baldy told him he would have to wait until after he finished his Foster Freeze. The murder suspect waited and when Baldy was done, he accommodated the suspect by booking him in the county jail. It was probably the best arrest by a Berdoo CHP officer that year or that decade, but cool Baldy couldn't be rushed.

Another day Baldy was at the office stirring up something, as usual. His Crestline resident partner, Don Hooper, was on days off and was painting his house when he received a phone call that there was a two-car property damage accident in the middle of Crestline Village that was blocking traffic. Hooper's wife had taken their four kids to Berdoo in their only car, a station wagon, so Hooper put on his uniform shirt, cap and Sam Browne gun belt and responded to the accident on his oldest son's bicycle. It is for certain that would never happen in today's world.

Barbara Graham had been convicted of brutally murdering an elderly lady named Monaghan and was sentenced to death. When it came time for her execution in the late 1950s, the CHP district commander, whose office was in the Berdoo squad office, received a request to escort the prison car from the Corona State Women's Prison to San Quentin Prison. Graham was a member of the notorious Santos gang, and officials feared the gang would attempt to rescue her on the way to San Quentin for her execution.

Although Corona Women's prison was in Riverside County, Berdoo Sergeant Barney Shell somehow got to take over the detail, and it was a top secret, two-officer CHP operation. Sergeant Barney Shell decided to get his old buddy Baldy to be his sidekick, so he contacted Baldy and told him not to tell anyone, including his wife Dorothy about the assignment. It could be dangerous and had to be absolutely confidential.

Two submachine guns were shipped down from Sacramento, and Sergeant Shell and Baldy met at the office to start their top secret mission. No one other than the captain and district inspector knew where they were going or why. Everything went well until Sergeant Shell and Baldy arrived at the Corona Women's Prison front gate. From there, they could see into the front area and saw that it was full of TV trucks. With that, everything went to hell, but since it was well over a decade before satellite TV, it wouldn't be on the news for at least a few hours, so they got a running head start and had no problems on the 450-mile trip to San Quentin.

Graham was to be executed the next day, and Sergeant Barney Shell asked Baldy if he wanted to see the execution. Baldy said he didn't want to see it, so they had a comfortable trip back to Berdoo with their two submachine guns.

> The Barbara Graham story was made into a Hollywood film in the 1960s. It was entitled "I Want To Live," and starred Susan Hayward as Barbara Graham.

When Captain Hollingsworth arrived in Berdoo to take command, he couldn't wait to tell us that Baldy fatally shot an armed robber who had shot and killed a Los Angeles County deputy sheriff. He said the fatally shot deputy had responded with his partner to an armed robbery in progress. Immediately upon arrival, the armed robber fatally shot the deputy. His partner radioed it in and numerous officers from different agencies responded.

Hollingsworth said he and all the other cops at the scene took cover behind their cars and were exchanging gunfire with the armed robber who was pinned down inside the store. He said Baldy drove up and stopped his car right in front of the store, got out, drew his service revolver and stood in the middle of the street in the open. He said all of them yelled at him to take cover but he ignored them. Baldy then took the usual Camp Perry target practice stance, took careful aim and fired one shot — and that one shot killed the armed robber and slayer of the deputy.

Despite Baldy's dauntless courage, he developed a haunting fear. Like all resident officers, he would receive calls in the middle of the night to respond to traffic accidents. In the Lake Arrowhead and Crestline areas there were many sparsely traveled back roads, and he had experienced some threatening situations and backup was about 30 minutes away in the middle of the night. So Baldy got a big black female Labrador and trained it as his immediate backup.

I could empathize with him because of one time I was called out about midnight on a Sunday night. The fire department dispatcher who gave me the location on Cushenberry Grade said it was a one-car, property damage accident with the car ending up in an embankment. Then he told me that the reporting party said the people involved told him not to call the police.

With the serious question of why they didn't want the police to be notified, I devised a plan as I drove to the scene. I decided I would drive by the scene to assess the situation. If it looked suspicious, I would continue past, go about a mile, stop and call for backup. The CHP radio did not reach the Berdoo dispatch on that side of the mountain, but it did carry to the Barstow CHP dispatch. By then, we also had a sheriff's two-way radio, which would reach the sheriff's dispatch in Berdoo through Rodman Peak.

But when I reached the scene, all that was there was a gouge in the embankment. They had somehow got the car back in running order in the hour from the time the reporting party saw them, reported the crash to the fire department and I got there. I was relieved, but it gave me cause to understand Baldy's concern.

Baldy's New Partner

The first time I saw Baldy's dog was one day when we met in Running Springs. The dog was in the rear seat, and the right rear window was rolled down about half way. Baldy proudly told me the dog was his new partner and told me to pet her. He didn't ask me to, he told me to.

When I got about ten feet from the dog, she started snarling, growling and showing her teeth. When I stopped, Baldy said, "Go ahead. She won't bite you."

My experiences with a few vicious dogs were ones that would walk up wagging their tails, then lunge and snap when they got close, and I didn't think Baldy was crazy enough to get me bitten, so I walked up and put out my hand. The dog licked my hand and started beating the seats with her tail. Baldy said he had trained her to do that, and she wouldn't attack and bite unless he gave her an order to do so, or if someone grabbed him.

The dog's first event was after a car had rolled off Highway 18 near the bottom end of the Crestline resident post area. It was not far from Berdoo city, so Sergeant Goodwin rolled to the scene to help Baldy.

For some reason, Sergeant Goodwin had to use a radio, and Baldy's car was the closest, but he didn't yet know Baldy had the dog. He got into the driver's seat and started transmitting on the radio. About halfway through his transmission, the dog reached up from the rear seat and licked his right ear. With that surprise, Sergeant Goodwin told me he dropped the radio mike, but he had a great sense of humor and thought it was funny enough to tell everyone.

The next episode was when Baldy's partner, Don Hooper, got tired of getting black dog hair on his uniform and complained to a sergeant about the dog being in the car, so Baldy was told to keep his dog out of the shared patrol car. That order went over about as well as if it had been given to the dog. In his usual manner, he disregarded it. He felt his safety was much more important than Hooper's dog-haired uniforms.

The final episode was the summer night Baldy arrested a DUI. He had his dog with him, so when he parked in the county jail parking lot, he left the car windows rolled down. About a half hour later, a young CHP officer with a DUI to book parked near Baldy's car. He also did not know about Baldy's dog, so as soon as he exited his car, the dog jumped out of the front window, crouched down, snarled, growled, showed its teeth and started toward the young officer.

Thinking the dog was vicious and belonged to Baldy's prisoner; the young officer pulled out his service revolver and shot the dog one time. Luckily, it hit the dog in the back, went under the skin, circled its rib cage and stopped, and the dog quickly retreated to safety.

Just about that time, Baldy walked out to the parking lot. When he saw what happened, there was much yelling and cussing. Baldy quickly put his wounded dog back in the car, turned on the red spotlight and siren and sped to a veterinarian's office.

When Baldy tried to submit the vet's bill to the captain for the shooter officer to pay, the captain told him he had been told to keep his dog out of the patrol car, so he would have to pay the bill. That added fuel to the already flaming situation. I was never there when Baldy and the shooter were in the squad room at the same time, but some who had been told me they quickly departed before a shootout erupted.

Shortly afterward, Baldy went on vacation. At the end of the next monthly pay period, I was told to go by Baldy's Twin Peaks home, get his time and activity report and deliver it to the office along with mine and my partner's. The next day I went to the office to get my paycheck and my partner's, and I was told to take Baldy's paycheck to him.

When I got to Baldy's I asked how his dog was doing. He told me to go see his dog and I could see for myself that she was doing fine. He said she was in his pickup truck. Not expecting anything unusual, I stood less than ten feet from the pickup driver's door when Baldy opened it. The dog jumped out, then froze in her tracks looking at me.

Baldy said, "Go ahead and pet her." I took a couple of steps, leaned over and patted her head. She quickly licked my hand as before. Baldy said, "That's what I wanted to find out. You're the first one she's seen in uniform since she was shot, and I didn't know how she would react." "Thanks a lot," I said, "so I had to be your lab rat to find out." We both laughed and I never again saw Baldy's sweet and amazingly well trained dog.

As much as Big Bear and Berdoo were full of so many hardships, I always considered it an honor and privilege to have known those legendary CHP officers. They were one of a kind in their own individual ways and are gone forever.

CHAPTER 32

Burned Out

Then in June, I was notified to report to the academy the first week in July for a 30-day trial period when a cadet class was to start. It was great news, because I had to get out of Big Bear. I was burned out from the whole mess.

On January 2, 1960 I went to my first in-service class at the CHP Academy. Those of us at a great distance from the academy shared the ride with another officer from an adjacent squad in an over-mileage car that was to be exchanged for a new one at the Motor Transportation Section behind the academy.

I rode with 20-year veteran Officer Harold "Hardhead" Simpson from the Banning substation in Riverside County. He picked me up at the Berdoo office and drove all the way to the academy at 45 miles an hour. Despite the fact that the state top speed limit had been increased from the 55 miles an hour "prima facie basic speed law" to 65 miles an hour maximum speed limit the day before.

His patrol car was a 1958 Mercury, one of the worst CHP cars ever put in service. They were great family cars, but were not suitable for law enforcement abuse or high speeds. When making sharp turns, the hub caps opposite the turning movement would fly off and roll down into a canyon. On the way at 45 miles an hour, I saw several 1958 Mercury CHP cars in the central valley on U.S. 99 with no hub caps. They had all been removed. To this day and forever, there are probably hundreds of those hub caps in California canyons and ditches.

Simpson had earned his nickname of Hardhead with much hard effort. He was much like Baldy, but more like Captain Yoder. He had complaints about every sergeant, captain and inspector who had ever told him what to do or how to do it, but he had some good sense in his own way. He told me about catching 29 Palms Marines in stolen cars returning to that desert base out in the middle of nowhere during World War II. He said he drove them to the front gate at the base and dropped them off. He would then return to the stolen car and recover it as an abandoned vehicle.

He said he did that because they were more important to the war effort, there was little or no transportation to the base from the big cities and they might be killed in action. If so, he wanted them to have the best last years of their short lives that he could give them. I admired him for that and favorably compared his actions with the San Diego police officer who had fatally shot a sailor in a stolen car who had tried to flee.

Infamous 1958 Mercury about a year before "Highway Patrol" decals were placed on doors and trunk lid.

There were about 60 officers in the two-week in-service class, and it was one laugh after another. All except for one sad and frightened officer from a small northern California squad with a lieutenant commander.

When he returned from exchanging patrol cars, he was sad. When he returned to class late, he couldn't hide his serious problem. When someone asked him if something was wrong, he said,

"You'll never believe what just happened." With everyone in the class most curious, including the instructor, everything stopped to hear his sad story.

He stood at the front of the classroom and said, "When I left to come here with the last Mercury in our office, there was a happy celebration in the parking lot as I drove out. Even the lieutenant was there cheering." When he paused, somebody said, "Well that was good to get rid of it," trying to cheer him up. "No, let me finish," he replied. "When I went out to get a new Dodge, they gave me a Mercury that our squad totaled almost two years ago. It was totally rebuilt by inmates at Folsom Prison and I have to take it back to the office, so I'm going to drive real slow and hope the lieutenant is gone for the weekend before I get there, because he is going to be pissed off, and it's not fun to be around when he's pissed."

One of the many clowns in the class said, "Maybe if you take the hub caps off and throw them in the trash before you get there, it might help." Everybody laughed except the very sad Mercury victim.

"No," he replied, "I'm going to call the office to be sure the lieutenant has left for the weekend. Then I'm going to put the keys on his desk and not answer my phone all weekend just in case he drops by the office and finds them. He'll really blow up when he sees it has only 9,000 miles on it with 66,000 miles to go." The others who had not yet turned in their cars for a new Dodge were very nervous until they were sure they were not getting an old Mercury.

The first week I discovered that one of the newer duty officers who had replaced John Pedri, one of the duty officers when I was a cadet, was going to transfer to a field office. Pedri was then the firearms and first aid instructor. He had a twisted sense of humor he used to confuse in-service officers. Every answer to the 50 first aid multiple choice questions was C. He loved to watch the officers when they had answered about half of the questions and looked puzzled. They couldn't believe the answer to every question was C.

But he had another test with mixed answers to keep it more confusing in case the all C answer officers told their buddies who were scheduled for in-service training.

As soon as I learned of the pending duty officer opening, I went to see Captain Overhouse. He was very receptive and said he would keep me informed about when the opening would take place, but he said it would be months away.

Simpson drove his new Dodge as far as Bakersfield, where we stopped for dinner at a nice family restaurant. All the way to that point, he drove 45 miles an hour. We almost stayed ahead of a big storm that at times overtook us. He said it was very important to not apply the brakes hard for the first 500 miles because they had to be broken in slowly.

He then made phone calls to try to locate his favorite sergeant who had been in Banning and was then assigned to the Lebec substation of the Bakersfield office, but he never got in contact with him. By the time he gave up, the storm had overtaken us.

I drove the rest of the way and drove as fast as possible to try to beat the snow falling on the Ridge Route over the Tehachapi Mountains. One time he told me to slow down, but I ignored him. About 15 minutes after we had cleared the snow on the south side of the mountains, the radio announced that chain control was being established. We didn't have tire chains and we just barely made it, thanks to his 45-miles-per-hour driving and about a half hour of phone calls.

The sergeant exam was given later in January 1960. I passed the written test with a score of over 80 percent, which I later learned was in the top ten percent. I also learned that only about ten percent ever studied very much. I only got 75 on my oral exam and placed 215 on the list. To have a chance for promotion to sergeant an officer had to be in the top 100 or 120 on the list, which was a four-year list with three veterans' preference points until 1968.

The oral rating was a sham. Great preference was given to officers with a college education or those who were military reserve commissioned officers or had been commissioned officers in the past. Resident officers were marked down because the oral exam panel got the wild idea that they were on the take for free coffee or whatever from local untouchables who gave gifts and gratuities.

It was also later revealed that there had been cheating on the written test. One source of cheating was from a State Police officer. The State Police function was solely to guard large state facilities. The State Personnel Board did not lock up or secure entrance employee or promotional written tests, so a State Police officer stole a sergeant's written test and gave copies to at least two CHP officers who placed in the top 100 — and one was in the top ten on the list.

When this was discovered, it resulted in a major State Police scandal. One of the corrective actions taken was the removal of the chief of the State Police. Later, the CHP fired the two former State Police officers, but their dismissal had nothing to do with their cheating on the sergeant exam. One was fired about two years later for having an affair with a CHP officer's wife. The other was fired for stealing a case of beer from the trunk of a DUI suspect's car.

Berdoo Captain Hollingsworth learned of a Berdoo officer who had copied answers from another Berdoo officer's answer sheet when he went to the rest room. He wanted to fire the cheater, but the witnesses, including the officer whose answers he had copied, refused to testify against the cheater, who was later promoted to sergeant and retired at that rank.

Until later in 1960, all CHP radio dispatch centers were on the same frequency. No more than once a year there was what was called a radio "skip condition" that was somehow caused by sun spots.

One day in my waning days at Big Bear while I was driving around the Arctic Circle, there was a skip condition. Clear as could be, I heard a northern California CHP dispatcher call a unit. The dispatcher said, "Unit so and so, report of a lion on the shoulder on the highway at so and so location." The unit officer responded, "10-9." (Repeat message). When the dispatcher repeated the message, the unit officer again responded, "10-9." Then another officer said, "You heard her, Lion, L-I-O-N. Go get 'em tiger."

The skip condition quickly ended, so I didn't hear any more of the lion story, but as I laughed, I could envision the dispatched officer taking a safe route in the opposite direction of the lion's reported location.

About three months after talking to Captain Overhouse about the duty officer position, he sent me a personal letter. He wrote that there was nothing new about when the position would be open. Then in his humorous way, he said you could never tell when a big decision would be made at the "Palace of Pooh," as he always called headquarters.

His letter was encouraging, but I knew very well that there was always a chance that some headquarters suck-up officer could beat me out. Headquarters was crawling with all kinds of officers — with not much road experience, but lots of politics and desk duty shuffling papers they didn't know what to do with.

Then in June, I was notified to report to the academy the first week in July for a 30-day trial period when a cadet class was to start. It was great news, because I had to get out of Big Bear. I was burned out from the whole mess.

CHAPTER 33

Never Kick a Cadet

The most important one was sort of a joke, but very true. It was, "Never kick a cadet because he might be your captain some day."

Duty Officer Orville "O.P." Johnson had been in that position for at least 12 years, and he tutored me on some of the academy policies and philosophies. The most important one was sort of a joke, but very true. It was, "Never kick a cadet because he might be your captain some day."

Although Captain Overhouse didn't have to worry about that happening to him, unless the cadet became his inspector, he definitely believed in treating all cadets with courtesy and respect. He was well educated and stressed that we were there to train and educate cadets, not to try to turn them into programmed robots with our ideas of how they should act or perform. He wanted them to think for themselves like adult men.

O.P. then told me of one officer in the past who had gone through a 30-day trial period and failed in every way. When O.P. told me the officer's name, I knew what he was going to tell me. That officer had been in my cadet class, and he was a big blow-hard who walked around with a lighted cigarette clamped between his teeth, even when he talked. Of the eight or so cadets in our class who were considered odd balls or know-it-alls, he was near the top of the list.

O.P. said he treated the cadets like Marine Corps boots and said he couldn't be bothered with answering questions about the department or clarifying some of the material presented in the classroom. That was the job of the duty officers — to answer all the questions they could. That was why they had been called "den mothers" for so many years.

It wasn't until I reported for my trial period that I was told I would assist O.P. with the motorcycle training and that the department had initiated advanced motorcycle training to qualify and test officers before being assigned to motors.

Since day one of the CHP, all cadets had to take motorcycle training. The problem was that when the academy staff recommended that a graduated cadet never be assigned to motors because of poor riding skills, their recommendation was ignored and cadets were assigned to motors if sent to a Los Angeles office. The result was that far too many officers were being seriously injured or killed.

With those motor accidents increasing, all officers assigned to motors had to pass the advanced motorcycle training and testing before being assigned, and motorcycle skill pay was initiated. For the first few years thereafter, they had to submit a daily report and were paid only for that riding day.

Not surprising, the motor pay gave some veteran officers new life. One was a 20-year veteran who had never ridden motors on the CHP. Another 20-year veteran had given up motors years before, but with the smell of money, these officers instantly became motorcycle hounds — and despite the fact that CHP motor officers always took their motors home and had free transportation to and from work.

Becoming a motor officer became a do-or-die goal for some. O.P. and I trained one young officer who failed advanced motor training miserably. When we took him in to the Duty Office and told him behind the closed door, he cried and sobbed. Even though he was denied a motor for his own good to keep him alive, he wanted a motor at any cost.

Captain Overhouse asked me if I could come to the academy if the department would not pay my relocation expenses. I told him I couldn't because I hadn't been able to sell my Big Bear home. At that time, the real estate market was depressed and Big Bear Lake was a mud puddle, which always depressed the Bear Valley real estate market. In addition, about ten school teachers had resigned from the Big Bear School District because of the ultra-liberal, progressive policies of the superintendent. Captain Overhouse said he would do what he could.

The next Sunday was halfway through my 30 days and I went home for five days. I drove a new Dodge to the L.A. zone office and picked up an over-mileage Mercury, which the zone fleet manager warned me not to drive over 50 miles an hour or the engine might blow out. That was just what I needed — another snail's-pace drive to the academy. Even with that, it was worth the trip to see my wife and two children, but there were still no prospects for selling our home.

I arrived at the academy just at the afternoon coffee break, so I went into the dining room where some of the staff members were taking their break. As soon as I sat down at the table with them, I was told Captain Overhouse had gotten approval for my relocation expenses. Then an officer who had just been promoted to sergeant and had applied for a transfer to an L.A. office asked me if I had ever used balloon intoximeters. "Yes," I said, "I used them for over five years in San Bernardino and Big Bear, and in Big Bear, I arrested more drunk drivers than any other officer in the Berdoo office month after month."

"Great," he said. "You can teach the drunk driver class." He then explained to me that drunk-driving accidents had increased so much starting in 1957 that Commissioner Brad Crittenden ordered the academy to start a drinking driver enforcement class to emphasize that enforcement, and he didn't want to teach it as an associate instructor and have to travel from Los Angeles to do it.

Up until that time, drunk driver laws were taught in the Vehicle Code class, but there was no instruction on how to detect, test and arrest drunk drivers. In that it was a new class, I had to start with nothing other than the drunk driver laws, and I had never written a lesson plan, which was required for the academy files. I had to rush to teach the class to the cadet class that was then in session.

DUI Laboratory

The class went well enough, and Captain Overhouse told me we should have a DUI laboratory as he so appropriately named it. It was actually getting two or three cadets drunk or half drunk and having them perform field sobriety tests in front of the class. The name of that exercise had to be most proper because it was illegal to drink alcoholic beverages on CHP property.

There were no more cadet classes until April 1961 because new California Governor Pat Brown put a stop to CHP expansion in 1959. With no cadet classes for six months, it gave me time to refine the class, so I went to the California Department of Justice Laboratory two doors to the west of the academy and recruited the criminologists for technical assistance. They tested for blood alcohol levels for many police agencies, and they were so interested in the class that they attended every so-called laboratory after that.

Captain Overhouse's original idea was to get one cadet to a level of about 0.15, the presumptive level of driving under the influence and give the second one just two beers, because it was common for DUI suspects to say they had only two beers.

In practice it didn't work very well because the two-beer cadet would finish his two beers before the 0.15 cadet finished his six or more whiskeys, so I increased it to three cadets and let the good times roll and got all of them drunk. And I let the cadet class select the participants because they knew which cadets were the class clowns much better than I did.

Then I got police equipment merchant George F. Cake's representative to provide an electronic intoximeter and we had a roaring good time. With the intoximeter, we tested the drunken cadets before taking them into the class room, so we knew what their blood alcohol levels were before giving them the field sobriety tests in front of the cadets. The participants did not have dinner until after the tests.

Drinking on an empty stomach is quite common in DUI cases. A person gets off work at about 5:00 p.m., goes to a bar without eating, drinks until closing time at 2:00 a.m., then gets behind the wheel. And from my experiences, they can be the most dangerous of DUI cases, because they are well under the influence in addition to being mentally and physically exhausted. With that combination, they are the ones most likely to fall asleep and hit another car head-on or run off the road.

At least one of the cadet drunks proved that was true. While anticipating putting on their sobriety show before their classmates, they were able to keep control of their mental faculties, but when they sat down in the dining hall and relaxed, everything started spinning. One cadet passed out and fell face first into his plate of food and didn't move, but we sat him up and saved him from suffocating.

Knowing that scenario from my more than eight years in the field, I told the first cadet class I instructed that it was my opinion that late, exhausted DUI suspects were the most dangerous.

Without knowing I had told them that, when I let the supervisor of the DOJ laboratory say his piece, he said just the opposite. He said the people who had several drinks and then drove were more dangerous because their inhibitions were lessened and they were still full of energy. I didn't say a word to contradict him during or after the class. For a couple of classes to follow, I didn't mention my theory of late, exhausted DUI suspects being more dangerous.

Then the DOJ criminologist supervisor who contradicted my theory was replaced by a young, sharp supervisor. Although I had not mentioned my theory to him, he expressed the same opinion, and he didn't have any actual DUI arrest experience. When I told him about the conflicting theories, mine and the former DOJ supervisor's, he said, "It's only common sense to figure that one out."

Obviously to be a DOJ criminologist it required no less than a Bachelor of Science degree. It again proved to me that police work can only be learned on the street, or some little bit can be acquired by a person with good common sense, but there are no "Common Sense 101" courses in colleges or universities. In more recent police academies, there is a course called "Problem Solving and Decision Making" that is as close to being a common sense course as possible. So, until institutions of higher learning start teaching common sense, much of their other teachings can be a waste of time. Common sense is essential.

The Drunk Driver Enforcement class turned out to be a huge success, thanks to Captain Overhouse's "laboratory."

One day when I was talking to John Pedri, the Academy firearms instructor, I asked him whey we didn't have shotguns. He said the legislature considered the CHP to be their "golden boys," and thought if we had shotguns we would be viewed as state troopers by the public and lose our image of being the protectors of all on the highways.

I said, "That doesn't make any sense, because most of our officers work alone and their safety is much more important than a Boy Scout image." "I know," John replied, "but that's the legislature for you. In the end, votes count more than CHP officer safety, and they don't want to lose any votes for turning the CHP into what might appear to be a general state trooper outfit."

The CHP Academy was a tour attraction for many. School children, CHP supporters and the curious often toured the facilities and asked many questions. Some questions were stupid and others quite intelligent, but they were all asked in good faith, so I did my best to answer them as well as I could, and those who asked appeared to be satisfied.

Princes of the Highways

One night during in-service training, I conducted a tour for the managers of the California Youth Authority (CYA), including the director of that department. As I always did after the tour of the facilities, I had them go into a classroom for a question and answer session. The first question was from the CYA director. He asked why CHP officers were so courteous and respectful as opposed to city cops, who were so rude and arrogant.

Putting on my best thinking cap, I answered that it started way back at the beginning in 1929 when the type of officers hired were called "princes of the highways" by many. I then said the oral panels that interviewed the candidates did an excellent job of screening out the social misfits.

I concluded that the academy staff set an example of authority over the cadets by treating them with the same courtesy and respect that they expected the cadets to treat the public on the highways after they graduated. The CYA director was most pleased with my lengthy, historic explanation.

At the front door while they were leaving, they all shook my hand, including one with no right arm who shook my hand with his left hand. Then they departed. With so much else to do, I dismissed that tour as just another demanding day on the job. Then about a month later, I was walking up the front hall toward the front foyer and Captain Overhouse and Inspector Bob Blossom were walking toward me from the captain's office. Just before I reached the foyer, Inspector Blossom said, "There he is now."

I thought, "Oh, God, what did I do now?" I already knew it didn't take much to screw up the touchy minds of headquarters brass. Too many were real nit-pickers. Inspector Blossom smiled and said, "You really made the training division and the academy look great."

By then the three of us were in the foyer and he told me what had happened. He said there had been a conference of all state department heads in Yolo County the week before, and Commissioner Brad Crittenden was the chief speaker. He said as soon as the commissioner got behind the lectern on the podium, one of the hundreds in the crowd raised his hand and asked the commissioner why CHP officers were so courteous and respectful when city officers were so rude and disrespectful. He said the commissioner hesitated and seemed to be at a loss for an answer.

Then the CYA director quickly raised his hand and said, "I think I can answer that for you commissioner. When my group and I toured the CHP Academy, Officer Nuttall told us why highway patrol officers are so courteous and respectful."

Inspector Blossom said the CYA director emphasized how the academy staff treated the cadets with courtesy and respect as an example of how they should treat the public. He said it really made the training division and academy look great and got the commissioner off the hook and saved him from embarrassment.

I was pleased for Commissioner Crittenden because he was liked and admired by CHP officers mostly because he had made it known that he was not in favor of all-out ticket writing — much to the unhappiness of the other headquarters brass. Also, he had only been commissioner for about a year and could not have a bright answer for every question.

The main result of that routine incident in my academy days was that I accidentally jumped to the top of Inspector Blossom and Captain Overhouse's hero list in one stumbling leap. It was all because the CYA director was such an avid CHP admirer that he would ask that probing question.

Val Bates was an officer when I attended in-service training less than a month before the sergeant exam. He did well on the exam and was promoted to sergeant and assigned to the Ventura squad office before I was transferred to the academy. About a year later, he transferred back to the academy, and he and I soon became friends. Our common factor was that we were not veterans and had to try to overcome the three veterans' point preference on promotional exams. He was also very intelligent and had a great sense of humor.

Look Out for the Rocks

In swapping humorous on-the-job stories, he told me about a 20-year-veteran Ventura officer who was always in hot water for not writing traffic tickets. He said for years the captain called the officer into his office every quarter and chewed him out for lack of enforcement activity. Every time, the officer told the captain that he knew his activity was low and he would really try to do better, but he never improved his activity.

Bates said he was sitting in the sergeants' office at the end of the day shift one day when the problem officer came in smiling to tell him about his big enforcement day. The officer always patrolled the steep U.S. 101 Conejos Grade at the east end of Ventura County. It abutted a hill to the south of the highway and rocks rolled onto the road. Bates said he was so surprised that he complimented the officer and asked him how he did it.

The officer replied, "You know all those signs that say 'Look out for the rocks?' Hell, nobody was looking for the rocks, so I wrote a full book of 25 tickets and could have written more if I hadn't run out of tickets." Bates said he was aghast, because the look out for the rocks signs were yellow advisory warning signs, not black and white regulatory enforceable signs, so he asked the officer to let him see them. He said the officer just turned and walked out of the sergeants' office and said, "I'll try to do better tomorrow."

Of course, there were no such tickets or any other kind of ticket turned in by the officer that day — just another trip to the captain's office at the end of the quarter was all he had to offer.

CHP Poster Boy

Bates pushed me to be the "CHP Poster Boy." First he took me to the Red Cross office for a publicity contribution campaign photo, then for the front and back covers of the first CHP informational recruitment booklet, and then for the CHP Annual Report and numerous training photos. It became clear to me why he pushed for me to be photographed so much in the late 1960s when I was the academy sergeant supervisor and instructor of the Riot Control course.

I took a graphic arts photographer in an unmarked gray Plymouth to the violent demonstrations at San Francisco State to take training films. I parked at the curb next to where a San Francisco Police Department sergeant had a squad of about 20 officers lined up on the sidewalk. They were known as the "Tac Squad," short for Tactical Squad, a highly trained riot squad.

When I asked the sergeant how to get to the Administration Building where we were going to set up on the roof, he gave directions. I thanked him and the photographer and I started to leave. Then he warned, "You'd better get ready to run like hell, because you've got cop written all over you." I hadn't told him I was a CHP officer, but he wasn't the first person to tell me that. Years before, a state DEA agent said the same thing when I showed an interest in joining the DEA.

The Deficient Twin

In April 1962, one of the most troublesome cadet classes started. It was from the top of a new eligibility list, and the general attitude of many in the class was that they were God's gift to the CHP. To make it worse, they were the first class to have their retirement contributions deducted starting with their first paycheck. Up until then, retirement deductions started after the six-month probationary period ended and officers became permanent employees. Most of all, it was the first 16-week cadet class after years of 12-week classes.

Aside from all that, one cadet stood out as not being qualified to be on any CHP eligibility list. I first noticed his lack of intelligence one night when I was working in the duty office and the class was in the classroom for their 6:00 p.m. to 8:00 p.m. study hall. I heard someone talking on the pay phone across the hall from the duty office, so I walked over and knocked on the door. The door opened and the deficient cadet was standing with the phone in his hand wearing civilian clothes and bedroom slippers. "Where are you supposed to be?" I asked, because study hall was mandatory. With a confused look on his face, he paused and said, "Oh." I told him to immediately get into his cadet uniform and go into the classroom.

For a little over a month, he sort of blended in with the many troublemakers who thought they had been put upon by the changes they had to suffer through. The cadets were required to take notes in every class and submit finished notes at announced intervals. They were then checked by a sergeant for spelling, grammar, punctuation and neatness.

The obviously deficient cadet's notes were horrible — so bad that the sergeant checking the notes looked in the cadet's employment records and found out which high school he had attended. The sergeant then sent a letter to the principal of that high school asking for a transcript of the cadet's grades. The principal knew why the sergeant had requested the transcript, so he sent a copy and a copy of his twin brother's transcript. The cadet had a "D" average and his identical twin brother had a straight "A" average. The cadet's twin brother had obviously taken the written test for him and probably the oral and physical agility tests that were conducted at the same time.

It would have been difficult if not impossible to prove, so the only practical recourse was to notify the State Personnel Board. That was done, and the board initiated a stricter proof of identification on future tests.

By some quirk of fate and probably by cheating on several written tests the twin graduated and was assigned to the South Los Angeles squad office. About a year later, Sergeant Howard Brutchy came to the academy for in-service training. He had been on the San Diego Police Department and had quit to join the CHP a year or so before I joined the SDPD. He was very intelligent and didn't shy away from doing his job as many sergeants were prone to do.

At the first opportunity, Brutchy asked me if I remembered the deficient twin when he was a cadet. I told him I could never forget the twin when he was cadet, and we were certain his identical twin brother had taken all the entrance exams for him — and to make it more obvious, he was in the first class from the top of the new list.

Sergeant Brutchy told me he quickly noticed the twin was dumb when he responded to a major injury accident Code 3 from the office one afternoon shift. He said the accident was at Artesia and Avalon, just a few miles from the office. All the twin had to do was drive north to Artesia and turn right, then go about a mile to Avalon and the accident scene. He said it shouldn't have taken the twin more than five minutes to arrive at the accident scene, but it took him about 25 minutes in broad daylight.

Sergeant Brutchy also said when the twin had to investigate an accident in the last half of his shift or had more than one to investigate in one shift, he always returned to the office at least an hour after the end of his shift and never claimed overtime. Brutchy said that made him suspect that the twin officer was going somewhere to have someone help him complete his accident reports — probably his wife.

With that suspicion, Brutchy said he told the captain what he thought the twin officer was doing and the captain agreed. They decided to test the twin by making him complete an accident report with Brutchy watching.

CHP accident reports required a diagram depicting the scene with measurements of the street or streets, skid marks, debris, the location of vehicles and any other evidence. In addition, all the information on the diagram had to be described in the Facts Section in narrative form, which required exact duplication.

Brutchy said he drew a simple diagram of a right-angle intersection with two cars at right angles in the middle of it with skid marks and debris in the roadway. He gave it to the twin, had him sit in the sergeants' office, told him to complete the Facts Section and watched him struggle with it. He said when the twin finally completed the Facts Section with much difficulty it didn't make any sense. It was a jumble of mess and confusion. Brutchy said he took it to the captain and they agreed to call the twin into the captain's office and offer him the opportunity to resign or be terminated. He resigned.

With that waste of CHP funds to employ and train a deficient imposter, it made me wonder what the odds were of that ever happening. How often could it be that identical twins could have such a wide range of intellectual capacity, and if so, how many would he so obsessed with becoming a CHP officer they would get their identical twin brother to take all the tests? And how many identical twin brothers would be dumb enough to commit fraud by taking the tests for their twins?

The odds were staggering. They had to be at least a million to one.

In November 1960, the one-year very unpopular training division inspector who was instrumental in creating the most shameful sergeant list in CHP history had O.P. Johnson transferred from the academy to his home town of San Francisco. It was his last disdainful act before being transferred to the Los Angeles zone headquarters, a transfer for which he had been waiting for over a year.

I was thrilled to see that inspector go for personal reasons. He never did me any harm, but he resided at the academy and I had to dine with him every evening. Every time I said anything and many times just to make conversation, he would ask, "Why do you say that?"

Then I would try to justify what I had said. It didn't take me very long to come to the conclusion that he was in his sneaky way trying to pick my brain to learn something he didn't already know. So I learned to eat my dinner in silence as fast as I could and get out of the dining room as soon as possible.

He was a health nut and worked out in the gym in tennis shoes. Any number of times when I was carrying on a private conversation with someone in the Duty Office, he would silently appear just outside the door in the hallway. I never knew how long he had been listening, but I suspected he had probably heard an earful before he appeared. He was a really creepy spy.

But his last-shot transfer of O.P. didn't pan out. When popular Deputy Commissioner Russ Magill and Inspector Bob Blossom, who replaced the sneaky inspector as training division commander, were sergeants, they had worked with O.P. at the academy and they were all very good friends.

As O.P.'s luck would have it, Deputy Commissioner Russ Magill made an extremely rare visit to the academy dining room to have lunch. It was the only time I ever saw him there to have any meal. I was sitting across from a very distressed O.P. when he got up from the table and walked over to talk to Magill. I watched as they had a short conversation. Magill intently listened and nodded his head then O.P. returned to our table in his usual playful mood.

A few days later, O.P.'s transfer to San Francisco was cancelled and he was transferred to the training division as the departmental motorcycle instructor. Shortly thereafter, Captain Overhouse called me into his office to tell me he wanted me to be in charge of maintaining the academy motorcycle fleet. He said with O.P. in training division, it was sort of an untenable arrangement, but to do what I could. Then in his usual humorous way he said, "I know you can do it without fighting with O.P," but it was worse than Captain Overhouse was aware of.

O.P. was a pack rat. The training division fleet consisted of 75 motors, including two 1955 or earlier hand-shift, foot-clutch motors O.P. saved as museum pieces to show cadets what they looked like. Of the other 73 motors, only nine were 1956 or later Duo Glides with hydraulic shocks on front and rear wheels. The other 64 were also 1955 or earlier Hydro-glides with hydraulic shocks on only the front wheel.

Because I thought it was best for officers being trained and tested in the advanced motorcycle classes to be trained on the same motors they would ride in the field, I wanted the entire fleet to be Duo Glides, so I went to Captain Overhouse and told him I thought the entire fleet should be Duo Glides and briefly explained to him why I thought it would be best for the trainees. I also told him the fleet could be reduced from 75 motors to 60 motors.

Without hesitation he agreed and said he would set the wheels in motion to get 51 Duo Glides, even if they had to be retired with less than 40,000 miles, which was the longstanding CHP lifetime mileage.

The Harley Davidson Scam

For years, O.P. had a so-called motor mechanic from the local Harley-Davidson dealership contracted to service and repair the motor fleet at $20 an hour. That rate was equivalent to more than twice the salary of the CHP commissioner. To make matters worse, the so-called motor mechanic spent most of his time with his hands in his overall pockets talking to the Emergency Vehicle Operations Course (EVOC) sergeant and officers. Then when I started putting the obsolete motors in a field to store them for sale, he spent much of his time inspecting and evaluating them to tell his boss which ones to bid on.

With all of that, I again went to Captain Overhouse and told him the mechanic had to go. Without asking any questions, he said to consider it done, and within a few days the mechanic was gone. But the timing was bad. It was winter when motors didn't sell very well.

By the time I completed the paper work to sell the 66 hand-shift and Hydro-glides, dozens of field motors were retired and there were almost 100 CHP motors to be put up for bid.

I didn't know it, but for some suspicious reason, only Harley-Davidson dealers could bid on and purchase over-mileage CHP motors, but that was about to abruptly change. When almost 100 motors were put up for bid and the bids were opened, every bid from the Harley-Davidson dealers was exactly $200. It was an obvious conspiracy to rob the CHP.

But it backfired. When the Department of Finance opened the sealed bids and saw almost 100 bids for $200, they quickly cancelled the sale. They also cancelled the longstanding agreement written by someone decades ago and opened up bidding to the general public.

Before that time, retired, over-mileage CHP motors sold for about $450 and after painting and being put into good running order, they were sold by the dealers for about $850. As it happened, it took the largest sale of motors in CHP history to correct that serious flaw in the outdated agreement, and the Harley-Davidson dealers had only themselves to blame.

The Overtime Penalty

In 1958 compensating time off of at least four hours overtime was initiated for officers who were called back from off-duty time to go to court. When Governor Pat Brown, who was not a friend of the CHP, instigated paid overtime in 1961, many officers were motivated to write marginal tickets that would lead to court appearances and earn them overtime pay and mileage expenses from home to court and back.

In the late 1960s when the CHP was trying to double its size from about 3,200 officers to about 6,400, many officers used paid overtime as a second form of employment. By the mid-1970s, 90 percent of paid overtime was for court overtime and some officers were grossing more than their captains — and some of their citations and arrests were suspect. In short, paid overtime changed the CHP for the worse forever.

Deadly Pursuit in Isleton

Isleton Resident Officer Charles "Chuck" Sorenson visited the academy one day to buy something from the PX. I waited on him, and we had a conversation about resident posts. Isleton is a small town at the southwest corner of Sacramento County with two CHP resident officers.

We discussed the differences between Big Bear and Isleton with two resident officers, and there was no comparison. Bear Valley had 4,000 permanent residents and on Labor Day weekends, there could be as many as 60,000 people in the valley with about 56,000 vacationers. Also, being a resort town with many visitors celebrating, there was much drinking and more than the unusual number of DUIs — and it didn't snow in Isleton.

With that and much more, Sorenson and I agreed he had a pretty soft touch compared to my years in snow and other problems that were unique to Bear Valley. Another difference was that because Big Bear was so isolated and had only two highways to access and exit, there was very little transient crime and never an armed robbery while I was there. So Sorenson appeared to be in good spirits as he departed.

Then on March 15, 1963, it all started changing for him when he received a radio call of an armed robbery in Lodi to the east of Isleton. He was heading toward Lodi when he saw the suspects' car. He made a quick U-turn and pursued the suspects into Isleton where the driver lost control and crashed. The two suspects jumped out and fled through some back yards of residences.

Sorenson left the keys in his patrol car and gave pursuit through back yards and fence gates. As he ran through an open gate, one of the armed robbers was lying in wait behind the gate and shot Sorenson twice killing him instantly.

The two armed robbers then jumped in Sorenson's patrol car and headed west toward Fairfield in Solano County. They were in their late teens and hell bent for whatever or whoever would have them.

A deputy sheriff had a truck tractor and semi trailer block the higher speed highway and parked his patrol car next to the big rig in the direction from which the CHP car and suspects were approaching. He turned on the red light and stood between the big rig and his patrol car. The stolen CHP car approached at about 90 miles an hour and crashed into the deputy's patrol car, crushing the deputy and instantly killing him.

Amazingly, neither of the armed robbers was injured. They later told investigators that they agreed to crash into the road block and shook hands as their last farewell.

As I had done since before joining the San Diego Police Department when I heard of officers being shot, I talked to my older cop friends to try to analyze how it happened and what could have been done better to minimize or avoid the threats involved.

On my first day on the SDPD, Officer Bob Richards taught me to always take the car keys when leaving the patrol car for any reason. Since that day, I never left the keys in the car. In the deputy's case, if the robbers hadn't been able to steal Sorenson's CHP car, they probably would have stolen a civilian car that would have been less identifiable and would have crashed that car into the deputy's car and killed him, so leaving the keys in the patrol car was likely of no consequence.

The most important issue in the tragedy was Sorenson's foot pursuit through back yards and gates. It was the natural action any dedicated police officer might take, so I couldn't conclude that it was a foolish mistake. Regardless, to this day when I watch police documentary TV shows, I shudder when I see cops chasing armed or possibly armed suspects through yards, over fences and through gates. This happens in large cities when dozens of cops are at the scene and could establish a perimeter to encircle the suspects and systematically hunt them down, but the heat of the pursuit almost always dictates bad decisions.

Alcatraz: A White Elephant

In the first quarter of 1963, U.S. Attorney General Robert F. Kennedy ordered the closure of Alcatraz Federal Prison. It was a very good decision. There was no fresh water on the island and it had to be transported by tanker, which was very costly. The prison facility was deteriorating and needed extensive repairs, and in its 30 years as a federal prison, it had never been filled to capacity with prisoners. As popular as it was as a landmark attraction, it was economically a "white elephant."

In May 1963, the U.S. Marshal in Sacramento arranged a law enforcement tour of Alcatraz and CHP Academy staff members were included, along with about 30 other Sacramento area law enforcement officers, so Captain Overhouse, two other staff members and I took the very informative tour.

Alcatraz was closed, but not yet decommissioned. The only prison officials on the island were Associate Warden Walker and the most senior guard who was going to retire as soon as it was decommissioned.

Warden Walker hosted the tour. He first gathered us in a large room and briefed us on a few points of interest. One of our group asked Walker if he was in favor of the death penalty. The death penalty had been a hot issue since Caryl Chessman, a rapist and kidnapper, was executed in San Quentin in about 1960 after being convicted under the "Little Lindbergh Act."

Walker was very impressive. He was about six feet two inches, raw-boned, broad-shouldered, weighed at least 200 pounds and was very direct in everything he said.

In response to the death penalty question, he asked, "Is there anybody here from the media?" The U.S. Marshal who was the leader of the group said "No, only law enforcement officers are here by special invitation." Walker said, "I won't say what my personal feelings are about the death penalty because I might be a warden someday and have to oversee an execution, and I don't want anybody to think it is a personal issue with me." He then said he would tell of an experience he had when he was a captain, and we could draw our own conclusions.

Walker said when he was a captain working the graveyard shift, he frequently discussed the death penalty with the prison chaplain, who was adamantly opposed to the death penalty. He said after several discussions he got a prisoner's file and told the chaplain to read it. It was the file of a prisoner who had with two others found a family in their disabled car on a highway and assaulted them. With the husband and children watching, the three repeatedly and brutally raped the wife and mother of the family. He said he left the file for several days for the chaplain to read and visualize the scene. When he retrieved the file, the chaplain didn't say a word about the death penalty, but about three months later, the chaplain resigned from the federal prison system.

Walker then showed us gouges with striation marks in all directions on the floor. He said they were made with military bazookas from the roof during the 1946 riot and attempted escape when the military was called in to quell the riot.

One person in the group asked why they hadn't been filled in so they would look better. Walker said, "We left them there as a reminder to the inmates of what happens when they try to riot and escape." Then he said, "I can't blame any of them for trying to escape, because if I was sentenced to 20 years, all I would do was think about escaping."

Birdman of Alcatraz

He then led us up to the second floor where the hospital was located. There he showed us the four-bed cell where the "Birdman of Alcatraz" had been caged. He said "the Birdman" Robert Stroud was housed there alone because he was so violent and dangerous. He said Stroud would shave himself from head to toe and parade back and forth the length of the cell naked, and they had a standing order that his cell door could not be unlocked without four qualified guards being present.

One of the group asked if Stroud was in the hospital ward because he was sick. Walker put his right index finger to his right ear and flipped it upward. Then he said, "Yes, he was sick from the ears up." "Then why didn't they put him into a mental hospital?" one asked. "Because if they had, some head doctor would have declared him cured and turned him loose in about five years to kill again," Walker replied. Robert Stroud was in federal prison for killing a man in Alaska when it was still a federal territory. Then in another federal prison, he had killed a guard.

As we were at the dock to board the boat back to San Francisco, Walker said, "Good luck. I don't envy you. You never know who you're dealing with, but we do, and we lock them up every night and know where they are."

Blowing Our Cover

On the way home, we stopped at a roadhouse in Yolo County to have a beer. We had been sitting at the bar for about five minutes sipping our beers when a half-drunk loser walked over and asked, "What are you police chiefs doing here?" We were wearing suits and ties, and that blew our cover. The loser quickly made us as cops because we were most likely the first men to go in there wearing suits and ties. "We're planning a vice raid," I said. His eyes got large and he straightened and quickly walked out the door to spread the alarm like Paul Revere.

Yolo County was then reputed to be a wide open vice capital somewhat like a small Las Vegas, with prostitution, gambling and whatever. In November 1954 while I was a CHP cadet, a CHP officer ran for Yolo County sheriff. His chief campaign platform was to stamp out vice in the county, but the Sacramento political powers backed his opponent, because if vice was stamped out in Yolo County, it would probably move east across the Sacramento River into Sacramento County. So the CHP officer lost the election.

Prepping for the Sergeant Test

The next sergeant test was going to be in January 1964, so I had to transfer to the Sacramento squad to have the time and energy to study. The duty officer position was very demanding and tiring. In addition to spending much time assisting cadets and in-service officers, I had to sleep overnight at the academy three or four nights a week and could only get about six hours sleep each night — and I required eight hours sleep.

About a week after I submitted my transfer request, Inspector Blossom came to the duty office just before breakfast and asked me why I wanted to transfer. As we walked to the dining room for breakfast, I explained my reasons and he readily agreed. I was transferred in July 1963 and, to my surprise, was replaced by two new duty officers, but it wasn't because I was worth two officers. Not long after I started as a duty officer, an Auburn sergeant filed a claim for the hundreds of hours he had to be on stand-by status at the direction of his captain. He had to be available at all times and inform the dispatch center where he could be contacted, even when he went out to eat or go to a movie.

The attorney general ruled in his favor, and that opinion also affected all duty officers who had for decades donated seven hours every night they slept, or allegedly slept, at the academy from 11:00 p.m. to 6:00 a.m. If I had filed a claim, it would have amounted to about $7,000, but like all the others, I didn't file a claim because it would have been career and political suicide. So I left the academy poor, but in good standing.

CHAPTER 34

Right-Side Approach

When I was in the San Diego Police Department Recruit Training Class, a motor sergeant suggested that we might consider making right-side approaches to violators' vehicles to protect ourselves from passing traffic.

Three of us transferred into the Sacramento squad the same day. One was assigned to replace slain Officer Sorenson in the Isleton resident post and the other, Jim Stamback, and I soon became friends.

The Sacramento squad had a history of being discontents and rebels. One of the problems was being under the gun of the state capitol and seeing the overt politics. Also, the zone commander's office was upstairs, and with the supervising inspector commander and two inspector assistant commanders, the brass couldn't stay out of the squad's hair.

Captain Julius Henry was the squad commander. He had been the first San Bernardino squad commander after Captain Freeman retired, and he and I got along very well when I was in Big Bear. I admired him very much as a commander, so we had a very good working relationship.

I always arrived at work earlier than any of the other officers. It was a habit I became accustomed to on the San Diego Police Department, when we were required to be in the squad room at least 15 minutes before line-up.

Before one shift, Captain Henry was in the squad room. When I walked into the squad room, he greeted me and asked me to sit down to talk. He didn't hesitate to tell me the problems he had with the inspectors always telling him how to run the squad. He said he had studied supervision and management for years to get where he was, yet the three political inspectors always knew more than he did about how to run the squad.

I honestly agreed with him and more than ever dedicated myself to study long and hard to get promoted to sergeant and move on to greener pastures, if there were any.

Within a week, I submitted my request for motor assignment. About a week later, the executive lieutenant who was rightfully called "Fearless Fred" by the officers as a joke called me aside to ask for my permission to pass me over for the next motor assignment. The other officer had less experience than I. It was a repeat of my San Diego Police Department days, so I was immune to it. And being new to the squad, I didn't want to make waves so I agreed to it.

It later turned out the best for me. A motor officer transferred out effective November 1, 1963 and I got his motor. Although he hadn't maintained it as he should have, it was as smooth and enjoyable as my San Diego motor. After I had the chains properly adjusted and lubricated and polished and waxed it, the motor was like a Cadillac to ride.

Bank Robbery in North Sacramento

When I was a few blocks from the office at about 5:40 p.m. on Friday, November 15, 1963, there was a broadcast of a bank robbery in North Sacramento. In those days, banks closed at 3:00 p.m., except on Fridays when they closed at 6:00 p.m. A description of the getaway car was given, but I figured it was a stolen switch car and it was already dark so I went the few blocks to the office to end my shift.

Soon after I got up the next morning it was on the news that CHP Officer Glenn Carlson of the Truckee substation had been fatally shot by the fleeing bank robbers.

There was snow on I-80 over Donner Summit, and when there was snow on the highway the speed limit was 25 miles per hour. Carlson had stopped the three bank robbers and cited the driver for exceeding that speed limit. He ran a check on the car, but it came back clear. A few minutes after he released the driver and two other bank robbers, radio advised that the car was stolen.

The robbers went about a mile and stopped to let the one in the right front seat get in the rear seat so he could shoot out the window if they were stopped again.

CHP Officer Dan Dixson was responding west from the direction of the Nevada state line to back up Carlson. For some reason that nobody will ever know, Carlson stopped behind the bank robbers in the stolen car. As he reached the front of his CHP car, Morgan, the one moving to the rear seat, opened fire on Carlson and hit him five times, driving him backwards across the highway and into a ditch.

The bank robbers then drove to Reno where they chartered an airplane to return to Sacramento. The charter service employee quickly became suspicious of the three and phoned the police. By then, the report of Carlson's slaying was known to law enforcement, so the Sacramento Police Department was notified.

When the chartered plane landed at the Sacramento Municipal Airport, the Sacramento police were waiting in force, and the robbers were arrested without any resistance or incident.

When the Placer County judge sentenced Morgan to life, he said, "Thank you, your honor." Morgan and the other two robbers had just been released from prison before they pulled the bank robbery and killed Carlson. Needless to say, all law enforcement officers were outraged at that hillbilly judge.

Despite the tragedy of it all, it led to the CHP getting shotguns. Assemblywoman Pauline Davis of Portola introduced a bill in the legislature to provide the CHP with those guns.

In 1964 the CHP received some shotguns, but only enough for about one-fourth of the officers. They cost only about $55 each, so it was only a token cost. Despite that, we were forever grateful to Assemblywoman Pauline Davis for her concern and effort. Even those shotguns were a blessing when 21 months later in August 1965 the Watts riots erupted. Then after that riot, the CHP was provided with enough shotguns for all on-duty officers.

At that time, I was looking for a car to replace my 1956 Oldsmobile Holiday club coupe with 75,000 miles on it. Eddie Reese, the academy motor and EVOC car mechanic had a Cadillac and had convinced me that Cadillacs were good quality, reliable cars.

Not long after the Carlson slaying, I was on my way to the Harley shop when I saw a beautiful white Cadillac Coupe Deville in the front row of a used car lot whose dealer specialized in low-mileage, showroom-condition used Cadillacs.

I parked and walked over to check the mileage on the white beauty. In less than a minute, a salesman approached and said, "You don't want that car. It's the one those bank robbers were driving when they killed your officer in Truckee."

It was bad news, because I really wanted that mint condition gem, but not after hearing about its history from that rare honest salesman. Then he said, "When we got it back, the rear window had been blown out. When the gunman fired a few feet from the rear window, the concussion in the below-freezing weather blew it out."

I knew he was telling the truth, because I knew the rear windows in some cars would fracture and disintegrate into very small pieces about the size of a pencil eraser when exposed to the warm morning sun after a freezing night. I had seen some in Big Bear. I thanked him and continued to the Harley shop.

We were in briefing in the sergeants' office when the administrative sergeant stuck his head through the sliding window and told us President Kennedy had been shot in Dallas. Going south on Watt Avenue on the way to my beat, the driver of a car next to me said something about how horrible it was that President Kennedy had been killed. That was how I learned he had died from his injuries.

Then I was at home watching TV before going to work when Lee Harvey Oswald was being led through the Dallas Police Department garage and Jack Ruby shot him. It was so shocking and I wondered what was coming next and when it would all end.

I had Sundays and Mondays off and a sergeant asked me on Saturday if I would work overtime at the governor's mansion to guard Governor Pat Brown and his family. He said there were two 12-hour shifts from 9:00 a.m. to 9:00 p.m. and 9:00 p.m. to 9:00 a.m. and I could work the 9:00 a.m. shift.

Guarding Governor Brown

When I arrived at the mansion at about 8:45 a.m. on Sunday, I was paired with Dick Hartley, one of the two Sacramento squad Hartley brothers. Three unmarked cars from headquarters were there with one each on H, I, and 16th Streets, a northbound thoroughfare to the North Sacramento Freeway. Hartley and I were assigned to the 16th Street car on the busiest street.

Sergeant Harold "Hal" Ruggles was our sergeant. He told us that Governor Brown wasn't there. He was in Washington, D.C. to attend President Kennedy's funeral services, but Mrs. Brown was in the mansion. He also told us the mansion was difficult to guard because of the two-story motels across the streets to the east, south and north of the mansion. He said he had contacted the managers of the three motels and asked them to contact the CHP immediately if any suspicious persons rented a room. This was not good. There were a lot of suspicious people in the area because the old mansion was on the fringe of skid row.

Sergeant Ruggles told us why we were there. He said Governor Brown's chief of staff, known as his executive secretary, was concerned that some crazy would try to kill the governor to get the same world-wide publicity that Lee Harvey Oswald was getting for shooting President Kennedy. So upon hearing of President Kennedy's assassination, he immediately called the CHP to protect the governor and his family.

Sergeant Ruggles told us that when Governor Brown saw the CHP officers in suits and ties with three undercover cars, he ordered his executive secretary to "Get them out of here," but the executive secretary refused to do so and explained why he thought we should be there, so we stayed.

We surmised that Governor Brown's objection to our being there was because when CHP officers were assigned to any details benefiting the governor, all costs came out of the governor's annual budget, not the CHP's.

The State Police was only a security outfit to guard primary state facilities. They had an office attached to the mansion garage, and there were two State Police officers on duty at all times.

One of the two who were on duty when I was there was an older officer with about 20 years of service who was very compatible and congenial and liked our being there. The other officer was about 25 years old and didn't try to hide his resentment of our being there. He thought the State Police should be protecting the Brown family and the mansion.

Just after dark, Sergeant Ruggles came to our car and told us that a man in a bar in Santa Barbara announced that he was going to Sacramento to kill Governor Brown. He said when he told Mrs.

Brown, she sent a pot of coffee and some store-bought cookies to the State Police office for all of us. Hartley and I weren't crazy about the store-bought cookies, so we passed on the nice offer.

About an hour later, Sergeant Ruggles again came to our car and told us the Santa Barbara big mouth had been arrested by some Santa Barbara cops and the threat had just ended. He also told us when he told Mrs. Brown, she told him to bring her coffee pot and cookies back to her.

It reminded me of my exchange about governors with Big Bear Lake Fish and Game Warden Dan Heenan when we had Thanksgiving dinner at our house the first year I was in Big Bear. Heenan was a great guy and we hit it off from the start.

Governor's quirks are always fun to talk about so we soon got on that subject. My cadet class had been told about Governor Earl Warren's maltreatment of CHP officers and his selfish ways. Heenan had a personal experience with Warren's ruthless ways, but he knew his would be better than my second-hand stories, so he let me tell mine first.

When Governor Warren was in Santa Barbara, which was his favorite stomping grounds, he required that CHP units relay the Warren family dirty laundry to the Sacramento mansion for free laundry service. Also, one morning when he had a 7:00 a.m. speaking engagement at the Senator Hotel, his CHP driver had to get up so early he didn't have breakfast. When the CHP driver dropped Governor Warren off at the hotel, he asked Warren what time he would like him to return to pick him up. Warren told him to stay right there until he was through and returned to the front of the hotel. The officer told Warren he hadn't had breakfast and would like to do so. Warren said that was his own fault and he was not to leave.

As soon as Warren was out of sight, the officer drove straight to headquarters, stormed into Commissioner Peterson's office, threw his badge on the desk and said he had enough. Commissioner Peterson quickly sent a headquarters officer to the hotel to pick up Governor Warren.

Thereafter, the newest CHP sergeant had to drive Governor Warren until he was appointed Chief Justice of the U.S. Supreme Court by President Eisenhower in 1953.

Heenan told of when he was a State Police officer just prior to becoming a fish and game warden. He said he was assigned to the governor's mansion with another officer for weeks before Christmas one year. He said a couple of weeks before Christmas, 25 beautiful Christmas trees were delivered to the mansion for Governor Warren. When his executive secretary asked Warren what he wanted to do with them, he said put one upstairs and one downstairs and burn the rest of them.

When the executive secretary asked Warren if he could give the other 23 to the mansion employees, he said, "Burn them." Heenan said it didn't take long for that to get around, and it only added to his and his partner's total disgust with Warren.

So he said on Christmas Eve, he and his partner proceeded to celebrate Christmas by drinking to drown their woes. Then he said just about dark, a large box was delivered. It had "Perishable" and other stickers on it, which told them it was food. He said they opened the box and found a large smoked turkey from the governor of Louisiana. He said they ate the whole thing and wondered what the governor of Louisiana thought when he didn't get a thank you of any kind from Governor Warren.

The next day as Hartley and I were walking to Sam's Hofbrau to have lunch, a skid row resident walked up to us and said, "Look there," pointing down at his shoes that didn't have any shoelaces. "You need shoelaces." I said. "I had shoelaces until I fell asleep on that bus bench," he angrily exclaimed, "and when I woke up, they were gone." Without saying another word, he clomped away with his shoes flopping up and down. That was the first clue that our cover was blown and everybody within blocks knew who we were and why we were there.

The only exciting action during our great guarding detail happened on the graveyard shift. The officers in the same car we used on 16th Street observed some attempted car thieves trying to break into a car in the used car lot across the street and arrested them, and that was it.

After studying every morning and every day on my month-long December vacation, I took the sergeant test in January.

Officer Friends Killed in Traffic Accidents

While patrolling east on Highway 50 at about 1:30 p.m. on March 23rd, I heard the call of a major injury accident involving one of our officers. A few minutes later, an officer frantically called to tell the ambulance operator to get an ambulance out there as fast as possible. It wasn't until the end of my shift that I learned that the injured officer was Jim Stamback and he was injured so severely that he probably wouldn't make it. He was on life support for 13 days and died of his injuries, which included massive brain damage.

He had stopped an elderly couple for having a long piece of lumber sticking out of the left rear window, because it was a Vehicle Code violation for anything to protrude to the left of a passenger car. Jim had stopped the violator on Auburn Boulevard on that sunny, clear day and was talking to the driver on the road side of the car. Then the six-times previously convicted DUI driver of a two-ton flatbed truck ran into the rear of the patrol car and ran over Jim — and he was driving under the influence.

Jim was the second good CHP officer friend I lost in my almost ten years in the department. The first was George Woodson, one of my cadet classmates, who was killed in a motorcycle accident exactly one year to the day after we graduated.

Woodson was about six feet four inches tall and had been an L.A. County deputy sheriff just prior to joining the CHP. I considered him to be one of the finest, if not the finest dedicated officer in our academy cadet class.

The Sunday before Christmas, which was also on a Sunday, Woodson, his wife and three daughters came to Big Bear to see me. We had an enjoyable visit and he asked if they could come up and stay with us when there was snow for his daughters to play in. Our rental home had four bedrooms with bunk beds in the two downstairs bedrooms, so there was plenty of sleeping space.

Woodson and I both had Mondays and Tuesdays off, so I said I would let him know when there was plenty of snow. He and his family were pleased with that arrangement and they soon left in good spirits.

The following Friday night, one of the other officers who had been in our cadet class and was assigned to Berdoo with me phoned me at the sheriff's office. He told me Woodson had been killed in a motorcycle accident. He said he mysteriously ran off of a freeway frontage road, landed on his head and his aorta had ruptured. I couldn't believe it or accept it. The three of us in Berdoo from our cadet class went to his funeral in Norwalk. There was an open casket, and it wasn't until I saw him that I could believe that he was really gone. It took me a long time to get over losing such a fine friend and fellow officer.

But Jim's death may have saved my life at a later date and probably the lives of some other officers as well. When I was in the San Diego Police Department Recruit Training Class, a motor sergeant suggested that we might consider making right-side approaches to violators' vehicles to protect ourselves from passing traffic, but the speed limits were mostly 25 or 35 miles an hour then and I had never heard of a SDPD officer being struck by a passing vehicle on the driver's side, so I didn't take heed.

Then in the CHP Traffic Enforcement Manual, it recommended the right-side approach. Again I didn't heed it because it was so much easier working out of a patrol car to make driver-side approaches. But it was just as easy to make right-side approaches when working on a motorcycle.

So from the day of Jim Stamback's tragic and unusual accident, I always made right-side approaches, and when I was promoted to lieutenant and assigned to the South L.A. squad office, I went on a campaign to sell the right-side approach.

Many times making right-side approaches I had to knock on the right front window to get the driver's attention. Most were looking over their left shoulder to see where I was. That gave me time to see if there were any guns in sight. I also realized that about 90 percent of people are right-handed and if they are ready to use a handgun, it would be in their right hand where I could easily see it from outside the right front window.

Most of all, when making a right-side approach, I always had the violator's car between the driver and me, and if he had a handgun in hand, I could duck down and move one way or the other and they wouldn't know where I was located. Also, if the driver thought I was still at the door and fired below the window, the bullet would have to penetrate the door to hit me and even if it did, it would have lost most of its penetrating power.

Then starting in the late 1960s during the riotous social revolutionary uprisings, when any number of violent groups were ambushing and shooting police officers and bombing police cars and stations, it was safer to be on the right side of a vehicle as cover from potential drive-by snipers. With all of those valid reasons to always make right-side approaches, I never again made a driver-side approach.

In my later retirement years, I have watched numerous TV "Cops" documentaries. At least three have shown state troopers in eastern states being struck by passing vehicles, including one struck by the large right mirror of a truck. Fortunately, none of the three was seriously injured, but I wonder how many others were killed but the TV producers didn't want to air the police car video camera recordings of those gruesome events. So there might be more than are publicized.

Also, I have seen TV "Cops" shows when officers are shot or shot at while making driver-side approaches when in the road with no chance of cover. Just from what I have seen on these TV documentaries my best estimate is that at least 10 to 20 uniformed law enforcement officers are killed every year only because they always made driver-side approaches. With that high-risk practice, the odds are not on their side. It's just no better than a crap shoot in a casino.

Close Call from Blown Tire

One sunny day I was stopped westbound on Highway 50 at Watt Avenue at a red signal. It was red in my direction for eastbound traffic to turn north on Watt Avenue on the green arrow. I was in the center lane when an old Dodge went east in the right lane at no less than 80 miles an hour. I quickly made a U-turn and pursued the speeder with red lights and siren. He was so far ahead of me it took a distance to get him stopped.

California rules of evidence allows experienced, trained traffic officers to testify to estimated speeds, so I finally pulled him over to write him a citation for 80 miles an hour.

He stopped on the dirt shoulder and quickly walked back to me on the right shoulder of the highway away from traffic. As he was trying to find his driver license in his wallet, the right rear tire blew out with a loud pop. I looked down at the deflated tire and could see fabric and inner tube exposed. He looked like he had just seen a ghost, and maybe his own ghost, but he didn't say a word thereafter.

I wrote the citation and left him to figure it out. The only reluctance I had in leaving was because there was a young girl in the right front seat, but I hoped it might have taught her a lesson about people she shouldn't ride with.

Highway 50 was two lanes in each direction with only a double painted center line divider. A blowout in the right rear tire is the most dangerous. When it blows, it causes the rear end to sharply swerve to the right and makes the vehicle swerve to the left. If I hadn't stopped him, when the tire inevitably blew a mile or two from where I stopped him, he would have crossed into oncoming traffic and crashed head-on into the usual moderate to heavy afternoon traffic, causing any number of fatalities.

As I rode away from the then-silent speeder, I had to believe that it had been another divine intervention. My beat south of the American River spanned over a hundred square miles, but why was I sitting there at a red signal when I saw him speeding? It was much like the armed, drunk, gambling loser in Logan Heights and the woman on the back of the motorcycle on 4th Avenue on Pill Hill.

CHP Flash Point

Unlike the San Diego Police Department which had no rational method of measuring an officer's work efforts and production, the CHP had Form 415 that listed numbers of activities and hours expended on patrol, accident investigations, court appearances, auto theft and so on. The number of citations and arrests were divided into only hours of patrol time to determine an officer's "flash point" as it was called. Also, unlike the SDPD, CHP officers were given credit for all citations, including parking, accident investigation and every other citation issued. And flash point was the primary measure of an officer's work efforts and production.

One sunny afternoon I was riding east on Highway 50 when I saw Officer "X" parked on the shoulder. He was a tall handsome officer who was bitter at the world in general and the CHP in particular. He didn't normally work south of the American River so I stopped and asked him how he was doing.

"All they want are tickets," he growled, as usual like a broken record. "That's our job," I said. "But that's all they want," he growled. "Think about it," I said. "They give us these expensive Hollywood toys to ride and take home with us like they're ours, and all you have to do is investigate one accident in a shift and write up the violator who caused the accident and you have a flash point of six. Then if you investigate a second accident and get a citation out of it, you have a flash point of four, and they won't get on you for four hours per arrest."

He looked at me and said, "See, it's just a numbers game." "Also," I said, "then you can go to a fire station like I do to complete the reports and get out of the hot or cold for about an hour." He didn't say anything, but I could tell the wheels were turning in his hard, anti-everything head.

A few days later, I received a call to investigate an accident in the center divider of the South Sacramento Freeway. When I arrived about ten minutes later, Officer X was hard at work on the accident and told me he would handle it. I thought it was comical because he had never figured it out in his six years on the job. He was like many Sacramento squad officers who would always try to get out of investigating accidents. I often thought that every one of their shifts must have seemed like two shifts while they were trying to get out of work.

Also, I had two locations where I would sit in at busy intersections to watch cars stop for the red signals to check for defective stop lamps. In addition to mechanical violations, about half of those I stopped did not have a driver license and said it must be in their other wallet. How many men have two wallets? None I ever knew did.

In April I was assigned to a special beat that some brainy inspector dreamed up. It was on Highway 50 in El Dorado County abutting Sacramento County to the east and Shingle Springs just west of Placerville on the way to Lake Tahoe. It was two lanes with a 65-miles-per-hour speed limit. In order to catch a good speeder, I would have had to go wide open at 95 miles an hour for miles, so I never wrote a speeding ticket all month.

Then one day on the way to El Dorado County I saw a dead deer in the center divider of the Folsom Freeway next to Aerojet in Sacramento County. I was certain if deer were that close to populated areas, they must be thick in El Dorado County. So when it got dark, I went back to well-lighted Rancho Cordova. Rancho Cordova had a shopping center on Highway 50 and was on my regular beat, so I knew there were no deer there.

After that unpleasant month, I went into Lieutenant "Pete" Peters' office and told him about the deer and that I thought the whole idea of Shingle Springs was a very bad nightmare. As always, he listened patiently but did not comment. Then I knew I had wasted my breath, because it was obviously the brainchild of one of the upstairs inspectors who was always telling Captain Henry how to run the Sacramento squad. So Motor Officer Joe Gere was assigned to the Shingle Springs madness for the month of May.

On May 4, 1964, it was cold so I had on my long underwear and Star leather jacket with a fur collar. I was sitting in south of Fruitridge Road on Sacramento Boulevard checking defective stop lamps and headlights way out of adjustment on northbound cars when they stopped for a red signal.

My Motorcycle Accident

At about 8:00 p.m. an eastbound Studebaker came within several feet of running the red light as it changed from amber to red and was going about 55 miles an hour in the 35 mile zone. I quickly started after it. It was a very long block to the first intersection at Mendocino. About halfway there, I glanced at my speedometer and I was going 65 miles per hour. As I approached Mendocino, there were two cars in the two westbound lanes — one in each of the two lanes. The one in the center lane had its left turn signal flashing.

As I had done about a hundred times before, I quickly saw that I would clear the intersection before the car got there and I moved from the center lane to the right lane as a safety buffer. The next thing I knew I was headed directly for the right front fender of the turning 1952 Chevrolet. I tightened my grip on the handle bars and locked my elbows to keep the front wheel straight as I applied the

269

front and rear brakes. I crashed into the right rear fender of the turning car and spun it around 180 degrees onto Mendocino and clear off of Fruitridge Road.

The next thing I knew I was lying on my back in the right lane about 80 feet east of Mendocino. I had flown and bounced that distance blacked out. All I could remember was the sounds of the skidding rear tire and the crash. I later figured my blacking out for those few seconds was a blessing. If I had been conscious, I may have tensed up and been injured much worse or had a heart attack while in flight.

Wanting to get out of the road before the traffic stopped at Sacramento Boulevard started my way, I tried to move, but I couldn't. As I tried to get up, the driver of the other westbound car stopped and ran across the street yelling, "Don't get up." "Hell, I can't," I replied.

As I was lying there, the 19-year-old driver of the car I had crashed into appeared. "What were you doing?" I angrily asked him. "I didn't see you," he lied. He later told the investigating officer that he thought he could beat me through the intersection. One way or the other, he lied.

My right leg was numb, so I thought it was broken, so when a sergeant asked me which doctor I wanted, I said, "Doctor Horn." Dr. Horn was one of three top orthopedic specialists I had heard of in Sacramento and his name was the easiest to remember.

When the ambulance arrived, it was a temporary fill-in. A few nights before when I was sitting in on Sacramento Boulevard, that ambulance crew stopped to talk to me. When I asked them what happened to their Chevrolet panel ambulance, they said they had wrecked it and the Pontiac was a loaner.

Before I was put in the ambulance, the sergeant said Doctor Horn's office said to take me to Mercy Hospital. With a wrecking ambulance crew and weak and aching from the neck down, I said, "Don't turn on the red lights or siren, go slow and don't hit any bumps because we'll probably get to the hospital before the doctor anyway."

When I was wheeled into the receiving room, a senior nurse said, "Oh, it's one of our boys." That made me feel good and I was happy to get away from the cowboy ambulance crew. Dr. Harold Gibbons sutured a one-inch laceration just below my right knee and found that my leg was not broken. Mercy Hospital was full, so I bedded down in the library with three others, and the only way we could call the nurses was with a chrome plunger bell like the ones on hotel reception counters.

Just before lights out time, a nurse came to me with sedative pills. She said, "Here, after what you've been through, these will help you calm down and relax." I was so weak and completely relaxed realizing that I was lucky to be alive, but I took the pills and didn't say anything so she would feel like she had done something merciful.

I was supposed to be there only one night for observation, but when Doctor Gibbons checked me the next morning, my left foot was swollen, so he had me stay one more day and night to x-ray my foot. The next morning he told me it was sprained, not broken, so I checked out and my wife drove me home.

By the grace of God, all I had was the sprained left foot, the laceration, back muscle spasms and a cracked rib, which was the worst. Sneezing with a cracked rib is a very painful experience as I later discovered.

A couple of days after I went home, a sergeant brought me a copy of the accident report. He said my motor helmet was so completely demolished that if I hadn't been wearing it I would have definitely been killed.

After he left and I studied the accident report, I was upset with it. It was classified as an intersection accident. The car officer who completed the report had never ridden motors other than during cadet motor training. He obviously did not know that the front wheel of a motor will not lock up and leave skid marks. If the front wheel does lock up due to a brake defect, it will violently pitch forward, go down and throw the rider to the ground, but I never heard of that happening.

So he wrote that my rear skid marks were the front wheel skid and had the point of impact in the intersection. When I later measured the length of a CHP motor, it proved that I had exited the intersection by about five feet when I crashed into the car. My best estimate was that the hotshot teen driver had cut the corner by crossing the center line about 30 to 40 feet before reaching the intersection, so it was a wrong-side-of-the-road collision, not an intersection collision.

Civilly, the way the report was written was not in favor of the CHP or me, but I didn't make an issue of it because I was certain the violator's insurance company had probably already bought a copy, so I decided to take my chances. It eventually turned out fine, despite the report errors.

I was off duty on injury time for seven weeks. In my second week off, I was told Joe Gere had struck a deer, run off the road and suffered a fractured leg working the Shingle Springs assignment. He had received a call to assist rangers at the Folsom Lake State Park with a report of shooting in the park, and he was on an isolated back road when he struck the deer.

Although I didn't like to hear Gere had a broken leg, I knew it could have been much worse. The blessing was that it finally put an end to the inspector's useless detail.

Motorcycle Safety Training Film

In October 1964 the CHP made the first police motorcycle safety training film ever made in the U.S., and O.P. Johnson and Inspector Blossom chose me to star in the film. It took about two weeks to shoot the film. The daredevil cameraman was named Wayne and had just returned from Vietnam where he had hung out of helicopters filming battles and other hair-raising scenes. When shooting near collision scenes he sat behind me on the radio box with his knees clamped to my sides. I thought it was kind of risky, but to him it was probably like kid's play after Vietnam.

Several months later, O.P., Lieutenant Art Murdock of training division and I went to Wayne's studio in Burbank to edit the film. A safety film called "Routine Stops" the CHP had made a few years earlier about the dangers of stopping unknown dangerous drivers won a national first prize for police safety films. Inspector Blossom was so eager to win another first prize for the CHP he submitted an unedited copy without the narration or background music of the "Highway Patrol March." Needless to say, it bombed out. If he had waited until it was completed and submitted it for the next year's contest, it may have had a good chance.

Protest in Berkeley

The first week of December 1964 the "Free Speech Movement" (FSM) activist radicals invaded the University of California at Berkeley administrative building Sproul Hall and about 1,350 protesters were lying passively on the second floor of the hall. The San Francisco Police Department already had its hands full with the hippies, flower children and San Francisco State problems, so when the small Berkeley Police Department called for mutual aid, the Alameda County Sheriff and Oakland Police Department got the job of dragging limp bodies down from the second floor.

I watched TV that night when the legally required unlawful assembly warning was announced to the 1,350 demonstrators. About 500 of the less dedicated protesters decided it wasn't such a good idea to end up at the sheriff's Santa Rita Detention Center, so they departed. That left about 850 to drag out, with a few exceptions who thought they should fight for their noble cause. Little did I know I would be working there the next day.

About 7:00 a.m. the next morning I got the call to report to the office as soon as possible to go to Berkeley. When about 20 of us from the Sacramento squad arrived in Berkeley, we were lined up in formation with other CHP officers. San Francisco Zone Inspector Ross Harris gave us strict instructions. He said we were to guard the perimeter and not express any opinions about what was going on. He said there were radicals with concealed tape recorders to tape everything we would say, so we were to ignore anyone who asked probing questions or give them a line of irrelevant babble.

I was assigned to what I thought was the west side of the perimeter. There was a wooden one by six board fence around a bare plot of ground about 100 by 100 feet with an opening for paddy wagons and buses to enter and depart on the opposite side from where I was located.

The university had been closed down for the day due to the disruption. There was a large crowd of spectators, including some assistant professors and students. They were all well behaved and friendly, all except a young radical on a platform about 50 feet away with a bullhorn. He did his best for about 30 minutes trying to incite anyone he could in the large crowd. Without any success, he finally disappeared.

After a few hours of watching limp bodies being stuffed into buses and paddy wagons, it got dull. Than just after an empty paddy wagon backed in, four officers came out grappling with a struggling demonstrator. Each officer was holding onto an arm or a leg. When the paddy wagon driver opened the rear doors, the four officers swung the fighting, struggling demonstrator back and forth then threw him into the prisoner compartment. About a second or two later, there was a loud boom sounding like a bass drum that had been hit hard. It boomed when the problem prisoner hit the front-end bulkhead of the compartment. With that, there was a loud cheer from the massive crowd.

A little later, a CHP officer who had gone into Sproul Hall to see what was going on told me about a great big deputy who was dragging demonstrators down the stairs. He said as the demonstrators' butts bounced off the steps, the big deputy was singing "Happy Days Are Here Again."

Not long after that an Oakland Police Department motor sergeant let some of the Berkeley football players parade around in the bare dirt area with their placards reading, "FSM, Free Sex Movement."

The whole event was turning into a side show when a foreign-looking pint-sized male subject elbowed his way through the crowd to get to me. It was in the 70s and was a warm day, but he was wearing a trench coat all buttoned and belted up. He may just as well have had a big sign on him saying he had a tape recorder under that sweltering trench coat. "What do you think about what is going on in there?" he abruptly asked like a Nazi interrogator. I almost laughed, but I kept a straight face and said, "I ain't got no idear, 'cause nobody don't tell me nothin'." The closest group burst into loud laughter.

With that, "Trench Coat" with tape recorder quickly spun around and pushed his way through the crowd and disappeared. When it all ended that day, the good guys had won by a score of about 850 to zero.

Unbeknownst to me, an assistant professor I had talked and laughed with most of the day took a photo of me leaning against the wooden fence with some friendly spectators. He noted my badge number and sent it to Sacramento headquarters addressed to my badge number. After I retired, I had it enlarged and hung it in my office with about a dozen other photos from my weird cop career.

The week before Christmas 1964 a gigantic storm struck northern California. The snow level in the Sierra Nevada mountains is usually about the 4,000 foot level, but that storm raised the snow level to 9,000 feet, so in addition to the heavy downpour, the snow melted and increased the runoff.

The overflow weir under the Yolo Causeway was opened to lessen the flooding, but it didn't help. The Sacramento River is higher than the level portions of Sacramento Valley, and rain runoff has to be pumped up into the river.

Rescue on a Bridge

There was a dirt-filled dam to the east of Auburn and it burst, sending a gigantic wave down the north fork of the American River. There was an old wooden bridge across the river connecting Auburn and Coloma, where gold was discovered sparking the California gold rush.

The CHP was notified that the dam had burst and dispatched a unit to the old wooden bridge. When the officer arrived, a teenage boy was standing on the bridge leaning on the rail of the down side with his back to the oncoming gigantic wave. A citizen had apparently heard of the dam failure and was there to take photos of the wave when it struck the bridge, so he was able to take photos of the CHP officer saving the teenager.

Just before the wave struck and completely destroyed the bridge, the CHP officer ran onto the bridge, grabbed the boy's hand and pulled him off the bridge. Within seconds, the bridge was gone. Newspapers printed the dramatic photo of the officer running off the bridge pulling the teenager to safety.

The storm continued off and on into the Sunday of the New Year's weekend. On Sunday it was raining hard and there was a light crew of officers on the 1:00 p.m. motor shift. Just after briefing, the sergeant received a phone call from Captain Henry. Motor Officer Dave Stolls and I were the only ones still in the squad room when the sergeant hung up. The sergeant stuck his head through the window between the sergeants' office and the squad room and said,

"We have to drive Governor Brown's daughter to Tahoe City. Stolls, do you want to do it?" Immediately Stolls said, "No, I've never driven in the snow." The sergeant then asked, "Nuttall, do you want to do it?"

Driving Governor Brown's Daughter

I said I would. I was dreading spending the shift racing from one traffic accident to the next alone, trying to keep the accident reports from getting wet. Working alone, we had to get out of the patrol car to clear the scene then in the patrol car dripping wet to interview the involved parties. In Big Bear I had driven in rain, wind, sleet, fog and all forms of snow, so I jumped at the chance.

The sergeant told me I had better take an overnight pack because I might get stranded in Tahoe City the way the storm was persisting, then to pick up Governor Brown's daughter at the mansion at 3:30 p.m.

I went straight home to get an overnight pack. When I arrived at the mansion, Governor Brown, his wife and daughter were waiting on the front porch. After a brief greeting, Governor Brown asked me if I could get his daughter to Tahoe City before dark. I could readily see that his daughter, Kathleen, was packed, ready and eager to go, so I lied and assured him I could.

It would have taken a helicopter to get her there before dark. It was also only about eight days after the shortest day of the year and was dark at about 4:45 p.m. Furthermore, it was almost a hundred miles to Tahoe City and most of the way on I-80 had snow on it and was a 25-mile zone. Despite all of that, he actually believed me.

So Kathleen and I headed for Tahoe City. She was wearing denims and a sweat shirt, which indicated to me that she was probably a down-to-earth sort of person. She started reading a comic book. It may have been Charlie Brown or Snoopy, but I didn't pay attention to it. I kept my eyes on I-80. She laughed a couple of times then asked me if I wanted her to read it to me. I said I did, so she read aloud until it got dark not long before we got to the Auburn CHP office to get tire chains.

It was not a Boy Scout "Be Prepared" operation. The Sacramento CHP office did not have tire chains. Also, the cars did not have air conditioning, so they did not have antifreeze in the cooling system.

I figured the request for the detail had probably gone through the commissioner's office then through one of the upstairs inspectors to Captain Henry, so I could only guess that it was most likely the same inspector who dreamed up the Shingle Springs fiasco that eventually ended up with Joe Gere having a broken leg.

The most sensible plan would have been for me to relay Kathleen to an Auburn unit and have them take her to Tahoe City, but that would have been too logical. As it was, I was happy I was taking her because she was such a delightful young lady.

After getting the tire chains, I drove to a Chevron contract station that was fully equipped to mount chains. The station had overhead hoists and the chains were on the rear tires in about ten minutes. Then we started the long 50-mile ride in an endless line of traffic in the 25-miles-an-hour snow zone to get to Highway 89 to go south to Tahoe City — and it was already dark.

Highway 89 had some surprises. The runoff at an angle across the roadway the week before was frozen under the layer of snow. Highway 89 was also slightly downgrade to Tahoe City and had some gradual curves. The first time I hit one of those icy slicks, I was turning slightly to the left at a curve. The front end swerved about two feet to the right before I could correct it.

Kathleen let out a light gasp, but didn't say a word. I could readily see she was a real trooper. I slowed down, but the second and last icy slick I hit caused about the same swerving reaction as the first one. Kathleen again lightly gasped but didn't say a word. When we finally arrived safely where she was going to stay with Brown family friends, she graciously invited me to go with her to meet the family friends. It was about 9:30 p.m. and almost five hours after dark. Sorry about that, governor, but we made it in one piece anyway. There were high snow banks on both sides of the highway, so I had to park in the roadway.

The hosting family was also very delightful. The husband and father of five very well-behaved children was a San Francisco attorney. He greeted me like an old friend and invited me to have dinner. The family had eaten hours before and Kathleen didn't want to eat, so I had a great roast beef dinner alone.

As I started eating, Kathleen stood on the other side of the table and went into her act of recreating the San Francisco attorney's Christmas party. The star character in her reenactment was Melvin Belli, who was probably the most prominent and flamboyant attorney in California at that time, and he was a dyed-in-the-wool performer.

The hosting family had not attended the Christmas party, so Kathleen's command performance was for their amusement. Acting it out in detail, Kathleen told about Melvin Belli making a grand entrance wearing a top hat, flowing black cape and carrying an adorned cane to represent his own world. We all had many good laughs until the very end of the show.

The gracious host then asked me if I would like to stay the night with them. The house was actually a mansion and probably had at least seven bedrooms and baths. It was about 11:00 p.m. and I wanted to stay, but the patrol car didn't have antifreeze in it and I knew from my Big Bear days if the skies cleared up that night the temperature would plunge below freezing. The last thing I wanted was to have a solid block of ice for an engine, so I graciously declined and thanked him for the invitation and for the wonderful meal. I said goodbye to all of them and left.

All went well going up Highway 89 until I tried to turn left onto I-80. The wheel wells were full of iced snow. Unlike Big Bear where the highways were mostly one curve after another and the repeated turning kept the wheel wells cleared of snow buildup, Highway 89 and I-80 were much straighter and the snow was soggy from the heavy rain the week before. I had to get out and kick the almost solid ice out from under the left front fender to turn left.

After I went over the Donner Summit, the storm quickly increased to a blizzard. Three times the 50-mile-an-hour gale caused a complete white-out of snow across the windshield. There was no other traffic in sight, and I had to quickly stop until the windshield cleared.

The third and last time it happened, when the windshield cleared I was stopped about 50 feet behind a large abandoned rental van truck without lighting. I radioed it to Sacramento dispatch, drove around it and headed for Sacramento.

When I got past the snow on I-80, I just kept going with the tire chains clattering all the way to the office. I'd had enough for one day. I left the chains where they were. It was 2:00 a.m. and I heard on the squad room radio monitor that I-80 was completely closed due to snow so deep it couldn't be cleared from the roadways. I had just made it.

Six months later I read in the paper that Kathleen Brown got married. I had always been a conservative Republican, but when Kathleen ran for governor in 1994, I voted Democratic for her. Unfortunately, she lost and disappeared from the political scene. It was very sad because if she had been elected governor, she could have kept Californians laughing for at least four years.

CHAPTER 35

Safe Cracker Family

Lawson told me that the Texas Rangers had classified the Anders brothers as the biggest safe cracking ring in the fourteen southern and western states.

While I was off duty on injured time after my motor accident, O.P. Johnson and my first Big Bear partner, Gil Stokes, phoned me at home to tell me I was 57 on the new sergeant list. My friend Val Bates was right. Only about ten percent actually study long and hard for promotional tests. About 1,350 had taken the test, and only the top 100 or 120 would be promoted to sergeant during the four-year eligibility of the list.

Then on my 35th birthday on August 6, 1965, Inspector Blossom phoned me at the office just before the start of my 1:00 p.m. shift. He said the legislature had passed a bill to double the size of the CHP in the following three years. He asked me if I would return to the academy to supervise the physical training, physical methods of arrest, baton and riot control courses.

It was like a great big birthday present. I would not have to move and the academy was only four miles from home. I jumped at the opportunity and told him I would gladly go back to the academy.

He said I would be promoted to sergeant on September 1, 1965 and would remain in the Sacramento squad until near the end of the year when the academy was staffed to train 3,000 to 3,200 cadets.

When I told Captain Henry of my pending promotion and my staying in the Sacramento squad for about four months, he said I could keep my motor until I left for the academy. I later heard that Commissioner Crittenden and Inspector Blossom had attended an International Association of Chiefs of Police Conference in the east. When the large group of police chiefs was told that the CHP was going to hire about 3,000 additional officers in three years, they all said it was impossible.

Knowing Inspector Blossom as I did by then, I could see that was like waving a big red flag in front of an angry bull. It gave him the opportunity to prove all of them wrong. He had spent his career building the reputation of the CHP and he was certain that reputation would attract more applicants than they had ever heard of in their police careers.

There was no graveyard sergeant in the Sacramento squad, so I was assigned to work the next worse shift from 7:00 p.m. to 3:30 a.m. Fortunately, my two children and all the other kids on the block went back to school a week later, so I did get some sleep later each morning.

I didn't ride my motor on that shift because of the greater hazard of DUIs, and I had to carry a camera to take photos of major injury and fatal accident scenes for evidence.

The maximum speed limit had been raised to 70 miles an hour on U.S. 99 south from Mack Road to the county line as a test. With it being a new maximum speed, all major injury and fatal accidents had to be photographed for study.

One night I roamed to the south of Elk Grove and was driving toward 99 on a country road when I saw a transient in dark clothing walking on the shoulder toward 99. I drove to the Town and Country area in the northern part of the county where there was more activity. After an hour of patrolling there, I heard a call of a fatal bus versus pedestrian accident on U.S. 99 not far north of the country road where I had seen the transient.

Fatal Bus Accident

When I arrived, I drove across a bridge over a creek and saw the body lying parallel with the railing next to the center lane. About a hundred yards north of the bridge, the bus was parked on the right shoulder with about 20 passengers standing next to it on the shoulder. As soon as I parked between the bridge and the bus, Officer Tom Drake met me. I knew something was wrong because he wasn't wearing his cap as required and he was visibly upset. "We ran over the body," he blurted. "Did anybody see you?" I spontaneously replied.

When I asked that off the top of my head I wasn't intent on hiding the fact for legal reasons, I was concerned about how it would look to the public to see a CHP car run over a dead body — not very good public relations.

"Yeah, all the passengers were standing there and saw us run over the body," Tom replied. He was so upset that when I told him I had to take photos, he said, "There's nothing to take pictures of," as if he wanted it all to go away and be forgotten.

I then got the camera out of the trunk and walked up to the front of the bus. The left turn signal lamp was broken out and there was a dent in the left front corner of the bus. That damage proved conclusively that the transient was walking in a traffic lane when he was struck. After the CHP car ran over him, his body was moved out of the center lane to against the bridge railing, so he was probably walking just inside the right lane when he was struck.

After the coroners did their thing and the bus departed, I told the deputy coroners we had to talk, and we drove north to a wide turnout on the shoulder. I told the deputies the CHP car ran over the body but it was a separate event and was not part of the fatal accident. They readily understood and agreed.

Then I said, "You probably know that the definition of a traffic accident is only where there is property damage, injury or death. A dead person cannot be damaged, injured or killed, so it was not a traffic accident when they ran over the dead body." The deputy coroners again agreed. "But I will write a memorandum explaining it all just in case the deceased has some family members who get dollar signs in their minds and want to sue," I explained. The deputy coroners were satisfied with that, and we all went our separate ways. I went straight to the office, wrote the memorandum and never heard any more about it.

The next night I was in the squad room before shift start when Bob Lane, the officer who was driving when they ran over the body, came in. We were the only ones in the squad room. When I said "Hi" to him and asked how he was doing, his reply was not good. He said he hadn't slept a wink that day and that all he could see when he tried to sleep was the body in the road. I tried to console Bob, but it was obvious that it didn't work.

Tom and Bob had been permanent partners for over a year, were excellent officers and were inseparable and the best of friends. When I was first able to get Tom alone to tell him what Bob had told me, he said he knew about Bob's distress. Tom then told me they had happened upon the accident before receiving the call. I knew that because the first I knew of it was when they called it in. Tom said he was looking at the bus and passengers when all of a sudden Bob said, "Oh, fuck," then they bumped over the body. Bob never mentioned it after that, nor did I, but I always wondered if he ever completely got over it.

The Wanted Car

One shift I received a car-to-car call from Officer Joe Story to meet him on the east frontage road of I-80 just south of Watt Avenue. When I arrived, Joe Barnes was standing about 20 feet west of a Lincoln club coupe holding a shotgun. Two men were out of the car and a large woman was still in the car. It was obvious this was a high risk stop, so I asked the woman to get out of the car. She was sitting in the right rear next to a pile of clothes on the left rear seat.

As Barnes guarded the three with his shotgun, Story and I stepped away so he could tell me what they had. He said he was pulling southbound out of the CHP Antelope Scales when he saw the Lincoln going south at about 80 miles an hour in the center lane. He said the Lincoln then quickly slowed to 55 miles an hour and moved to the far right lane. He thought it looked suspicious, so he radioed in a check for wants on the vehicle. It came back that the car was wanted along with two Anders brothers for safe burglary in Salem, Oregon, so he called for backup before he stopped the Lincoln.

But further checking with the Oregon police revealed that the two wanted Anders brothers were already in prison in Salem. The Oregon State Police had failed to cancel the APB for those two Anders brothers, but the two he stopped were also Anders brothers. He called me to figure out what to do with the two Anders brothers who were not wanted but were driving a car that was still listed as wanted. I said, "I'll talk to them to see what they have to say."

The older one was 40 years old, about five feet ten inches, had black wavy hair and brown eyes, and his name was Neil Anders. The younger one was about 20 years old, five feet eight inches tall with blond hair and blue eyes. His name was Billy Joe Anders. I had Joe take Neil Anders back to his patrol car about 30 feet from the Lincoln and I told Billy Joe to stay next to the Lincoln.

Thinking Billy Joe might be less con-wise, I decided to question him first. When I asked for identification, he pulled out his wallet and started fumbling through it for his ID. As I had learned to do in the San Diego Police Department I did my best to see what was in his wallet. A small canary yellow paper was usually an unpaid traffic citation and almost always led to a failure to appear (FTA) warrant. As I gawked into his wallet, I clearly saw the business card of a New Orleans bail bondsman. When he finally produced his Texas driver license, it was expired and had no photo.

He was very nasty and hotheaded. Whenever I asked him a question, he snapped answers back at me. When I asked him if he had ever been arrested, he snapped that he had been released from an Oklahoma prison six months before. With that and the bail bondsman's business card, I figured we had something hot. I mentally noted Billy Joe's birth date and returned his worthless driver license to him. Then I walked back to Joe and Neil Anders. I pointed back at Billy Joe and asked Neil who he was. "He's my baby brother Billy Joe," he replied like a proud father.

I asked Neil what Billy Joe's birthday was and he answered with the wrong day and month. I told him it was wrong and told him to try again. He gave me another wrong date and then failed again on the third try, so I gave up. My impression was that they had different fathers and with the 20-year age difference, he probably wasn't within a hundred miles when Billy Joe was born. I then asked Neil what they had in the Lincoln. I was dying to search it.

"Just those clothes, go ahead and look if you want to," he replied without batting an eye. It was a consent to search in language as far as I was concerned and just what I was hoping for. I also thought it was a bluff, so I quickly took him up on his offer.

I looked in the glove compartment and found two small transceiver radios — burglar and lookout equipment, I thought. I then walked around to the driver's door, opened it and looked under the driver's seat and saw two paper bags. One had a half-empty pint of whiskey in it and the other was full of rolled coins.

I took the keys out of the ignition and opened the trunk. There was a large black leather satchel overflowing with rolled coins. On the other side of the trunk was a large drill motor and next to it was a new-looking small pruning saw with a smear of orange paint on the handle. I put my hand on my service revolver and said, "Nobody move."

Joe clutched his shotgun tighter and stood at the ready and none of the three moved an inch. I radioed for a sheriff's detective to meet us there. About 15 minutes later the Detective Sergeant Don Lawson arrived and parked on the other side of the frontage road. As he walked across the street, I could see he was over six feet tall and at least 250 pounds of lean Texas beef. When he asked what I had, his Texas drawl confirmed it was Texas beef.

In reply to his question, I pointed into the trunk at the large drill motor and asked, "Do you want this?" When he saw it he said, "I sure do."

In a complete search of the Lincoln we found two handguns. One was an unloaded Derringer hidden at the back of the right front seat under the backrest. The other was a loaded .38 revolver concealed under a floor mat.

When the three were handcuffed and under control, I went to the office to make out my critical report of the details of Neil's giving me his consent to search the Lincoln. If the search was ruled unconstitutional by some ultra-liberal judge, the entire case would fall apart.

About five months later in February 1966, I received a subpoena to appear in a Salem, Oregon, Superior Court to testify in the Anders' case. Don Lawson contacted me and said there was a problem with the Sacramento County sheriff. The sheriff was very controversial and demanded that Oregon pay for Lawson's and his partner's salaries, retirement contributions and other employee benefits for every day they were in Oregon on the case.

A few days later, Lawson contacted me and said a California Superior Court judge ruled that Oregon only had to pay for the deputies' traveling expenses, but he also ruled that Lawson and his partner could be in Oregon for only one day on the case. Amazingly, the California judge also ruled that Lawson and his partner could not be arrested while in Oregon for any reason. It was just like diplomatic immunity for foreign diplomats.

I sat next to Lawson on the milk-run flight to Salem in a driving rainstorm. He immediately asked me how I got consent to search the Lincoln. I told Lawson how Neil had said I could look through the car when I asked him what was in the car. Lawson said, "From my police experiences, you are probably one in ten who would have taken him up on it. Most officers I've known wouldn't have called his bluff and would have just let it go." Lawson told me that the Texas Rangers had classified the Anders brothers as the biggest safe cracking ring in the fourteen southern and western states.

He then told me there had been a grocery store safe burglary on Florin Road in the town of Florin some months before and a sheriff's patrol unit had contacted some of the Anders brothers in the store parking lot that same night. Lawson was certain the Anders brothers had also pulled that job. I had read about it in the paper and I agreed with him.

I told Lawson how Officer Joe Story had first seen the Lincoln speeding at about 80 miles an hour and then it slowed to 55 miles an hour and moved to the far right lane and that it all came together because the Oregon State Police hadn't cancelled the APB on the two Anders brothers who were already in prison.

Lawson and I laughed at how stupid criminals were to speed or commit other traffic violations that draw attention to them and end up arrested like the Anders brothers. Lawson told me all they could book the three on without proof of a burglary was concealed weapons charges. He said when they searched the very large, buxom woman they found $850 in her bra between her large breasts.

He said Neil made one phone call and a local bail bondsman had them out soon after they were fingerprinted and mugged. I didn't say anything at the time, but I thought the New Orleans bail bondsman wired the bail money to the local bail bondsman.

Lawson said one of the three chucks was partially broken off the drill motor and was missing. He sent a teletype to all stations describing the drill motor and pruning saw with the orange smear on the handle and got no response until the next morning when the Oregon State Police responded with a hit, then they had to scramble to locate the Anders brothers.

Lawson phoned the local bail bondsman and asked him if he knew where the Anders brothers were. When the bail bondsman said they were in his office, Lawson asked him to stall them, and he and his partner went there and arrested them for the Salem safe burglary.

An Oregon State Police officer and a deputy sheriff met us at the Salem Airport. As they drove us to a hotel to register and leave our luggage there, they briefed us on the evidence they had collected at the scene. They said they found a broken piece of a drill motor chuck in front of the safe and an orange pry bar on top of a stack of boxes.

They said it was a skylight entry job. The pry bar was probably dropped as the burglar's tools and the money were being lifted up after one of the brothers pulled himself back up on the roof and he didn't want to bother to go back down and get the pry bar.

We all agreed that only a young, agile, strong man could have climbed a rope and done all that, so we all concluded it had to be Billy Joe who did the safe cracking and all the lifting. Billy Joe was short and stocky, so it fit.

After going to the hotel, we were driven directly to the court. With only one day to testify, it was to be a rushed trial and would probably extend into the night. We learned that Neil Anders had an alibi for the case, because he had some proof he had been in the state of Washington at the time of the burglary.

The elected district attorney personally prosecuted the case, and Billy Joe's attorney was a high-paid Las Vegas shyster.

With other witnesses excluded from the court room, Officer Joe Story testified to his probable cause to stop the Anders brothers in the Lincoln included in the APB. Then I testified two times. The first time was while the jury was absent from the court room so the defense attorney could argue against the constitutionality of my consent search. The judge ruled that my search was legal and admissible. Then I repeated my testimony to the jury. As I had learned early in my cop career, when I answered questions, I looked directly at the jurors and tried to pick out the one I thought might influence the others or be selected as the foreman.

It wasn't difficult in that case. There was a man about 65 to 70 sitting at the top left corner of the jury box. He looked like a hard working retired farmer and intently listened to every word I said. I looked directly at him during most of my testimony, and as I concluded my testimony, he looked directly at me and slowly nodded his head. With that, I would have bet ten to one we had the conviction in the bag and sealed shut.

Joe Story and I were dismissed by the judge and taken to the hotel by a deputy sheriff. We had a couple of drinks, watched TV and solved the problems of the world for hours. At about 8:00 p.m. Don Lawson and his inspector partner came to our room. The inspector was outraged at the district attorney. He said the D.A. belabored the issue that $8,500 was taken in the burglary but only $4,500 was returned by the Sacramento sheriff's office. I told him it was probably just the district attorney's tactic to impress the jury that he was honest for future votes and we would never see any of them again, so enjoy the trip.

With $4,000 allegedly missing, I mentioned that the store owner may have padded the loss amount, as some do. Then I saw a good reason to tell them about the New Orleans bail bondsman's business card in Billy Joe's wallet. I told them about the business card and said, "I think he's their banker and they probably wire him about half of their take from every job. Then all they have to do is call him collect to get bailed out like they did when you booked them for the concealed weapons charges." They all agreed and the inspector cooled down.

We then went to a nice night club to eat and celebrate. We had been at the diner for about an hour when the district attorney appeared and greeted us as though there had never been a money shortage problem. I told him about the New Orleans bail bondsman's business card and our belief that he has the $4,000 and he agreed. Then he invited us to go to his attorney friend's lavish office with a well stocked bar. We had to make the most of our one-day trip, so we went and all became friends.

We spent a few hours at the lavish office and finally got to bed in the wee hours — so late that we missed our scheduled flight out of the Salem Airport, so the state police drove us to the Portland International Airport to get a flight home.

About two weeks later, I received a letter from the Salem district attorney, who said Billy Joe pled guilty to the safe burglary charges and was sentenced to only two years in prison — even though he was a two-time loser and would be in prison with his brothers to plan their next heist. With that I decided what Oregon needed was judges like San Diego's Judge John Hewicker.

CHAPTER 36

Three from the Ring

One defensive action when standing an arm's length from a potentially threatening subject while interrogating him is called "Three-Count from Baton-Ring Exercise," or "Three from the Ring" for short.

When I reported to the academy on December 1, 1965, the only lesson plan I inherited was a one-page list of callisthenic exercises, and no assistant. The courses had to be built from the ground up except for the FBI Methods of Arrest Course. The FBI would instruct their eight come-along holds and carotid sleeper hold, and my assistant and I were to drill the cadets afterwards to ensure they could properly apply the holds.

The women's rest room in the gym was converted to our office with a phone and two desks. I had until the first week in January to get an assistant and plan a practical exercise and running schedule.

There was an obstacle course designed like the Los Angeles Police Department's course, but the LAPD six-foot wall had been cut down to five feet because too many cadets in the past had injured their private parts going over the wall. There was no dirt running track, so I had to have the maintenance crew grade one that would drain in rainy weather.

I planned a progressive exercise and running schedule for even the most out-of-shape cadets. It increased for twelve weeks then leveled off for the remaining four weeks.

For years after I graduated from the academy officers complained about being required to run five miles or more as cadets and it was so miserable they would never run again. Two of the physical training instructors they complained about were extreme conditioning fanatics who apparently thought all CHP officers should be Olympic competitors. One was a lieutenant who wore lead weights in his shoes while running. A few years later when he was running one morning with the lead weights in his shoes, he fell over dead from a massive heart attack, and I did not want to kill any cadets.

My goal was to condition the cadets to be able to run a mile in eight minutes without any extreme effort in the hope it would encourage them to continue running after graduating, so the schedule started with a quarter of a mile and progressed up to a mile. The first two weeks were the hardest.

I also made it mandatory that my assistant or I would lead every class in calisthenics and running, but not the obstacle course, so we could time them. I believed we should be able to prove we could do everything we required them to do, not just walk around yelling at them to do more. I was 35 years old while most of them were 10 years younger, so I tried to show that age shouldn't slow them down.

There would be three classes of 120 cadets in each class. Three months from the first Monday in January there would be 360 cadets to train. Each class had to be divided into two companies of 60 each, because the gym would accommodate no more than 80 with space for calisthenics.

We were told the 3,200 officer expansion was for additional officers to man 100 Passenger Vehicle Inspection (PVI) teams. The PVI operation was an attempted end run around President Johnson's newly passed Highway Safety Bill that required annual safety inspections of all passenger cars by licensed auto repair shops.

His bill was a political farce. Many states already had those requirements, and they were a gold mine for dishonest auto repair shop owners. It was like blackmail. Crooked shops would allege all kinds of phony problems and overcharge the victim car owners. They had to pay or they got no car registration.

Also, CHP annual reports for years listed only three percent of traffic accidents as being caused by mechanical failures, so it was obvious that it was much more politically expedient for President Johnson to try to blame cars for traffic accidents instead of the driver voters.

It didn't take long for us to figure out that the additional 3,200 officers were to establish a statewide riot control force, not for 500 PVI officers. Most interesting was that Governor Pat Brown had never been a friend of the CHP. As soon as he became governor in 1959 he immediately discontinued the CHP expansion of the 1950s. From then until this 3,200 officer expansion, he had not given the

CHP any additional officers despite the approximate 50 percent increase in traffic accidents during those years.

But his political home base was in the San Francisco Bay area where most of the riots, demonstrations and revolutionary activities were taking place. Conversely, Los Angeles County had about 15,000 officers on the LAPD, L.A. Sheriff's Department and dozens of smaller police departments, so it was obvious the new CHP riot force was for Governor Brown's home political turf. L.A. County did not need our help after the Watts riots in 1965.

Despite Captain Overhouse's long-term commitment to quality education and training of cadets, there was a small force of about three staff members who thought otherwise. Their battle cry was, "Get rid of the culls." In my CHP career I was never treated with a threat like that hanging over my head, nor had I seen other CHP cadets or officers exposed to that kind of cold-blooded threat.

From August when Inspector Blossom phoned me to offer me the academy position until I reported in December, he was promoted to chief of staff and was replaced by a newly promoted inspector. The new inspector had been the captain commander of the same Southern California squad where the three "Get rid of the culls" had been assigned under his command for years. It was not a healthy situation. The direct information pipeline had been laid, and one of the three informed on anybody if it would enhance his image in the right eyes.

I also learned that the sneaky snitch wanted to have my physical training supervisor position, but Inspector Blossom wanted me to have it. It also came to my attention that the one who had wanted my position criticized me behind my back because he thought the physical training should be the primary operation to flunk out cadets who couldn't perform to his "Superman" standards. So I was very pleased that I could probably save any number of potentially fine officers from his axe.

It was January by the time I was assigned an assistant. He was a former marine, had played semi-pro football, was in great physical condition and was very popular with the cadets.

Then in March as we were drilling a cadet class in the FBI holds they had already been shown by FBI agents, an overzealous cadet became violent and fell on top of me. It fractured and slightly displaced my first lumbar vertebra. I immediately requested my motor accident orthopedic surgeon, Dr. Harold Gibbons. He told me he believed he could manipulate my vertebra back in place without surgery. He did and I was very pleased with the results.

I went home after ten days in Sutter General Hospital. I was in a cast for five weeks, then in a brace for about four months. While I was wearing the brace, there was an academy staff party at the home of a staff member. During the party, one "Cull" advocate seriously asked me if I was going to retire on a back disability. I said "no" much to his obvious disappointment. The three were itching to get my job for the number one "Get rid of the culls" advocates.

When I returned to work after five months off, I was assigned for one month as vacation relief of the cadet supervisor. My supervisor was Lieutenant Steele. One morning we were called to a classroom where a cadet had suffered a seizure. When we arrived, he seemed okay then another cadet called me aside and told me he had been a Los Angeles County deputy sheriff and had seen epileptic seizures. He said he was sitting directly behind the cadet who had the seizure and said it was definitely an epileptic seizure.

We had an officer take the seizure victim to a specialist for an electroencephalogram (EEG) to determine if he had suffered an epileptic seizure. The results came back positive; he was an epileptic victim.

Lieutenant Steele and I took him into the lieutenant's office to tell him, and he cried, sobbed and shook violently when he was told he would have to be medically terminated. In just a few hours, that cadet's life crashed forever, and just before I returned to work another cadet had also had an epileptic seizure and had to be terminated. One occurred while he was watching a First Aid training film wherein ketchup was used to imitate blood. The other was watching an old film shown when I was a cadet of an old heroin addict probing his needle-marked leg with a needle trying to find a vein to inject heroin.

Watching that cadet cry, sob and shake made me wonder how the "Get rid of the culls" pushers would feel about ending the CHP dreams of other cadets who had become one of the chosen few. I thought one or two of them might have a change of heart, but the third one who wanted my job would probably never change his cold-blooded stance.

After drilling a few classes in the FBI holds, I learned that about ten percent of cadets were impervious to pain. No matter how much their wrists were bent back or elbows twisted, they would mock the holds by laughing. These were very old FBI methods that I was taught in Recruit Training Class on the San Diego Police Department. I had used them many times not knowing they were seriously flawed.

The Koga Methods

Also after many baton training sessions, I came to realize the age-old batons with the traditional leather thongs left much to be desired along with our riot control formations. I phoned the Los Angeles Sheriff's Academy and asked about their methods, but they were the same as the CHP methods. Then I phoned the LAPD Academy and was quickly connected with Officer Bob Koga, a Japanese/American officer who held two or three martial arts belts. He explained his methods, and it took only about ten minutes for me to realize I had hit the mother lode of police physical methods.

Koga said he and his assistant were coming to an instructors' conference in Sacramento in a couple of weeks and they would demonstrate his methods to my assistant and me. When we met at the academy, something came up about my back injury and I told Koga I had returned to the physical training to try to get my back in shape. When I told him how it happened, he laughed.

He said that was the number one danger of being a physical methods training instructor, because every cadet class has at least one who wants to prove he can lick the instructor. After seeing Koga's methods, I wrote a memo recommending the CHP adopt his baton, methods of arrest and riot control formation methods.

A couple of days after I submitted my memo my lieutenant told me I should have submitted two memos. He said one should have been for the baton and riot control formation methods and the other for Koga's Twist-Lock control. He didn't explain why I should submit two memos and not being a politician, it took me a while to figure it out. Koga's more effective Twist-Lock control hold would replace the FBI's eight come-along holds training and that FBI training would be discontinued.

At that time and for years before, the CHP Academy had a highly respected world-wide reputation. While I was a duty officer from 1960 to 1963, five Indonesian Federal Police command officers attended an entire 12-week cadet class. Also, even though the CHP Academy was open only to law enforcement officers, the U.S. State Department pulled rank and a young civilian Iranian man attended a complete cadet class. Years later I had to conclude that he was probably a member of the Shah's family. He was a delightful young gentleman, and we all loved him.

Also, during the same period a North Carolina State Highway Patrol lieutenant and a captain from Finland visited and lodged at the academy. Considering all that and more, instructing at the CHP Academy was a big feather in the FBI's cap and very political, so I was headed for number one on the FBI's most unwanted list.

Commissioner Harold Sullivan was a retired LAPD deputy chief. The scuttlebutt came from somewhere that he did not like Koga. I wasn't sure if it was from a source who didn't want me to get credit for improving methods or the truth, but I didn't care. We had hundreds of officers battling demonstrators, dissidents and violent activists at the Oakland Army Induction Center, San Francisco State University, Berkeley and other hot spots, and they needed the best methods possible.

Then almost two months later, my assistant and I were ordered to attend a three-day Koga methods in-service class at the LAPD Academy. It was encouraging and proof that someone had concocted the tale about the commissioner not liking Koga.

The three-day training was excellent and convinced me more than ever that Koga's methods were far superior to what the CHP had and probably the best ever in law enforcement. At the conclusion of the training, Koga gave me a split bamboo training baton that would sting trainees but not injure them.

I had to submit a memorandum evaluating Koga's methods and training. Months went by without any decision one way or another. Then one day the training division inspector phoned me about some unrelated issue he wanted to clarify.

With that direct call not known to anyone who wanted to sabotage my efforts, I was able to ask the inspector the status of my Koga methods recommendations. He didn't know, so I asked him if he could get an appointment for me with Chief of Staff Inspector Blossom so I could demonstrate the methods. I said it was difficult to understand the methods from two memorandums. They had to be seen. The inspector said he would speak to Inspector Blossom.

About a week later, the training division commander inspector and I went to Inspector Blossom's office and I demonstrated Koga's methods. Inspector Blossom's only objection was the movements that involved thrusting ends of the baton toward an adversary's eyes, but when I explained that it was solely a distraction tactic, he quickly withdrew his objection.

Inspector Blossom was impressed, but said he would like me to get the approval of the training committee which was composed of inspectors who hadn't been on the road for years and had never had a baton. He also wanted to get the opinion of the physical methods supervisor I had replaced. This was not a good idea; he never tried to improve anything and left me with a one-page list of calisthenics and a box of plastic batons that cracked and broke during training when struck against the tire targets on cold mornings.

Almost two weeks later, I demonstrated the methods to the training committee in the academy library. They were impressed but didn't commit themselves one way or the other to me. Inspector Blossom must have reconsidered when he had time to think about the previous physical methods supervisor's qualifications, because he never got involved.

Then another long wait ensued. Captain Overhouse was exactly right in calling headquarters the "Palace of Pooh." Paper was shuffled from one desk to another with lower grade brass afraid to make recommendations that wouldn't be in accord with top brass' ideas. So many plans ended up at the bottom of a pile of other mind-boggling political bombs. Bureaucracy in action!

While waiting for a decision, a two-day workshop for all instructors was conducted. The lecturer was USC Professor Dr. Ascot. He explained his instructional methods and was very impressive. He told of a night student he once had who was working full time during the day. As hard as the student studied, he didn't pass the course and Dr. Ascot had to fail him, and despite the fact he had no choice, it had seriously bothered him ever since he failed that student.

Near the end of the second and final day, I asked him what he thought about pre-testing cadets the first week of each class. Dr. Ascot completely agreed with that concept. He said if he had pre-tested the failed student's class he was certain the student would have passed the course. He said it was later obvious to him that the student had no knowledge of the course subject matter when the class started and had to grope his way through the entire semester.

As we walked down the hall after the completion of the two-day course, the number one advocate of "getting rid of the culls" disagreed with pre-testing because it wasn't done in colleges. I knew it wasn't worth my time arguing with him because he was intent on firing cadets, not teaching them with the best methods possible.

The hypocrisy was that all of us who had gained promotions had a loose-leaf binder full of past promotional test questions to study for months before tests. We also had studied Ken or Arco books of copyrighted supervision and management questions and answers that were repeatedly used on state tests. But he was so intent on flunking cadets he apparently never heard a word of Dr. Ascot's lecture.

There was an FBI special agent who had instructed at the CHP Academy for over ten years and was sort of the dean of FBI instructors and head FBI liaison with the CHP Academy. He was also very communicative and made it his business to know what was going on at the academy. He had obviously heard of the pending CHP consideration to adopt the Koga methods that would end the FBI instruction of come-along holds.

He came into our small office with fire in his eyes. He didn't mention Koga's Twist-Lock control hold that would replace the FBI's eight control holds. He challenged the claim that a Koga baton could not be pulled from an officer's hand if properly gripped by the officer, so he challenged me to try to keep him from pulling it from my hand.

I picked up the baton Koga had also given to me and held it out for him to grab. He was about six feet 1 inch tall, weighed 180 pounds and was wiry and very strong. He started violently pulling, jerking, pushing and twisting in the small office. "Whoa," I said, "let's go into the gym before somebody gets hurt in here." He agreed and we went into the gym and got on a mat. He resumed his violent pulling, jerking, pushing and twisting for about three or four minutes with no success and then spun around and stomped out of the gym without saying a word. I had no idea that episode would end his FBI career.

FBI Director J. Edgar Hoover took great pride in the FBI instructing local and state agency officers. So much so that he initiated the FBI National Academy in 1935 to educate and train law enforcement officers from other agencies and departments. It was in part of the FBI Academy and was located in Washington, D.C. until the late 1960s or early 1970s when a beautiful new FBI Academy was built on the Quantico, Virginia Marine Corps Base.

Not long after he lost the tussle over the Koga baton, the longtime FBI

Bob Koga demonstrating three finger and thumb grip of Koga baton — creating "Chinese handcuffs" tightening effect when pulled.

instructor at the CHP Academy was gone, but I couldn't concern myself with his possible early retirement or transfer to some other post. The CHP needed the best methods and Koga's were by far the best.

About a month later, the commissioner approved the Koga methods. Then about two weeks later the deputy commissioner issued a memorandum mandating that all CHP officers up to and including the rank of lieutenant be trained in the Koga methods within 90 days.

Sergeants were sent to the academy from all areas of the state, and my assistant and I trained about 40 of them. They returned to their squads and divisions, and the training was completed in less than 90 days.

GEORGE C. NUTTALL

The Koga baton is dense wood and about 29 inches long, has a diameter of 1 ¼ inches and is fitted with a rubber crutch end with the end cut out to make a grommet that will fit snugly about 7 inches from the end. The tapered portion of the grommet is pointed toward the long end of the baton and serves as a grip and a stop when the baton is slipped into a baton ring attached to the officer's Sam Browne gun belt.

One defensive action when standing an arm's length from a potentially threatening subject while interrogating him is called "Three-Count from Baton-Ring Exercise," or "Three from the Ring" for short. The officer has his hand on the baton at all times. If the subject becomes a threat, the officer suddenly thrusts the baton end toward the subject's forehead to strike or distract him. Then in one sweeping arced motion strikes the subject in the chest with the other end of the baton, then in another sweeping arc motion strikes the subject in the stomach. The three strikes take only about two to three seconds.

Not long after all CHP officers were trained in the Koga methods, several officers from a Los Angeles County CHP squad were confronted by a mob of about 20 angry activists. One person in the mob became a threat to the officers and one officer quickly used the Three from the Ring method and struck the subject a hard blow on the forehead with the short end of his baton. With that one blow, the subject was knocked unconscious and fell to the ground and the other activists saw what happened and quickly dispersed. Thereafter, the Koga methods were known throughout the CHP as "Three from the Ring."

During a later in-service class, an officer came to our small office in the gym and said, "Thanks, George, I've been on the department for ten years and this is the first time I ever knew how to use my baton." Needless to say, it made me feel good to know that all my long efforts were worth it.

When the FBI special agent who had instructed at the CHP Academy for over ten years suddenly disappeared, he was replaced by a veteran special agent to instruct the one remaining FBI class of "Techniques of Arrest."

The FBI instructing such a class was questionable to even my cadet class. It was reported that of the 80 in my cadet class, 40 were

298

former cops. We could not figure out why the FBI was instructing the class that had to do with making felony stops. The FBI policy was well announced to be "Superiority of manpower and superiority of fire power" when going after known fugitives, but until 1964 when the CHP was finally provided with shotguns, most CHP officers worked alone with no more than their personally-owned six-shooter. Even with shotguns when traffic stops are made, officers don't know if they are dealing with a fugitive or not. Furthermore, the FBI Techniques of Arrest class was more of a "dog and pony show" to entertain the cadets than a serious officer survival course. Also, a CHP sergeant instructed a companion class of "Enforcement Tactics" that stressed officer safety much more when making traffic stops.

The replacement FBI Techniques of Arrest instructor conducted the classes in the gym. Two times just before his class, he stuck his head in our office and moaned about having to instruct the class. He was only a few years from retirement and was obviously burned out.

The second time he moaned about instructing the class, my assistant and I looked at each other in disgust as soon as he left to go into the gym. Almost simultaneously, we both said the same thing: we were certain that class would some day lead to a major CHP disaster.

Four CHP Officers Killed in Newhall

About two years later on April 5, 1970, it happened. Four Newhall squad CHP officers were fatally gunned down by two ex-cons. There had been a broadcast about one of the two brandishing a gun at another motorist. The first two officers stopped the two ex-cons in a lighted roadside area where there was a restaurant and a service station, but one officer did not use proper tactics, and he and his partner were killed.

My assistant who agreed with me about the sloppy Techniques of Arrest class had been promoted to sergeant and was then instructing the CHP Enforcement Tactics class, so I didn't bother to speak my piece about the probable cause of the tragedy because I knew him well enough to know he would tell everyone about our mutual prediction. He obviously did, because the FBI Techniques of Arrest class was quickly discontinued.

I knew the Newhall captain commander very well and had a few discussions with him about the worst tragedy in CHP history. At a much later time, he told me of the saddest part of the disaster. He said three of the officers' wives were able to rebuild their lives and remarry, but the wife of the officer who made the tactical error assumed his guilt and hadn't recovered from it as of that time.

As a result of that tragedy, the CHP issued a new order entitled "High Risk and Felony Stops" that gave officers much more latitude than ever before to draw their weapons if there was any indication they were dealing with a dangerous subject. Prior to that time, if a citizen so much as complained that an officer even had his hand on his sidearm during a traffic stop, the complaint could be sustained against the officer as being offensive to the complainant. As sad as it was that the tragedy happened, some small good did come out of it.

CHAPTER 37

The Dyer Act

There were two Redding resident FBI special agents who frequently came to the Yreka office to get information about Dyer Act stolen vehicles that had crossed the state line and been recovered by our officers.

Because I was not a military veteran and did not have the three veterans' preference points for promotional tests, I was certain I could never reach the rank of captain, and lieutenant was the worst position on the CHP. Lieutenants were mostly small squad commanders or field operations officers in large offices where they were caught between the captain and sergeants and blamed by both sides for everything that went wrong. So I decided to stay at the academy until my children were in college, then transfer to Auburn or Placerville where there were no graveyard shift sergeants.

Then about six months before the next lieutenant test, the legislature limited the veterans' preference points to only Vietnam veterans who had served in that wartime period in the past ten years. It was like a shot of new life for me.

I began studying and came out 39 on the lieutenant list. The same year the CHP retirement plan was improved and the mandatory retirement age was dropped from age 65 to age 60. With the improved retirement and lower mandatory retirement age, dozens of officers who were ranked lieutenant or above retired after it went into effect on December 1, 1968.

Effective January 31, 1969, 39 sergeants were to be promoted to lieutenant. One ahead of me was in a small lieutenant command office and waived his promotion at that time because his lieutenant commander had applied for retirement. He would then be number one on the list and could become the commander.

It only made good sense, but not to the top brass. The word quickly came down from the top that it was not favorably looked upon by the commissioner or other top brass to waive a promotion, so when I was offered Yreka, I accepted. Yreka is inland on I-5

301

about 25 miles from the Oregon border — not to be confused with Eureka on the north coast.

There were two Redding resident FBI special agents who frequently came to the Yreka office to get information about stolen vehicles that had crossed the state line and been recovered by our officers. I asked one of them why they wanted the information when our office had already taken credit for the recoveries and in nearly all cases arrested the thieves. He replied that they had to report all Dyer Act recoveries and arrests within their area of responsibility and emphatically asked that I notify them of all Dyer Act cases.

It sounded fishy to me, so I ignored his request. Also, when I was a sergeant in the Sacramento squad office one of our officers recovered a mysterious stolen Corvette that had switched state of Washington license plates. It was a Sunday and I radioed for the FBI to respond because it was obviously an out-of-state stolen vehicle and a Dyer Act case handled by the FBI. But radio replied that the FBI said they wouldn't respond unless there was evidence of other out-of-state crimes in addition to auto theft.

I then requested a National Auto Theft Bureau agent to assist us at our location. He arrived in about 30 minutes and started tracing the stolen Corvette through NATB records. Within 30 minutes he determined the car had been stolen in Alabama and had crossed numerous state lines. Our further investigation revealed the thief had numerous forms of identification with different names and a loaded revolver in his quickly abandoned apartment. That snubbing by the FBI and the fact that the double reporting sounded dishonest to me, led me to ignore their request.

About a month later, the same FBI agent came to the office and said he heard one of our officers had recovered a Dyer Act stolen vehicle out of Oregon and asked me why I hadn't notified him. I replied that I didn't know about it, which I didn't.

The FBI had a long history of "all take and no give" with local and state law enforcement. I had better things to do than to quiz our officers every day to find out if they had recovered Dyer Act stolen vehicles.

> The reason the Redding FBI special agents were so determined to get information about all our Dyer Act stolen vehicle recoveries and arrests became clear many years later — in April 1976 — when a Congressional investigation revealed that FBI Director J. Edgar Hoover had been padding his annual budget requests for decades by taking credit for Dyer Act recoveries and arrests made by other local and state law enforcement agencies.

One morning when the captain was home in San Luis Obispo, I was the acting commander. Officer Bill Dorsey came in to tell me about a stolen motorcycle he had recovered and the thief he had arrested. The I-5 Freeway was being constructed and the I-5 still ran through the city of Yreka with one signal in the middle of the city.

The Motorcycle Thief

Officer Dorsey said he was stopped at the signal when he noticed a motorcycle in the rear of a station wagon stopped next to him, so after the light turned green, he stopped the station wagon to check out the motorcycle. It came back stolen out of Orange County, California. He said there were also several boxes of stereos still in the shipping boxes, so he called for the Yreka Police Department and turned the stereos over to the police officer to check if they were stolen.

Dorsey said the motorcycle thief tried to convince him the motorcycle was not stolen because an Orange County Police Department had already checked it out and determined it wasn't stolen. He said the thief told him the Orange County police had arrested him and impounded the motorcycle to check it out. Then the police released him and returned the motorcycle to him as being clear.

Dorsey said the Orange County Police Department officers had run the wrong number to check it for stolen. He said there is an engine number and a transmission number and they didn't run both numbers to be sure. With a 50/50 chance, they ran only the wrong number. We both laughed and I commended him for such a good arrest.

About two hours later I received a phone call from the Yreka Police Department chief's secretary. She said the chief wanted to talk to me and put me on hold. When he came on the line a few minutes later, he asked me to come to his office to discuss a problem. When I arrived at his office, the secretary asked me to take a seat and wait until the chief had time to talk to me. With that, I was beginning to get irritated. It was like I was going to have the honor of meeting with FBI Director J. Edgar Hoover, and I supervised 4 sergeants, 29 officers and 6 civilian employees compared to his 10-officer police department.

When I was finally allowed to enter the chief's office, I met the 65-year-old politically appointed chief and he looked distressed. Nervously, he told me about CHP Officer Dorsey's turning several boxes of stereos over to his sergeant to check out. He said his sergeant was the only officer on duty and they were not equipped for or familiar with checking for stolen goods, and it created a big problem for his department.

I told him Officer Dorsey had told me about his arrest of the motorcycle thief and his turning the stereos over to the sergeant and asked the chief what he wanted me to do about the problem. He sort of stammered then asked me if I would order my officers not to stop anyone in the city of Yreka again. He said they should wait until the violators or suspects left the city limits before stopping them. As crazy as it sounded, I lied and told the chief I would do what I could. He actually believed me and thanked me.

As I left his office I thought this is worse than Big Bear. There was no way I would do such a crazy thing, so I canned the whole bizarre idea and never mentioned it to anyone. If I had, it could have caused strained relations between the CHP and Yreka police officers.

Pursuit to the Border

One Sunday a young man obviously under the influence of drugs stopped at a Weed service station and hung around. He was from San Francisco where drug use was rampant at that time, and he babbled incoherently for about two hours before heading northbound toward Yreka in his VW Super Bug. As soon as he departed, the stressed out service station attendant phoned the CHP and reported the wild acting young man.

A younger and less experienced CHP officer observed the Super Bug at the south Yreka city limits and gave chase. In about the middle of Yreka, the officer made a reckless move and pulled up to the right of the VW. The driver swerved to the right into the CHP car and it went off the road into a parking meter. The CHP car then went out of control, swerved across the highway and came to rest disabled in a grocery store parking lot.

A sheriff's captain and a Yreka police officer gave pursuit through what is called "The Canyon," which was four lanes of divided highway all the way to the Oregon border. The drugged driver of the VW stopped a few times after going around curves, stood up through the sunroof and fired a handgun at the captain and Yreka police officer. The captain returned fire, and the pursuit continued to the Oregon border where they discontinued their chase.

The Oregon State Police was notified of the pursuit and quickly set up a road block several miles north of the border. When the VW approached the road block at high speed without slowing, the Oregon State Police opened fire on it. The wild VW driver was mortally wounded and later died at a hospital.

The sheriff examined the captain's car and discovered that the windshield had not been shattered by shots from the pursued gunman. The shots had come from inside the captain's car. The sheriff later told me he gave the captain a commendation for his valor in pursuing the dangerous gunman. He also gave the captain a censurable report for shooting out the windshield.

The CHP Tule Lake resident officer then reported a problem to me. He said Siskiyou County and bordering Modoc County had entered into an agreement with the Tule Lake Police Department to build a new police station and jail. The agreement was that the two counties would pay for the building and the Tule Lake Police Department would always provide an officer as a jailer whenever a CHP or sheriff's prisoner was in the jail. The problem was that the written agreement did not include a clause requiring the Tule Lake Police Department to provide a jailer.

The Tule Lake resident officer phoned and told me the Tule Lake police chief said he didn't have the manpower to provide jailers and wouldn't do so. He asked me what he should do when he made physical arrests. Somebody had scammed the two counties. I told him I would call the sheriff and get back to him.

I called the sheriff and he said to turn prisoners over to his Tule Lake resident deputy and he would transport them to Yreka to the county jail. I then called the CHP resident officer and told him what the sheriff said to do. By then Big Bear was beginning to look like a well-oiled, precise law enforcement operation. Nothing seemed to go smoothly in Yreka and it was like trying to put out one brush fire after another.

Then one late morning a sergeant phoned me and said one of our officers had arrested a Catholic priest for driving under the influence and the Weed Police Department chief would not let him book the priest in the Weed jail. The sergeant mentioned the chief's name, and he had an Italian surname. I figured being of Italian descent, the chief was probably Catholic and that was why he wouldn't book the priest. I told him to book the priest in the county jail. Less than two weeks later, the Weed police chief was fired. I couldn't help but believe it had something to do with the CHP arrest of the Catholic priest that he couldn't quash.

Interviewing Candidates

About a month earlier, the sheriff had me sit on an oral panel with him and the publisher of the local newspaper to interview and appraise deputy sheriff and jail custodian candidates. After we had interviewed about half of the 15 candidates, the sheriff said he had to leave to take care of a pressing matter and for me and the publisher to continue.

I asked the sheriff if he would be satisfied with our appraisals. He said he would leave the tape recorder on and we could discuss the interviews he missed after all the interviews were completed. The two of us interviewed one candidate and gave him a passing score.

The sheriff then returned and we suddenly noticed he had not turned the tape recorder on before he left. There was no discussion of that one candidate and the publisher and I never knew if he passed the sheriff's fine screening or not.

The sheriff then asked me to sit on a panel with him and the Weed City Council to interview candidates for chief of police. I couldn't very well refuse, so I did so with a plan to closely watch the sheriff and his tape recorder.

There were five candidates to interview. We met in a small conference room in the Weed City Hall. The five city councilmen entered the room in a group. The only one wearing a suit and tie was the mayor, who was the father of a Yreka CHP officer. Another councilman was wearing blue bib overalls with a dress shirt buttoned all the way up to the collar. I thought this should be a rare experience.

The seven of us interviewed the five candidates, and it wasn't even close, so we selected a former sergeant of a Los Angeles county beach police department. He told us he had high hopes of someday becoming the chief of that beach police department, but when a new chief was appointed from outside the department, he resigned in disgust.

I readily voted for him because I knew how he felt. I had always opposed political appointments from outside. I felt that if a law enforcement agency does not have qualified personnel to promote from within, there's something seriously wrong with that department. About two years later I was told the chief had been fired.

One day a memorandum came from the headquarters unit that processed the originals of all traffic and parking citations. It listed three citation books that were missing about half of the citations. When I looked at the three lists of missing citations, it was obvious they hadn't yet been issued. Despite the obviously stupid query, I gave it to the very efficient day sergeant to unravel.

Later that day he returned with the answers to that great mystery. He said one of the citation books was his and he hadn't yet completed issuing all of the citations. He said one was issued to the PVI team that almost always issued written warnings and wrote few citations, and the book wasn't completed. He said the third was issued to an officer who was off duty on injury time and was only partially completed.

With that ammunition, I wrote a lengthy memorandum in very certain terms about forwarding all citations to headquarters. That process had started in 1929 when the CHP first became a sole statewide agency as the enforcement division of the DMV. The purpose was to collect data for the annual report, account for all citations and check for errors on citations.

Then in 1962 the CHP initiated a Data Process Unit and officers submitted daily Form 62 reports in codes for all citations issued, accidents investigated and the number of injuries and deaths. With those reports, data was computer collected for the annual report. The old accounting method was useless. Fixing a ticket was very simple; you could just destroy the court copy and forward and file the other copies as required by the Headquarters General Order.

"That's the Way We've Always Done it."

I wrote the memorandum with all the explanations clearly stating why the 40-year-old process was obsolete and no more than an expensive make-work exercise in futility. Then I sent it upstream to the Redding zone office. About a week later one of the zone inspectors visited the Yreka office. The first thing he asked as soon as he sat down in the office I shared with the captain was, "Why did you write that memo?" "I thought it was self explanatory, Inspector," I replied "and forwarding all citations to headquarters doesn't make any sense. It's a waste of time and money." "But that's the way we've always done it," he said.

I later served in three offices as a lieutenant and captain and heard that same hollow excuse any number of times when I discovered useless procedures that had been established by a captain 20 years earlier. It may have made sense at the time, but by then we had put a man on the moon. Times had changed.

Seven months later, a new Headquarters General Order was issued stating that citations were no longer to be forwarded to headquarters. The originals of citations that in the past had been forwarded to headquarters were to go to the courts. I had never paid any attention to which citation copy had been sent to headquarters and was surprised that the courts had been receiving carbon copies for 40 years. I'm not an attorney by a mile, but I always thought courts should have original documents if available.

When the order came out I kicked myself. The unit that was disbanded by that order processed about 2,000,000 citations a year. The savings to the CHP was probably about $100,000 a year. If I had submitted a Merit Award Board Suggestion form for money savings suggestions, I would have received ten percent of the first year's savings, or about $10,000. In lieu of that award, I made myself very unpopular. Of the approximate 4,500 people on the CHP at that time, including dozens of pencil pushers in headquarters and the commissioner, nobody ever put two and two together to see that it was a useless process, probably because "That's the way we've always done it."

CHAPTER 38

Chaos

The South L.A. office was the largest and most complex CHP office. The area included the Carson Scales, the affluent Palos Verdes Estates area and the largely black-populated areas of Willowbrook, Florence and Athens Park.

My family was still in Sacramento and I had waited for a promising opening in the Sacramento squad office, but in June it was obvious it wouldn't become a reality, so I went to see Deputy Commissioner Jim Bryant, who was a straight shooter and didn't pull any punches. He had worked his way up from the bottom and I knew him very well from both times I had been at the academy. The only thing louder than his booming speaking voice was his laughter.

I told him I had to get out of Yreka before my children went back to school in September, and I asked him where there were lieutenant openings. He said Baldwin Park, Barstow and South Los Angeles and I could have any one I wanted. I told him I would discuss it with my wife and get back to him the next day.

Although I had never wanted to be assigned to a Los Angeles County squad office and especially South L.A., it was closer to the ocean and cooler than the other two inland areas. My wife was a Pacific Bell business office supervisor and had attended Pacific Bell training in the South Los Angeles area while I was in Yreka and had made some key contacts. She was certain she could transfer to that area as a supervisor.

When I told Deputy Commissioner Bryant I would go to the South L.A., he graciously told me I could use the relocation expenses I had not used when I went to Yreka. I told him the only expense I hadn't used was the household moving expenses. He told me to see the head of the accounting section and tell him he had approved my moving expenses.

That was typical of his looking out for those he thought deserved it, because expenses were not allowed when an officer or employee

310

requested a transfer. Expenses were allowed only for administrative transfers, including initial promotional relocations. The South L.A. office was the largest and most complex CHP office. There were 23 motor officers, plus six motor officers using their injury time and sick leave to retire on disability. The area included the Carson Scales, the affluent Palos Verdes Estates area and the largely black-populated areas of Willowbrook, Florence and Athens Park.

The facility had been built in 1960 as a fortress, with no windows, to accommodate 100 officers. There was no overflow drain for the men's restroom, and when the urinals overflowed the water went into the officers' locker room. It was reported that the contractor who built the facility committed suicide not long after it was completed.

When I arrived in August, there were 200 officers, including about 25 who were banked for the Central L.A. office that was under construction and about 27 more banked for the Westminster office that was also under construction. Every 16 weeks when cadet classes graduated, up to 19 new officers arrived from the academy along with two or three newly promoted sergeants, and about the same number of officers transferred out.

My first assignment was as night Field Operations Officer (FOO) supervising eight sergeants and 88 officers on the three night shifts. There were two other senior lieutenants who had spent most of their 21 and 18-year careers in L.A. County squad offices, and we shared the same dingy office. From the beginning, I was treated like the third man out.

The first of many CHP vehicle accident reports to hit my desk was a motor accident involving a 12-year veteran motor officer. I checked his personnel file for his accident record and found that this was his 11th motor accident in 12 years. He claimed it was caused when the siren fell off and got tangled up with the rear wheel. The 18-year CHP officer lieutenant had been a South L.A. motor sergeant before being promoted to lieutenant. I asked him if it was fashionable in South L.A. to go down once a year for a vacation on injury time, and he just shrugged his shoulders.

He and I then went to the Harley shop where the motor was sent for repairs. Our inspection clearly showed the siren was hanging loose and there were gouges on the rear wheel and tire. The siren had fallen off as the officer had said. I told the lieutenant that if the officer had one more motor accident, he could kiss motors goodbye forever.

When I tried to locate the officer to interview him about checking his motor for loose parts, I was told he was in Hawaii with his wife. I also learned that there was a very generous doctor who nearly all the injured South L.A. officers went to who gave them extra long injury times off. It was like a country club environment for the officers.

After the officer returned to duty, he filed a civil suit against the Harley dealer for negligent servicing. His motor had been serviced by that Harley dealer not long before, so he claimed it was their fault. The Harley dealer quickly notified the office that he had banned that officer and his motor from that shop forever, so we had to have him take his motor to a Harley dealer in Inglewood.

In addition to all the other confusion in the South L.A. office, there were eight courts to service with cases and officers' subpoenas — and only one court officer.

My night schedule included working days every Monday to deal with the extra work generated over the weekends when I was off duty. On my second Monday in the office, the captain gave me a complaint from two deputies in the sheriff's Firestone substation. The complaint was filed against two black CHP officers who had created an explosive situation and then departed, leaving the deputies to calm the outraged victims and witnesses. The complaint included the names and phone numbers of the alleged victims and witnesses.

Excessive Force

The captain assigned the complaint to me to investigate because an L.A. zone inspector had held a meeting with the sergeants not long before I arrived. The sergeants complained that they were overworked and didn't have the time to investigate the many citizens' complaints. That was a questionable administrative decision. There were 15 sergeants and only one of me. The sergeants supervised 10 to 15 officers and I supervised 96 sergeants and officers.

I already knew from the CHP grapevine that one of the officers involved had fatally shot his roommate's friend about a year before, so I reviewed his personnel file. It happened when he got off duty and went to the room he shared with his roommate. When he arrived there, his roommate's friend was sitting on the officer's bed, and there were a couple of other friends of his roommate in the room. With no substantial evidence to prove otherwise, the LAPD concluded that it was an accidental shooting. It was easy for me to imagine that after seeing one of their friends being fatally shot by a CHP officer, they didn't see anything.

I first interviewed the three young black men separately to get their versions of what had happened. Their accounts were all the same. Two had been punched by the officer and knocked to the ground. The one who had been in the right front seat and appeared to be the most physically fit laughed and said the officer really had a powerful punch. They all said the two CHP officers stopped them because the driver's car was lowered too far to the ground.

They said the first officer approached the driver and told him why he had stopped them. The driver gave the officer some sass then the punching officer walked up to the right front passenger's window, stuck his head in the open window and said, "Your mother." Anybody who knows anything about black culture should know that mothers are the most sacred of all in a black person's life. Just to mention mother in that way is offensive. When the right front passenger stepped out of the car to object to that offensive remark, the officer struck him in the face and knocked him to the ground.

There was a construction site at that location, so the rear seat passenger picked up a brick to defend himself against the punching officer. The aggressive officer then drew his service revolver and pointed it at the one with the brick in his right hand. After a few seconds of that potentially deadly standoff, the reporting deputies stopped to offer any needed help. Without discussing the situation with the deputies, the two CHP officers got into their patrol car and quickly departed.

That Saturday night was the final event of the Watts Festival commemorating black pride and solidarity after the August 1965 Watts riot. The celebration was about a mile north of the CHP officers' incident location. If that punching officer had shot that young black man, there was no way of knowing if it would have ignited a second Watts riot.

313

I interviewed the witnesses, including a Caucasian bread-truck driver. All of their statements were the same as those of the three young black men. There were no he says or she says. Their statements fit together like a six-piece jigsaw puzzle.

The captain had told me to interview the punching officer's past partners for witnesses to any other brutality or deadly threats by the officer. Two said they hadn't seen any incidents, but I got the impression they were afraid of his deadly tendencies and didn't want to get involved, and I couldn't prove they were lying. The other officer told me of an incident when the punching officer pulled his service revolver on a black driver after a short pursuit when the pursued man's vehicle ran off the roadway onto a lawn. He said the pursued driver was then very submissive and he didn't see any reason for the officer to draw his revolver. He said the officer's behavior was scary and unpredictable. That officer was able to give me enough information for me to identify and locate that pursued driver.

When I interviewed him in a patrol car in front of his home, he told me the same story that the identifying officer had related to me. Then he told me about the offending officer stopping his brother and striking him with a baton because his brother sassed him. Sass from violators is everyday police stuff.

I didn't bother to interview his brother because I had enough to end the investigation with an interview with the punching officer, so I just listed the brother as another victim/witness to the officer's excessive use of force.

During my then 17 years on the San Diego Police Department and the CHP, the administrations of both departments strictly forbid any use of excessive force. It was also denounced by the vast majority of officers on both departments. Those few officers who had a tendency to use excessive force or condoned its use were considered to be sadistic and even mentally disordered.

So by the time I interviewed the punching officer, I had formed the opinion that he was inclined to be homicidal more consciously than unconsciously. It was also very clear to me that he had been terrorizing the black residents of Willowbrook that abuts Watts to the south. Watts was in the city of Los Angeles and Willowbrook was unincorporated.

When I interviewed the punching officer, I tape recorded it. Based on all the witnesses' supporting statements and my opinion that he was homicidal, I had only one question for him to answer, "If the young man had made a motion to throw the brick at you, what would you have done?" I asked looking him directly in the eyes. "I would have taken the necessary action to defend myself against his threat of deadly force," he answered like he had rehearsed his justifiable homicide defense. When I asked him the same question a second time, he repeated the same obviously canned answer.

"Would you have shot him?" I asked to get to the most critical issue of the entire investigation. "Yes," he answered as though he had previously justified that action with his two former rehearsed, canned answers. "That's all I wanted to know," I said, and I told him he could leave.

Charges were quickly filed to terminate his CHP employment. He appealed to the State Personnel Board, a lengthy hearing was conducted and he was terminated. He was then gone and no longer a deadly threat to the public, so we thought.

All personnel investigations are strictly confidential within supervision and administration. I could not tell any officers of my findings and conclusions. Most of all, I could not so much as indicate that I suspected he was homicidal.

It had always puzzled me why good officers would band together against the administration when an obviously deficient or otherwise undesirable officer was investigated, punished or terminated. When I was an officer, it always pleased me to see supervisory action taken against officers I knew were not a credit to the department and worthy of public service, protection and trust. Also, I figured while supervision was busy going after them, they didn't have time to nit-pick what I did or didn't do — and there were some real nit-pickers on the CHP that I had the misfortune of working under. So without any details of the investigation findings and conclusions, some officers deemed that I was a hatchet man and let their opinions be known.

When I went to work on a Monday morning about a year later, there was an L.A. Times article on the office bulletin board. The headline was something like "Ex CHP Officer Kills Mother of Girl Friend." It went on to say the Santa Monica Police Department was searching for the killer and named our terminated punching officer. While I was reading the article, more than one officer expressed his relief that the man was no longer a CHP officer.

A few minutes after I returned to the lieutenants' office, a sergeant told me that another sergeant had told him at the time of my investigation that the terminated punching officer had said he was going to kill the witness officer and me. The witness officer had transferred to the Oceanside CHP office, so I wanted to alert him to the threat. As I was looking up the Oceanside office phone number in the state directory, the same sergeant told me the ex-officer killer had been apprehended.

When I learned the details of his capture, it was almost comical. He still had his CHP uniform and had worn it without a badge or cap piece to his girl friend's home in Santa Monica to kill her. When her mother interceded to protect her, the imposter CHP officer beat her to death with a lamp. Then he fled to Needles at the Colorado River and the Arizona state line more than 200 miles to the east.

Still wearing his CHP uniform, he reportedly went to a phone booth in a service station and phoned the Santa Monica Police Department and asked about the condition of his girl friend's mother. When he was told she was dead, he fainted in the phone booth. The service station attendant closely watched all of it because in the small city of Needles, he knew there were no black CHP officers, so when the fugitive fainted in the phone booth, the attendant called the Needles Police Department and the suspect was arrested.

That confirmed my original opinion that he was homicidal and then convinced me that he was completely crazy. Fleeing from a homicide in a CHP uniform across an open desert where traffic was very light and he could have been spotted easily by CHP officers was enough to make the dumbest criminal cringe. But with the timing as it was, he probably went through the Barstow CHP area at shift change time when no units were on the road.

The final event in the case was about three years later. I was walking through the public office to my private office next door when I saw the ex-CHP officer/killer leaning on the counter, all buffed up from three years of lifting weights in prison.

He smiled and said, "Hi, lieutenant," like we were the best of friends and it was old home week. I smiled and said, "Hi, --------," and kept walking into my office. I closed the door, put on my Sam Browne belt, unsnapped the holster strap and faced the door for several minutes. I wasn't about to have my career and my life ended by a crazy man who had already threatened to kill me. But he happily departed several minutes later and that was the last time we saw or heard of him.

Ambush Shooting

I had just completed that case when I got a tragic one. On a Sunday night one of our officers was shot during a traffic stop. Newer Officer Leslie Clapp and his 14-year-veteran partner stopped three Black Panthers in a VW bug in Willowbrook for light equipment violations. It was a little over halfway through the 1965 to 1972 era of violent social unrest — civil rights demonstrations, riots, and violent racial activist actions against all of law enforcement.

Officer Clapp contacted the driver, told him why they had stopped him and obtained his driver license and car registration. Clapp walked several feet back toward the patrol car then returned to the driver's door to ask the driver if the address on his driver license was still correct,

As soon as Clapp got back to the driver's door, the right front passenger leaned over and shot Clapp in the lower chest with a .45 automatic pistol. Clapp fell to the pavement near the rear of the VW bug, paralyzed from the waist down, but he tried to draw his service revolver. The driver then stepped out and fired several rounds at Clapp with a .38 revolver. Amazingly, all of the rounds hit the pavement, fragmented and caused only scratch wounds on Clapp's arms and chest. Outnumbered three to one and thinking Clapp was dead his partner fled across the rear of a corner service station and took cover on the opposite side of the lot.

Thanks to the inspector who actually believed the sergeants when they told him they were over-worked this case also was assigned to me to investigate. When the captain told me to handle it, he said Deputy Commissioner Jim Bryant had said he couldn't make any snap decision about the older officer fleeing and leaving wounded Officer Clapp behind. Bryant said all situations are different and he wasn't sure he wouldn't have done the same.

GEORGE C. NUTTALL

Having read of Jim Bryant's heroism in the "Highway Patrolman" magazine in my early days on the CHP, I knew he was not one to make excuses for a possible coward. When Jim Bryant was a lieutenant commander of a small CHP office in central California in about 1955, there was an APB aired for five armed and dangerous robbers. With few CHP units on the road in that rural area, Bryant went on the road to help search for them. It didn't take long for him to get behind the five wanted armed robbers and stop them.

As reported, he took cover behind the patrol car driver's door and announced his intentions: "I intend to retire from this job in good health, so if any of you *$#&%#@%s think otherwise, you'll be the first to go," he boomed, "and I've got six rounds here for you and there are only five of you, so who wants to go first?" Probably thinking he was completely crazy, the five armed robbers didn't move. They sat still until backup officers arrived and rescued them from that crazy trigger-happy cop.

Shortly after the captain assigned the case to me, a sheriff's detective phoned me from the Firestone substation and told me he had a problem with Clapp's partner. I told him I already knew about it and would take care of it. A sergeant then came into the lieutenants' office and said Clapp was the only officer who would work with his fleeing partner because the unpopular partner was going to take Clapp deer hunting with him.

Like so many other times after an officer's tragic death, I learned about conditions or circumstances that were known to some but they didn't say anything about it until it was too late. Although I didn't make an issue of it at the time, my instant mental reaction was if the sergeants all knew that, why did they assign a newer officer to work with him? But based on my knowledge of the events of the shooting at that time that were later confirmed, even the best partner most likely could not have prevented Clapp's being shot as it was.

Before I could break away and go to the shooting scene to start my investigation, we were told sheriff deputies had apprehended the three Black Panthers. They had fled into a nearby neighborhood and holed up in an unoccupied residence.

We later learned the three were to be arraigned in the Compton Court before Judge Homer Garrott, the first black CHP officer and

318

the only black officer from 1942 to 1955. We also quickly learned that the LAPD had arrested the same three Black Panthers a few days before Clapp's shooting but had to release them on bail.

When I finally arrived at the shooting scene, I walked across the rear of the corner service station to see if I could find any empty cartridge casings or unexpended cartridges that the fleeing officer may have dropped in his haste. At the fourth rear yard of a row of residences abutting the service station the rear fence was broken down and lying on the ground among some weeds. I walked in to look for anything I thought might be related to the officer's flight. I had been in the yard for no more than two minutes when the resident of the property came out and somewhat angrily asked me what I was doing in his yard. When I told him why I was there and what I was looking for, he quickly calmed down.

Then he told me he had seen the fleeing officer after he heard several shots. He said the officer had run all the way across the service station rear lot and gone behind a masonry wall behind a small store west of the service station. He said he later spoke to the extremely upset officer and felt sorry for him. I wrote down the cooperative man's name, address and phone number and thanked him for his important information. With that credible account of the primary issue in the investigation, I returned to the office to inform the captain of the witness and my findings.

When I told the captain, he said the fleeing officer had been assigned to the day shift because he did not have a graveyard partner and also so that he would be readily available for me to interview him at any point in my investigation.

With the witness's credible account of the fleeing officer's actions and state of mind, I told the captain I didn't see any reason to interview the officer at that time. I also told him that in my opinion it was an unpredictable ambush that could happen on any traffic stop and the fleeing officer in no way contributed to the shooting of Clapp.

The captain agreed and told me to start writing my report to be forwarded to the zone office and CHP Headquarters. He said he didn't think any action would be taken against the fleeing officer based on what Deputy Commissioner Jim Bryant had expressed about who knows what he or any other officer would have done in that situation, and especially if they thought Clapp was dead.

The next morning the captain came into the lieutenants' office and told me the fleeing officer had asked him if he could be assigned to the front desk to clear PVI forms. He said the officer said every time he saw a VW bug with black occupants he froze up and broke out in a cold sweat. The captain said he told the officer he would not take him off the road and he would have to find some way to overcome his fear because he couldn't spend the next ten to fifteen years until his retirement behind a counter or desk. A few days later, the captain told me the fleeing officer had just signed his resignation papers.

For several Sundays, I visited Officer Clapp at the special county hospital for paraplegic and quadriplegic patients. It was very depressing, and my visits didn't appear to help him in any way. One time I visited, his parents were also there. The last time I visited Clapp, the patient in the bed next to him was a Hell's Angel. That was too much for me. I wondered who the fool was who made that stupid arrangement. How could they place an honorable law enforcement officer next to a Hell's Angel? That was the last time I visited Officer Clapp.

Years later I learned that he had received State Compensation Rehabilitation Training and had become a gunsmith in Missouri. Then in the late 1990s I read in the California Association of Highway Patrolmen (CAHP) newsletter, the "APB," that he had died in Colorado at about 55 years of age.

The Auto Theft Specialist

One day the South L.A. office auto theft officer came into the lieutenants' office to say something to the senior lieutenant who was the executive officer and supervised the special duty officers. The auto theft officer was a small black officer I remembered from the academy when he was a cadet. His name was Ernie Browne and even a mind reader couldn't have guessed he was a CHP officer. The first thing I noticed was his unpolished non-uniform black cowboy boots with very pointed toes.

After he left the office, I asked the senior lieutenant how Ernie ever got to be selected as the office auto theft officer. I also commented on his non-regulation cowboy boots and sort of unkempt appearance. The senior lieutenant said Ernie was selected because he recovered more stolen cars than all the other officers put together. He said Ernie had grown up in Willowbrook and several officers reported seeing him in an alley there talking to some black kids. Then not long after they would hear Ernie get a hit on a stolen car. The kids were telling him where stolen cars were parked in rear yards. He said Ernie dressed as he did because some Willowbrook residents had horses and his cowboy boots and sort of shoddy appearance made him fit in and relate better with his kid informants. Knowing the value of public informants, I couldn't dispute his appearance or tactics.

A few months later, Ernie was transferred to the L.A. zone auto theft unit and about a year later at an annual CHP Day Luncheon at the LAPD Academy, Zone Commander George Reinjohn told the hundreds of officers about Ernie's latest escapade. He said Ernie was standing in line at a bank not far from the zone office on North Vermont to deposit his monthly paycheck. Supervising Inspector Reinjohn humorously interjected that Ernie was on his lunch hour, which aroused much laughter. He said while he was standing in line, a black armed robber jumped up on a counter and ordered everyone to lie down on the floor. Inspector Reinjohn said the bank security camera showed the best part of the event. As everyone else was dropping to the floor, Ernie remained standing, drew his small revolver and fired one shot that instantly killed the armed robber.

Inspector Reinjohn said Ernie later told him he suddenly noticed he was the only black male in the bank and he knew the LAPD would be responding, so he ran over to the bank manager, told him he was a CHP officer and asked him to tell the LAPD when they arrived that he was not the robber. He said Ernie was certain the LAPD would shoot the first black man they saw in the bank, and he was the only one there.

A couple of years later, I overheard Ernie's sergeant talking to him on the phone. He told Ernie which case he wanted him to work on and told him to wear his "Pimp suit." In my over 31 years in law enforcement, I never knew or heard of a more capable or well suited undercover cop. To make it even better, Ernie had a great sense of humor and was always ready for a laugh, even when he was the brunt of the joke. Like Jim Bryant and so many other classic CHP officers of all ranks, he was one of a kind who could never be replaced.

Escorting Barry Goldwater

Effective October 1, 1969, the captain transferred to the Baldwin Park office and we got a new captain commander. About two weeks later I received a phone call from a man who requested we provide an escort for their limousine that was to transport U.S. Senator Barry Goldwater from the Long Beach Hyatt House Hotel to LAX Airport. It was to be on the following Saturday night at about 8:00 p.m.

Assuming the man was a Goldwater aide, I agreed to provide a security escort. Also, I was willing to do it because I admired Senator Goldwater for his honesty when he ran for president in 1964. During his campaign when the Vietnam War was starting to drag on with no end in sight, he openly declared that he would bomb Hanoi. That resulted in his being labeled a "hawk" and most likely caused him to lose the election to President Lyndon B. Johnson. Johnson had made an issue of Goldwater being a hawk during his campaign. Then when the war continued to drag on, Johnson ordered the bombing of Hanoi.

Being very busy with a new captain who was nervous and was causing extra work I didn't need, I intended to assign a two-officer evening unit to the Goldwater escort detail. Then a couple of nights later, I received a second phone call from the man I thought was a Goldwater aide. In my haste to get back to more pressing matters, I didn't clarify if he was a Goldwater aide or who he was. I got the impression he thought we would provide a red light and siren escort from Long Beach to the airport.

The California Vehicle Code strictly limits red light and siren escorts to preservation of life situations. The more I thought about it, I feared the caller might demand a red light and siren escort and the two officers might not want to refuse a U.S. Senator's Aide's demands and provide an illegal and potentially unsafe escort. So I decided to take a sergeant with me and make it clear to everyone that there would be no illegal red lights and siren and the sergeant and I would provide whatever was needed.

The sergeant and I arrived at the front area of the Hyatt Hotel at about 7:30 p.m. and parked directly in front of the main entrance.

About ten minutes later, a man in a tuxedo ran out of the main entrance like a fleeing robber, went by us without saying a word and ran into the parking lot. A few minutes later he drove up in a big black Lincoln and parked behind our patrol car. Then Senator Goldwater walked out the main entrance carrying an attaché case and accompanied by another man in a tuxedo. The sergeant and I were standing by the trunk of our car and Senator Goldwater walked directly up to me and asked, "Where do you want me to ride, lieutenant?" "They have a limousine for you, Senator," I replied. "No," he said, "I'd rather ride in your car if I could and with no siren, red lights or any of that crazy stuff."

"Would you like to ride in the right front?" I asked. "Oh, no, this is good enough," he said as he reached for the left rear door handle of the patrol car. Then I asked him if he wanted to put the attaché case in the trunk, and he handed it to me. The sergeant put it in the trunk and I started walking around the car to the right front door to get in and sit down. The little man in the tuxedo stopped me and asked if he could ride to the airport with us. Still not knowing who he was, I said he could.

Before we were out of the parking lot, I knew from the strange conversation he was trying to strike up with Senator Goldwater that I had made a big mistake. It was only then that I learned from his rambling that he was the president of the U.S. Air Force Reserve Association. Senator Goldwater was a general in the Air Force Reserve and had been the chief speaker at the association's meeting.

On the I-405 Freeway, Goldwater started freely talking. Perhaps to keep the USAF Reserve president quiet, Senator Goldwater directed his remarks to the sergeant and me. He somewhat angrily said if people only knew what was going on in Washington they might revolt. He was not specific about anyone or any thing, but it was President Nixon's first year in the White House and less than three years before the Watergate scandal erupted. As we approached Century Boulevard to turn off the 405 to LAX, the tuxedo-clad association president asked Senator Goldwater if he could walk to the gate with him. "Oh, no," Goldwater quickly replied, "I do this every night and these officers have work they have to get back to."

It was obvious that he wanted to get away from that political pest as soon as he could and wanted to be as inconspicuous as possible to avoid autograph hounds. When we stopped at the terminal, I opened

323

the trunk and gave the senator his attaché case and he shook my hand and thanked me for the ride.

As he walked across the sidewalk to the terminal door, the USAF association president asked me if we would wait for him while he walked to the gate with Senator Goldwater. He said he had some important things to tell him. "No, Senator Goldwater made it very clear that he wanted to walk to the gate alone," I said.

I walked back to the right front door of the patrol car and got in. I thought if you want to walk to the gate with him, you can walk back to the Hyatt Hotel. He quickly climbed into the rear and I told the sergeant to go directly to the office. I'd had more than enough of the little pest and decided to have a graveyard unit take him to the Hyatt House Hotel. Then I went into the lieutenants' office and closed the door.

About a month later the Central L.A. office was completed and 25 banked officers, including 19 new officers who had just graduated from the academy were transferred to the station, which was built under a freeway interchange. The office would be the site of the TV show "Chips" less than ten years later.

Then effective January 1, 1970, the nervous captain and the lieutenant assigned as the day field operations officer transferred to other offices. The new captain was George Goodwin, who had been my first sergeant when I graduated from the academy and was assigned to the San Bernardino squad office, and we had been good friends since that time.

A South L.A. squad sergeant was promoted to lieutenant and took my place as night field operations officer (FOO), and I became the day FOO. With Captain Goodwin for the commander I for the first time had an ally since I went to South L.A. He was very relaxed and content with his new assignment. He soon assumed his primary duty of putting his feet on his desk, crossing his ankles and working very hard on crossword puzzles. But he didn't bug me every day with questions as the nervous captain had done, so things started to slow down.

Among other slowdowns, there was only about one CHP vehicle crash a week. During my first month in South L.A. there had been seven CHP crashes in a seven-day period — not one a day, just an average of one a day including the motor accident caused by the siren falling off and into the rear wheel. The pace was slowing down to a frantic speed.

Tanker Explosion

It was almost getting boring when one morning at about 9:00 a.m. there was a tremendous explosion. It sounded like it was nearby, so Captain Goodwin put down his crossword puzzle and we went out front to see if we could see where the sound had come from. There was a huge billow of black smoke rising from the area of the Harbor and 405 Freeways crossing.

Captain Goodwin and I got in a patrol car and went to the scene. A tanker truck was completely burned in about the middle of the Harbor Freeway tunnel under the 405 Freeway and was still smoldering.

I saw a large smudge of light green paint on the large concrete support of the 405 Freeway. It was far to the right of the roadway, and I recognized that unusual green color as Linde Air which had a plant in Etiwanda in the San Bernardino area. As I recalled, that tanker company transported oxygen as its exclusive product, and oxygen is highly explosive.

When the smoke cleared from the tunnel, we ran the license numbers of the truck tractor and semi trailer for registered ownership and found that both vehicles were registered to Union Carbide, apparently the parent company of Linde Air.

Amazingly, the truck and trailer were the only vehicles in the tunnel of that usually heavily traveled freeway. Although the truck driver was killed, it was a blessing that he was the only victim. If the accident and explosion had occurred 30 to 90 minutes earlier, there would most likely have been several San Pedro and other South Bay commuters' vehicles in the tunnel. With the massive explosion that shook the CHP office more than a quarter of a mile away, there could have been several more people killed.

The I-405 Freeway over-crossing tunnel structure had to be closed for 24 hours to inspect it for damage, and it caused a monumental traffic jam for tens of thousands of commuters in that 24-hour period. Fortunately, the tunnel was not damaged and opened up late the next morning.

It wasn't until I arrived at the office on Monday morning April 6, 1970, that I learned four CHP officers had been killed the night before near Newhall. It was the worst tragedy in the 40-year history of the CHP. The fearful prediction that my academy physical training assistant and I made about two years before had finally happened. My assistant and I had trained the four officers when they were cadets.

Four CHP Officers Killed

The tragic scenario ended when one of the gunmen broke into a farmhouse not far from the shooting scene and held the occupants hostage. For some reason, he released one of the hostages, who notified the sheriff. It was reported that when the sun rose, the farmhouse was surrounded by an army of deputies. After more than an hour of negotiations, the deputies stormed the farmhouse and as they entered, the gunman reportedly committed suicide. As it was reported, there were suspicions that the deputies might have aided and abetted the gunman in his suicide.

The second gunman was captured about five hours later in a stolen pickup truck with a camper he had carjacked from the owner. During the carjacking there was an exchange of gunfire between the owner and the gunman. When captured, the gunman was wounded and was taken to a hospital. It was never reported if he had been wounded in the shootout with the pickup truck owner or with the CHP officers. Unfortunately, a Supreme Court had ordered a moratorium on death penalty executions a few years earlier, so the second gunman was tried and sentenced to life in prison.

The Right-Side Approach

From the time I first arrived in South L.A. I preached and preached the right-side approach and encountered much resistance. Like most human beings, cops are creatures of habit and do not want to change what they have been doing for years or decades. It becomes their comfort zone. When I was an instructor at the academy, most of the staff did not look forward to in-service classes because many of the veteran officers openly displayed an attitude of "I dare you to try to teach me anything I don't already know."

But clearly recalling how Jim Stamback had been killed and what I had learned from using the right-side approach for nearly two years afterwards, I persisted. Some listened and others didn't. One who didn't was killed some years later.

When the Westminster CHP office was completed in June 1970, about 27 banked officers transferred to that squad and jurisdiction over portions of the I-405 and Long Beach Freeways and small county islands within the city of Long Beach were also transferred to the Westminster office. The transfer of those officers and the Long Beach freeways was a major relief for the South L. A. office. The Long Beach Freeway was reported to be the busiest truck freeway in L.A. County serving the Long Beach and Los Angeles Harbors.

Fiery Protest in Isla Vista

One night early in 1971 Captain Goodwin and I and our wives had just returned to our home after having dinner out together when we received a phone call for Captain Goodwin. He took the phone and then angrily said, "They just burned the Bank of America in Isla Vista, and we have to send 33 officers and 11 cars to Isla Vista Code 3."

He had been the lieutenant commander of the Buellton office in Santa Barbara County where Isla Vista was located. It served as a dormitory and housing community for University of California at Santa Barbara students. Being there for many years, he was well aware of the unruly conduct of many of the out-of-control students, and it angered him to learn that they had finally resorted to such blatant anarchy.

As luck would have it, the timing was perfect. It was about 9:00 p.m. and the afternoon shift of about 35 officers went off duty at 10:15 p.m. and the graveyard shift of 20 officers went on duty at 9:45 p.m. Captain Goodwin immediately went to the office and had no trouble getting about 33 of the approximately 55 officers to travel the 100 miles to Isla Vista with red lights and sirens. We later learned that the Isla Vista Bank of America was a temporary prefabricated building that was easily torched.

Although the Isla Vista anarchy persisted for about a year, several weeks after it started Zone Commander Supervising Inspector

George Reinjohn assigned me to attend a six-week live-in POST Police Community Relations Leadership School at San Diego University. I was one of four lieutenants assigned to attend at four different universities throughout California. It was the first time CHP officers were ever included in POST training courses.

I was pleased I would attend in San Diego because I was very familiar with the law enforcement in that county and the problems the San Diego Police Department had started experiencing before I left to go on the CHP.

A Mexican activist group had demonstrated to keep law enforcement officers off the San Diego State University campus, so we were housed and classes were held at the Mission Valley Howard Johnson's Motel. The classroom was directly across the hall from the room I shared with a Tehachapi Police Department officer who was much fun.

The first day of class we had to introduce ourselves to the other 21 in the class and tell them which department we were from. When I said I was a highway patrolman, one of the other class members said, "What are you doing here? The CHP doesn't have any public relations problems." "They sent me here, so somebody must believe otherwise," I replied with a smile.

There were dozens of very informative lecturers including blacks and Hispanics from ghettos and barrios. They were able to give us insight into the problems in their communities they believed were caused by the police, but we weren't so sure. One session was conducted by two psychologists and I knew one from Hoover High School. He had been two years ahead of me when I was a sophomore and he was a senior. I distinctly remembered he wore dress slacks, Florsheim shoes and sport shirts to school when my friends and I from the other side of the tracks wore Levis, T-shirts and surplus marine boondockers and Army combat boots. I didn't remember him being an athlete or seeing him in a gym class. We were from two different worlds.

He and his almost silent partner had the 22 of us sit in a large circle for a debate about whether the most intellectual or toughest street fighter in a street gang would be the gang leader. The question almost made me laugh. I grew up in borderline criminal and violent East San Diego and I was very familiar with some of the sociopaths in the "Jim Town Gang." The biggest and toughest one in the gang was always the undisputed leader. He was always in the lead when they paraded down the street, and the others followed behind him like sheep.

One of the others in our class was in his second year as the president of the Peace Officers' Research Association of California (PORAC), an older peace officers' lobbying group. He was a very energetic police sergeant who liked to argue any side of an issue — like politicians who want to get attention and hear themselves talk. Also, he was on a small local police department that was noted to be a community for retired Navy officers, not street gangs.

He immediately started the argument by taking the side that the most intellectual member would be the gang leader. With that, I couldn't control myself and immediately took the opposite side and gave my reasons. I said, "Have you ever seen a street gang member in a library?" I then related my years of daily observations of the Jim Town Gang members in Junior High School from the 7th to 9th grades. None of them ever made it to the 9th grade. They were expelled and ended up at privately-owned Snyder Continuation School that we called "Snyder Crime School" or in a juvenile detention center. The San Diego Police Department juvenile officers were at the school so often we learned all of their last names from the gang members.

After about an hour of that foolishness, my schoolmate psychologist called time. He gave his conclusions based on his observations of the debate. He said the PORAC president was the emotional leader and I was the logical leader. He then said the PORAC president was correct in that it had been proven that intellectuals are the gang leaders.

I was as stunned as the rest of the class, including the PORAC president. He had obviously taken his position just for the sake of argument. It again proved to me that what goes on in colleges and universities should stay there and not get involved in street police work. It reminded me of when one of my older brothers started at USC to earn his master's degree. He majored in speech therapy and minored in psychology and he told me of a new theory. He said that one or more of the professors in the psychology department had been inspired by the revelation that a healthy defecation could be more enjoyable and satisfying than an orgasm. I told him if that were true, the sales of laxatives would boom and the population would bust in the civilized world.

When I was a CHP cadet, Sacramento State College Professor Robert Gordon taught psychology to my class. He was a really sharp and squared-away psychologist, and he started by telling us what every psychologist needs is a good psychologist. And from my years of hearing their theories, I believe his was correct, and this street gang fantasy further convinced me it was true.

One field trip I went on with a classmate was to visit an assistant to the assistant city manager. He was a retired Navy fighter pilot and took us to lunch at the North Island Naval Air Station Officers' Club.

The week before our classes started, a new San Diego Police Department chief had been appointed from within the ranks of the department. He was an officer when I was on the police department and I knew him. He was sort of a bulldog officer. We had been told there were so many problems on the police department that the mayor and city council ordered him to have his office at city hall and let the deputy chief, whom I also knew and highly respected, run the police department.

The deputy chief was Bill Gant, a most capable detective when I knew him and no doubt an outstanding administrator and one I thought might finally be able to correct the many faulty policies and practices of the police department. Our host told us of the many police department problems that the mayor, city council and city manager were trying to correct. When he finished telling us, I told him about a major problem that started evolving when I was in the department from 1952 to 1954. I told him the whole story about Chief Jansen's promise to the city council to increase the issuance of traffic citations to cover the cost of 50 additional officers in 1953. I also told him the police department did not have any system or method to measure officers' work efforts, activities and production other than citations, and that the CHP had an excellent system since I joined in 1954. He listened intently and made notes. When we finally left his office, he thanked me for the information.

I never knew if he was able to make any use of the information. It was well known by all the officers who were on the police department when I was there, and many were still there to confirm what I had told him. Although he was very sincere, I had my doubts he could break old bad practices.

When I returned to the South L.A. office, the Isla Vista uprisings were still persisting now and then. With the transfer of about 52 banked officers to Central L.A. and the transfer of Long Beach responsibilities to Westminster, activity slowed for the remainder of 1970 and the first half of 1971. We were down to about 150 officers and 15 sergeants in the 100-officer building.

Then in July 1971, Captain Goodwin transferred to the Visalia squad office and the senior lieutenant retired. One new lieutenant transferred in but didn't stay long, but no captain in the state showed any interest, so I had to be the acting commander for two months. On the first of September Captain Jack Cowan transferred in after attending USC for a year to get his master's degree on an all-expenses-paid educational leave. He had been my lieutenant at the academy for over a year, so we knew each other very well and had no problem communicating.

High-Stress Cadet Training

In one of our discussions, we got on the subject of high-stress cadet training, which I strongly opposed. He said an L.A. County sheriff's captain was in his master's group and set out to prove high-stress training was superior to no stress. Cowan said the captain conducted extensive research comparing the performance of officers who had undergone high-stress academies such as the L.A. Sheriff's Academy as cadets with officers who had attended other police academies where there was no-stress training.

He said the captain was shocked when his research proved that the officers who attended no-stress academies performed better on the job than those who had undergone high-stress cadet training. With that conclusion, he wrote his thesis confirming his findings and filed a copy in the USC Library. Despite that research, findings and conclusion, the L.A. Sheriff's Academy never changed its high-stress training to no-stress training. Furthermore, nearly all Southern California academies and the CHP Academy persisted in high-stress training much like Marine Boot Camps.

Ban on Carotid Sleeper Hold

A month later, Zone Commander George Reinjohn held the quarterly squad office and zone inspector commanders' conference at the South L.A. office. Being the senior South L.A. lieutenant and second in command, I attended. The first item on the agenda was Commissioner Sullivan's order to prohibit any further use of the carotid sleeper hold. He ordered the ban because a DUI suspect died after the hold had been applied.

Although I liked and agreed with all of Commissioner Sullivan's enforcement policies, I could not accept his ban of the carotid sleeper as being reasonable. I was first taught that method on the San Diego Police Department. It was also included in my CHP Academy cadet training by the FBI and was part of the LAPD/Koga physical methods of arrest. Both with the FBI physical methods of arrest and later with the Koga methods I had trained about 2,000 CHP cadets in its proper use.

I never used it during my years on the street, but I did use it one time on a cadet when some other cadets told me it didn't work on him. I decided to try it on him to see if it would work. In training, the cadet is told to put his hand on the upper arm of the one applying the hold from behind then when he starts to feel the effects of the blood not flowing to the brain, he is told to tap the arm of the person applying the hold.

When properly applied, the forearm and bicep of the one applying the hold are pulled together around the neck to compress the two carotid arteries and shut off the flow of blood to the brain. Then in about three to five seconds, the victim subject becomes unconscious, goes limp and falls to the ground.

I went over and instructed the cadet where to put his hand. We were on a gym mat and there were about eight cadets watching me as I applied the hold. In about three seconds the difficult subject went completely limp. I was surprised because he hadn't tapped my arm. I gently lowered him to the mat and he lay there for about 20 seconds then started batting his eyes and looking at all of us in a state of daze and confusion. About 15 seconds later he said his first impression was that he had forgotten to go to training, was on his bed in his dorm and we had come to get him.

Although I had not in any way intended to put him out and down, it was a learning experience for me. It proved that when the carotid sleeper is properly and successfully applied, it gives an officer at least 20 seconds to handcuff the prisoner before he regains consciousness, then another 15 seconds or more for the prisoner to reorient himself.

The carotid sleeper is so effective it works on everybody, including those under the influence of any and all drugs, alcohol and those suffering from violent mental disorders. When the flow of blood is stopped from going to the brain, it puts everybody out and down. I was certain the commissioner had greatly over-reacted.

I didn't think the death of one prisoner out of hundreds or thousands after the carotid sleeper is successfully applied justified the ban of that valuable method. I wondered if the commissioner had bothered to study a copy of the autopsy report to determine the actual cause of death. There were two most likely causes of the prisoner's death: one being that he had a serious physical ailment such as a heart condition; the other that the officer didn't apply the hold properly. There was also a choke hold that was applied to the front of the throat and cut off the airflow to the lungs, but it took minutes to render a person unconscious and was much more dangerous because it could severely damage the fragile windpipe. Because it was less effective and more dangerous, it was not included in the FBI or Koga methods and was not taught at the CHP Academy.

The three zone inspectors had 20 to 30 years in the CHP and none had been on the street for 10 to 20 years, so they were not even aware of the CHP training and use of the carotid sleeper hold. When one of them questioned what it was and how it was used, I went to the sergeants' adjacent office and got the CHP Unarmed Defense Manual. When I returned with it, I handed it to one of the inspectors opened to the page illustrating the hold with one academy sergeant applying the hold on another sergeant.

The sergeant pictured applying the carotid sleeper hold was then the captain commander of the Lancaster squad office in the desert — the most undesirable office in that zone. He was well reputed to be very vocal and his outbursts were seldom well received by others of any rank, so Inspector Reinjohn had told him he would remain in Lancaster until he learned to keep his mouth shut.

When I tried to defend the use of the carotid sleeper, the Lancaster captain didn't say a word. Yet he had preceded me as the academy physical methods supervisor and had instructed the carotid sleeper hold to cadets. But that subject discussion was short lived and Inspector Reinjohn moved on to the next agenda item, and that was the end of more than 20 years of CHP use of the carotid sleeper hold. It again proved to me that effective police work and methods are learned on the street, not in a classroom or behind a desk.

In the months to follow, Inspector Reinjohn developed a brown growth on his left shoulder. It was diagnosed as melanoma cancer and he died a few months later. In the interim, Deputy Commissioner Jim Bryant retired. Their departures were saddening to me. They both spoke their minds as honestly and constructively as humanly possible. They didn't hold grudges, and after chewing out subordinates, they would forget the matter unless the mistake or misdeed was repeated. We always knew where we stood with them and there were never any questions about what they thought or what they expected. They could never be replaced, especially Reinjohn. He was my chief supporter and knew how difficult the South L.A. squad office was to manage. He also appreciated my efforts to correct the many long-lasting deficiencies in its operations, despite the prevalent "That's the way we've always done it" attitude.

Passenger Vehicle Inspections

The South L.A. office had three passenger vehicle inspection teams that issued hundreds of written warnings for safety equipment, driver license, vehicle registration and defective smog control devices violations every weekday. The violations corrections had to be certified by licensed light, brake or smog stations or CHP officers depending on the violation. There were so many issued that the South L.A. office had two officers assigned to the public office to certify corrections every Monday through Saturday.

The office also had to test applicants for light, brake or smog licenses every Friday morning starting at 8:00 a.m. The tests were administered by Elva, an office clerk who was about 64 years old but looked more like 80 with her wrinkled face. She had been born into a carnival family and her mother, who was in her 80s and didn't believe in retirement, still owned and operated a "kiddie-land" ride concession in the city of Hawthorne.

With much showmanship in her blood, Elva conducted the light, brake and smog licensing tests like a Marine Corps drill instructor. She wore a whistle around her neck on a chain to keep the 30 to 50 applicants in line and in order. She told me the reason she wore the whistle was to call for help in case one of the applicants attempted to sexually assault her.

A couple of Friday mornings when Elva was parading the applicants through the hall past my office in single file, one of them would stick his head in my office door and ask in a lighthearted manner, "Do we have to take this?" "Only if you want to pass the test," I replied with a smile. "That's all I wanted to know," one of them replied with a laugh.

One Friday morning before 8:00 a.m. a PVI written warning recipient for defective lights arrived in front of the office to have it cleared by an officer. When he saw the 30 to 50 applicants in front waiting for Elva to let them in, the warning recipient took his place at the end of the line. A week later on a Saturday I was working in my office to catch up on paper work. My office was next to the public office and I could hear everything said in that busy place. I heard a man say he wanted to get his PVI written warning cleared by an officer. Then he told his long, sad story. He said he had come to the office the Friday before to get it cleared and was directed into a large room to take a light test with a bunch of others by a hardboiled old woman. He said he failed the test and told the woman he wasn't a truck driver and didn't know how many clearance lights had to be on a semi-trailer, and she told him he would have to study harder to pass the test. Hearing all of that, I had to keep from laughing out loud.

He then said he knew he could never past the light test, so he told a Torrance Police Department officer friend about his dire situation. The Torrance officer told him the correct way to get the written warning cleared and he was there to get it done. The officer cleared the PVI form and the poor man left like he had just been paroled.

Within minutes, the Elva story spread throughout the office like a fire alarm. When a sergeant heard it, he said he would write the story and send it to the editor of the "California Highway Patrolmen" magazine for publication.

As soon as Captain Cowan arrived at the office on the following Monday I told him about the man's experience with Elva's strict testing procedure. I also told him about the sergeant wanting to write the story and send it to the association magazine and asked him if he thought that would be a good idea because it might make the South L.A. office look like it was being run by a bunch of clowns.

Cowan laughed and said if the top brass didn't yet know how screwed up the South L.A. office was, it was time they found out the truth. The story was published in the next edition of the "California Highway Patrolmen" magazine and Elva enjoyed the carnival-like publicity.

The last chapter of the Elva story was when she turned 65 and applied for retirement. She told me in the coffee room that her mother didn't believe in retiring, and her mother phoned her every day in the office. She was worried about what her mother would do when she was told Elva had retired and wasn't there any more. I told Elva we would tell her mother she was on a very long vacation and would return her call when she got back.

Elva retired, and that was the last we heard of her. I could only imagine Elva was probably working at her mother's "kiddie-land," wearing her whistle and ordering little kids to shut up and enjoy their ride or else.

As the day field operations officer I supervised the day shift patrol officers and sergeants, the Carson scales officers, the three PVI teams and the sergeant supervisor of both of those operations.

At a quarterly PVI meeting at zone headquarters conducted by an inspector, the first item on the agenda was that the Department of Finance had denied the CHP's request for minivans for the PVI teams. This request had been made because for about six years the rear seats had been removed from the second patrol car used by every team to carry the signs and other PVI equipment. This restricted the use of the $5,500 patrol cars to the 40 hours per week of the PVI teams, and very little mileage accrued.

Without thinking about the Merit Award Board Suggestion award payments of up to ten percent of the first year's savings, I stupidly suggested replacing the equipment-carrying patrol cars with trailers. Within months, about 100 trailers were purchased at about $1,500 each to replace the patrol cars, and the only maintenance cost of the trailers was greasing the wheel bearings.

Patrol cars were retired and sold by sealed bid at 75,000 miles and 18 months service. For the remaining three years of the PVI teams' existence before they were discontinued by newly elected Jerry Brown in 1975, I figured the trailers saved the CHP about $500,000.

Like my suggestion to discontinue sending all citations to headquarters three years earlier, I wondered why one of the college-educated desk jockey officers in headquarters hadn't thought of trailers, but as one candid inspector once said, "If they can't do their job, they are promoted." I also knew from personal observations that it wasn't politically expedient to make suggestions that would make the brass look bad because they hadn't thought of it first.

I was later assigned as the executive officer and supervised the clerical staff, office special duty officers, automotive technicians and janitors. In taking inventory of the CHP forms, I discovered we had six cases of "CHP 180 Stolen Vehicle- Stolen Vehicle Recovery-Storage Forms." All forms were subject to occasional revision, so they could all go to waste if the Form 180 was revised. There had been no system for requisitioning forms and there was a six-year supply on hand.

With the work load as it was, I delayed sending some back to the Stores Section in Sacramento. Then one afternoon I was told a Firestone sheriff's sergeant was on the phone. The sheriff's substation sergeant rather sheepishly said they had run out of Form 180s and asked if we could loan them two pads. There were 25 forms to a pad, so all he asked for was 50 forms.

It made me so happy to hear that request and I said, "I've got a deal for you. How would you like two cases that our hyperactive requisition clerk ordered that we'll probably have until we die." He instantly said he would be off the hook with that many, so I told him to send a car over and have the deputy meet me in the rear parking lot by the carport and we would smuggle them out.

The deputy soon arrived and I was happy to see the two cases go and be put to good use. I considered it to be a good gesture because we booked our prisoners at the Firestone substation, we were all in the big mess of law enforcement together and what are a couple of cases of 180s between friends? I wasn't too sure what the top brass would think about it, but what they didn't know wouldn't give them ulcers or heart problems.

Officer Killed in Freak Accident

It was late afternoon Sunday, July 4, 1972, when my phone rang at home. When I answered, an obviously upset sergeant said, "Paladini's dead," and then hung up before I could get any details. I told my wife an officer had been killed and I was going to the office and didn't know when I would get back.

On the way to the office, I was most upset because Officer Paladini was such a fine young man and officer. Only about a week before he had asked me to help him try to find something in his patrol car. When I found it in his glove compartment among some junk he said, "That's why you're a lieutenant" in a cute, humble way — and now he was gone.

The captain lived on the opposite side of Los Angeles from my home in Seal Beach, so when I got to the office he was gone and the office was almost deserted. Captain Cowan had gone directly to the scene and on to the hospital where Paladini had been taken, but the officer had died en route. The sergeant who had phoned me was in the office and was able to tell me how Paladini had been killed. He said a horse had been struck by a car and its leg was so severely broken it had to be put out of its misery. An animal control officer responded to the scene with a horse trailer but did not have a tranquilizer gun or any sedation to lessen the horse's extreme suffering. With much effort while the horse owner and spectators yelled for them to put the horse out of its misery, the horse was finally forced into the animal control officer's trailer.

With the crowd yelling at him, a deputy sheriff climbed onto the trailer hitch and fired a shot aimed at the horse's head. The horse was thrashing around and just as he fired his revolver, the horse jerked and the round glanced off the horse's forehead, went across the street and struck Officer Paladini in the chest. It was a freak and tragic accident.

Other CHP officers at the scene quickly placed Paladini in the rear of a patrol car and raced with red lights and siren to the nearest hospital, but he died on the way.

In analyzing the tragic event, I could not fault the deputy. He was under extreme pressure from the boisterous onlookers to end the horse's misery. The only blame I could direct was at the county of Los Angeles for not equipping its animal control officers with tranquilizer guns or any other form of quick-acting sedatives.

Officer Dana Paladini's hometown was Sacramento, and Captain Cowan attended the funeral services in that city. Although I was the executive officer and did not supervise the field officers at that time, Paladini's death was the only one I ever had to experience as a supervisor in any office.

With record speed for headquarters, a general order with illustrations was issued describing the proper and safe methods of shooting large animals to end extreme pain and suffering.

Not long afterwards one of our newer officers contracted poison oak in a Palos Verdes Estates canyon. There were rolling hills and canyons throughout that affluent community, and a car had run off the road and into a canyon a few nights before. When the routine injury report was forwarded to zone headquarters, it was scrutinized and questioned, "Where in the South L.A. office area is there poison oak?"

After Captain Cowan explained the Palos Verdes Estates area to the inspector, he hung up the phone and shook his head. He said he thought every inspector should ride along with beat officers for 30 days to see what was going on out there in the streets. I completely agreed with him. Much like the banning of the carotid sleeper hold, the inspectors had been behind desks for so long they were out of touch with the real highway patrol.

At a retirement dinner for one of the San Bernardino officers I had worked with, the new deputy commissioner told some of us what Governor Reagan had said about appointing a new CHP commissioner when Commissioner Sullivan retired. He said Commissioner Sullivan had advised Governor Reagan to never again appoint a CHP commissioner from outside the ranks of the department. Sullivan said it took him over two years to learn CHP policies and procedures and get to know the capabilities of the top administrators.

With that I thought that's why he appointed Jim Bryant deputy commissioner. Bryant worked his way up from the bottom on the CHP and knew where the bones were buried and who had buried them.

Governor Reagan had said he would not appoint a CHP commissioner unless he had at least a bachelor's degree and the deputy commissioner nervously said he had only 90 college units with only one college semester remaining before Commissioner Sullivan was to retire.

Studying for the Captain Test

I took a month of vacation to study for the upcoming captain test. About halfway through my vacation I went to the office for some reason. When I went to see Captain Cowan to find out if there had been any new minor or major disasters, he told me a new testing was to be used for the captain test. He told me the State Personnel Board and CHP had agreed to use the Employee Development Appraisal (EDA) testing procedure for the first time. He said it had a pass or fail written test and commanders' appraisals for ranking the applicants.

My heart sank. I knew a rat when I smelled one and it was obvious that this was an end run around the merit system that had been in effect for about 40 years — a system that had given the CHP objective, competent administrators like Jim Bryant, George Reinjohn, Floyd Yoder and many others, who had built the CHP into the best state traffic law enforcement agency in the nation.

The merit system promotional test written scores were weighted 60 percent and the oral scores 40 percent for an average on the sergeant and lieutenant tests, and they were weighted 50 percent for both the written and oral scores on captain, inspector and supervising inspector tests. With the pass or fail written test, less qualified favorites would have a much better chance of competing with the more experienced and qualified applicants.

The lieutenant position was the worst rank on the CHP. Caught between the captains and sergeants and officers, the lieutenants were blamed for everything that goes wrong or isn't popular.

New Promotion Process

Shortly after I went back to work, the deputy commissioner made one of his visits to the South L.A. office. I asked him about the new EDA testing for captain. When he briefly explained it to me, I knew it was an internal political spoils system.

He said those who passed the test would have their commander's appraisals forwarded to headquarters. Then the commissioners and the zone commanders would confer in a private session to rank all the applicants and establish a preliminary list. The applicants would then go before the oral qualifications appraisal panel for a score, but no applicant could move up more than three positions from their position on the preliminary list.

That information confirmed my original belief that it was a political maneuver to promote the less qualified applicants who had their noses in the right places. To me, it was the first big step in the destruction of the CHP I had loved and joined when it was at its best, and I didn't think it would be the best in the nation in years to come.

More than once when I was on the academy staff in the late 1960s one of the other staff members boasted that the CHP was the best law enforcement agency in the country. Not completely joking, I responded, "If we're the best, I would hate to see what the others are like." That remark that I was sure Jim Bryant would have made in jest was not well received by the high and mighty staff members, but I was certain if Jim Bryant had said it, they all would have laughed. I also remembered many stories about the top brass in headquarters. One was an ambitious, controversial and unpopular inspector who didn't know when to laugh if he couldn't see if the commissioner was laughing.

After hearing about the new EDA testing, I knew I was in trouble. My strongest and most vocal supporter had been Zone Commander George Reinjohn, but he had died months before the captain test. When the captain list was publicized, I was 25 on the list, and only the top 18 to 20 were certain to be promoted.

About a week later, Captain Cowan told me the new zone commander wanted to talk to me. Captain Cowan had received notice that he was going to be transferred to headquarters, so I put in a transfer request for the Westminster office, which was much less complex and only four miles from my home.

At the appointed time, I went to the zone commander's office. He told me the system had failed in my case and I would be transferred to the Westminster office when a pending opening came about when one of the two lieutenants retired on disability. He said if Captain Bill Berry gave me a good appraisal he was certain I would come out much higher on the 1974 captain list.

The deputy commissioner obtained his bachelor's degree in some amazing manner that didn't remain a mystery very long and was appointed CHP commissioner by Governor Reagan. It was later reported at the first senior staff meeting of the commissioner and the 12 or so headquarters and zone commanders the new commissioner made a rather enlightening announcement. He said if any of them hoped to be appointed commissioner after his term was over, they must have at least a bachelor's degree — and none of them had that degree.

For decades the CHP had enjoyed the reputation of being the finest state traffic law enforcement agency in the nation, but it had been managed by mostly self-educated high school graduates who started on the street and worked their way up through the ranks based on experience. Despite that, college degrees suddenly became the new CHP claim to success.

I did not have any college units, so I decided to enroll in administration of justice classes at Golden West Community College when I was transferred to the Westminster office — not because I expected to learn much from the 101 classes, but to make it look good on my application for the next captain test.

During 1972, the Los Angeles Sheriff Department experienced an unusual number of shootouts, so they made a video training film to better prepare their deputies for such events. The film mostly included interviews with deputies who had been involved in shootouts to identify mistakes made and how they could be avoided in the future.

Functional Blackouts

One deputy interviewed had been observed by other deputies when he ran about 15 feet from behind the cover of a sheriff's car and took cover behind a large bush. Obviously, the car was the best cover and the bush was no protection at all. He was asked why he gave up his best cover and exposed himself by running about 15 feet to the bush with no protective cover. He replied that he wasn't aware of what he was doing and didn't remember anything from the time the shooting started until sometime after it was over.

That functional blackout condition did not surprise me. It had happened to me two times in my career. The first time was when I was removing handcuffs from a belligerent drunk in the door of the Big Bear Jail. I had just removed the cuff from his right wrist when he said, "You son of a bitch." I was lucky he said that, because I looked up just as he swung at my left jaw. I moved my head to the right and his fist barely grazed my left jaw. The next thing I knew he was sitting in the corner of the cell. For approximately two seconds, my mind went blank. I knew I couldn't hit that hard, so I could only assume that I had pushed him as hard as I could because that was what I had mentally conditioned myself to do to get away from any threat.

The second time I blacked out for two seconds or more was when I had my motorcycle accident. I had instructed in-service motorcycle trainees to always lock their arms and keep the handlebars and front wheel straight if they were going to crash into a passenger car. It was so ingrained in my mind that I automatically locked my arms when I knew I was going to crash into the right-rear fender of the wrong-side-of-the-road car.

I had discussed functional blackouts years later with an officer who had served in Vietnam. He said one time when he came under fire he put his automatic rifle over the top of the trench and didn't remember anything until he was repeatedly pulling the trigger of his empty rifle.

For both of my functional blackout events I could thank the sharp San Diego Police Department lieutenant who advised us on our first day in the police department to imagine every threatening or emergency situation and mentally condition ourselves to take the best action. I followed his good advice, and it worked for me.

There is no way of knowing if it would have worked for the interviewed Los Angeles Sheriff Department deputy or other peace officers, but it is one way to survive and retire in good health.

CHAPTER 39

The Shell Game

It was obvious that it was no more than a political shell game — with no pea under any of the three shells.

The Westminster office was much simpler to operate than the South L.A. office. There were no motorcycles or commercial scales and only two courts to deal with. About 90 percent of the highways of office responsibility were freeways, including the high truck-traffic Long Beach Freeway. The area included Santa Catalina Island, but the Los Angeles County Sheriff took care of the island, because the CHP did not have a boat.

Although it was like a country club compared to South L.A. it didn't take long for me to see that there were problems, especially with court overtime. This indicated that there were probably many "bounty hunter" citations being issued by officers for court overtime. Since 1958 all officers received a minimum of four hours compensating time off for all call-backs, including court on their time off. Then starting in 1961, officers had the option of taking compensating time off or overtime pay. Also, when officers went to court in their own cars, they were paid mileage from home to court and back.

My main concern was that some officers were issuing bum citations for profit and motorists were getting a bad rap. In addition to the interest of true justice, this practice could destroy the decades of fine reputation of the CHP, so I started keeping track of citations issued versus citation subpoenas received. DUI cases were not included, because those arrests nearly always generated more subpoenas due to higher fines, jail sentences for repeat offenders and possible driver license suspensions.

It didn't take long for the statistics to confirm my suspicions. The worst ratio was that of an 18-year veteran officer with one subpoena for every 5.7 citations issued. He was not a model officer and had a bright red nose that made me think he was a heavy drinker. The best ratio was that of a young officer born in a foreign country who had

344

one subpoena for every 72 citations issued. The rest of the officers had ratios between those two, but none even close to the 5.7 ratio.

When the officers were told the ratio statistics were being compiled and would be included in their annual appraisal reports, my popularity hit bottom, but I didn't care. My intent was to get them to issue quality citations that would prevent accidents, not reward them financially. As a result, the ratio 5.7 officer improved to a 10.0 ratio the first year — nothing to celebrate, but some improvement.

As a supervisor I never pressured officers for arrest activity because I believed in quality citations and arrests. I also believed in in-view patrol, which is very effective because every speeding motorist who sees a CHP patrol vehicle nearly always slows down. But when a citation is issued, the cited speeder is probably the only one who slows down for a while afterwards.

One of the first issues the new commissioner addressed in a public message was about citations and arrests. He clearly stated he was not interested in high CHP citation and arrest activity. Needless to say, that made him very popular with all California residents. Then he issued an internal order that the decades old "Flash Point" was to be discontinued. Flash point was the measure of an officer's arrest production derived from dividing the number of citations and arrests into the number of patrol hours, and he thought the term sounded too much like a football score or some other bloody competition.

The senior lieutenant chose to be the night field operations officer because his wife worked evenings, so I was the permanent day field operations officer and acting commander when the captain was absent from the office on vacation or for some other reason.

I was scheduled to attend a large conference on ocean oil spills one morning and was ready to leave the office when we received the report that one of our officers had been shot but was only slightly injured. I told a sergeant to take care of it until I got back from what I thought was an important conference.

Oil Spill Conference

The ocean oil spill conference was conducted by the California Office of Emergency Services (OES), which was called Civil

Defense during World War II. It was non-civil service and the only known emergency service it had provided was to purchase hundreds of fire trucks, place its emblem on them and assign them to fire departments throughout California.

There had been some ocean oil spills in other parts of the world, so systematic cleanup procedure planning was of importance. The procedure was explained by an OES manager, who said if oil washed onto beaches they would spread straw over it and wait for the straw to absorb the oil. Then the oil-soaked straw and sand would be loaded into dump trucks by skip loaders and transported to a location about 50 miles inland in San Bernardino County.

My first reaction was that straw is shiny and is not absorbent and even if it was, the straw would not be lying flat on the ground like sawdust, so it wouldn't be in complete contact with the oil. Worst of all, there would be at least dozens of dump trucks traveling about 50 miles on freeways dripping oil on the roadways — and causing any number of traffic accidents, especially after the first rain. There were at least 200 in the audience, including some Cal Trans state highway employees and superintendents, so I looked to see if any of them would raise their hands, but nobody did.

I was the only CHP officer there, so I raised my hand. When recognized by the OES manager, I explained the probability of oil slicks on the freeways from dripping crude oil. Despite the straw absorbency problem, I suggested the loads be dumped on the already-contaminated Hellman Oil Field nearby until it dried out and could be safely transported to San Bernardino County. There was no agreement response from the OES manager, and the conference was quickly adjourned.

I was familiar with slippery roadways since I was a CHP cadet and we were told of sugar beet pulp being transported for many miles in dump trucks. The pulp dripped sugary juice on the roadways, and in the first rain there were vehicles sliding in all directions and crashing, so transporting sugar beet pulp in leaky trucks was quickly prohibited.

That was the last I heard of any plans for ocean oil spill cleanups. Either that was the last conference or the last one the CHP was invited to attend. If the OES had just done some research, it would have saved a lot of state time.

Burglar Suspect Shoots Officer

As soon as I returned to the office I got the details of the officer's shooting from the sergeant. The officer had just completed issuing a citation on the southbound shoulder of the Long Beach Freeway when a Long Beach police officer looked over the fence and told him of a burglary that just happened. The Long Beach police officer said the burglar was a young black man and was last seen walking south on the freeway shoulder a few minutes earlier.

Without radioing the information to other CHP units, the officer headed south to look for the burglary suspect. At the Willow Street off-ramp he saw a young black man who fit the description of the burglar walking away from the freeway. He overtook the possible burglary suspect and asked him if he was the one who just knocked over the house by the freeway and spread eagled him against the hood of the patrol car.

Just as he started to search the suspect, the man pushed away from the hood, swung at the officer, knocked him to the ground and took his service revolver from its holster. The suspect then walked about 20 feet, turned around and said, "I'm going to shoot you." He fired two shots, and one round hit the officer in the buttocks. Then he fled with the revolver.

The officer had initially been in the South L.A. office before the Westminster office opened while I was stressing officer safety and the right-side approach, but with about 175 officers in the office, he was sort of lost in the crowd and I didn't know much about him.

It was easy for me to identify the careless mistakes he had made. First of all, he should have radioed the burglary suspect information and description to all other CHP units on the car-to-car channel. Then when he saw the suspect who fit the description, he should have called for backup officers before stopping the suspect. Then above all, he should not have accused the suspect of being the burglar to his face. He should have told the suspect he stopped him for illegally being a pedestrian on a freeway and obtained his identification. Then if he had called for backup he could have tried to stall him until another officer arrived. He took none of those precautionary measures and could have been killed if shot in a vital area instead of in the buttocks, or he could have been shot six times instead of one.

Being the acting commander, I had to decide the best corrective action. Not knowing at that time that he was one of about five officers in the Westminster office who were anti-supervision, nonconformist, complaining types, I thought getting shot should be sufficient corrective action.

He was off duty on injury time recuperating at home and I thought he would have ample time to realize how close he had come to death and the careless mistakes he had made — and would correct them on his own. So I decided to write a censurable Form 2 Incident Report clearly explaining all the mistakes he had made and the correct measures he should take in the future.

Not long after I made that decision, the zone assistant commander phoned me and said the zone commander wanted the officer to be suspended for five days without pay for his carelessness, because he had endangered Long Beach police officers by letting the burglar escape with his service revolver. I told the assistant zone commander the action I had decided to take and the reasons for that action. He didn't make any comment, but I got the impression he agreed with me. He was a veteran street cop and was reasonable and empathetic.

Long Beach police officers identified and arrested the burglar and recovered the officer's service revolver the next day. I phoned the Long Beach Police Department and spoke with a detective, who said the burglar lived in North Long Beach, was well known to them and was a bully and tough street fighter. Since he pulled a burglary in broad daylight, walked illegally on a freeway where he could be cited and identified, walked about 20 feet before deciding to shoot the officer, I was convinced the burglar wasn't very bright, and I told the detective I thought his I.Q. was probably in the low 80s. The detective laughed and said, "No, that's way too high."

When the wounded officer returned to work after 11 days off on injury time, he was issued the Form 2 Incident Report. His true nature emerged because he didn't think he had done anything wrong. He thought it was a job hazard to be shot and that he should get sympathy, if anything.

In the seven following years while he was still in the Westminster office I saw him for what he was. He was bitter at the world in general and the CHP and me in particular, but I never told him or anyone else I had saved him from being suspended for five days without pay. It wouldn't have made any difference anyway.

In 1980 he transferred to a Central California office and was killed about a year later. He was issuing a citation on busy, high-speed U.S. Highway 99 on the driver side of a violator's vehicle when an elderly man fell asleep at the wheel, drifted off the roadway and struck him. He was killed instantly. He had been in both the South L.A. and Westminster offices when I stressed and preached the right-side approach, but like so many others if a supervisor with 15 to 20 years of traffic enforcement experience told them to turn right, they would turn left just to show that they do what they want to do. In his case, it cost him his life.

Rapid Transit Plan

There was an Orange County Enforcement and Engineering Committee composed of a CHP lieutenant from each of the three Orange County offices, traffic engineers from Cal Trans and the Orange County Highway Department and an Auto Club representative. Being the Westminster day field operations officer, I was on the committee. There were quarterly meetings to identify highway engineering defects and recommend corrections.

After a couple of quarterly meetings, one of the Cal Trans engineers phoned me and asked if he could come to my office and discuss an important issue with me. When he arrived, he had two other Cal Trans engineers with him. They all looked like they didn't want to be there and needed a stiff drink. After a few minutes of rather senseless talk the one who had requested the meeting handed me a beautifully bound manual. The lettering on the cover said it was the suggested plan for rapid transit systems in the Los Angeles Basin. I looked inside and saw that the credits for composing the plan did not include the CHP, so I knew immediately he had slipped me a political bomb. Then the three engineers excused themselves and gracefully departed.

Before they were out of the parking lot I was in the captain's office. I handed the manual to him and told him he should take care of it. As I had done, he read the cover, opened it up and read the credits for composing the plan. "Where in hell did you get this?" he exclaimed. As soon as I explained how and where I got it, he got on the phone to the zone office.

Before the end of the day the commissioner's office was buzzing and all hell broke loose in Sacramento. Cal Trans had gone behind the CHP's back and composed the manual. From what I had seen there were seven different plans and some were contributed by Los Angeles County supervisors.

When the smoke cleared in Sacramento, a CHP inspector was assigned by the commissioner to oversee the rewriting of the plan. It was completed about a year later and its new title included the CHP. When Cal Trans was caught cheating and trying to upstage the CHP, they were willing to let the CHP commissioner name it anything his heart desired.

Mapping Traffic Accidents

There was also a Cal Trans engineer named Rick Snow who loved the CHP and made regular visits to our office to see if he could do anything for us. Historically, all CHP offices had pin maps to show the location of all traffic accidents, but the pins did not show which way the crashed vehicles were traveling, how many vehicles were involved or the time of day the accidents happened. I asked Rick Snow if he could have large maps copied if I provided him with an original detailed map.

I identified an officer who had drafting skills and had him draw a straight-line map of all the freeways and unincorporated islands in the Westminster office area. It was to be much like highway engineers' collision diagrams but was on heavy butcher paper measuring three feet by four feet.

It was a difficult task and took the officer about a month to complete the map. It took much thought because I had told him to include all freeway lanes, shoulders, center dividers and off-ramp gore points. When he completed the map it was perfect.

The next time Rick Snow came to the office I gave it to him to make 100 copies. They were to be posted on the bulletin board with one for each of the three shifts for each quarter of the year, because officers were assigned to quarterly shifts. It would take 12 copies per year, so the 100 copies would be an eight-year supply. About a month later, Rick Snow returned with the 100 copies and said they had cost about $850 but there would be no charge to us.

Seventeen-year veteran officer Harold Whitney was the staff accident investigation follow-up officer and compiled precise property damage, injury and fatality statistics. I told him to mark each accident exactly where it occurred with green for property damage, red for injury and black for fatal accidents.

At about the same time I got copies of the accident statistics from Whitney to reevaluate the deployment of the day shift by day of the week. When I arrived at the office the deployment priority was equal for all days of the week for the day shift but there were high and low accident frequency days. Without much time and effort, I amended the deployment priorities to match the accident frequencies by the day of week and beat.

When Captain Bill Berry saw my new deployment schedule, he directed the night field operations officer lieutenant to do the same for the evening and graveyard shifts.

When a new quarter started, we posted the new map on top of the previous quarterly map or maps so newly assigned officers could refer to them. Amazingly, it worked better than I had dreamed, thanks to the officers who actually studied the maps and directed their in-view patrol and enforcement efforts toward the higher accident locations.

The very first full quarter the graveyard map clearly showed a cluster of solo-vehicle, ran-off-roadway accidents southbound on the I-405 Freeway in the northern part of Orange County. Those accidents clearly indicated DUI drivers from Long Beach or other parts of Los Angeles who had fallen asleep or otherwise missed the roadway in their impaired condition. Of those accidents, a few had crashed into the gore point guard rails at off-ramps. Crashing into gore points or other fixed objects results in what is called "intolerable deceleration" in the traffic business and can cause severe or fatal injuries.

With the use of the maps and strategic deployments, the results were incredible. In 1972, the year before I transferred to the Westminster office, there had been a total of 2,986 traffic accidents, 796 injury accidents and 36 fatal accidents. In 1973, the first year of the maps and new deployment, there were

2,581 accidents, 634 injury accidents and 30 fatal accidents. Then in 1974, the total dropped to 1,905 accidents with 593 injury accidents and 15 fatal accidents.

Some other office commanders said the very low 1974 accident statistics could be attributed to the new 55-mile speed limit that went into effect on January 1, 1974, but the quarterly zone accident report statistics by office showed only minimal or no reductions in accidents for any of the other offices. None were even close to the Westminster reductions.

Captain Berry was elated with the 1973 accident statistics and credited me with the improvements. The zone commander had told me if Captain Berry gave me a high appraisal I would do much better on the next captain test, so I felt very good about my chances.

Then a few months before the captain test, the zone commander visited the Westminster office. He made it a point to come into the lieutenants' office to tell me about the 1974 captain test. He said there would be no written test, it was not mandatory that applicants appear before the qualifications appraisal panel and the list would be established based on commanders' appraisals.

I knew it was an end run around the merit system to give the favored headquarters and zone lieutenants who had failed the 1972 captain test a free ride. It would also give the lieutenants who were too lazy to study for the written test the same free gift. But I only told the zone commander what I thought about the lazy ones. I said it would probably increase the number of applicants from about 60 to about 90. I also said if any didn't know enough about departmental policies and procedures to pass a pass-fail written test, they shouldn't be lieutenants, much less captains, so I thought it was a very irresponsible idea and would severely impact the department.

It was obvious that it was no more than a political shell game — with no pea under any of the three shells. When the test results were mailed out, I was 27 on the list, despite the zone commander's promise.

Fiery Accident

Shortly thereafter, I responded to a fiery double fatal accident involving a truck and two cars on the Long Beach Freeway. It was in the northbound lanes and they were closed at the I-405 Freeway. I had to enter the freeway at the next off-ramp to the north of the accident and drive southbound in the closed northbound lanes. There was a fire chief's car ahead of me and I followed the battalion chief to the scene.

The sergeant at the scene was complaining to an officer about the firefighters continuing to drown a large pile of black hotdog buns in the middle of the northbound lanes. A Cal Trans skip-loader was standing by to bulldoze the pile off the roadway. When I asked a firefighter why they didn't get out of the way and let the skip-loader get the pile out of the roadway, he replied that his captain hadn't told them to quit hosing the drowned buns down. They had to have orders from above.

I looked over to where the captain was talking to the battalion chief and Cal Trans Highway Superintendent Dick Holt, who was an outstanding manager and he and I had a wonderful working relationship. I went over and told the captain I wanted the pile of buns out of the roadway so we could open the freeway. He immediately went over and told his firefighters to stop soaking the buns and let the skip-loader doze them into the drainage ditch on the shoulder that was already full of water.

After the freeway was opened to northbound traffic, the battalion chief and Dick Holt called me over to discuss a problem. The chief said the problem was that there were no fire hydrants on freeways. Holt had offered to dispatch his 6,000-gallon water tanker truck to all freeway fires, but the chief persisted in addressing the issue of no fire hydrants on freeways.

The freeways had water lines to irrigate the landscaping, so I asked the chief and Holt if fire hose fittings could be affixed to the irrigation lines. I knew that fire hose fittings were unique to fire services, so I asked the chief if his department would provide the fittings. The chief and Holt agreed it could be done, but the chief would have to get the approval of the fire chief to provide the fittings.

A couple of weeks later, the battalion chief, Holt and I met with the assistant fire chief. After a brief discussion of the proposal the assistant chief agreed to provide the fittings and necessary labor to install the fire hydrants on the Long Beach and I-405 Freeways in the city of Long Beach.

About a year later, I rode to a meeting with the Seal Beach fire chief. On the way back from the meeting I told him about the Long Beach Fire Department and Cal Trans installing fire hydrants. He was very interested, but I never knew if he had fire hydrants installed on the I-405 Freeway in the city of Seal Beach.

Fire Trucks Cause Traffic Tie-ups

In 1974, the Long Beach Fire Department started a paramedic program that included department-owned ambulances. It was an instant nightmare for us. They insisted on responding to minor injury accidents with an ambulance and a fire truck. They would park the fire truck in a freeway lane blocking traffic and leave the overhead red lights flashing, which caused traffic on both sides of the freeway to slow down to a crawl. That always led to the possibility of rear-end crashes.

I phoned the captain in charge of the paramedic program two times to complain about their responding with fire trucks. One time he said the truck was necessary to carry enough firemen to provide adequate medical treatment for the injured. I told him CHP officers had been administering first aid to injured traffic accident victims since 1929 and officers were always there to help, so they needed only the two paramedics in the ambulance.

The second time I phoned him he had a different excuse. He said there wasn't enough room in the ambulance to carry the respirator, so it had to be delivered to the accident scene in a fire truck. I told him in my over 20 years in police work I never knew of a traffic accident victim who needed to be administered with a respirator, but he paid little attention.

Another serious problem was that more than one officer reported to me that the paramedics had on more than one occasion tried to force accident victims with minor injuries into the ambulance when the injured did not want to go with them. For any number of reasons, including religious beliefs, no adult can legally be forced to receive medical treatment. Forcing them could be a civil rights violation of depriving people of their freedom, so the CHP officers rescued the slightly injured parties from the paramedics.

354

That was only the beginning of the paramedic problem for the CHP. In years to follow, the paramedic intrusion into traffic accident scenes spread throughout California like wild fire. Agreements between fire agencies and police agencies had to be formally established. The result was that fire trucks respond to every traffic accident including minor fender benders and create traffic slowdowns on freeways and other high-speed highways.

Bad blood between the Long Beach Fire Department and law enforcement was stirred up in 1970 by a large billboard sign. The billboard at the south end of the Wilmington curve next to the I-405 Freeway was most conspicuous. It pictured a fireman in soot-covered turnouts and the large caption read, "Firemen Fight Fires Not People."

I saw it a few times and it angered me. In 1970 California law enforcement was only a little past the halfway point in the 1965 to 1972 era of violent civil rights demonstrations, ambush shootings of police officers, bombings of police stations and cars and other anarchy.

When I mentioned the billboard to a Long Beach Police Department lieutenant who was in my 1971 six-week live-in POST class in San Diego, he erupted. He said it had been posted by the firemen's association and the police department immediately demanded that it be removed. He said it was removed within days and there had been bad blood between the police department and the fire department for over a year.

The FBI National Academy

In 1975 I was selected to attend the FBI National Academy at the FBI Academy on the Quantico Marine Base in Quantico, Virginia. I was asked by the training division lieutenant if I would go to the 11-week summer session from July to September. He said most of the others going did not want to attend during the hot summer in Virginia, so they preferred to go in the winter, spring or fall.

I knew it snowed in Virginia and I had my fill of snow in Big Bear, driving Kathleen Brown to Tahoe City and in Yreka during the major winter of 1968-1969, so I quickly agreed to go to the summer session.

The day after we arrived, it was raining in Washington, D.C. and Quantico. Being a lifelong California resident, I wasn't aware of the summer weather conditions on the East Coast. Then I remembered a song that included, "and it doesn't rain in Indianapolis in the summer time," which was a joke.

I had known since childhood that the Civil War was still a sore subject with those from the Confederate States and I had been told by other CHP lieutenants and captains who had attended the FBI National Academy that the "Rebs" still thought, "The South will rise again."

On Sunday night, our first night at the academy, the FBI inspector in command of the National Academy assembled our group of 250 attendees in the auditorium for our orientation. His first announcement was, "I would like you to know that the Civil War is over."

That drew massive applause from about 80 percent of us from the Union States and several from throughout the free world, but the Rebs didn't think it was so funny.

Later in the 11-week session, I made friends with a Texan who had a great sense of humor, but the term "Civil War" was not proper or funny to him. He said it was "The War Between the States" or "The War of Northern Aggression," not the Civil War. I thought that was funny because he didn't mention that the Confederates had started the war at Fort Sumter. All through our session the Civil War, Rebs and southern moonshiners were the brunt of many jokes told by the FBI instructors.

The inspector commander also told us that we had all been investigated the same as applicants for the position of FBI special agent. He said all of the academy employees, including janitors, had also been cleared by the same intense background investigations. He said if we left any money on our beds, when we returned there might be more money because some might have thought it was a collection for a good cause and contributed their fair share.

There were two adjacent rooms with a shared bath between them. One of my concerns about going to the academy was the possibility of being in the same room with a big jerk, but I was most fortunate. My roommate and the two men we shared the bath with were all great officers, gentlemen and fun.

The 250 in the session were divided into five sections, each on a different floor of the seven-story National Academy wing of the FBI Academy. Each section was to elect a leader who would run for class spokesman to deliver a speech at the graduation ceremony, along with being the direct liaison with the National Academy inspector commander and staff. Each section had an FBI special agent counselor.

The next day we were told we had to contribute $37.50 for three separate funds. One was $17.50 for three sectional social functions and dinners. The second was $10 for a session legacy to commemorate our 102nd Session, and the third was $10 for the FBI Recreation Fund.

That first day of classes, we were given pretests in three of our classes to measure our prior knowledge of the subjects. About a week later, I happened to get in the long line at the dining room for lunch directly behind the head of the management department, a Japanese/American called "Toke."

Mentioning the pretest in the management class, I asked him if he had gone to USC and knew a professor named Dr. Jack Ascot. He replied that he was from Colorado, hadn't gone to USC and had never heard of Dr. Ascot. I explained Dr. Ascot's workshop at the CHP Academy about seven years before and that he had stressed pre-testing of all CHP cadets the first week of the 16 weeks of classes. Toke wholeheartedly agreed with that learning process and said pre-testing was the future of law enforcement training, and especially for cadets. Despite his enthusiasm for pre-testing and his prominent position at the FBI Academy, that was the last I ever heard of pre-testing in law enforcement.

There was a San Diego Police Department captain in my section. A few days into our first week, he came to me and told me about a problem in another section he thought we might be able to help defuse. He explained that a NYPD sergeant and an LAPD lieutenant were having a heated argument over which one of their departments was number one in the nation.

I laughed because I thought it was childish and stupid. I told the SDPD captain they should put on the gloves and slug it out in the gym like two junior high school kids would do to settle who was number one. That was the end of our problem.

There was a large beer and pizza hall in the academy. I figured it was included in the academy to encourage the FBI cadets and National Academy students to drink on campus rather than in public where they could get into conflicts with cop haters. Also, we were told by instructors to mix with those from other departments to learn how they operated. The beer hall was the best place to mix with those from other sections. All one had to do was buy a pitcher of beer, walk around looking lonely and lost and someone would always flag you down to talk shop.

My roommate didn't drink, so I usually went alone to the large and very noisy beer and pizza hall where everybody was trying to talk over the others. A few nights after the NYPD and LAPD squabble was apparently resolved without bloodshed, a Boston Police Department captain waved for me to sit at his table. He introduced himself and asked me where I was from. "California," I briefly answered. "Which department?" he asked. "Highway patrol," I replied. "My God," he exclaimed, "you guys are number one in the country." "Thank you," I replied. I felt like telling him that reputation was built by deputy commissioners, supervising inspectors and inspectors who didn't have college degrees.

At our first sectional social function and dinner at a pizza parlor our FBI counselor told us we would then elect our section representative. One Texan nominated another Texan who was a deputy U.S. Marshal, and another Texan seconded his nomination. Then a third Texan made a motion to discontinue nominations. The FBI counselor did not call for a vote of the section and that was the end of the so-called election. Our FBI counselor was from New York and was a great guy but obviously did not know the first thing about running a democratic election.

A few weeks later, a copy of the latest monthly edition of the FBI Bulletin magazine was placed on each one of our beds. As I thumbed through it, I saw that the class spokesman in the previous session had been the number one advocate of "Get rid of the culls" at the CHP Academy when we were both sergeants there in the late 1960s. Because of his cold-blooded attitude toward cadets and his denouncing pre-testing of cadets to help them learn, he was at the bottom of my list as a human being.

His being the previous class spokesman aroused my competitive spirit to a fiery high. It was like waving a red flag at a mad bull, but our section representative had been elected. When I told my roommate of my personal feeling about the previous class spokesman, he asked me if I would like to run for class spokesman of our session. I told him I would for no other reason than to put the anti-cadet "Get rid of the culls" advocate in his place.

There was a Chicago Police Department lieutenant who had started openly campaigning for class spokesman our very first day at the academy. He first passed out book matches with his name inscribed on them; then gave each of us a small bottle of whiskey like those on airline flights, then a can of Tannery leather softener and conditioner. Although he drove a brand new Cadillac convertible, we all had no doubt that he never paid so much as a penny for any of the payola trinkets.

About a week later, our FBI counselor told us to gather in a classroom to elect our section representative. My roommate nominated me, and there were five others nominated, including the previously so-called elected representative. We each gave a short speech and I was elected,

After another week my new Texan friend told me his friends were so mad about the second election and were so sure the Chicago lieutenant had caused it that they had poured sugar in his bed to get even.

The same day I was elected the National Academy inspector commander called me to his office to give me some tips on what kind of speech I should deliver at the election for class spokesman. I thanked him and was somewhat surprised that his subject was almost the same as the one I had used to get elected section representative. It was a personal speech to thank many people, especially our wives and husbands for tolerating our being away from our homes and families for 11 long weeks.

The big election was held the next week. Although I was in Section 2, I was the last of the five candidates to speak. It turned out to be a definite advantage for me. The four others had higher ranks than mine in their departments, but their speeches were all on dry, cold law enforcement subjects as though they were running for sheriff. I was fairly certain that if I had delivered my heart-warming family speech second in line, the three who followed me might have tried to amend their speeches to parrot mine.

None of us could get a majority vote because of the loyalty of nearly all to their section representative, so the one with the most votes would be elected. It took about 15 minutes for staff members to count the votes and announce I had won. As I walked back to the podium to thank the session members for electing me, I shook the hands of the four other section representatives.

I had to believe that my speech was just one part of the reason I had been elected. As the Boston Police Department captain had said to me in the beer hall, the California Highway Patrol was number one in the country. I couldn't help but believe that had swayed his vote along with many others to the CHP and me.

That night my section held a California champagne celebration to honor my election. It was held in the middle of our floor next to the elevator area. Everyone attended in great spirits except the Chicago lieutenant, who sullenly pushed his way through the crowd and got on an elevator, and then returned and again pushed his way through the crowd and went back to his room. His ugly behavior and his personal self-glorifying interest made me think the Texans just might have done the right thing by putting sugar in his bed.

The National Academy inspector commander then arrived to congratulate the section and me for winning the election for the highly prestigious position. I thanked the inspector commander for giving me tips on what kind of speech to deliver. "I gave the others the same tips, but none of them listened to me," he said with a smile.

Late the next afternoon when I was walking to the dining room for supper, a session member from another section stopped me to ask a question. He wanted me to find out what the required ten-dollar donation to the FBI Recreation Fund was all about. I hadn't given it much thought, so I told him I would find out and get back to him. I went straight to the inspector commander's office and asked him that question.

He grabbed the phone, punched some numbers, said he was sorry for running late and would get there in a few minutes. Then he quickly left his office without saying a word. It was obviously a question he could not answer. I located the session member who had posed the very valid question and told him how the inspector had reacted when I asked him about it. He was as suspicious and displeased as I was, but it was all I could do to find out.

The FBI Recreation Fund remained a mystery until April 1976, seven months after our session graduated. It was reported in my local newspaper, the "Orange County Register," that the $10,000 a year collected from the FBI National Academy attendees was a fund for the recreational activities of the top FBI executives. It was a report based on a Congressional investigation of the FBI after J. Edgar Hoover's death. It made me wonder why the FBI Recreation Fund collections were still being mandated from my session when slow-moving Congress certainly knew about them long before we were scammed.

Earlier in our session, we had been told that after FBI Director J. Edgar Hoover died in May 1972, Congress had lowered the FBI mandatory retirement age from 70 to 55 years of age. Our instructor had indicated that Congress had taken that action to get rid of Hoover's top executive cronies who could have assisted him in compiling his well-known files on those who could impact his political actions and his career.

Nuttall is shown giving his "Spirit of Unity" speech at the FBI National Academy's 102nd Session graduation ceremony in September 1975.

The day after the recreation fund question came up a session member from another section stopped me in the hall and asked if movie star John Wayne could speak at our graduation ceremony. I told him I would talk to the inspector commander about the possibility. It sounded like a great idea to me because I knew John Wayne, Ronald Reagan and U.S. Senator Barry Goldwater were staunch law enforcement admirers and supporters. Also, as luck would have it, one of my younger cousins who lived in Newport Beach was one of his three secretaries.

I went to the inspector commander's office and asked him if we could invite John Wayne to speak at our graduation ceremony. He immediately said he could not be included in our graduation ceremony because the chief speaker was going to be the president of the International Association of Chiefs of Police (IACP). He then jokingly said that the scheduled chief speaker was the chief of police in "Slippery Rock." I later learned he was the chief of police in a small, obscure, unknown town equivalent to a wide place in the road. With that in mind, it was obvious that his being the president of the IACP was the highest point in his otherwise mediocre police career.

But it was also obvious that there was another reason. It was FBI Director Clarence M. Kelley. If John Wayne was on the FBI Academy grounds he would upstage everybody in Virginia and nearby Washington, D.C., and if he attended the graduation ceremony, he would be the center of attention and few if any would hear one word of the chief speaker's or FBI Director Kelley's speeches.

I told the inquiring session member what the inspector commander had said, but I didn't tell him my thoughts on the matter. In only two days as the class spokesman, I had batted zero with the FBI to represent the session members. I considered talking to the base commander of the Quantico Marine Base to act as John Wayne's host because he had starred in some Marine Corps movies, but I figured he would ask too many questions about why the FBI Academy wouldn't host him — and I was not in a position to buck the FBI and especially Director Kelley. Although it was clear to me that it would be an exercise in futility, I later regretted that I didn't pursue it.

A few days later, the inspector commander phoned me in my room. He directed me to notify the sections representatives that Director Kelley was going to tour the academy that day. He said Director Kelley was going to lead a group of dignitaries through the academy and asked me to tell the four section representatives to tell their members to be sure to have their quarters in tip top inspection condition. It was the lunch break, so I was able to contact the four other section representatives in just a few minutes.

FBI Director Clarence M. Kelley presents certificate to George C. Nuttall at FBI National Academy graduation.

The next day, one of the section representatives said as soon as he told his section members of Director Kelley's grand tour, they dumped their waste baskets in the hallway. I never heard anything about that childish prank from the academy staff, so I had to assume Director Kelley and his tour group did not go to that floor.

But after the inspector commander's evasiveness about the required donation to the FBI Recreation Fund and denying our request for John Wayne to be at our graduation ceremony, I couldn't blame the session members for their overt rebellion.

Also, it was pretty clear from the beginning of our session that few if any members were FBI fans. Most were there because graduating from the FBI National Academy was a feather in their cap for future favorable assignments and promotions. It was and is the best police academy in the world and selection to attend was in itself an honor.

Session Member Dies

Before I finished writing my graduation ceremony speech a few mornings later I was called from the classroom and told of the tragic death of one of our session members. Just after completing the physical training class of calisthenics and running, he collapsed in the shower room and died of a massive heart attack. He was the first session member to die while attending the National Academy in its 40-year history.

I went directly to the classroom of his section, sat in the rear of the room and listened to the members of his section tell what had happened and how they had tried to revive him. He had been taken to the Marine Base Hospital by a Marine Corps ambulance and pronounced dead by the attending Marine Corps physician.

Without any great ceremony the session members voted unanimously to give his widow the $2,500 for a legacy to commemorate our session and decided that our legacy would be a photo of him that would hang in the academy chapel.

The deceased session member was a St. Louis, Missouri, Police Department detective, and the inspector commander told me that he, the deceased's roommate, section counselor and I would fly to St. Louis to offer our condolences to his widow and children and I would present the widow with the $2,500 check. It was not a trip I was looking forward to in any way.

Section counselor Dick Tibbs drove us to the Washington National Airport and asked me about the CHP motorcycle training course because he wanted to attend so he could work undercover as a street motorcycle thug. We all laughed, because he was about six feet two inches tall, weighed 230 pounds, had played college football and had cop written all over him.

Being from the Santa Ana, California FBI field office, Tibbs was very familiar with the 1970 slaying of the four CHP officers. As in so many major police events, the story of what happened and how it happened got twisted as it went from one person to another. He told me what he had heard and although his version had some flaws in it, I didn't want to make an issue of any of the errors.

I was in FBI territory and did not want to venture into that minefield of finger pointing at the deficient FBI training at the CHP Academy that had contributed to the greatest disaster in CHP history, so I played dumb, let Tibbs' version stand and let the subject move on to that of our deceased session mate.

We were met at the St. Louis Airport by an FBI agent who drove us to the Catholic Church the deceased attended where a wake was being held. We met in a private room with the widow and children. Since my father had died when I was five months old and I had grown up without a father, it was very difficult for me to see the five children ranging from seven to fifteen years of age and envision what their lives would be like. Trying to control my emotions, I told the widow that the session members wanted her to have the legacy funds and I handed the check to her.

It was a Sunday and St. Louis had a "Blue Law" that prohibited drinking, dancing and even working on Sundays. The FBI agent driving us was at a loss to find a restaurant where we could have supper, but after a half-hour of driving he finally found a fine steak house owned and operated by a sinner and it was open for other sinners. After spending the night in a nice hotel, we flew back to National Airport. On the way the inspector commander told us he had spoken to the St. Louis Police Department chief about the widow receiving a survivor's pension. The chief said he was chairman of the Fire and Police Retirement Board and had the last say and would see that the widow definitely received a survivor's pension. That was our main concern, so we were happy to hear that.

After going from the FBI Recreation Fund, John Wayne and tragic death events in addition to attending classes, I finally finished my graduation ceremony speech. The theme and title was "The Spirit of Unity," which had so clearly been exemplified by the session during the death crisis. I turned it in to the inspector commander for review and approval.

Before the ceremony, many photos were taken including one of my wife and me with Director Kelley. The ceremony went very well and in my speech I thanked everyone who had made it a pleasant 11 weeks at the academy and especially our wives and one husband who had to endure our absences and support our career efforts.

When I returned to the real world of being a lowly CHP lieutenant, the CHP deputy commissioner requested a copy of my speech. About a week later I received a memorandum of commendation from him for my outstanding representation of the department and a commendable memorandum from the CHP commissioner that ended with "You have served the public, your profession and the department in an exemplary manner" the week after that.

However, those commendations and the one from Captain Berry giving me the credit for reducing fatal accidents from 36 to 15 didn't matter. When I took the 1976 captain test I again came out 25 on the list — about five positions too low to make captain.

During my oral interview the panel made a big issue of the high rate of CHP vehicle accidents, officer injuries and officers' overtime in the Westminster office. I was the day field operations officer, and nearly all of those statistics were generated by officers on the evening and graveyard shifts. Also, Captain Berry was the commander and had overall responsibility for the entire office operations. Despite that obvious chain-of-command structure, Captain Berry placed number two on the 1974 inspector list with the same dismal safety and overtime records at that time.

Captain Berry and I had become good friends, and he was promoted to inspector from that 1974 list three months after I returned from the National Academy. He told me I was as competent, or more so than the others but I wasn't a politician.

I thanked him on both counts because the last thing I ever wanted to be called was a politician. Starting on the San Diego Police Department, I had seen so much in the way of cheap politics that it made me wonder how law enforcement could ever protect and serve the public with the honor and respect it deserved.

With the third replacement captain commander of the Westminster office to follow Captain Berry, I came out 14 on the captain list. It was high enough to get promoted. Jack Cowan, who had been the fourth of five captains in the South L.A. office when I was there, was then the deputy commissioner. I was certain he had influenced my higher ranking on the list. We had also become good friends because I had been in the South L.A. office for two years before his arrival and was able to easily tell him where the problems were and who was or had been responsible for creating them. He was very capable of identifying them on his own in due time but my advice expedited the correction of many flaws.

In 1981 and 1982 I was selected to serve on three Qualification Appraisal Panels to interview and grade applicants for the position of CHP officer. Each of the three times I had to go to the academy for interview orientation and to meet the State Personnel Board and public members who were to be on the same panels with me.

High-Stress Training at the CHP Academy

At the academy I quickly became disgusted with the manner in which the cadets were being treated by the staff. The cadets were wearing their Sam Browne gun belts and batons to classrooms, so I asked a staff member why. He said the staff felt they should wear them to classes so they could get accustomed to wearing them. "What a bunch of crap," I thought. Starting on my first day on the San Diego Police Department I became comfortable wearing my Sam Browne belt including a loaded service revolver. For about the first two weeks I felt conspicuous wearing a police uniform in public, but that was the only mental adjustment I had to make.

I also noticed the cadets acted like frightened rabbits when they said, "Good evening, sir," when I met them on the grounds. I was well aware of the scare tactics of the academy staff and was certain they had told the cadets lieutenants would be there for the orientations, so be on their best behavior. When they greeted me like I was a threat to them, I always smiled and replied, "Hi, how are you?" to try to make them feel at ease, but it never did any good.

Then one evening on the way to the dining room I saw an academy lieutenant yelling at three cadets on the walkway. There was a staff officer with him and he was chewing out the three cadets as though they had committed a felony. On my way home I thought the entire academy staff was crazy. I knew most of them had college degrees to be there and it made me wonder if they had learned anything in college about psychology. I also wondered why at least one of them hadn't gone to the USC Library and made a copy of the master's degree thesis Cowan told me about in South L.A. which proved that no-stress cadet training produced better-performing officers than high-stress training.

Not long after, Deputy Commissioner Cowan phoned me at the office and the subject soon turned to academy cadet training. He said one of his sons was in CHP cadet training and he was concerned about what his son was telling him about the training methods at the academy and he didn't like what he was hearing. I told him what I had observed while I was at the academy and that I thought it was outrageous.

Unfortunately, the new governor elected in 1982 announced all department heads would be replaced like a "take no prisoners" policy. That rash action resulted in the CHP commissioner and Cowan leaving the CHP and being appointed director and deputy director of the Department of Justice by the attorney general.

To make it worse, not long after the commissioner was appointed to that position by newly elected Governor Jerry Brown he announced his policy of "humanitarian" supervision to the entire CHP. I could only conclude that the academy commander and staff had missed that one, or they thought they were somehow exempt.

Tanker Truck Fire

I had just changed out of my uniform one night when the phone rang. The CHP dispatcher abruptly told me a gasoline tanker truck had burned and the trailer was on fire on the 22 Freeway at Brookhurst. She said the captain wanted me to manage the scene and he would meet me at the office. I quickly changed back into my uniform and drove the four miles to the office. The captain and I then responded to the scene only a few miles east of the office.

The captain had only about two years on the road as a CHP officer and then was assigned first to a desk job, then to the academy and then to headquarters. He had never managed a major accident and, as usual, was dressed in civilian clothes.

As soon as we arrived and parked west of the fiery scene, a battalion fire chief came over the center divider wall toward us and asked me if I was the scene manager. "Yes," I replied. "We have foam coming from Los Alamitos," he said. "I don't want foam," I replied. "Let it burn out."

Los Alamitos was a former U.S. Naval Air Station that was then the regional military reserve training center and still an active military air base. I then walked to the freeway off-ramp to the east where two CHP sergeants were standing. I asked them where the command post was located. The newer of the two sergeants said in a childish, joking manner that the fire department wouldn't come to their party so they wouldn't go to the fire department's party — and pointed down to the bottom of the off-ramp.

With the captain following me, we walked down to the bottom of the ramp and I saw a battalion chief wearing a turnout coat with "EMERGENCY SCENE MANAGER" printed in large letters on the back. He was leaning in the open rear door of a station wagon talking on a radio. There were two large firemen in regular uniforms standing like guards to keep anyone from getting near the battalion chief.

Before I could get past the two bodyguards the fire went out, just the opposite of what I had directed. The battalion chief then slowly walked away from the station wagon and toward the freeway embankment like he was in a daze. I was very angry, so I asked, "Now what are you going to do?" Still slowly walking in what appeared to be a dazed state, he said, "Re-ignition," as though he had just realized that if the fire reignited there could be a massive explosion.

Gasoline is flammable and is also an explosive when it is hot or otherwise vaporized. When we had a boat and my family attended a Coast Guard safety training class, we were told one teaspoon of gasoline vaporized in an enclosed engine compartment was equivalent to one stick of dynamite if ignited.

"I told your other battalion chief to let it burn out, so why didn't you?" I abruptly asked. "He's an Orange County Fire Department battalion chief, not one of ours," he replied. My God, I thought, this turned into a firemen's party something like an American Legion or Shriners' convention, and I could no longer fault the sergeant for making his snide comment about "their party and ours."

There was no re-ignition, but the roadway was damaged. The top of the tanker trailer had collapsed from the intense heat and was like a large bathtub. The firemen had directed the stream of water into the tank instead of at the bottom of the tank to keep it from collapsing and to keep the concrete roadway cool. Their streaming the water into the tank not only put the fire out, it caused the mixture of gasoline and water to overflow and run down the storm drains into an adjacent residential area.

There was a manager from a hazardous materials disposal company at the scene to offer his services to remove the gasoline and water from the tanker trailer. His estimate for the removal was $4,000. I told him to get started so we could get it out of there and open up the busy freeway.

Then the Cal Trans superintendent who was also on the scene told me the eastbound lanes of the freeway were so damaged they would have to keep the freeway closed the next day to resurface the lanes. He explained to me that intense heat causes concrete to pop like popcorn and that is what happened to the lanes.

I was completely disgusted. Just directing the stream of water in the wrong direction had turned the simple tanker fire into a major disaster, even without a re-ignition explosion. I later learned from the CHP officer who investigated the accident that the tanker driver had been cut off by an unsafe lane changer and caused him to go out of control trying to avoid crashing into the lane changer — but the unsafe lane changer had continued on and couldn't be identified. That made me think the owner of the gasoline tanker and trailer would probably be liable for the $4,000 hazardous material removal fee, in addition to the Cal Trans resurfacing of the freeway lanes.

A few days later, the captain told me the fire department officials wanted to have a meeting with us to critique the management of the tanker fire. He told me to be our spokesman because I had been the emergency scene manager. When we arrived at the fire department headquarters, I was asked to sit across a table from their spokesman. He was a battalion chief in charge of their training unit. He started the meeting by telling me that he didn't think the CHP knew very much about managing highway emergency scenes.

That not only irritated me, it made me believe that the meeting had been called to try to fix civil liability blame on the CHP to avoid the liability for their own inept management. I told them the CHP had very successfully managed major accident scenes for over 50 years and in my over 30 years in police work I had never seen or experienced such a confused scene. I then asked why the Orange

County Fire Department battalion chief was at the scene representing himself as their scene manager and I told him to let the fire burn itself out.

It was obvious the battalion chief did not know about that impersonator. I told him the CHP has to manage an average of two or three gasoline tanker fires a year and it had been the practice for years to let them burn out to avoid re-ignition explosions. The battalion chief who had mismanaged the tanker fire scene was also at the meeting with a few other city employees. He spoke up and said that fire was the biggest emergency event he had experienced in his 25 years on the department.

Then a city police lieutenant spoke up and started moaning about the massive traffic jam it had caused in their city when the CHP diverted all of the freeway traffic onto their streets. "What did you want us to do with that commuter traffic?" I asked, "It had to go somewhere and your city was the only accessible detour route." He just sat there and didn't answer.

The training unit battalion chief then asked me about the command structure of the CHP and how many officers a CHP captain commanded. It surprised me that he apparently had no idea how much fire and police agency supervision and administrations differed. I then told him I was from a San Diego Fire Department family and knew that a fire captain immediately and directly supervised an engineer/driver and no more than four firefighters, but CHP captains commanded from one lieutenant, four sergeants and 25 officers up to three lieutenants, 15 sergeants and 150 officers. I added that firefighters were always directly supervised and didn't have to make critical decisions as opposed to CHP and other police officers who worked alone without direct supervision and had to make any number of critical decisions every shift. With that, the meeting came to a rather sudden ending.

As the captain and I drove back to the office, I told him that was the most meaningless meeting I had gone to with an outside agency since the one when the Office of Emergency Service conference had a straw plan that could have spilled crude oil on about 50 miles of freeways. He just laughed. I told the captain I thought they wanted to try to get whatever information they could to cover their ass civilly and blame us for their expensive bungling.

In 1975, the year after the Long Beach Fire Department started its paramedic program, a Riverside County state assemblyman introduced a bill to empower fire agencies to be the scene managers at all highway traffic accidents, but that bill was defeated and never became law. Then in 1976 a legislative bill was introduced to permit fire agencies to respond to all highway traffic accidents. That bill passed and became law. It clearly read that the police agency responsible for investigating the accident would be the scene manager. It also stated that the police agency scene manager could give the fire agency orders on what to do but could not tell them how to do it. The law also mandated that fire and police agencies in the same jurisdictions that would respond to the same accidents must enact formal agreements to define specific responsibilities.

The three Orange County CHP captains and the many city police chiefs negotiated with the fire chiefs in Orange County for more than two years without any agreement. The fire chiefs demanded more authority than the police officials were willing to concede to them.

Within a month after the fiery gasoline truck and trailer accident that the fire department bungled, the formal agreement was enacted and immediately went into effect. It was my own personal opinion that the bungled gasoline tanker fire prompted our meeting and all the fire chiefs learned from that incident that there could be civil liability involved, so to lessen their liability, they agreed to less authority — then any blame could be attributed to the police scene managers.

Danger: Propane Tankers Can BLEVE

At about 2:00 a.m. a month later the phone rang and woke me from a sound sleep. The CHP dispatcher said there was a tanker fire in the northbound lanes of the Long Beach Freeway just south of Del Amo Boulevard, and the captain wanted me to manage the scene. Assuming it was a gasoline tanker fire I quickly dressed in my uniform, drove the four miles to the office, got into a patrol car and headed for the scene. Just as I was approaching the Long Beach Freeway on the San Diego I-405 Freeway, the CHP dispatcher announced that the registered owner of the tanker was "Petrolane."

My God, I thought, it's a propane tanker that could BLEVE. I quickly radioed on the car-to-car channel to the sergeant at the scene that it could BLEVE and to get at least a quarter of a mile away and take cover. BLEVE is the acronym for bottled liquid energy violent explosion. When the fire from the safety release valve heats the propane to an expanded explosive level, it can cause it to BLEVE.

About a year earlier on a training day we viewed actual footage of a very large propane distributor's storage tank BLEVE in Arizona. There was a fireman at the top of a truck ladder hosing the tank to keep it cool. Suddenly there was an immense explosion that blew him off the ladder about 20 feet to the ground. He wasn't killed, but the cameraman was killed and the movie ended. They reportedly found a large piece of the tank two miles away in the desert.

Just as I stopped where the sergeant and two officers were standing at least a quarter of a mile south of the tanker fire, a Long Beach police car squealed rubber in a quick U-turn and accelerated southbound in the northbound lanes. I asked the sergeant if they had just received an emergency call. He laughed and said, "No, I just told them what a BLEVE was all about and they couldn't wait to get out of here."

Pleasantly surprising to me, an investigator for the California Industrial Safety Department arrived on the scene. He introduced himself and said he wanted to inspect the tank after the fire was extinguished to determine how close it came to having a BLEVE.

The daredevil Long Beach firemen stood about 50 feet from the tank, hosing it and the 20-foot flame until it was out. The industrial safety inspector and I closely examined the welds fusing the two convex bells to the ends of the large cylindrical tank. We could plainly see that there were hairline cracks in the welds. The inspector told me he would microscopically examine the welds to determine how much more heat and expansion of the tank it would have taken for it to BLEVE.

About two weeks later, the inspector came to our office and gave me a copy of his final report. He said he had concluded that the welds were at a critical stage of completely failing and would have caused the tank to BLEVE. It was then obvious that if it had violently exploded as clearly illustrated in the Arizona storage tank BLEVE, several Long Beach firemen would have been blown to pieces.

I had discussed the possibility of a BLEVE with the captain and told him the inspector was going to give us a copy of his report, so as soon as the inspector left the office, I took the report to the captain. He was so intensely interested that it was like I had given him a pot of gold. I didn't ask him what he was going to do with it, but my best guess was that he was going to send a copy to the Long Beach fire chief.

PART THREE
Protecting President Reagan

CHAPTER 40

Rawhide

They told the 200 law enforcement officers that the Secret Service assigned every president a code name and President Reagan's was "Rawhide."

I was offered promotion to captain effective August 1, 1982, as commander of the Santa Barbara office. That position included being the CHP Coastal Division Protective Services Coordinator with the Secret Service for the protection of President Reagan and other dignitaries when on a highway.

The Protective Services assignment was automatic with the Santa Barbara commander position because President Reagan's "Rancho del Cielo" ranch and Western White House were in the Santa Barbara office area.

About a month before I was to report to the Santa Barbara office, the Secret Service conducted a protective services class in Camarillo in Ventura County. I attended with Santa Barbara Sergeant Doug French who did nearly all the routine coordination with the Secret Service when President Reagan made frequent visits to his mountaintop ranch.

The class was very informative about the lengths to which the Secret Service goes to protect all presidents, although one instructor admitted it was impossible to protect any president from all of the "crazies" as they called them. He said the only way they could protect the president with any measure of certainty was to keep him in a metal box from one election to the next.

We were told every motorcade included an ambulance and TV satellite trucks from the three network stations. The TV trucks were referred to by the Secret Service as the "Death Watch" because their primary purpose for being there was to cover possible assassination attempts. It was important that the TV trucks rotated in position every other motorcade.

They explained some of the precautions taken in planning motorcade routes. One was, if at all possible, to use only streets that were wide enough for the limousine carrying the president or other dignitaries to be able to make a quick U-turn in one sweep to flee in the event of a threat. They also told the audience of about 200 law enforcement officers that the Secret Service assigned every president a code name and President Reagan's was "Rawhide."

Not long before my promotion to captain, the title of supervising inspector was changed to chief; inspector was changed to assistant chief; and zone was changed to division. On my first day as the San Barbara commander and Coastal Division Protective Services Coordinator, I reported to the division chief and assistant chiefs in San Luis Obispo.

The division chief told me of a few operational corrections needed in the Santa Barbara office. He emphasized his concern for the safety of President Reagan by saying he did not want another "Dallas" in Santa Barbara. I assured him I would do everything possible to protect President Reagan, not only because he was our president, but because like almost all others I loved and respected him as a wonderful, caring gentleman.

CHP officers had driven governors since 1929. In later years, there had been a governor's driver and limousine in Los Angeles and Sacramento. From the late 1960s until he retired in the early 1970s, CHP Officer Willard "Barney" Barnett had been then-Governor Reagan's Los Angeles driver. When Barney retired, Governor Reagan served as the chief speaker at his retirement dinner, gave him an $850 model train set and hired Barney as his personal driver and bodyguard. When I saw Barney in early 1980, I asked him if he still worked for Reagan. He said he had to quit because he and his wife didn't want him to be away from home for the nearly ten months of the upcoming presidential campaign with all of the travel involved. Then a few days after Reagan was elected president, a news article reported he was going to rest at his Santa Barbara ranch and cut brush and chop wood with his friend Barney.

That was the kind of man President Reagan was. He chose his friends according to their character and personalities, not for his personal or political benefit.

I had known Barney since 1955 when he and another L.A. County motor officer were assigned to assist my partner and me in Big Bear over the hectic Labor Day weekend. He was just a typical rough-and-tumble veteran motor cop with a great personality and sense of humor. Knowing Barney as we all did, we could see what kind of man President Reagan was to choose Barney as one of his closest friends. All of us thought it was an honor to protect him, especially the Secret Service agents and officers.

Some of the Secret Service agents assigned to the ranch said that when President Reagan couldn't sleep at night, he would go to the Secret Service prefab facility on the ranch and play cards with them. How many U.S. presidents would do that? He was one of a kind.

Conversely, when President Lyndon B. Johnson visited Sacramento in 1964 I was assigned to traffic control on Highway 50 near Aerojet where he was to make an appearance. The Secret Service agents told CHP officers in the motorcade how Johnson treated them with ugly disrespect and even elbowed them in the back and cursed them when he forced his way out of their inner circle to go into a crowd to shake hands.

The Johnson motorcade was about 30 minutes late reaching my location, because President Johnson had told the armored limousine driver to stop in front of the crowd at the Rancho Cordova strip mall. Then he got out of the limousine alone and went into the crowd shaking hands. This bizarre action caused his Secret Service bodyguards to go into a near panic.

Because of my protective services coordination duties I was assigned an unmarked patrol car with no spotlights or other visible equipment. However, there was a shotgun mounted on the inside of the trunk lid, and the car was painted a very distinctive, ugly brown. CHP officers and Secret Service agents could identify it from blocks away, but other than that, it was an undercover car.

About two weeks after my arrival in Santa Barbara, Sergeant Doug French and I were invited by the Secret Service to the ranch to watch a demonstration of their bomb-sniffing dogs in action. Sergeant French and I went to the ranch in a marked patrol car to be more easily identified by the video camera at the ranch gate. It was my first trip to the ranch a little over six miles up Refugio Road from U.S. 101. On the way, Sergeant French told me of his one panic experience on a very foggy night.

He said it was so foggy they had to transport President Reagan from the Santa Barbara Municipal Airport to the ranch in the standby armored Crown Victoria usually kept in the hangar next to the helicopter tarmac. He said it was so foggy he could see no more than 15 feet ahead. Then all of a sudden it struck him that he was leading and responsible for the safety of the most important and powerful man in the world. If he made the wrong turn off the roadway, the Crown Victoria would follow him and crash. He said he had to get a grip on himself and do the best he could to see the obscured roadway, but he did it.

Refugio Road was a challenge even on a clear day in bright sunlight. About the first two miles east of U.S. 101 was a first class, wide roadway that dipped through two paved rain runoff creek beds that were dry except when it rained. Then the road narrowed to about 20 feet just before a very sharp right curve where a large oak tree was located no more than three feet from the roadway. Not far from that sharp curve, there was a sharp, blind left curve that was only 18 to 20 feet wide and required a near stop to negotiate the curve and see if there was any oncoming traffic.

The road then straightened and went about a quarter of a mile through a run-down settlement of old houses and rusted farm equipment — definitely not a rose garden path to President Reagan's over 600-acre Western White House.

Then the road curved to the left and up a narrow grade cut into the side of a rock mountain. The road was about 18 to 20 feet wide and the shoulder on the downgrade side was less than a foot wide overhanging a canyon up to about 100 feet deep. Being a rock mountain, there was no brush or other natural growth to reflect headlights at locations where the roadway curved away from the deep canyon. About halfway up the mile of mountain grade was an almost 90-degree right curve with only about 30 feet of sight distance to see if there was any oncoming traffic. It required honking the horn and coming almost to a stop before negotiating the curve. At the top of the grade, the roadway straightened for about two miles to the ranch gate.

When we arrived everybody was gathering at the Secret Service prefab facility where their communications center was housed. After the 50 law enforcement officials had arrived, we all started walking to the area where the bomb-sniffing dog demonstration was to take place.

A Secret Service supervisor walked next to me and asked if I could do anything to make the road to the ranch safer. He said they had asked the county road department to do what they could to mark the roadway to make it safer, especially when there was dense fog. He said the road department told him they couldn't paint a center line in the roadway because it was so narrow that vehicles going in opposite directions would both have to be left of the painted center line and that marking would not conform to established highway engineering standards known as warrants.

The county road department representative said any improvements requested and completed would have to be paid for by the Secret Service. For that reason the Secret Service supervisor asked if I could figure out how to make the road safer and request that it be done without cost to the agency.

I told him I had already seen enough of that road to know it needed some safety improvements. I said the best measure I could think of would be to install white paddle markers at the large oak tree at the sharp right curve, on the downgrade shoulder next to the canyon and some other places I thought needed them. I told him I would pursue these improvements and the Secret Service wouldn't have to pay for them.

The bomb-sniffing dog demonstration was very impressive. The dog was an older German shepherd with an ailing right hip that was going to be retired and retained by its handler as a family pet. We were told Secret Service dogs were trained at Andrews Air Force Base and up until a few years before had to be returned to them to be destroyed when they were no longer serviceable, but due to the hue and cry of the handlers who treated them as part of their families and constantly refreshed their training, that merciless policy was changed and they were able to keep their beloved dogs.

The demonstration was very brief. An explosive device had been placed in the exhaust pipe of a minivan to mask its odor, and the dog did not see where it was placed. The handler then released the dog from about 30 feet to the rear of the minivan. The dog hurried with a slight limp to the right of the minivan, quickly sniffed the exhaust tailpipe, continued about three feet, returned back to the tailpipe, stuck his nose in the tailpipe and groaned. It took no more than five seconds for the dog to detect the explosive device despite the exhaust pipe odor masking it.

Then they had a chase dog pursue a Secret Service agent in protective clothing up the side of a hill and bring him down with one leap and grab. Both demonstrations were very impressive and convinced all of us that President Reagan was in good hands with the Secret Service.

As soon as we returned to the office, I phoned the county road department and requested paddle markers be placed at certain locations on Refugio Road, but my request was not well received.

The next day a county road department foreman and two of his assistants arrived at the CHP office to go to Refugio Road to see what I thought they should do to make it safer. We all got into my ugly brown undercover car and went to Refugio Road. As I pointed out the critical locations where I was convinced about a dozen white paddle markers should be installed, one of the assistants in the rear took notes.

It was obvious that the foreman was not thrilled with my request for about a dozen paddle markers. Before I had pointed out all the locations on the narrow grade next to the deep canyon, he said if they installed them, somebody would probably shoot them full of holes. "Better than a CHP, Secret Service or other car going into the canyon," I replied. "The markers can be replaced, but lives can't," I emphasized. He didn't say another word about gun crazies shooting holes in their precious paddle markers.

About a month later, an elementary school student was struck in a school crossing crosswalk about a tenth of a mile south of the school. The mother of another student contacted me and asked if I would inspect the school crossing and attend a county road department meeting with my recommendation of how it could be made safer.

I told her I would be happy to do so and drove to the school location. It was on the east side of a higher speed open road, and the residential area where the students lived was west of the road. The school crossing crosswalk was to the south about a tenth of a mile and on the other side of a blind crest in the road between the school and crossing. It was obvious to me that it was unsafe because southbound motorists could not see the crosswalk until after they had crested the hill. Also, the average motorist expects school crossings to be in front of schools or at other adjacent streets. The school crossing should be moved to a location directly in front of the school.

I arrived at the county road department offices about 30 minutes before the scheduled meeting. As soon as I walked into the office, the county road department superintendent introduced himself and asked me if I would like to go to the employees' lunch room for coffee. As soon as we sat down with our coffee and Danish, he asked me if the Secret Service had initiated the request for the paddle markers on Refugio Road. "No, it was my idea from the beginning," I replied.

His facial expression in response to my honest answer was not one of joy. In fact I had seen the need for safety measures on my first trip to the ranch before the Secret Service supervisor addressed the issue. I told him I had made recommendations for many highway engineering improvements during my 30-year police career and thought this one was as valid as the others. I stressed the civil liability of the county road department if a car ran off the grade into the canyon when it was common knowledge to be a fogbound area at times.

It was obvious that he had not considered civil liability and was focused solely on his annual budget, but if one person was seriously injured or killed in a crash into the canyon in the fog, the settlement could eat up many years of his annual budgets. A sharp attorney and the right jury could award a judgment of millions from the county's "deep pockets."

At the school crossing crosswalk hearing the mother who had requested my recommendation and I offered the same solution, and the superintendent complained that there was no sidewalk on the west side of the roadway and if our recommendation was accepted and acted upon, they would have to install one. I suggested they cover the dirt path with pea gravel to serve as a sidewalk to keep the students' shoes clean. When they heard that simple, cost-effective solution, they decided the crosswalk should be moved and they were delighted that it was far easier than drilling paddle markers into the rock mountain.

President Reagan's ranch was about halfway between the cold Pacific Ocean waters about four miles to the west and the very warm air of Santa Ynez Valley about the same distance to the east. When the hot and cool air collided over the mountain area of the ranch, dense fog could be generated at any time of the day or year.

This unpredictable condition frequently prevented the two Marine One helicopters from seeing the ranch tarmac and attempting to land. There were always two Marine One helicopters, so when in flight they could alternate positions to prevent anyone other than those in the helicopters from knowing which one President Reagan was occupying.

The fog could roll in over the ranch in 30 minutes or less, about the same length of time it took for the two Marine One helicopters to load and transport President Reagan to the ranch from Point Mugu where he arrived on Air Force One. So Secret Service and CHP units were nearly always on a standby alert at the Santa Barbara Municipal Airport to transport President Reagan to the ranch by car if the fog rolled in and obscured the tarmac in less than 30 minutes.

About 90 days after I took command of the Santa Barbara squad office, we moved from the old leased office to a newly-constructed, CHP-owned office adjacent to U.S. 101. The new office was in Goleta, north of Santa Barbara proper and directly across 101 from the Santa Barbara Municipal Airport.

Some standby alerts at the airport did not appear to be necessary, so the Secret Service agents did not always advise the CHP of the possible need for car transportation and protective escort for President Reagan. There were two working Secret Service agents who were not directly involved in the protection of the president. One named Gus was hard working and usually had a fast-food lunch with a can of soda and threw the empty cans onto the rear floorboards of the car, where they accumulated.

One of the nights when it was improbable that the fog would roll in over the ranch he did not notify the CHP of the president's flight. When he returned to his office the phone rang to tell him the fog had rolled in over the ranch and President Reagan was waiting at the airport to be transported to the ranch. In his haste to get to the airport, he did not want to notify the CHP due to the lateness and did not remove the empty soda cans from the rear floorboards. He just raced to the airport to arrange for transportation for President Reagan.

The next day Sergeant French told me about Gus's unusual night transporting President Reagan. Gus said when he arrived at the airport the only ones there were the Marine One flight crews and President Reagan. There were no other Secret Service agents in sight, so President Reagan climbed into the rear of Gus's car, kicked the soda cans to the other side of the floorboards and said, "Let's go." Gus said President Reagan acted like it was an everyday event to ride in a car littered with empty cans and never said a word about the mess. He just chatted on the way to the ranch.

Along with the events involving President Reagan, there were occasional anti-nuclear demonstrations at Vandenberg Air Force Base and at a nuclear power plant under construction in the northern part of Santa Barbara County, and CHP officers from several squad offices in the areas surrounding Santa Barbara had to be deployed to control the mobs.

With those disruptions in normal operations, it was almost like the late 1960s and early 1970s when everyone seemed to be demonstrating, rioting, shooting or bombing in protest of the police, civil rights, the Vietnam War, racism or some other noble and just cause.

Then there was the Santa Barbara Law Enforcement Committee (SBLEC). Before I reported as the Santa Barbara squad office commander, the CHP commissioner told me about the committee and one extremely powerful woman member whose husband owned a bank in that city. He told me to do my best to get on her good side, because I would automatically be a member of the committee and she had great power over it.

The SBLEC met quarterly with the sole function of selecting an officer of the year from one of the Santa Barbara County law enforcement agencies and presenting a coveted award to him or her at an annual banquet in May. The chairperson was a dedicated and pleasant lady whose husband was the administrator of a local medical center. It didn't take much discussion for me to see they gave only one award each year for anything from an officer who dreamed up a bicycle safety program to one for valor in the line of duty.

I couldn't identify the politically powerful woman the commissioner had told me about in the group of about ten members, but it didn't make any difference to me. I couldn't help but tell them that they should not give the same award to an officer for a bicycle safety program and an officer who risked his or her life in the line of duty. I said there should be different classifications of awards for outstanding performance and no limit to valor awards each year.

I explained to the committee that from my 30 years of experience and observations in law enforcement that there could be five years during which no officer performed any life-threatening act that qualified for an award of valor. Then in the year to follow, five officers could risk their lives with extraordinary courage to deserve an award for valor.

A deputy sheriff sitting directly across the table from me quickly nodded his head and openly agreed with me. No other members expressed either agreement or disagreement.

The meeting soon adjourned and I left not knowing that one fine member later volunteered to design a new standard for awards based on different levels of outstanding performance, including an exclusive award for valor.

Not being an advocate of officer or employee of the year with so many other demands of my job and not knowing another member was going to work on new levels, I didn't think to give a copy of the State of California Awards Program to the chairperson or committee. At the next meeting, the volunteer was called upon to present his version of the new awards level standards. When he finished his presentation, the chairperson asked for a motion to adopt his amended awards level standards.

Before there was any motion to adopt the new standards, a small, frail elderly woman stood up and expressed her adamant opposition to any changes in the standards. She then said she had a dental appointment and immediately left the room. There was a deathly silence and the chair person turned pale and stood like she was frozen.

The outspoken elderly woman had not attended previous meetings and I had not seen her before, so I asked who she was. The chairperson tried to regain her composure and said that is Mrs. So and So — the political powerhouse the commissioner had told me about and asked me to get on the good side of.

Captain Nuttall presents CHP western belt buckle to President Reagan at the Reagan ranch helicopter tarmac.

Her obvious power play to intimidate the rest of the committee members and control the entire awards program really irritated me, so I immediately made a motion to adopt the amended standards. The motion quickly restored some sanity in the room and another member seconded my motion. The chairperson had regained some color in her face and called for a show of hands in favor of adopting the amended standards. All hands went up and it passed without one word of opposition or any comment about the elderly woman who tried to squelch any change of any kind.

After the meeting adjourned, I asked one of the other members what he knew about Mrs. So and So. He told me what little he knew, including the fact that her husband was the manager of a local bank. Oh, I thought, he doesn't own a bank, he just works for one. It amused me that someone had conned the commissioner into believing her husband owned a bank and she was to be feared and catered to in every way. It also disgusted me to think that some people were so power-crazy they would go to almost any lengths to gain control over others.

That was the last time I saw or heard of her. The awards banquet was held on schedule the next May, and one local police officer was awarded a medal of valor plaque and several others were awarded lesser awards for outstanding achievements.

The sheriff chaired a quarterly meeting of Santa Barbara County law enforcement chiefs and other administrators and I was invited to attend. These meetings were always enjoyable, interesting and informative, except for one disturbing meeting. That meeting evolved into the sheriff chewing out the county marshal for not keeping his arrest and arrest warrants current when he learned that there had been two or more arrests of a person on the same warrant.

The sheriff explained that it not only caused his jailers to spend valuable time unraveling the confusion, it could also make the county civilly liable for false arrests. When the marshal stood up and tried to justify his outdated records, it made me feel like I was back in Big Bear or Yreka, not affluent Santa Barbara County.

One late afternoon after attending a meeting, I went to the Montecito shopping center to get a haircut wearing a suit, not my CHP uniform. As I was walking from where I had parked my ugly brown undercover patrol car to the barber shop, my mind was miles away in deep thought about something. A young lady walked at an angle across the parking lot in my direction and when she was about 20 feet from me she smiled and said "Hello." I smiled and said "Hello" and immediately realized it was Jane Fonda. My photo had been in the local newspaper two times so it dawned on me that she knew who I was and in her very sweet, cute way wanted me to know she was no longer "Hanoi Jane."

CHAPTER 41

The Queen's Visit

Early in December 1982 the Secret Service invited all of the Santa Barbara law enforcement administrators to lunch to tell us about the Queen of England's scheduled visit to Santa Barbara on March 1, 1983.

They told us the queen was to make stops in San Diego and Los Angeles before going to Santa Barbara to meet with President Reagan. For some unexplained reason at that time, they told us to keep it strictly confidential.

We had an office uniformed supervisors' meeting scheduled for the next week. With no explanation for the secrecy of the queen's visit by the Secret Service, I thought I could trust the lieutenant and sergeants to keep it confidential, so I told them and ordered them not to tell anyone about it. I later learned from a Secret Service agent that there was an Irish Republic Army (IRA) chapter in Santa Barbara and that was the reason they did not want the queen's visit to be publicized too far in advance.

The following week I had to go to the CHP Academy for a week of training for new captains. Somebody in headquarters or the academy with nothing else to do dreamed up that waste of a week of my time. It was the most useless excuse for training I had ever experienced in law enforcement. One hotshot who later climbed his way up to the rank of chief wasted about eight hours of our time allegedly instructing a course in "Emergency Scene Management." The only experience he could relate was when he was the captain in South L.A. in 1979 and an officer fatally shot an unarmed subject. It was obvious that he had never managed an emergency scene as I had done several times, but he had enough people fooled to retire as a chief. To make it worse, the cadets were still wearing their Sam Browne belts and batons to class and marching around like cookie-cutter robots and frightened rabbits.

The only benefit from my boring stay at the academy was sitting in my room documenting how many contingencies we would have to manage with two simultaneous motorcades during the queen's visit. I came up with seven. They were as follows:

- Clear, calm weather with no fog at the ranch, so the queen's ship, the Britannia, could anchor off the coast, she could be brought in by motor launch, and President Reagan could be flown by helicopter to meet her.

- Calm weather but fog at the ranch, so President Reagan could be taken by motorcade to meet her at the dock.

- Rough seas make it necessary to dock the Britannia at Port Hueneme about 30 miles south of Santa Barbara in Ventura County. No fog at the ranch, so President Reagan could be taken to Port Hueneme by helicopter.

- Rough seas make it necessary to dock the Britannia at Port Hueneme, but fog at the ranch, so President Reagan would be taken to Port Hueneme by motorcade and return with the queen.

- Rough seas keep the Britannia in Los Angeles, so the queen would be brought by motorcade from Los Angeles to Santa Barbara. With no fog at the ranch, President Reagan would be taken by helicopter to meet the queen in Santa Barbara.

- Rough seas keep the Britannia in Los Angeles but fog at the ranch, so motorcade President Reagan to Santa Barbara to meet the queen.

- Seas rough with the Britannia in Los Angeles and fog at the ranch with Refugio Road creeks raging and the queen and President Reagan have lunch at the Sheraton Hotel where two suites had been reserved, instead of going to the ranch for a taco lunch.

It was an extremely rainy winter known as an El Niño year and by the time of the queen's visit there were 16-foot seas and the ocean waters between Los Angeles and Santa Barbara were known to be treacherous at times, so every contingency had to be considered and prepared for.

When I returned to Santa Barbara from the academy, everyone in the office knew about the queen's visit including the janitor, but it didn't matter because it was the talk of Santa Barbara far beyond the walls of the CHP office. It again proved to me that if one wants to spread a juicy rumor or any confidential information, tell it to anyone and tell them to keep it a secret. It's like putting it on the TV news for days.

For the next two months I was mentally consumed with the queen's visit. There were so many things that could go wrong, most of all the weather. It didn't take long in my cop career for me to recognize that Murphy's Law was a fact of life, and if anything could go wrong, it would.

About a month before the queen's visit, I calculated how many Los Angeles County CHP officers would be needed to assist with the two motorcades. Based on the worst-case scenario of two simultaneous motorcades from Port Hueneme to Santa Barbara and the queen's motorcade turning off U.S. 101 to stop at the scenic courthouse and President Reagan's continuing up U.S. 101 to the ranch, I estimated it would require 55 L.A. County officers.

With that maximum number of officers needed, I phoned my assigned assistant chief and gave him the earthshaking news. The next morning my excitable assistant chief phoned me. In a stressed, crackling tone of voice he said the deputy commissioner's assistant blew his lid when he was told that as many as 55 L.A. County officers would be needed. He said the deputy commissioner's assistant, a chief, had complained that so much overtime pay had been expended in San Diego and with much more in Los Angeles for the queen's visit, the annual overtime allotment was nearly exhausted.

"I didn't invite her here," I replied, "and the Secret Service completely depends upon us to help them protect the queen and President Reagan, so let it be on the shoulders of the deputy commissioner's assistant if we have another Dallas in Santa Barbara." He didn't respond, so I left him with that to consider.

A week before the queen was to arrive on Tuesday, March 1 the Secret Service conducted a preplanning meeting at their downtown office. Our assigned assistant chief attended the meeting with Sergeant French and me. We were first introduced to Secret Service agent Rick Scott who was assigned with us to coordinate and manage the queen's motorcade.

After the meeting, the assistant called me aside and rather sheepishly confessed to me that he had asked the division chief if he could take over the management and coordination of the queen's visit. He said the chief flatly denied his request and said it was my area of responsibility; I had a rapport and working relationship with the Secret Service, and he should stay out of it. The chief did tell him he could attend and view the operations but should not interfere in any way.

The next day Sergeant French and I met with Secret Service agent Rick Scott to view and assess the potential alternate routes for the queen's motorcade. We had to try to avoid streets that were not wide enough for a one-sweep U-turn to escape from a threat of any kind, streets without easily accessible escape routes, railroad tracks and any other locations that could pose a security risk. Railroad tracks had to be avoided if at all possible because train schedules were not reliable. Like most forms of public transportation, including airlines, they are notorious for running late.

During our inspection tour, Rick Scott told Sergeant French and me about the Secret Service's preplanning coordination with the British Secret Service security for the queen. He said the British Secret Service agents were oblivious to any threat to the queen. One of them said, "Nobody would want to 'arm the queen." Rick said even when he told them there was an IRA chapter in Santa Barbara, they were undaunted.

Agent Rick Scott told us if the queen's ship the Britannia could anchor offshore, President and Nancy Reagan were to have dinner on the ship that night, but the British Secret Service told him that if the Reagan's boarded the ship they could have only two U.S. Secret Service agents with them and those agents could not be armed. Rick said he told President Reagan about the restrictions and said he was not going on that ship for any reason. He said President Reagan readily agreed because he had barely survived an assassination attempt just two years before.

The Los Angeles County CHP Protective Service Coordinator lieutenant sent a motor sergeant to Santa Barbara to become familiar with the planned routes and operation. Sergeant French and Rick Scott accompanied him.

As soon as their tour was completed, Sergeant French told me the L.A. motor sergeant had openly criticized my plan to close off the southbound on-ramps south of Santa Barbara with Cal Trans trucks and CHP officers as a special precaution if we had to lead both motorcades from Port Hueneme to Santa Barbara in one long procession. I immediately phoned the L.A. Protective Services Coordinator lieutenant and told him not to send that motor sergeant to Santa Barbara again as long as I was in command

Agent Rick Scott also told Sergeant French and me that the Santa Barbara meeting of the queen and President Reagan was the most complex operation in U.S. Secret Service history. He said with the only highway from Santa Barbara to the ranch being U.S. 101, with narrow streets, railroad tracks, an IRA chapter, two simultaneous motorcades, threatening weather and seven operational contingencies, it was a first for the Secret Service.

With the complexities of the operation and an assistant chief trying to take over, I did not need some cocky L.A. sergeant trying to dismantle months of planning. Years later I learned from other retired CHP officers that the sergeant was noted for his God-like attitude and demeanor.

A few days before the queen's visit the Secret Service held a meeting of all the local law enforcement supervisors and administrators who would be involved in the unpredictable operation. The first announcement the host Secret Service agent made was that the meeting was exclusively for law enforcement personnel. He asked if everyone present was from a law enforcement agency.

I had already seen at least one fireman not far from where I was seated, but he remained seated and did not respond to the question. He had absolutely no reason for being there. His rude intrusion in a restricted meeting was only a small example of the community frenzy that had developed in the weeks leading up to the queen's visit. Far too many people were trying to get into the act. One well-meaning gentleman actually came to the CHP office to offer me two tickets to the heads-of-state meeting ceremony. I graciously told him I had enough and thanked him.

Another day three women came to see me to discuss something about the queen's visit, but before they left the office I could not recall what it was about. My mind was on seven contingencies.

For five days after the first planning meeting at the Secret Service downtown office, agent Rick Scott, Sergeant French and I had scoured the Santa Barbara area for motorcade routes and any potential danger spots. On Sunday afternoon we agreed that we had done all we could and it was then up to Scott to convey the information to all involved and put the plan into action.

At about 9:00 p.m. Sunday night, about 36 hours prior to the queen's arrival, Sergeant French phoned me at home and told me the seas were so high and rough they could not take the Britannia out of Los Angeles Harbor, and the Queen would fly into Santa Barbara Municipal Airport on Air Force Two.

On the morning of the queen's visit it was pouring rain as it had for most of that El Niño winter. When I arrived at the office the parking lot was wall-to-wall vehicles and my reserved parking space was the only one that was still empty. The ambulance was parked behind other vehicles near the rear office door and it blocked my view of what was in front of it. Also, I hurried to get out of the rain and didn't look around.

The interior of the office was packed with CHP officers and Secret Service agents. I had no sooner made it to my office when an excited CHP officer rushed over to me and told me the queen's limousine had broken down in Malibu. I quickly found agent Scott and told him I had heard the queen's limousine had broken down in Malibu.

He laughed and said the queen's limousine was in the parking lot in front of the ambulance. He laughed again and said the car broken down in Malibu was full of White House staff members and he hoped they wouldn't be able to get it going again and come to Santa Barbara. That was only one expression of disgust for White House staffers that I heard from Secret Service agents. Before that day was over, I got a taste of White House flunky arrogance.

Sergeant French had selected a senior officer to be my driver of the CHP command car and two Secret Service supervisors were assigned by agent Rick Scott to ride in the rear of the car. About an hour prior to the queen's scheduled arrival Rick told us to head for the Tracor hangar at the airport and to gas up on the way, if needed.

We gassed up at a Chevron station on the way and parked close to the rear pedestrian door in the parking lot behind the hangar. The immense aircraft entry doors at the opposite end of the hangar were open and we could see seven National Guard or Army cannons about 200 feet north of the hangar.

The concrete floor of the hangar was wet from foot and vehicular traffic that had moved about before we got there. We soon learned that water on top of the oily jet fuel residue made the floor as slippery as an ice rink.

The civilian viewers' area was directly across from where we were positioned near the rear pedestrian door. There was a magnetometer metal detector and Secret Service agents checking all of the viewers just inside the door.

About 30 minutes before the queen's arrival, President and Nancy Reagan arrived in a limousine. They walked over to us and graciously greeted us then went to the viewers' area where President Reagan greeted people and shook numerous hands.

Shortly thereafter Air Force Two slowly turned into the hangar and taxied up to a red carpet about 30 feet long flanked on both sides by personnel from all branches of the U.S. military services in dress blues.

We had earlier been told that Air Force Two was initially Air Force One and had been used to transport the body of President John F. Kennedy to Washington D.C. after his assassination in Dallas, Texas.

Cannons fired a 21-gun salute as the president and the queen met, and the welcoming ceremony lasted about 15 minutes. Then agent Rick Scott hurriedly said, "Let's go," and we all rushed out the door to get the motorcades under way. Unbeknownst to me, President and Nancy Reagan were taken by motorcade back to the ranch as we escorted the queen and Prince Phillip to the landmark Santa Barbara courthouse.

As my driver, the two Secret Service supervisors and I rushed to our car I slipped on the wet jet fuel-coated parking lot asphalt and almost fell down. Even though it had a rough surface, it was almost as slippery as it was inside the hangar.

I did not learn until the next day that my lieutenant with a back ailment had slipped and fallen inside the hangar and his injuries ended his CHP career. He went off duty on injury time and sick leave and retired on disability.

When we were inside the patrol car my driver turned the ignition key to start the engine. The Dodge engine just let out a slow, sick groan and stopped. The driver frantically turned the key a second time and the engine repeated its groan like a last gasp. The third time he turned the key the engine roared to life. That again proved the truth of Murphy's Law, since it was the first time in my 30 years of police work that a patrol car engine had performed in that manner — at the worst possible time imaginable, but there was more to come down the road.

We got quickly on our way to the courthouse and as we exited the U.S. 101 Freeway there were rows of excited spectators lined up six deep on the sidewalks. As soon as we came into sight the massive crowd erupted into near deafening applause for the queen.

We brought the motorcade to a stop in front of the courthouse where a large group of civic leaders and officials greeted the queen and presented her with a gigantic bouquet of about six dozen red rose buds.

As I stood in front of the patrol car watching the excitement, a young man who looked to be about 18 years old approached me and said he was on the White House staff. When he told me his name I immediately recognized it as being the same as that of a former governor of an adjacent western state.

He asked me if I could have one of my CHP cars drive him to the ranch. It was so ridiculous, I told him I didn't have a car to spare and wondered what he was doing there in the first place. Already aware of agent Rick Scott's sentiments about White House staffers, I told him to see Secret Service agent Rick Scott as I was certain he would provide a ride for him to the ranch.

First of all, I did not know at that time that President and Nancy Reagan were on their way to the ranch. Even if they were, was he invited to go there and what did he think he was going to do when he got there? It was obvious why agent Scott had no use for White House staffers. It was also obvious that the kid had no idea what Refugio Road was like and that it went through two raging streams that could not be traversed by standard model passenger cars. They were too low to the ground. He scurried away and that was the last I ever saw of him.

We drove around the corner and parked eastbound next to the north edge of the courthouse yard. As I looked around for any unusual activity or persons, I saw several Secret Service agents on residential rooftops to the north of the street. They all had black leather carrying cases strapped over their shoulders and they looked alert but casually inconspicuous. I knew those black leather cases contained Uzi submachine guns that could fire an amazing number of rounds per second, so I relaxed and waited for the next order from agent Scott and wondered what he had done with or to the White House staff hitchhiker.

Soon agent Scott ran down the street yelling "Let's roll." When he got close enough I asked him, "To the right to the Sheraton or left to the ranch?" "Left to the ranch," he replied.

As soon as we entered the U.S. 101 Freeway, the Secret Service supervisor in the rear asked if we could keep the speed down to 25 miles an hour all the way to Refugio Road. He explained that the four-wheel-drive Dodge Rams that had to be used to drive the queen to the ranch were still on their way to the ranch with President and Nancy Reagan, and they had only two Dodge Rams.

Although the engine had not played dead again, the self-generated stress throughout the operation was something I hadn't experienced or witnessed since the San Diego police shootout in Linda Vista in 1954. It was electrifying for too many.

I could tell our car was very gradually gaining speed over 25 miles an hour. I looked at the speedometer and it read slightly over 30 miles an hour and still rising. I told my driver to slow down and keep the speed at 25 miles an hour. He was so stressed that it happened two more times before we reached Refugio Road. When we arrived at Refugio Road there was already a large group of Secret Service agents waiting to transfer the queen and Prince Philip to a Dodge Ram when it returned from taking President and Nancy Reagan to the ranch.

About 15 minutes later the two Rams returned. Looking closely at them, I didn't think they looked like they were armored or equipped with bullet-resistant glass, and there were brush-covered hills on both sides of Refugio Road where a sniper with a scope could easily be concealed.

It wasn't my job to protect the queen against those potential exposures, so I put my trust in the Secret Service to know what they were doing. They had already proven how good they were at their job so I didn't let it stress me.

As soon as the transfer was completed and they were on their way to the ranch, we drove to a large parking lot to the west of U.S. 101, parked and got settled for a one-and-a-half or two-hour wait for their return. The rain had subsided but it was humid and stuffy sitting in the patrol car with four others. The windows were all fogged up, so I got out of the car. When agent Scott walked over to our car, I asked him if we could sit in the queen's limousine.

He said it was a good idea so we went back to it and got in. I sat in the right rear seat where the queen had ridden. Rick and I joked about being in a royal environment in the limousine, and it was probably as close as we would ever get to the queen.

A few days later, newspapers reported that the mayor of San Diego had created an incident during the queen's visit by touching her. While she was climbing some stairs, the mayor had put his hand on her back to help her. Despite his honorable intentions and gentlemanly gesture it was a very bad idea. According to British custom, the only time any commoner could touch the queen was when she initiated a handshake by extending her hand. The queen did not make a big scene about it, but we were warned not to touch her.

Sitting in the queen's seat, I looked at the gigantic bouquet of red rose buds on the floorboard at my feet and plucked two of them for a lifelong souvenir of that exciting, crazy day. There were so many buds I was certain she would never miss them, and I also thought she was so busy that one of her aides would probably take care of the bouquet for her.

When the queen and Prince Philip returned and were settled back in the Lincoln limousine, we started south on U.S. 101 for the last stop at the Santa Barbara Mission before leaving on Air Force Two. Nancy Reagan was with them and was reportedly going to San Francisco with them, while President Reagan had remained at the ranch.

We had gone about three miles when it was aired on the CHP car-to-car frequency that the Secret Service station wagon carrying Nancy Reagan's piles of luggage had just rear-ended the ambulance, but the station wagon was still operable and would continue to the airport.

The official heads-of-state meeting of Queen Elizabeth and President Reagan at the Santa Barbara Municipal Airport.

I had to laugh and think that Murphy must have had this day in mind when he proposed his law, but it wasn't over. As we slowly traveled south on U.S. 101 to the old mission, Sergeant French was in the scout car about a quarter of a mile ahead of my command car as he had been throughout the motorcade route. About every mile or so a CHP car would pass us in the far right lane at about 90 miles an hour and stop and observe spectators standing near the freeway for security assurance until we passed that location. That hop-and-stop security continued until we left the 101 Freeway.

As we reached the top of the sloped driveway up to the mission I saw a large one-inch hemp rope strung from one large tree to another tree lengthwise in the parking area — reducing the width of the parking area and the U-turn space by about one third.

"Rawhide" President Ronald Reagan

"Oh, s---," I muttered to myself. It looked like somebody may have strung it there to trap the queen's limousine and prevent it from making a one-sweep U-turn to escape. Then when we entered the parking area I could see all of the spectators were at least a hundred feet away, across a large lawn and controlled by Santa Barbara Police Department officers.

As soon as I saw there was nobody close enough to pose a threat to the queen or Nancy Reagan, I assumed one of the many self-appointed do-gooders took it upon himself to keep assassins away from the queen.

During our pre-inspection of the queen's proposed routes the week before, Agent Scott had carefully measured the width of the parking area in front of the mission for a one-sweep U-turn, so whoever strung that rope should have had it put around their neck, as far as I was concerned.

All went as planned and we took the queen, Prince Philip and Nancy Reagan back to the airport and saw them depart on Air Force Two.

With all the confusion and surprises, I never did get to count heads to determine how many L.A. County CHP officers arrived to assist, but I did later learn that one of them hydroplaned off U.S. 101 in Camarillo into the flooded center divider and was last heard of when his patrol car was axle-deep in mud and water. I never knew if he made it to Santa Barbara, but without him my best guess was that there were about 24 L.A. officers assisting us.

As it turned out, the torrential rains were a blessing in that they simplified the most complex operation in Secret Service history by isolating the entire event in Santa Barbara and the ranch. That was the same as having perfect weather, except for the need for the Dodge Rams to get to and from the ranch.

We were all relieved, satisfied and pleased until two days later when we heard of a Secret Service tragedy near Yosemite. After the queen's stop in San Francisco, she was being driven to Yosemite National Park in the Sierra Nevada Mountains. On a two-lane road near Yosemite, a large sheriff's four-wheel-drive pickup truck crashed head-on into a Secret Service car occupied by three agents, and all three were instantly killed. It was reported that the impact of the collision was so great that it drove the engine of the Secret Service car into the rear seat and killed the agent who was lying asleep on the seat. The sheriff's pickup truck was occupied by a sheriff's deputy and a sergeant, who was driving. To make the tragedy even worse, the queen reportedly witnessed the collision.

Knowing the excitement and near frenzy generated by being involved in the queen's motorcade, I assumed the sheriff's sergeant was excited, traveling too fast for a curve, drifted to the wrong side of the road and crashed into the much lighter Secret Service passenger car. Then some time after that tragic crash a controversial retired CHP lieutenant reconstructed the accident and reportedly concluded that the Secret Service driver was at fault, but I wasn't convinced that he was correct in his findings, because I had known him since I was an academy duty officer.

He was a CHP cadet at that time, and our paths crossed a couple of times when we were both lieutenants in L.A. County squad offices. One reason I doubted his conclusion was based on my experience of investigating over a hundred collisions, including many involving high speeds. It requires a terrific amount of speed to drive the engine of any car into the rear seat, so I had to conclude the sheriff's pickup was traveling at a high rate of speed — too fast for the road conditions, especially around curves.

Also, during my career and after my retirement from law enforcement, I have seen a number of so-called experts in any number of fields testify to their expert opinions that are in direct conflict with another so-called expert witness's expert opinions. In most expert witness cases, the expert is more than adequately compensated for favorable testimony — it's one of the many inherent flaws in our judicial system.

After we all went back to normal routines in the office, President Reagan's Secret Service detail agents and CHP officers resumed trading CHP and Secret Service baseball caps. We came out on top, because ours only cost $4.50 and theirs cost $10. They knew it but didn't care. One of the agents told me that the most prized possessions around the White House grounds were CHP baseball caps. He said the CHP was the most cooperative, congenial and popular department they had to work with, and they all appreciated the fraternalism.

Not long after that expression of gratitude, one agent told me of escorting President Reagan in a motorcade through a small city in a Midwestern state. He said the chief of the small city's police department greeted them with his hand out for prepayment of any kind for his department's assistance. The agent said it was a pleasure and joy to get out of that state and back to California.

CHAPTER 42

Rancho del Cielo

With all its features and activities, I had to conclude that the Reagan Ranch was just like a big, happy loving extended family topped off with a petting zoo for good measure.

I had an open invitation to visit the ranch and did so one Friday afternoon when an agent told me a big event was to take place that day. When I arrived I was told by the agents that the big event was Barney, President Reagan's former CHP driver and brush-cutting and wood-chopping buddy, was bringing a new, red jeep to the ranch for Reagan. It was to be the second jeep at the ranch, but more stylish. The other jeep was an old military model that had been lengthened about three feet and was not even close to being a show piece.

The agents were as excited as kids on Christmas morning — not only because of the jeep but because they were going to get to see Barney, who didn't make many trips to the ranch.

While waiting to see Barney again, I visited with a few agents near the front door of their prefab facility. Trying their best to intrude in our meeting and get our attention were two dogs and a few horses. I was told the larger dog belonged to the Reagans' daughter but had become a permanent resident. One of the horses was a beautiful, large white stallion that had been given to President Reagan by the president of Mexico after Reagan had given him an expensive high-powered rifle as an expression of lasting friendship between the two nations. An agent told me the stallion had been so mean and abusive to other horses he had to be gelded, and then he had become as gentle and snuggly as a kitten.

As the dogs and horses rubbed and nuzzled against us, the agents told me there were sensors installed around the grounds that could sense and alert the communications center to any movement as small as a jackrabbit up to a distance of a quarter of a mile. They said the only breaches of security they had experienced were deer hunters unknowingly wandering onto the over 600-acre ranch in search of game, but they were easy to chase off.

There was a large mobile home near the Secret Service prefab where the permanent, full-time maintenance man had lived before President Reagan had a new home built for him about 100 feet east of the ranch house.

I had known the name of the maintenance man from the beginning of my visits to the ranch, and his surname sounded like that of a Native American Indian. Just like his lasting friendship with Barney, President Reagan obviously chose his friends, close associates and employees based on strength of character and convictions, not politics.

I also knew the ranch house had been a stage stop before and after the turn of the century. That clearly explained the narrow, treacherous roadway cut into the side of the rock mountain. The ranch house had what looked like a red clay tile roof, but the agents said it was a form of light plastic or other synthetic material because the old stage stop building would not bear the weight of clay tile. They said a friend of President Reagan had it installed as a gift.

There was a large pond about 100 feet in diameter south of the ranch house where President Reagan paddled Nancy around in a canoe strumming a ukulele and singing to her.

With all its features and activities, I had to conclude that the Reagan Ranch was just like a big, happy loving extended family topped off with a petting zoo for good measure. I knew for certain there had never been nor probably ever would be another U.S. president to match his charm and warmth.

The agents also told me of the hot afternoon that President Reagan and Barney were cutting brush and chopping wood when Barney got flushed and red in the face and looked like he was having a heart attack. President Reagan and the agents tried to persuade Barney to call it a day and rest, but he waved them off, took a short break and resumed cutting and chopping as always.

When Barney finally arrived after fighting the heavy Friday afternoon L.A. County commuter traffic, it was as though Santa Claus and the vice president combined had landed. There were numerous handshakes and much loud laughter as all greeted their old friend Barney. After a warm handshake and some friendly exchanges with Barney, I decided it was time for me to leave so he and the agents could celebrate alone and check out the new jeep.

A couple of months later I decided it was time to retire from the CHP and move on to new endeavors and challenges. One motivator was the internal political system of Employee Development Appraisal (EDA) that had replaced the true merit system eleven years before in 1972. With that shell game was a new ivory tower mystery being stressed called, "self-improvement." After studying law enforcement subjects and practices for more than 30 years, managing CHP offices for over 14 years and being part of the two percent of CHP officers to attain the rank of captain, what improvement did they want?

One shining example of the so-called EDA system was a mediocre officer who was in the Westminster squad when I was a lieutenant in that office. He very shrewdly teamed up with one of the commissioner's well-known pets and went to college with him. He was soon transferred to headquarters, got one promotion after the other and several years later was promoted to captain and assigned to a Coastal Division squad office.

At a commanders' conference in San Luis Obispo, one of his two lieutenants I had known for years took me aside and told me how incompetent the headquarters captain was in every way. He said he and the other lieutenant spent much of their time keeping the captain out of trouble because of his senseless, off-the-wall decisions and actions.

That was only one example of many that convinced me the CHP was not the same elite organization I joined and enjoyed for most of my career. It again proved Captain Overhouse was correct when he called headquarters the "Palace of Pooh." There were too many pet people in that place with nothing to do other than dream up ways to jerk around the troops in the front-line trenches with the latest senseless brainstorming ideas — and it got much worse after Captain Overhouse retired in 1968, four years before EDA was imposed to destroy the merit system.

Another more important reason for retiring was the shortage of supervisory personnel in the Santa Barbara office. The lieutenant who had slipped and fallen at the queen's greeting in the hangar remained off duty on injury time and had not been replaced. To lower costs only commanders were replaced when permanently off duty pending disability retirement. Also, one of the four sergeants was permanently off duty using up his sick leave until his service retirement.

Throughout my CHP career the department had operated on "penny-pinching" budgets, and I was tired of taking up the slack for the Sacramento "pork-barrel" legislators who knew nothing about police work and squandered state funds on the pet projects of their constituents. So despite my otherwise enjoyable CHP career and the pleasure of working with the Secret Service and other fine Santa Barbara law enforcement agencies and civic organizations, I submitted my application for service retirement effective August 7, 1983, the day after my 53rd birthday. That date was significant because state retirement pensions were based on age and years of service at the time of retirement.

Touring the Reagan Ranch

About two weeks before my retirement date I asked the ranch supervising Secret Service agent if my wife and I could have a tour of the entire Reagan ranch and we set a date when the president and Nancy wouldn't be there.

When we arrived at the Secret Service facility over a quarter of a mile from the ranch gate we were greeted by our tour guide. He was a very congenial retired former LAPD officer who was then a Secret Service officer. His primary duty was to guard presidential properties, including the White House. After a warm greeting he asked if we would like to see the inside of the ranch house, even though it was not usually allowed.

The interior of the ranch house was very casual, quaint and homey with personal knickknacks displayed on tables and walls throughout. We looked inside the door of the Reagan's bedroom and saw a pair of well-worn, scuffed tan boots about 12 inches high inside the open wardrobe closet. Our guide said the first thing President Reagan did every time he arrived back at the ranch was go change into his Levis, a shirt and those boots. Then he was the real "Rawhide" and his true self.

As our tour guide drove us toward the helicopter tarmac at the north end of the developed part of the ranch we saw a few head of cattle on the other side of a barbed-wire fence. He said President Reagan had them on the ranch because they were some sort of tax deduction as a cattle ranch. One was a Texas longhorn that looked more like another part of the ranch zoo to me than a tax deduction — but not a petting zoo.

At the helicopter tarmac we could see the black armored Ford Crown Victoria in the large hangar. Our guide said the car was so heavy with all the steel armor in it that the brake linings wore out quickly and had to be replaced about every 4,000 miles.

He then drove us on a bumpy dirt road encircling the more level northern part of the ranch and returned to the ranch house area that looked to be deserted except for the communications center, where the agents were no doubt intensely watching the TV camera screen covering the gate and listening for the sensor warning of any jackrabbits within a quarter of a mile. As he stopped the old extended jeep, the Reagan daughter's dog trotted up wagging its tail. Our guide patted its head and said he usually took the dog with him in the jeep when making his rounds of the ranch. He said one time when he was walking from the jeep to open a locked gate the dog went crazy barking. He looked down and saw a coiled rattlesnake about a foot from where he would have had to stand to unlock and open the gate. He said he had always taken the bright, alert dog with him since that time, except on visitor's tours. Hating rattlesnakes as I do, I said the dog could go with us anytime, even if it had to sit on my lap.

Our tour guide asked if we would like to see the hanging tree that was the best kept secret on the ranch. He drove a couple of hundred yards to the north of the ranch house, stopped and opened a locked gate. It was a very large oak tree with a cross chopped in the trunk bark for administering last rites. There were 14 notches chopped in the bark to designate how many had been hung there. Silent proof of the hangings was a scar in the bark of a large horizontal limb about 12 feet above the ground — just about the right height for a condemned man sitting on a horse to swing on a three-foot rope after the horse was taken out from under him. It was really chilling to envision.

The ranch had been a stage stop in the late 1800s and very early 1900s, and I was certain no Santa Barbara County Superior Court judge would travel by horseback to preside over a trial of any kind in the desolate place the ranch had been at that time, so I had to

GEORGE C. NUTTALL

conclude that the hangings were the result of very brief "Judge Roy Bean law west of the Pecos" vigilante justice trials.

I could also visualize that the trials were over almost before they started with no defense attorneys in the neighborhood or yellow pages. Then the quickly convicted were probably strung up less than an hour after the so-called trial started, and the executioner and his enthusiastic posse returned to the stage stop to drink up to the next hanging.

With those gloomy thoughts, I could clearly understand why the hanging tree was the best kept secret at the ranch, even though President Reagan was definitely a staunch law and order advocate. When he was California governor during the late 1960s and early 1970s when the rioters, demonstrators and anarchists were calling cops "Pigs," he stood up for us. He turned it around on the crazies of all kinds and said "Pig" stood for "Pride, Integrity and Guts." We all loved him for that bit of wit.

Even with his law and order stand, a hanging tree less than a quarter of a mile from his Western White House might have been a little over the top, so I kept it a secret until he left the White House.

About two weeks later my wife and I departed from Santa Barbara for retirement and new adventures, but not in my wildest dreams did I ever envision writing this book 25 years later as so many had suggested during the San Diego Police Department end-of-shift, hunt-and-peck typing and entertainment hours. And this book would never have been written if I had flunked the 25-words-a-minute typing test and been fired. It had to be divine intervention for me, but maybe not for you.

CHAPTER 43

D.B. Cooper

Gary's theory that Cooper's scattered remains were on one of the Columbia River islands was based on the fact that $5,800 of the ransom money had been found on a bank of the Columbia River about 16 miles downriver from Government Island.

Soon after my retirement I attended a reunion luncheon of San Diego Police Department veterans and saw Gary Gray, my old Beat 8 partner from 1952 to 1953. After he retired from the police department, Gary worked as a Naval Intelligence investigator for 11 years and then in the San Diego District Attorney's organized crime unit for 10 years. At the time of our reunion he had his own private investigation agency.

After the luncheon we went our separate ways until about nine years later, when I heard he had retired and moved to Washington State. Since he was the most knowledgeable, hard-working and dedicated officer I had ever worked with and had a great sense of humor, I wrote to him to renew our friendship. After exchanging letters and phone calls for about a year, I asked him if he lived near where D.B. Cooper had bailed out. I said that case had always fascinated me and asked what he knew about it.

His reply arrived a week later, saying I was a man after his own heart, because he had been working on the D.B. Cooper case since he moved back to Washington in 1986. Then about a week later there was a large parcel post box at my front door. It was full of his seven-year collection of D.B. Cooper books, news articles and maps, Columbia River tide tables and sketches related to Cooper's jump area.

In a follow-up letter about a week later Gary wrote, "You're the analytical one, you figure it out." Then he added that he had concluded with at least 90 percent certainty that Cooper's scattered remains were on one of the Columbia River islands.

For over a year I read the D.B. Cooper books and tried to make some sense out of them. One was so bizarre — about a woman finding Cooper alive on her property — that I quickly disregarded it. The most complete, logical and factual one was written by a former FBI special agent turned attorney and investigator of unsolved crimes. I used that one to work from as a starter, although I did not agree with his theory that Cooper had landed safely in the Columbia River and drowned when the 21-pound money bag pulled him under. Another was authored by a retired Portland FBI agent who wrote that he had been the chief Cooper case agent, but I later learned that the Cooper case had been assigned to the Seattle FBI field office. The fourth book was written by a retired Utah U.S. chief probation and parole officer who was assisted in research by a retired Salt Lake City FBI agent. Their book contended that a later ransom bailout skyjacker named McCoy was actually Cooper, but I also disregarded it.

I studied the two books authored by the attorney turned investigator copyrighted in 1984 and the 1986 copyrighted book written by the retired Portland FBI agent. The two books contained much conflicting and contradictory information that was reported to be factual. For example, one book said Cooper sat in Seat 18C, an aisle seat, while the other book reported he sat in Seat 18E, the middle seat of three seats to the right of the aisle. The book by the attorney was more concise and didn't digress by touting the investigative expertise of the FBI as the other did.

Despite all of the confusion, I was able to profile Cooper as a former Green Beret and a compulsive gambler over his head in debt to Las Vegas Mafia loan sharks who had given him his final warning — "Pay up or else," alluding to the only more horrible death I could imagine in comparison to his desperate 5-to-100 odds suicide jump.

My profile of Cooper was based on my knowledge of the Mafia loan sharks, their sadistic and deadly methods of dealing with welshers, and the fact that Las Vegas was still controlled by the Mafia at that time. In addition, Cooper's clothing was unusual for several reasons. He was wearing a dark suit with narrow lapels, a narrow black tie, white dress shirt, black raincoat and slip-on loafer shoes. Narrow lapels and ties had gone out of style in the late 1950s or early 1960s. His dress convinced me he was wearing a service uniform much like those worn by limo drivers, bartenders and other service personnel in hotels and high-class resorts. This attire was not suitable for parachute jumping in the freezing weather and indicated to me that he was on the run from a deadly threat and had not had time to dress appropriately for the jump.

Cooper had purchased a one-way ticket to Seattle at the Portland International Airport on Thanksgiving Eve, November 24, 1971 for Northwest Airline Flight 305 departing at 3:00 p.m. He gave his name as Dan Cooper for the flight manifest and asked the clerk if the plane was a 727 — the only commercial aircraft that had a rear staircase that lowered for passenger boarding and exiting. The 727s had been used by the CIA in the Vietnam War to drop personnel and supplies, and I had learned that the CIA had used Green Berets to do some of their dirty work, including assassinating heads of enemy countries.

The Vietnam War was still in full swing at that time, so I figured if Cooper had been a Green Beret it was likely he had been terminated with a bad conduct, dishonorable or other less than honorable discharge.

Out of curiosity I referred to my dictionary for the definitions of Dan and Cooper. There are not many definitions of men's given names in the dictionary, but the definition of Dan is "Title of honor equivalent to master or sir," and the third definition of cooper is "to furnish or fix up."

Those definitions convinced me beyond any doubt that my profile of Cooper was absolutely correct. I had to conclude that it was a coded message to the Las Vegas mafia loan sharks that he was honorable and would pay his gambling loss debt to them. The Mafia code of live or get killed stresses honor, so I was convinced it was a well chosen code message to the Las Vegas loan sharks to call off the sadistic, torturous hit that had been ordered for him.

Later in the search for Cooper's identity, a news reporter at the Portland Police Department overheard the name "D.B. Cooper" and put it on a national news wire, and Dan Cooper forever became D.B. Cooper.

Before Flight 305 received clearance from the tower to take off, Cooper slipped an envelope containing a note to a flight attendant to take to the pilots. Then he opened his attaché case and showed her what he claimed was a bomb. The reported sticks of dynamite were red, not tan, and appeared to be highway flares, but the flight attendant nor any of the other flight crew members wanted to challenge his claim.

Cooper told the flight attendant to return the envelope and note to him after showing it to the pilots. The note asked for $200,000 cash, a backpack and four parachutes and demanded that the plane should not land at the Seattle SeaTac Airport until the money and chutes were there and could be given to him without delay.

The retired Portland FBI agent reported that Cooper refused military chutes because they would automatically deploy after the parachutist had fallen a certain distance from the aircraft. The attorney turned investigator reported three civilian chutes and one military NB-8 emergency pilot's chutes were provided, and Cooper jumped with the NB-8 chute.

Although Cooper's profile convinced me why he jumped, it gave no clues to the whereabouts of his remains, and locating them was our sole objective at that time. Gary was convinced Cooper's remains were on a Columbia River island, and he recruited me to join him in the investigation to confirm his theory. He was obsessed with finding Cooper's remains because of his previous success locating the scattered remains of a Navy ensign years before.

When Gary was a Naval Intelligence investigator, a Japanese/American Naval ensign had gone on leave and never returned. His abandoned car was later found by a CHP officer near Campo Lake in the Laguna Mountains east of San Diego. The Navy searched the area and used divers to search the waters of Lake Campo with no success, so the ensign was classified as a deserter and the case was closed.

Gary knew about Japanese honor and was certain the ensign would not desert, so for about a year he tried to convince his supervisor to reopen the case and conduct a more thorough search of the area where the ensign's car had been found. The supervisor repeatedly rejected Gary's pleas and told him to forget it because the case was closed and another search would be a futile waste of money.

Being the thorough and determined investigator he was, he recruited some other Navy rank-and-file investigators to join him in a new search on a Saturday day off. When they arrived at the location where the CHP officer had found the ensign's car, his instincts pointed him to the most likely route the ensign would have taken to a remote location where he would commit suicide in a traditional Japanese manner of honor.

When he and his associates had continued about a quarter of a mile beyond where the Navy personnel had searched the year before, they found the scattered remains of the ensign. His wallet was near some of the remains and positively identified the remains as being those of the ensign. Gary said he felt so good about solving the case that he was determined to find Cooper's remains. After that, he jokingly said, he would try to find "Bigfoot."

As I tried to visualize the area where Cooper had jumped, I phoned Gary a couple of times to offer my opinion of the most likely location of Cooper's remains. Each time I related a location, Gary said that I had to come up there to become familiar with the terrain and learn about the area, so we set a tentative date for me to fly to Portland and join him.

The attorney turned investigator reported in his book that he had interviewed some of the flight crew of Cooper's skyjacked 727, so I obtained the home addresses and phone numbers of the pilot and copilot through Northwest Airlines and the Federal Aviation Administration (FAA). My letters to them went unanswered, so I phoned the copilot's home on two Saturdays. Both times a woman answered and told me he wasn't there and she didn't know when he would return.

It was obvious that the copilot did not want to talk to me, and since the pilot had not replied to my letter, I had to assume he didn't want to talk to me either. When I told Gary about getting no response from the pilot or copilot, he somewhat angrily said, "You would think everybody would want to solve the case, especially them."

One of the books reported that one of the flight attendants he interviewed was a cloistered nun in an Oregon convent at the time he interviewed her. Gary wanted to interview her because she had been required by Cooper to remain on the plane in Seattle when he allowed the other two flight attendants and 35 passengers to deplane. He wanted her to remain in the event he needed help with anything. After he had expertly donned the NB-8 chute, she had seen him cut a line from another chute and tether the 21-pound money bag to his waist with a six-foot length of the line. That was a routine practice of paratroopers — so the weight of the load would hit the ground before they did — and all Green Berets are paratroopers.

Gary had been a devout Catholic since I had first worked with him in 1952, so he wrote a letter to the diocese in Oregon requesting to get in contact with the cloistered nun who had been a flight attendant on Cooper's skyjacked plane in 1971. He never received any response from the diocese.

Gary's theory that Cooper's scattered remains were on one of the Columbia River islands was based on the fact that $5,800 of the ransom money had been found on a bank of the Columbia River known as Tina's or Tena's Bar about 16 miles downriver from Government Island. The partially decayed bills were found on February 10, 1980 by an eight-year-old boy digging a fire pit to roast hot dogs on a family picnic.

After the FBI identified the bills as being some of the Cooper ransom money, they used a backhoe to dig for more of the money. They found small pieces of $20 bills as deep as three feet down in the area where the $5,800 was found. From these discoveries, Gary concluded that the full money bag had slowly sunk as it got saturated and traveled about 16 miles down the river from Government Island and settled on the bottom of the river in front of Tina's Bar. Then when the Army Corps of Engineers dredged the Columbia River in October 1974 they flushed the money onto Tina's Bar, and the bulldozer that followed to level the dredged soil buried the pieces of the $20 bills three feet deep.

Before skyjacked Flight 305 took off from the Seattle SeaTac Airport, the pilot asked Cooper where he wanted to go and he replied "Mexico City." Chicago Mafia boss Sam Giancana, who was reported to be in control of all Mafia loan sharks in the U.S., had lived in the Mexico City area since 1966 when law enforcement made it too hot for him in Chicago. I concluded that Cooper's Mexico City destination was the second part of his coded message to the Las Vegas Mafia loan sharks who had given him his last warning "or else."

About a month before my trip to meet Gary, he applied for and was issued permits to visit the no public access islands owned by the Port of Portland. He told port officials why he wanted to search the islands, and they were very interested and cooperative — even somewhat excited about his searching.

At the same time, Gary was able to get the business phone number and address of the retired Portland FBI agent and author of one of the books I had studied. Gary gave the information to me and I sent a letter that included some questions and the date I would be arriving in the area.

Gary phoned the author's business and spoke to his daughter. She said her father was out of town and would return the following day. The next day Gary received a phone call from a total stranger who said he was a retired Green Beret sergeant and had been searching for Cooper's remains for years. He said he was searching the Washougal River Drainage area where there were many marijuana growers who guarded their crops like moonshiners. He said it wasn't safe for strangers to go there, but the growers knew him and what he was doing so it was safe. Gary told him he was searching the Columbia River area.

Gary had always been a news junkie, especially when it came to cops and crimes reported in newspapers and on TV — so much so that he subscribed to both of the major newspapers in the Portland and Vancouver areas. He knew that the Washougal Drainage area was crawling with hunters and fishermen much of the year and he had never heard of anyone having been shot or killed. Gary knew the caller was trying to con him and scare him off from searching, so he told him about the Columbia River area. The caller immediately said he had already searched the Columbia River area and had found nothing related to Cooper.

Knowing what the caller was trying to do, Gary asked him to describe the location of some landmarks along the Columbia River. The caller responded with inaccurate locations and bogus information, convincing Gary the caller knew nothing about the area and had never searched there. Gary also said when he was talking to the caller there was much noise in the background that sounded like a hippie commune.

The most interesting and disturbing issue about the stranger getting Gary's home phone number was that it was unlisted, and he protected his identity and location almost as though he were in the witness protection program. It was because his life had been threatened by some deadly hoods he had put away. Also, starting in the mid-1960s when rioters, anarchists and other crazies were ambushing and shooting law enforcement officers and bombing police stations and cars, cop's phone numbers and addresses became strictly confidential — so much so that there had been a CHP order to shred squad office rosters into at least four pieces lengthwise before disposing of them.

Being as cautious as he was, Gary gave his phone number only to family and close friends. The only other person he ever gave it to was the retired Portland FBI agent and author's daughter.

The evening before I was to meet Gary, the retired Portland FBI agent phoned me. Early in our 30-minute conversation about the D.B. Cooper case, he said it was his opinion that Cooper's attire was a service uniform. I hadn't yet mentioned that I had come to the same conclusion, so it reinforced my profile of Cooper. He said he thought Cooper's remains were probably in the Washougal Drainage area as he had said in his book. Other than that, he didn't tell me anything I didn't already know.

The one question that Gary had asked from the beginning was why there had been no report of Cooper's skyjacked plane being tracked by the Portland International Airport control tower radar. That was the mystery of many mysteries.

Gary had gone to flying school in the late 1940s on the G.I. bill and earned his pilot license. He was familiar with FAA rules, control towers and aircraft safety. The two books I studied reported that Cooper's skyjacked 727 was tracked on radar by Seattle SeaTac Airport, McCord Air Force Base and Auburn Central, all about 100 miles to the north. As a result, it was estimated from the time he had jumped at 8:13 p.m. that the 727 was over an area near Woodland about 25 miles north of Portland.

That area was searched by FBI agents and 400 Fort Lewis soldiers, as reported by the attorney turned investigator. They

414

searched for about two weeks and did not find anything related to Cooper.

Then when the $5,800 was found, it proved they had searched an area about 25 miles north of where Cooper had jumped — unless the discovered money had floated upstream against the five-mile-an-hour flow of the Columbia River.

The retired Portland FBI agent wrote that the mistaken search of that area cost the taxpayers a great amount of money, but he never wrote anything about why the skyjacked 727 was not tracked on radar by the Portland International Airport traffic controllers.

He did write that there were many FBI agents at the Portland Airport, so it seemed strange to me that the traffic controllers at that airport had not tracked Cooper's skyjacked 727, especially since the retired U.S. chief probationary and parole officer said the Salt Lake City FBI skyjacking plan had been approved by FBI headquarters in December 1970. The plan called for Team One to work out of the air traffic control tower of the most advantageously positioned airport. And Cooper's 727 had taken off from Portland and was headed back right over the west runway of that airport if it was on automatic pilot Vector-23. Even if it was not on automatic pilot, Portland International Airport was by far the closest airport to the 727's flight path.

The same book reported that J. Edgar Hoover had ordered every FBI agency to develop a skyjack plan in 1970, and it was well known that when Hoover ordered that something be done, it had better be done or there was always an opening in Butte, Montana.

If the Utah skyjacking plan had been approved by FBI headquarters, it would be reasonable to believe that all other plans would have to be as good or better.

During my first evening at Gary's house, he told me more about the strange caller who had mysteriously acquired his well-protected phone number and called him at 11:00 p.m. one night after he and his wife had gone to bed. He called the man during the day a few times to ward off any more late night calls, and he said each time there was loud noise in the background and sometimes a woman answered.

Gary called the man and told him his D.B. Cooper partner would like to speak to him about his searches. When I took the phone, the man told me about the marijuana growers and their deadly threat to strangers as he had told Gary. Then he told me about the items he had found in his searches that he thought might prove Cooper had been in the Washougal Drainage area and his remains were still there. One item he told me he had found was a pair of Ray Ban aviators' sunglasses with one lens missing. After hearing that, I politely ended the conversation. The sunglasses find told me he was somewhat strange and knew little or nothing about the Cooper case. Cooper had reportedly worn horn-rimmed sunglasses with very dark lenses like those worn by Mafia hoods and movie stars. Ray Ban aviators' sunglasses have lighter shaded lenses like the ones I wore when I rode motorcycles. That was the last time Gary or I spoke to the mysterious man.

Gary took me to the Washougal River to convince me that the recovered Cooper money could not have made its way from the Washougal Drainage area to where it was found. I took numerous photos of the river that had many large rocks in the middle of its bed and was somewhat of a white-water river, even though it was June and there had not been any heavy rains in the prior weeks or months. There were also many small still water areas on both sides of the river where anything floating could be forced into and would remain there until the river force greatly decreased.

We then went to the confluence of the Washougal and Columbia Rivers. At the foot of the Washougal River, there was a large, deep calm settling pond almost a quarter of a mile in length with a few islets in the middle. That convinced me that the retired Portland FBI agent's Washougal Drainage theory was implausible. For Cooper to have reached the Washougal Drainage area, he would have had to deploy his parachute and drift up to ten miles. Then if he had been able to deploy his chute, he would most likely have landed in the top of a very tall pine tree, and if he had made it safely to the ground, it would have been difficult or impossible to remove the chute from the pine tree with its prickly pine cones and needles. If he couldn't have removed it from a tree, it would have been visible to the many people who reportedly searched the entire area from aircraft.

With all those factors combined, I had to conclude that searching the Washougal Drainage area would be no more than a wild good chase.

The following Saturday Gary drove us to the home of the parachute expert who had provided the chutes for Cooper's jump. He graciously agreed to meet with us — the only key witness related to the Cooper case who responded to our request for an interview.

His home was east of Seattle. When we arrived, he agreed to our tape recording the interview and told us he thought we were crazy to get involved in the Cooper case.

The parachute packer confirmed that the only parachute of the four he provided that wasn't returned to him was the NB-8 emergency pilot chute. He said the ripcord handle was in a pocket to the rear of the right shoulder and was difficult to reach even under the best of conditions.

He then stood up and demonstrated the face-down position a parachutist had to get in to deploy the chute without getting tangled up in the shroud cords. He said when Cooper jumped into the 212-mile-an-hour headwind he would have tumbled "ass over teakettle," his long raincoat would have been flapping around and the 21-pound bag of money would have been bouncing around so much he was certain Cooper would not have been able to reach the ripcord handle and deploy the chute. From the plane's reported 10,000 feet elevation and falling at about 126 miles an hour, Cooper would have had less than a minute to deploy the chute. Considering that and all of the other conditions he had demonstrated and explained, he concluded that Cooper had plummeted to his death.

During a slight pause in his explanations and demonstrations I asked him how far Cooper would have drifted. He said without deploying the chute in the approximately 45 miles an hour-headwind he would have drifted about a half-mile to a mile to the northeast. If he had been able to deploy the chute, he would have drifted about 10 to 15 miles to the northeast.

The un-deployed chute distance fit perfectly with Gary's theory that his remains were on one of the Columbia River islands. To make it more interesting, it also indicated that Cooper had bailed out one or two miles east of the Portland International Airport in order for the money to end up in the Columbia River as it had.

The parachute packer then took us into his garage where he showed us some of his parachute buckles and other hardware. He said parachutes are unique to the makers and he could positively identify any chute as being his or not being his. He said if we found any parachute parts to bring them to him and he could confirm if they were part of one of his chutes.

He also said that one of the civilian parachutes returned to him was missing its outer canvas case. He said he figured that Cooper had used it to put the bank money bag in because bank money bags are like pillow cases with no securing device. He said he could also identify that chute case if we found it. After a few more laughs, I gave him a CHP baseball cap as a reminder of the two Cooper crazies before we departed.

As Gary drove us back to his home I told him that I was convinced he was right about Cooper's remains being on one of the Columbia River islands. In that I had made it clear that I wanted to independently investigate the case to confirm his Columbia River theory, Gary for the first time told me he was certain Cooper's scattered remains had to be about 50 to 100 feet from the main channel of the Columbia River. He said Cooper probably crashed into a tree top at about 126 miles an hour, causing the money bag to break loose and be propelled no more than 100 feet into the Columbia River.

In that I had previously tested dry paper to find out if it would sink or float and it initially floated until it was completely saturated, we agreed about how the money ended up at Tina's Bar. Since Tina's Bar is about 16 miles downstream from Government Island and the Columbia River flows at about five miles an hour, it would have taken a little over three hours for the money to slowly get saturated and sink, then stop on the bottom of the river even with Tina's Bar.

As we had done for two days before that Saturday, Gary and I resumed searching for anything related to Cooper.

Gary's search plan was to start in the most accessible areas of land and work his way toward the more likely areas and complete his search for Cooper's remains on the islands. A boat would be needed to get to the islands, and Gary would need someone with him on the islands, because he had a heart condition. This plan would take weeks, and I was going to return home after my nine-day stay with him and his wife.

Washington and the entire Pacific Northwest is scattered with wild blackberry vines. On the edge of the forests where they are exposed to the sun, they are immense and dense — some growing more than 20 feet high and over 10 feet deep. But in the interior of the forests where they are always shaded, they are spaced apart, allowing for walking a zigzag route between them. We searched some areas within the forests without finding anything but beer and soda cans.

When my nine-day stay was over, all we had accomplished was to confirm Gary's Columbia River island theory, but there were some reports in the D.B. Cooper books I had studied that raised some serious questions in my mind. Gary had solely focused on finding Cooper's remain and hadn't gone beyond that issue.

I had studied the books for over a year and analyzed every word to learn all I could about the case. There were some reports that clearly showed some FBI investigative irregularities or deficiencies that raised questions and suspicions. The most obvious deficiency was that FBI Director J. Edgar Hoover did not release the serial numbers of the ransom bills until about ten days after Cooper's skyjacking, and then only to banking institutions. He died in May 1972 and the list of serial numbers was not released to the press by his successor until the second anniversary of Cooper's crime. Yet Seattle FBI agents had the list of 10,000 serial numbers before Cooper's skyjacked 727 took off from Seattle SeaTac Airport.

The second most obvious deficiency was that Cooper's skyjacked 727 was never reported to have been tracked by Portland International Airport traffic controllers. Only three other radar tracking stations about 100 miles to the north tracked the plane from behind, but only tracking path not distance.

Then after the money was found, Continental Airlines Captain Tom Bohan voluntarily posed a very valid question when he visited with the retired Portland FBI agent turned author. He told the author he was four miles behind and 4,000 feet above Cooper's 727 in one of the worst storms he had experienced in his nearly 24 years as an airline pilot. He said his reason for meeting with the author was to suggest using infrared photography to locate Cooper's remains. Infrared photography was being used in Vietnam at the time to detect Vietcong shipments from Laos. It had also been used to locate the graves of itinerant farm workers killed by Juan Carona around 1969, but the FBI did not use infrared photography.

419

In the same author's book, copyrighted in 1986, he stated that the FBI was profiling Cooper. One of the pioneer FBI profilers reported that the FBI Academy behavioral science profilers received about 50 profiling requests from other police agencies in 1979, but as late as 1994 I could not find nor did I ever hear of an official FBI profile of Cooper.

Despite all my research and increasing suspicions, I pretty much put the Cooper case on hold. Being a TV cops and crimes documentary and biography junkie, I just happened to watch a TV documentary three years later in 1998 and the graphic details made all the pieces of the puzzling Cooper case fit together without any doubt whatsoever. It answered all the lingering questions I ever had about the Cooper case.

That chance discovery explained why Gary and I had run up against a stone wall in our attempts to contact and interview the flight crew as the attorney turned investigator had done in his book. It also answered the questions about why the Portland air traffic controllers had not tracked the skyjacked 727, why Hoover did not immediately release the 10,000 serial numbers to the press, why no FBI profile had been publicized, why the FBI did not use infrared photography to search for Cooper's remains and why the FBI and Army troops had searched an area about 25 miles north of where Cooper jumped.

I looked through my library and found two books that I had never bothered to read because I didn't have any idea they were related to the Cooper case. The TV documentary that had answered my questions was based on one of those books. The other book was co-authored by the brother and nephew of Sam Giancana. In addition, I later read a book authored by a retired former Chicago FBI agent that reinforced the critical information in the other two books.

The information in the TV documentary and the three books clearly proved to me why Cooper's skyjacking was the only unsolved skyjacking out of more than 2,111 reportedly committed in the 1960s and 1970s. But it would take an entire book about the size of this one to explain and clarify all the details of the Cooper case that I discovered and documented.

CHAPTER 44

National Cop Shame

During my 31 years as a California peace officer I observed and experienced the disgraceful lack of cooperation and communication between law enforcement agencies. This detriment to effective crime fighting and the solving of major cases was due to childish inter-agency resentments, competition, rivalries, arrogance and glory-grabbing by various agencies.

The theme of my FBI National Academy graduation speech was "The Spirit of Unity," and I meant it because it was manifested during our 11 weeks at that fine educational institution. Although I later received a few phone calls from other session mates from out of state asking for assistance on cases and I honored and accommodated those requests, we did not work in the same area or state. The calls were all from Michigan, Kentucky and other eastern or southern states.

My belief has always been that all law enforcement officers have the same responsibilities and the same purpose, so we should all bend over backwards to assist other law enforcement officers in every way possible, but I couldn't do anything about it. Then in 2000 vice presidential candidate Dick Cheney opened an appointment office in Virginia.

Although they were still counting, recounting and again recounting "hanging chads" in Florida to determine who was to be our next president, Dick Cheney optimistically opened the office to receive applications for about 6,000 presidential appointments.

Just to see what would happen, I typed a lengthy letter of application to be appointed as a presidential law enforcement advisor or member of a presidential law enforcement commission that I was certain was needed. I added if there was no such advisor or commission, which I was certain there wasn't, I strongly recommended that an advisor or commission be created. I stressed that the advisor or commission members should be retired law enforcement officers with no fear of retaliation from superiors in rank and should be retired from highly reputable agencies. In addition, I stressed that the advisor or most of the committee members should be rank-and-file street or detective cops.

The only response I received was a post card advising me to get a copy of an application from their website and submit it as instructed. I did so and mailed it to the McLean, Virginia address. That was the last I ever heard about it.

I wasn't offended by being stonewalled, but I knew from years of experience in Sacramento and Santa Barbara that elected politicians appoint inexperienced and inept political cronies as aides and staff members. I could envision some lowly political junkie sorting through piles of applications with the sole purpose of getting rid of them as quickly as possible — bureaucracy in action.

Then for months after the terrorist attack on 9/11/01, there was report after report of the CIA and FBI not communicating and even reports of FBI field offices not communicating with other FBI field offices. Children, get your heads on straight and do the job as you swore under oath to do it.

And to the next and succeeding U.S. presidents, create a presidential advisory committee as suggested and find out what is going on our there in the streets and police stations. Until that action is initiated, crime will climb and climb to new heights and terrorists will have a field day. Please select committee members based on their street cop experience, not on how many college degrees they possess. True, effective police work is learned on the streets, not in colleges, and law enforcement must communicate, coordinate and work as a team in a true "Spirit of Unity."

EPILOGUE

Law Enforcement Reform

U.S. law enforcement is in dire need of reform in many areas — policies, procedures, methods and tactics. The most obvious causes are "We have always done it that way" or overzealous officers, academy staffers or administrators trying to reinvent the wheel to fix something that isn't broken. The result is that officers are unnecessarily injured or killed; police-community relations are strained; police officer recruitment is more difficult; and taxpayers' money is wasted.

The most obvious reforms needed are as follows:

Right-Side Approach: After decades of CHP officers being injured or killed making driver-side approaches on traffic enforcement stops, the agency changed to the right-side approach about 20 years ago and the lives of many officers have been saved.

In the last ten years of viewing TV cops shows, I have seen three eastern and Midwestern state troopers struck by passing vehicles on the driver-side of violators' vehicles — and recorded by their patrol car video cameras. The safety benefits of right-side approaches are clearly explained earlier in this book. Thus, all law enforcement administrators should mandate that the right-side approach be utilized on all traffic stops.

Sam Browne Gun Belt Shoulder Belt: The San Diego Police Department and the CHP discontinued the wearing of the shoulder belts in the late 1930s or early 1940s because they are a safety hazard. The belt can easily be grabbed from the rear by a criminal and used to control an officer and violently swing him or her around and to the ground.

As I have seen on shows, many eastern and Midwestern state troopers are still wearing these hazardous shoulder belts. They are no more than traditional adornments that resemble dress parade enhancements and should be dispensed with.

423

Koga Baton and Physical Methods of Arrest: The Koga methods are by far the most effective of all baton, physical methods of arrest and riot control methods. In the decades since his retirement from the LAPD, Bob Koga has continued to teach his methods to law enforcement officers through his nonprofit institute. Every U.S. law enforcement agency should avail itself of this remarkable methods training. Bob Koga's office is in Fallbrook, California.

Merit System: Every U.S. law enforcement agency should have or initiate the merit system in preference to political cronyism or nepotism systems for entry positions and promotions. The CHP and California State Personnel Board replaced the merit system with an internal political system in 1972, with demoralizing and devastating effects since that time.

College Education and Degrees: Hiring and promotions should not be based on college educations and degrees. Police work is effectively learned through street experience and on-the-job training by well qualified veteran training officers. It is not learned solely in classrooms, nor does any college degree prove competency by itself.

Two-Officer Units: The primary reason for two-officer units is for the second officer not making an arrest or contacting a traffic violator to be a backup in the event the first officer needs physical help. The second officer should always remain behind a patrol car door and advance only if needed to control a resisting or violent subject. It does not require two officers to issue a traffic citation.

Not following these procedures is what led to the four CHP officers being killed in Newhall in 1970. The driver of the CHP patrol car that stopped the two gunmen had removed the driver and was searching him for weapons at the left rear fender of the gunmen's car. The passenger officer did not remain behind the right front door of the CHP car. With the un-cocked shotgun at port arms, he approached the passenger's right side door. The passenger gunman quickly opened the door and fatally shot the passenger officer. The CHP driver officer was then outnumbered by the two gunmen and was fatally shot.

The two CHP officers in the second patrol car to arrive as backup were not aware of the first two officers having been killed and drove into an ambush and were fatally shot.

Unless it requires two officers to control a resisting or combative subject, the two officers should always maintain a reasonably safe distance between them to avoid being an easier combined target.

Credit Sharing: Every law enforcement officer should willingly, actively and openly give credit to the other officers or agencies that significantly assisted in the solving of a case and/or the apprehension of the perpetrator of a crime.

To take complete credit for a successful investigation and identification or apprehension of the perpetrator or perpetrators when significantly assisted by another officer or agency creates a strong resentment and discourages future inter-agency coordination and cooperation.

Pre-Employment Background Checks: All law enforcement agencies should conduct extensive background checks of applicants for all positions. In addition to checking criminal and driving records, they should also contact neighbors, friends, co-workers and family members.

In California, fingerprints of all law enforcement position applicants are sent to the Department of Justice Criminal Identification and Investigation (CII) unit. If an applicant is rejected by a law enforcement agency because of adverse information discovered in a background investigation, the applicant's CII record of fingerprints should be flagged "Rejected" for the information of other agencies.

Law Enforcement Salaries: All law enforcement officers should receive a reasonable, competitive, livable salary. Historically, most California peace officers in large departments have received higher salaries than those of average workers due to the hazards of the job. Every traffic enforcement stop can pose a deadly threat because cops never know if they are stopping an armed and dangerous fugitive.

At the FBI National Academy I was dismayed to learn of the substandard salaries and benefits some officers received — including officers and supervisors of law enforcement departments of some Midwestern states.

Criminal Cops: All law officers who commit crimes should be prosecuted. They not only commit a crime but more importantly they violate their sacred oath of trust to uphold the law. If you can't trust a cop, who can you trust?

When prosecuted, a crime becomes a public record for the media to report, and when the general law-abiding public learns of a cop being prosecuted, the public is assured that their police agency is honest and rids itself of rogue cops.

Traffic Citation Revenues: Historically, California law provides for 50 percent of traffic violation fines to go to the city or county where the violation occurred. If in a city, the revenue goes to that city and if the violation occurs in an unincorporated area, the revenue goes to the county.

I believe this archaic law is legally questionable. I am not an attorney or appellate court justice, but based on the true intent and spirit of common law, I believe it could be judged a conflict of interest — and even bounty hunting. Many government officials have been successfully prosecuted for using the power of their offices to bring about financial gain for themselves or others, and I believe this form of revenue collecting could be called a conflict of interest if nothing else. I can only wish a very competent attorney would pursue it as such to the highest court of the land.

Traffic citations should be issued for potential accident-causing violations, not technical or petty borderline violations for revenue.

Jail Custodians: Law enforcement departments with jails should have jail custodian positions to free trained officers to perform actual police duties. Jail custodians require much less training than law enforcement officers. Many could be retired military personnel who already have health insurance and other expensive retiree benefits that the police agency would not have to provide. If supervised at all times by a sworn officer or supervisor, they could perform as well as a sworn officer jailer.

Retired Officer Cold Case Investigators: When experienced veteran police investigators retire, their expertise is lost. Many play golf, go fishing, travel in their RVs, become private investigators or do nothing. Their years or decades of investigative experience and expertise are lost to the benefit of the general public, and this is a waste of very valuable resources.

There are reportedly thousands or tens of thousands of unsolved cold cases these retired officers could investigate without the normal phone calls or other interruptions that detract active law enforcement investigators from their thought processes. They could even work out of their homes to give them the time and quiet to concentrate on the smallest details of a case.

I saw two homicide cold cases on TV that were solved by retired, experienced detectives. One case involved four retired detectives who put their heads together and solved an old cold case. They wore cowboy hats and looked like retired farmers, but they knew what they were doing.

Also, much the same as jail custodians, they would have their health care and other retiree benefits from their previous law enforcement agencies, and their wages could be much less than those of active police investigators. Most of all, they wouldn't need any training whatsoever.

Cadet/Recruit Academy Training: Starting with the Los Angeles Police Department Marine Corps boot camp high-stress recruit training when a retired Marine Corps general was appointed chief in about 1950 to discipline the LAPD after what the Los Angeles Times called the "Christmas Eve Massacre," that irrational, brutal bullying method of berating and desensitizing recruits has spread like wildfire to nearly all California police academies.

It should have proven to be a complete failure decades later by the Rodney King criminal beating and ensuing riot that cost more than 50 people their lives, the "Rampart" corruption scandal and the bungled O.J. Simpson homicide case investigation.

Police officers are humans and deserve to be treated humanely the same as they should treat the public when they graduate and enforce the law. Putting cadets and recruits through concocted forms of stress like college fraternity pledges during "hell week" to see if they can take it and be tough enough to be one of us is not only cruel, but childish. It may make the bully instructors feel like "super cops," but it only makes them look like insecure, pathetic street gang members. No bully should ever be allowed to wear a police badge and gun.

Most recently, a TV show entitled "The Academy" has been aired. It is a true, live documentary of recruit training at the Los Angeles Sheriff Academy and is very disturbing. The instructors demand that the recruits be mentally and emotionally in unison with all of their classmates and think the same like a team. This is the purest form and evidence of a police academy trying through fear to produce "cookie-cutter robot cops."

Police officers must be intelligent enough to make valid, independent decisions every shift, and some decisions must be made instantly in situations that are life-threatening to themselves and others. Trying to make decisions based on what others may think is not rational. Strong, intelligent people make decisions on their own, not by vote of a group, period.

Furthermore, a high-stress environment is not conducive to learning. If it was, all colleges and universities would employ it.

Based on what Captain Cowan told me in 1971 about the Los Angeles Sheriff's captain's master thesis proving non-stress cadet/recruit training produced much better performing officers in the field than those enduring high-stress training, I obtained a copy of that thesis at the USC Doheny Library.

Much to my disappointment, the thesis did not conclusively prove one or the other was a better training method. It only presented more of the controversy. And that was probably the reason the thesis was not filed at USC until 1974, indicating that it took the captain four years to complete.

The most disgusting training mentioned in the thesis was one form of instruction wherein the recruits watched video lectures wearing headphones instead of listening to live instructors. That state-of-the-art method probably put any number of recruits to sleep. Also, the thesis reported the highest recruit dropout rate was prompted by the requirement to frequently run two miles.

Modified physical training is essential to keep cadets and recruits in good physical condition while at the academy because they are physically inactive sitting in a classroom most of the time. But it should not be overdone. From my 29 years on the CHP, I can attest to the fact that about 90 percent of officers never ran more than a city block at one time after graduating from the academy. And excessive physical training takes away from the time the cadets could be receiving valuable classroom training.

For anyone interested in the LASD captain's thesis, it can be obtained at the USC Doheny Library as follows:

Pu '75035 – Oglesby, Edgar Wixon. The effect of police academy training on the social attitudes of police recruits by Edgar Wixon Oglesby. — December 1974. v. 138 leaves; 28 cm.

Police Written Entrance Tests: Police pre-employment written tests should be on knowledge of laws that a police officer must know to effectively apply as a law enforcement officer. General I.Q. or other copyrighted tests from some university composed by a professor who knows nothing about police work should never be used. All questions should be relevant to law enforcement.

The CHP entrance test I took in 1953 was an I.Q. or general knowledge test that had nothing to do with law enforcement. One CHP test question I will never forget was "Why is ethyl gasoline red?" Who cares? And what did that have to do with being a CHP officer?

Pre-testing of Cadets/Recruits: As USC Professor Jack Ascot advocated and FBI Academy Instructor "Toke" said, pre-testing should be a learning method of the future. I wholeheartedly agree with them.

If cadets and recruits were given the entire course's written tests the first week of training, it would open up their minds to look for the correct answers. Then when they heard the classroom lectures, the correct answers would in most cases jump out at them. But they would never be told until the end of their cadet/recruit training what their pre-test score was. It would also be valuable to the academy staff to measure the knowledge improvement each cadet/recruit made from the start to the finish of the training course.

Police Motorcycles: Although I loved motorcycles and loved being a motor cop, they should be abolished or minimized to the lowest number possible. They are cripplers and killers. Since the CHP became a solely state-controlled traffic law enforcement agency in 1929, over 80 CHP motorcycle officers have been killed. And in nearly all cases, if they had been in a patrol car they would not have been injured or would have been only slightly injured. In addition, there have been many more than that who were so severely wounded that they had to be retired on disability. Also, CHP figures show it costs two and one-half to three times more to operate a motorcycle than a patrol car.

Police Licensing: In California, private investigators, real estate agents and any number of other professional positions of trust require a state license. The applicants for those positions must be fingerprinted for criminal and DMV record checks and must pass a written test based on relevant laws.

But there is no required license to be a law enforcement officer in California, even though these officers have the most awesome legal authority to arrest and deprive persons of their liberty and are granted the special power to use deadly force.

One California sheriff appointed two assistant sheriffs for political reasons. One had a few years experience on a smaller department and the other had no police experience, but was very wealthy. After years in those two positions, they were both indicted and one served a year in jail. Then as this book is being written, the sheriff himself is under federal indictment for bribery and corruption and his trial is up-coming.

Currently in California, any police chief or sheriff of an agency without civil service — and some with civil service — can appoint anybody to become a sworn peace officer, even his unemployable brother-in-law or a high school dropout friend or relative.

For the most part, the only requirements mandated when California Peace Officer Standards and Training (POST) was legislated in 1959 was fingerprinting of police applicants and required training as established by POST.

Until no later than the 1980s that I know of, California law enforcement was reputed to be the leader in the United States, so if California does not require police licenses, it is most likely that no other state in the nation has that requirement. If that is the case, there are probably a great many U.S. police agencies that are as bad as or worse than the ones I had to endure in Big Bear and Yreka in the 1950s and 1960s.

Concealed Weapons Licenses: California Penal Code Section 12050 has historically empowered the sheriff of a county or the chief of a municipal police department with the exclusive authority to issue concealed weapons (CCW) licenses to private citizens.

This law has many flaws. Most of all, it grants every sheriff the discretionary right to issue CCW licenses to all of his more generous reelection campaign contributors and other political supporters. Then there is the issue of the chief of a one-officer police department to give out CCW licenses to every adult in the chief's small city. In 1969, there were two one-man police departments in Siskiyou County when I was in Yreka. In one of those rural cities, the police chief reportedly enforced traffic laws on commuters in the morning and operated the road grader and did other maintenance work the remainder of the day. The chief was a very nice gentleman, but the few times I saw him he was wearing everyday work clothes.

Florida was the first or one of the first states to enact a common citizens (CCW) law, and it was reported that the first year that law was in full effect, the state's homicidal rate dramatically dropped. This was a strong indication that cowardly criminals — and nearly all criminals are cowardly — feared taking the chance of encountering an armed intended victim. In the last several years, it has been reported that there are over a dozen states that have also enacted similar common citizen CCW laws.

It was also reported in recent years that after Australia enacted law to ban citizen-owned firearms, the crime rate soared in that British Commonwealth nation, but Britain hates guns!

After decades of squabbling, the constitutional right of Americans to bear arms was finally resolved by the U.S. Supreme Court in 2008. The court ruled the U.S. Constitution protects the right of every citizen to bear arms, so the good guys finally won that long battle with the ultra liberals. With that clear court decision, every state should enact a common citizen CCW law to help protect the law-abiding citizens and reduce crime.

Much as reported in Florida, every applicant for a CCW would have to pay $50 or more for a one-year license. The applicant would be fingerprinted for positive identification and to check for a criminal record, and if no criminal arrests or convictions are found, the applicant would have to take a firearms safety and competency test, which would include qualifying on a target range.

Citizens in many professions such as medical doctors, nurses and other emergency personnel must work all hours of the day and night, and many hospitals are in high-crime areas. These at-risk people should be the first to receive CCW licenses.

Firearms are no more dangerous than motor vehicles. The danger lies in the irresponsibility of those controlling them, so let the CCW licenses roll for the good guys and gals!

Citizen Complaints: All citizen complaints should be thoroughly investigated by administrators of law enforcement agencies — not by police officers, who may not be closely supervised or who may have covert immoral, unethical or illegal tendencies.

Most of the citizen complaints lodged against CHP officers during my tenure as a lieutenant and captain alleged that the officer was "rude." The investigation usually disclosed that the only act of rudeness was the officer's issuing the complainant a citation, and those complaints were not sustained. If complainants alleged that they were innocent, we usually referred them to the court to determine innocence or guilt, unless there was an apparent or obvious miscarriage of justice or the officer had a history of similar complaints. If so, the allegations were investigated.

While these were normal, routine complaints, there also are serious complaints of brutality, excessive use of force or improper sexual conduct. For example, during my first two years in the Westminster CHP office, two officers were terminated for their inappropriate sexual suggestions or physical advances toward young women.

Then in 1982 in the Barstow CHP squad, the "1981 Officer of the Year" shot a beautiful young woman who aspired to be a movie star to silence her. He was convicted of murder and sentenced to life in prison, where he died of a heart attack a few years later.

I had known the Barstow office captain commander since he was a CHP cadet, and it did not surprise me that something like that could happen in a squad that he commanded. About ten years later, and after he had retired, he was arrested for child pornography and reportedly served 18 months in a federal prison. So, who was watching the man who was entrusted with supervising the raping, murdering officer?

Then about ten years later, a San Diego CHP squad officer murdered a beautiful young woman, and the officer was the model officer for that squad. It was later learned that he would direct young female drivers to leave the I-15 Freeway onto a dead-end, incomplete off-ramp named "Mercy Road." In this case, he threw the young woman off the Mercy Road Bridge to her death after she threatened to report him for his sexual advances and inappropriate sexual conduct. To compound that tragedy, an investigation by the San Diego Police Department revealed that two other young women had reported that same officer's inappropriate sexual conduct to the CHP. However, the CHP did not pursue those complaints, and the officer went on to cause the horrific death of a fine young woman.

In their investigation of the homicide, the San Diego Police Department reviewed all the office copies of citations issued by the officer for the previous seven months and interviewed all the female citation recipients. They found at least a dozen who related that the officer had directed them to leave the freeway at Mercy Road and made sexual remarks to them. After incriminating physical evidence was discovered in his patrol car, the officer was sentenced to 25 years to life in prison.

As only one of nearly 200 CHP lieutenants and captains, I saw, heard and experienced more than enough to convince me that every citizen complaint must be investigated. More than one investigation started out with an isolated insignificant event, but this proved to be only the tip of the iceberg and evolved into a gigantic can of worms. Another started out with a questionable accident report and evolved into the second largest personnel investigation in CHP history at that time — and the involved officer was terminated for years of dereliction of duty.

Citizen complaints are no doubt the most dreaded aspect of police work and are hated by all cops, including me. I was very unpopular for demanding the investigation of all complaints, but I could never live with myself if I had ignored a citizen complaint that ultimately resulted in the tragic death of anyone. And despite the thousands of dedicated and honorable officers of the CHP and other local and state police agencies, it takes only one bad officer to slip through the screening process and make hell for all the others.

It is the personal and professional responsibility of all police supervisors and administrators to be ever vigilant for the warning signs and take appropriate action without delay when indicated.

General Summary: All of these reforms are attainable, but none of them will be acted upon for three reasons: First of all because of the American public's complacency and disinterest. The average American does not care one bit about law enforcement efficiency or safety until they or one of their family members or friends is burglarized, robbed, raped, murdered, or becomes the victim of some other crime.

The second reason is because law enforcement administrators are not normally open-minded to suggestions or recommendations from external sources. One age-old, worn-out reason is because, "That's the way we've always done it." The other classic excuse for rejecting new improved methods is, "If it is a good or better way of doing anything, we would have thought of it first and done it long ago."

Accordingly, all seasoned elected politicians know all of the above and direct their efforts toward satisfying the whims of their constituents and getting reelected. Many do not even know what statutes are in the numerous codes they are responsible for enacting, amending or deleting.

A class case of that blindness became clear to me several years ago when I discovered that the home addresses of California law enforcement officers were public records on the Registrar of Voters' computers for anyone to see, so I urged the California Association of Highway Patrolmen (CAHP) to lobby for legislation to remove all cops' addresses from those records.

The legislature's quick corrective action amused me. The 120 California state legislators obviously didn't know that their home addresses and those of the governor, judges and other elected officials and their family members with unlisted phone numbers were also public records on the Registrar of Voters' accessible computers.

At the end of the year when new laws passed by the legislature go into effect, I stopped by the Orange County Registrar of Voters office and checked the name and information of a civilian friend not connected in any way to law enforcement, and there was no address information. That proved to me that they panicked. It was vividly clear to me that when they became aware of a governmental practice that personally affected them, their privacy and their security, they acted with great haste.

But don't even think about asking a California elected official to enact a safety ordinance or law for the public welfare. I have a few times and was stonewalled or received a "sorry" written response that would insult the weakest of minds. So, although I felt compelled to present all these reform issues, I am certain nothing will change, and honorable officers will continue to be unnecessarily killed — but I tried.

During my 29 years on the California Highway Patrol, there were 93 officers killed — over an average of three each year. Twenty-five were killed on motorcycles, twenty-eight were killed by shootings, eight were killed in aircraft crashes, and thirty-two were killed in traffic. The most tragic was that five of those killed by traffic were on the driver's side of the violator's vehicle or were returning to their patrol vehicles from the driver's side next to traffic.

A few years before I joined the CHP a national auto magazine conducted a study of the CHP and concluded that based on the number of CHP officers at that time — in about 1950 — it was the most dangerous occupation in the nation.

But for some crazy reason, I would never have been contented or satisfied with doing anything else for a living. Just like the thousands of others before, it was my most enjoyable, exciting, interesting and entertaining career.

I have no illusions that anything presented in this book will improve law enforcement policies, practices and/or officer safety because of the following truth:

"Great spirits have always encountered violent opposition from mediocre minds." — Dr. Albert Einstein.

This author sincerely welcomes your written comments, criticisms, suggestions and recommendations and will respond with my considerate and respectful agreement or rebuttal. If enough comments are received, I will author a second book of those letters and responses. If you wish your name to be used, please include your name and address and I will send you a release form to sign indicating your consent. If no consent form is returned, letters will be published anonymously.

So feel free to write because law enforcement needs all the new ideas it can get, and I am certainly not one who hangs his hat on "But that's the way we've always done it," or "If it was such a good idea, I would have thought of it long ago."

Send your comments and questions to the following address:

George C. Nuttall
P.O. Box 2749
Laguna Hills, CA 92654-2749

Don't Let What You Cannot Do
Interfere With What You Can Do.

— John Wooden

SOURCES

San Diego Police Department:

Castanien, Pliny. *To Protect and Serve.* San Diego: San Diego Historical Society, 1993.

California Highway Patrol:

California Highway Patrol Badges of Honor. Sacramento: Headquarters Office of Public Affairs, 1997.

D.B. Cooper:

Gunther, Max. *D.B. Cooper What Really Happened.* Chicago: Contemporary Books, Inc., 1985.

Himmelsbach, Ralph P. and Worcester, Thomas K. NORJAK: *The Investigation of D.B. Cooper.* West Linn, Oregon: NORJAK PROJECT, 1986.

Rhodes, Bernie. *D.B. Cooper The Real McCoy.* Utah: University of Utah Press, 1991.

Tosaw, Richard T. *D.B. Cooper Dead or Alive.* Ceres, California: Tosaw Publishing Company, Inc., 1984.